D1129761

mo

MULTIVARIATE APPLICATIONS IN THE SOCIAL SCIENCES

Edited by
NANCY HIRSCHBERG
University of Illinois at Chicago Circle
LLOYD G. HUMPHREYS
University of Illinois at Urbana-Champaign

LEA LAWRENCE ERLBAUM ASSOCIATES, PUBLISHERS
1982   Hillsdale, New Jersey

086820

Lawrence Erlbaum Associates, Inc., Publishers
365 Broadway
Hillsdale, New Jersey 07642

Library of Congress Cataloging in Publication Data

Main entry under title:

Multivariate applications in the social sciences.

   Includes bibliographical references and indexes.
   1. Psychology—Statistical methods.   2. Multivariate
analysis.   3. Social sciences—Statistical methods.
I. Hirschberg, Nancy.   II. Humphreys, Lloyd G.
BF39.M849   150'.72   82-5069
ISBN 0-89859-152-X   AACR2

Printed in the United States of America

Contents

Introduction

Textbooks in multivariate methods proliferate, but there are few books concerned with their application. This is unfortunate, as students may learn the techniques without having any idea how to conceptualize or design a study that can be analyzed by multivariate methods, nor how to apply these methods to particular sets of data. In his 1957 presidential address to the American Psychological Association, Lee J. Cronbach lamented the bifurcation of psychology into two distinct groups: the experimental psychologists and the correlational psychologists. Experimental psychology and its associated method of statistical data analysis, analysis of variance, has tended to dominate psychological thinking even in such areas as social and clinical psychology, two areas that are particularly ill-suited to simple analysis-of-variance statistical models. Social and clinical psychology typically study situations that involve the myriad of psychological factors that cause a person to behave in a particular way. Unlike experimental psychology with its emphasis on the manipulation and control of relatively few variables in a laboratory setting, correlational, or multivariate psychology is designed to handle many variables and to determine the relevance of those variables to behavior.

Thus the recent emphasis of clinical and social psychology on applied research relevant to social problems requires that more attention be paid to multivariate methods and appropriate research designs. There is every reason to believe that the classic experimental research designs are inadequate to cope with the complexity of human behavior as it occurs in natural settings. Despite the fact that the two types of statistical models, the analysis-of-variance model and the multivariate model, share a common algebraic base, psychologists still show a prejudice in favor of one or the other. Although this book illustrates and examines the multivariate approach alone, this does not imply that a multivariate approach combined with an experimental approach would not in the long run provide the best overall research design.

Before a useful combination of the two research approaches can be attempted, however, the researcher must be aware of the limitations and advantages of each approach. We have long had lucid accounts of experimental research designs, with associated analysis-of-variance statistics and applications of those statistics. This has not been the case for multivariate analysis.

The present collection of multivariate applications introduces some of the kinds of research problem that can be tackled by means of multivariate statistical analysis. These readings do not begin to exhaust the possible applications of multivariate statistics nor the various types of multivariate models. Rather, each contribution represents an interesting and important application of multivariate technique to a different substantive problem in psychology.

In the present collection of readings, clinical, personality, and social psychology applications predominate, whereas experimental applications are underrepresented. This imbalance simply reflects the fact that most contemporary research employing multivariate methods is in the former area. There is no conceptual or methodological reason for the imbalance to continue; indeed, it is hoped that a better appreciation of the utility and versatility of multivariate applications in the social and clinical fields will encourage experimental psychologists to recognize the merits of multivariate analysis.

Among the various types of multivariate models, we may distinguish between structural models and process models. Structural models attempt to reproduce the static mental map that a person has of the objects in his or her world. An example of a structural model would be a multidimensional scaling model that attempts to mirror a person's theory about the ways in which various external objects are related to one another. Process models, on the other hand, attempt to capture the ongoing mental operations that take place as a person deals with new information about the environment. Models that attempt to simulate personality qualify as process models. The present group of readings tends to represent structural, rather than process models. The reason is not that process models are innately less important or interesting, but that they are almost certain to be more complicated than structural models and have therefore been less studied. Where structural models deal with states of mind, process models attempt to account for changes in these states; put in this simplified way, it is clear that structural models have a certain logical priority. Huesmann in the final chapter of this book laments the paucity of process models and explains their importance to the science of behavior.

Were this book to be dedicated to a single person that person would be Kern W. Dickman. Dickman supervised the applied computer center at the University of Illinois at Champaign during the heyday of multivariate research there. Dickman was primarily responsible for the development of SOUPAC, a canned computer system particularly designed to perform complicated multivariate analyses. The use of any portion of the system was surprisingly simple and it was an easy matter to string together a large number of suboperations within the system. Despite its simplicity, SOUPAC represented the most complex development in multivariate analysis at that time. For example, there were programs for various designs in multivariate analysis of variance, discriminate function analysis, canonical correlation analysis, various types of factor analytic programs including alpha factor analysis, image analysis, maximum likelihood factor analysis and three-mode factor analysis, and a large number of factor analytic rotation programs including the Binormamin rotation, an oblique analytic rotation developed by Kaiser and Dickman. These programs were already operating around 1960. Whether or not the students of multivariate at Illinois could have survived without Dickman's expertise or vice versa is an unanswerable question; the two went hand in hand. The result was some of the model ingenious applications of multivariate analysis long before multivariate models were part of the zeitgeist. It is not surprising that so many psychologists who have contributed to this volume had some relation with SOUPAC either at its inception in Illinois or at one or another place that students traveled along with SOUPAC. In spirit, at least, this book can therefore be considered a product of the legacy left by Dickman and SOUPAC.

Nancy Hirschberg
February 10, 1979

* * * * * * * * *

Note: This book was conceived by its editor, Nancy Hirschberg. It was she who invited the authors of the papers who have contributed, and she who completed a large part of the editorial work before her tragic death at the age of 41 on February 21, 1979. It was characteristic of her devotion to her friends and to her discipline that she worked on the manuscript almost to the day of her death. She had planned a more extensive introduction but was unable to complete it.

Major credit for much of the final editing goes to Professor Lloyd Humphreys, who had been a colleague of Nancy Hirschberg for many years at the University of Illinois at Champaign, and to Professor Anthony Conger who had been an Illinois student. Thanks are due also to Professor Larry Grimm, her colleague at the University of Illinois at Chicago Circle, who helped in many ways to bring together the material in this volume.

Donald Davidson

1 Multivariate Reliability: Implications for Evaluating Profiles

Anthony J. Conger
Purdue University

A variety of psychological and social science problems involve the use of test batteries or instruments that provide scores for an individual on several attributes. The more commonly used measurement devices include achievement and intelligence tests, vocational and interest inventories, and personality questionnaires. Instruments of this kind are used in both theoretical and applied research as predictor variables, covariates, and dependent or criterion measures. Test batteries also provide, often in the form of profiles, the basic information for many applied activities, including differential diagnoses, selection, and classification. Although test batteries are used for such a variety of purposes and with varying methodologies, there is a common problem inherent in their use; namely, to what extent do the scores of purportedly distinct attributes provide independent and reliable information?

The purpose of this chapter is to describe a procedure specifically developed for investigating the reliability of test batteries that yield scores on several more or less distinct attributes. But because the scores on the different attributes are usually correlated, problems arise when attempts are made to interpret or derive diagnostic significance from a particular pattern of scores. Problems in research, interpretation and diagnoses can, of course, be avoided by using empirically derived and validated score combinations but unless such score combinations are themselves uncorrelated or used in the form of discriminant functions, the problem of interpretability has just been shifted to a new set of scores. For example, Robb, Bernardoni, and Johnson (1972) present nine separate composite scores for the WISC but one of their composites, *G,* can be derived from three other composites (Verbal Comprehension plus Anxiety minus Fluency). The development of empirically validated patterns should of course be encouraged, but unless the patterns or score combinations are uncorrelated and exhaustive of the inter-

5

ests of test battery interpreters, the problem of what a test battery can reliably measure will persist. The current use of test batteries and profiles by clinical, counseling, and personnel psychologists is hardly limited to exhaustive and uncorrelated test score profiles or composites.

In order to illustrate the concept and use of multivariate reliability and the related concept and use of maximally reliable composites, this chapter focuses on research done by Conger, Conger, Farrell, and Ward (1979) on the WISC–R (Wechsler Intelligence Scale for Children–Revised: Wechsler, 1974); however, before getting into specific applications, a review of some fundamental concepts seems warranted.

Profiles and Score Vectors

A profile is typically a visual representation of test battery scores that have been standardized; that is, scores on different subtests have been transformed so that they have a common mean and common observed score variance. Standard scores for WISC–R subscales, for example, all have a hypothetical mean of 10 and a hypothetical standard deviation of 3, whereas the three IQ scores have a mean of 100 and standard deviation of 15. Visual inspection of profiles proceeds by noting the overall level of the profile (the "central tendency"), the amount of scatter (how high the peaks, how deep the valleys), and the pattern (location of peaks and/or valleys). Verbal labels generally have not been associated with Wechsler profiles, but Minnesota Multiphasic Personality Inventory (MMPI) profiles are frequently identified by labels such as "4–9" and "neurotic triad." Simple visual scrutiny of profiles may satisfy some test battery interpreters, particularly persons with years of experience in administering and interpreting the same test; however, naive diagnosticians and statistically sophisticated testers eschew simple visual perusal and value summary statistics. Thus, level is measured by the mean of the profile elements (test scores), scatter can be measured by the standard deviation or variance of the elements, and shape can be measured by some sort of correlation with a target profile (for example, r_c developed by Cohen, 1969). Except for profile level, mathematical and statistical properties have not been fully investigated for these characteristics used in profile interpretation.

More emphasis has been placed instead on the properties of the score vector underlying the profile. Most of the major theoretical articles on profile and pattern scores (Cattell, 1949; Cohen, 1969; Cronbach & Gleser, 1953; Gaier & Lee, 1953; Osgood & Suci, 1952; Overall, 1964) have focused on methods of calculating profile similarities and differences. The general approach assumes that a profile can be handled as a vector of scores with no loss of information. Furthermore, two well-accepted techniques of profile comparison are generally used: the Cronbach and Gleser D^2 (Cronbach & Gleser, 1953), which ignores intercorrelations among profile elements and the Mahalonobis D^2, which does not ignore the intercorrelations (Overall, 1964). Both procedures consider the total distance between two profiles and include differences arising from level, shape, and pattern. Harris (1955) demonstrated that both functions are related to the principal components of the population (or estimated population) covariance matrix, with the Mahalanobis function weighting the independent information equally, whereas the Cronbach–Gleser function gives more weight to the redundant information. At this point this may not seem important, but the difference leads to some interesting consequences, as discussed later.

As stated earlier, there is an alternative to global profile analyses, that of predetermined patterns or composites. Actually the use of predetermined patterns does not solve the problem of what to do with a profile unless every observed profile clearly coincides with one of the established patterns. If such is not the case, then an observed profile must either be left uninterpreted or a choice needs to be made as to which pattern it most closely resembles. This is a problem in its own right and is not further addressed in this chapter. The use of composites of profile elements represents the other choice. Except for the problem of interpreting profiles of composites, the characteristics of composite scores have been extensively investigated.

A composite is nothing more than a weighted sum of scores. If X_{ij} is the score for person i on subtest j and if W_j is the weight given to a score on subtest j, the composite score Y_i could be written:

$$Y_i = \sum_j W_j X_{ij}.$$

If each subtest score is assumed to have an underlying true score T_{ij}, a composite true score could similarly be described as

$$T_i = \sum_j W_j T_{ij}.$$

The measurement characteristics of such a composite score can be easily derived under a standard assumption that errors of measurement are random, have an expected value of 0, and are independent of the true scores and one another (see, for example, Lord & Novick, 1968). Under these assumptions the reliability of a composite score based on J subtests having equal variances is simply:

$$\rho_y = \frac{\sum_j W_j^2 \rho_{x_j} + \sum_{j \neq j'} \sum W_j W_j{}' \, r_{x_j x_{j'}}}{\sum_j W_j^2 + \sum_{j \neq j'} \sum W_j W_j{}' \, r_{x_j x_j}{}'} \tag{1}$$

where ρ_{x_j} is the reliability of subtest j. For readers familiar with matrix algebra, this may be written:

$$\rho_y = \frac{W' R_{tt}^* W}{W' R_{xx} W}$$

where W is the vector of weights, R_{xx} is the intercorrelation matrix, and R^*_{tt} is the intercorrelation matrix with reliabilities substituted into the diagonal.

This formula is even simpler to use when the weights are either $+1$ or -1, a fact that has led to its being recommended for routine use by test interpreters (Tellegen & Briggs, 1967). Unfortunately its routine use for analyzing *discovered* patterns of scores rather than *a priori* patterns may be inappropriate. Consider for a moment the typical WISC-R profile comprised of 10 subtest scores. Each subtest score could be described by one of three terms, depending on its relationship to the population mean or the person's own mean: "above average" (i.e., $W_j = +1$), "average" (i.e., $W_j = 0$), or "below average" (i.e., $W_j = -1$). This simple procedure would result in 59,049 (i.e., 3^{10}) distinct patterns or 29,524 different composites.[1] Before computing the reliability of a discovered pattern or composite for a single individual it seems prudent to consider the likelihood of having obtained it.

The interpretation of profiles and score vectors thus seems highly susceptible to capitalization on chance. In order to provide some guidelines to profile users Conger and Lipshitz (1973) developed a general index of reliability that could be used with any method of computing differences among profiles. Using their general formulation, multivariate reliability indices were derived for Cronbach–Gleser distances and Mahalonobis distances. Bock (1966) independently derived a measure of reliability for test batteries using a multivariate analysis of variance procedure that was shown (Conger, 1974) to be a special case of the Conger and Lipshitz general index.

Defining Profile Reliability

The basic unit of analysis for investigating profile or test battery reliability is a score vector X_i for an individual i. This score vector is assumed to have an underlying true score vector T_i and a random error vector E_i. The errors are assumed to be independent random variables and are uncorrelated with one another and with true scores. Under this assumption, the covariance matrix of observations in the population under study can be expressed as:

$$\Sigma_{XX} = \Sigma_{TT} + \Sigma_{EE},$$

where Σ_{EE} is a diagonal matrix of error variances.

Profiles of different individuals i and i^* (note i^* could be a target or idealized profile) are compared first of all by taking a difference between them. Let this difference be

$$d_{ii*} = X_i - X_{i*}.$$

---

[1] Composites that differ only in sign are effectively equivalent and the composite comprised of all zero weights is irrelevant, thus the number of composites is $\frac{1}{2}(3^{10} - 1)$.

Thus if person 1 has a score vector (2, 1, 1) and person 2 has a score vector (1, 2, 3),

$$d_{12} = \begin{pmatrix} 2 \\ 1 \\ 1 \end{pmatrix} - \begin{pmatrix} 1 \\ 2 \\ 3 \end{pmatrix} = \begin{pmatrix} 1 \\ -1 \\ -2 \end{pmatrix}.$$

The difference vector is then transformed into a distance function by either the Cronbach–Gleser method

$$D_{ii*}^2 = d'_{iii*} d_{ii*}$$

or the Mahalonobis method

$$D_{ii*}^2 = d'_{ii*} \Sigma_{xx}^{-1} d_{ii*}$$

where Σ^{-1} is the inverse of the observed score covariance matrix.

Using the 3 element score vectors given above:

$$D_{12}^2 = (1 \quad -1 \quad -2) \begin{pmatrix} 1 \\ -1 \\ -2 \end{pmatrix} = 6.$$

To continue this hypothetical example, let

$$\Sigma_{xx} = \begin{pmatrix} 3 & 1 & 0 \\ 1 & 2 & 0 \\ 0 & 0 & 2 \end{pmatrix}$$

Based on this Σxx, the Mahalonobis function would be

$$D_{12}^2 = (1 \quad -1 \quad -2) \begin{pmatrix} .4 & -.2 & 0 \\ -.2 & .6 & 0 \\ 0 & 0 & 5 \end{pmatrix} \begin{pmatrix} 1 \\ -1 \\ -2 \end{pmatrix} = 3.4.$$

The definition of profile reliability is an analog of univariate reliability. That is, univariate reliability can be defined as the ratio of true score variance to observed score variance (Guttman, 1945), and by analogy Conger and Lipshitz defined multivariate reliability as the ratio of multivariate true score variance to multivariate observed score variance. For the Mahalonobis function applied to standardized variables this turns out to equal

$$\rho_p = \frac{1^{-1}}{J} T_r (R_{TT}^* R_{XX}^{-1}), \tag{2}$$

where T_r denotes the trace function and J is the number of subtests. R_{TT}^* is as previously defined, and R_{XX}^{-1} is the inverse of the correlation matrix. In case the observed scores are uncorrelated, or the Cronbach–Gleser function is used, the index of multivariate reliability becomes the simple average of the subtest reliabilities. Conger and Lipshitz (1973) reported that the average subtest reliability is also the upper limit for the more general Mahalonobis index. They preferred the Mahalonobis index for two major reasons—despite its computational complexity. First of all, it functions analogously to a univariate index in that it is mathematically identical to a test–retest, parallel form, squared correlation between true and observed score, or ANOVA definition of reliability, whereas the Cronbach–Gleser index is not. Second, the sampling distribution of the Mahalonobis index is well known (Conger, 1974).

Maximally Reliable Composites

The index of multivariate reliability as discussed so far actually has limited application. It does represent the reliability of all possible comparisons and thus of a randomly selected (or discovered) profile. The index can also be shown to function as an analog to a univariate index and in fact has been used in a Spearman–Brown prophecy formula for comparing short form MMPI profiles to full-scale MMPI profiles (Newmark, Conger, & Faschingbauer, 1976). Despite these uses, it seems to have more limited application than a univariate index. For example, given a score vector how does the index help to interpret the score and what is the standard error of measurement of a profile?

There is currently no direct answer to these questions. Instead, Conger and Lipshitz (1973) and Bock (1966) both resorted to deriving a series of composites for score vectors. These composites have been described as either canonical composites (because of the equation used to find them) or as maximally reliable composites (because of their reliability maximizing characteristics).

Earlier in this chapter a composite was described as a weighted sum of test scores. Suppose that the weights were not numerically specified but instead were to be derived in such a way as to maximize the reliability. This can be formulated as: let $Y_k = X W_k$ and $\tau_k = T W_k$. The problem is to find the vector W_k that maximizes the ratio of true score variance to observed score variance, i.e., find W_k so that ρ_{y_k} is a maximum, where

$$\rho_{y_k} = \frac{\sigma^2_{\tau_k}}{\sigma^2_{y_k}} = \frac{W'_k \Sigma_{TT} W_k}{W'_k \Sigma_{xx} W_k}$$

The procedure for finding the weights has been known for a long time, but except for Bock, and Conger and Lipshitz, no one bothered to look beyond the most reliable composite. Another analogy seems appropriate at this time. In principal components analysis and in canonical correlation analysis, equations similar to the one above are used. In both cases, weights are found to maximize some function. In principal components analysis, the variance of a composite is maximized, and in canonical correlation analysis the correlation between two composites is maximized. Furthermore, in both of these procedures subsequent composites are sought that: (1) are uncorrelated with one another; and (2) provide a maximum variance (or correlation). In a similar fashion, a series of score composites can be established for a profile that are uncorrelated with one another and provide a maximum variance. Actually the solution to the equation provided above is given by an eigenvalue–eigenvector equation:

$$\Sigma_{TT} \ W_k = \lambda_k \ \Sigma_{xx} \ W_k , \tag{3}$$

where the eigenvector W_k associated with the largest root λ_k gives the maximally reliable composite, the eigenvector associated with the second largest root gives the second most reliable composite, which is uncorrelated with the first, and so on. As it turns out, the reliability of each composite formed in this way is precisely equal to the corresponding root. And a little matrix algebra will demonstrate that the average reliability of the maximally reliable composites is equal to the multivariate reliability index. That is,

$$\rho_p = \frac{1}{J} \sum_{K} \lambda_k = \frac{1}{J} \sum_{K} \rho_{y_k} .$$

The maximally reliable composites thus provide the same information as the overall index, but because each composite is simply a univariate score, its interpretation is facilitated and a standard error of measurement $\sqrt{1 - \rho_{yk}} \ (\sigma_{yk})$ could be computed. In addition, statistical tests are available to establish the number of dimensions that can be statistically relied upon. The test (after Bock, 1966) is a χ^2 approximation to a likelihood ratio criterion for establishing the significance attributable to the J-s smallest roots:

$$\chi^2 = n_b + n_e - \frac{n_b + K - 1}{2} \sum_{j=s+1}^{K} n_e \left(1 + \frac{n_b \lambda_j}{n_e} \right) ,$$

where $n_b + 1 = N$ (number of subjects) and $n_e = (K-1) \ (N-1)$. However, because the derivation of maximally reliable composites probably would be done for large numbers of subjects relative to the number of variables, the decision as to how many composites to retain would be based on the magnitude of the reliability coefficient rather than on statistical significance alone. In either case, the resulting subset of s composites would yield a profile with uncorrelated scores that would have a multivariate reliability of

$$\rho_{p_s} = \frac{1}{s} \sum_{k=1}^{s} \rho_k . \tag{4}$$

Before taking up one other topic that facilitates the understanding of test batteries or profiles, a much needed illustration is given.

Profile Reliability of the WISC–R

The Wechsler intelligence scales, unlike the Stanford–Binet, provide a profile of subtest scores and more global Verbal, Performance, and Full Scale IQs. Despite caveats about the unguided interpretation of profiles or differences among subscales (Anastasi, 1968; Conger & Conger, 1975; McNemar, 1957; Tellegen & Briggs, 1967), clinicians are encouraged to use the Wechsler scales for various diagnostic purposes. Recent examples encouraging such use are offered by Robb, Bernardoni, and Johnson (1972), and Sattler (1974), who make liberal use of subscale comparisons in their quest for "psychodiagnosticity" from the Wechsler scales. The Wechsler manuals themselves encourage such procedures by providing tables of values necessary to say two subscales are significantly different while providing no cautions about the large number of possible pairwise comparisons.

The question remains, however, as to how reliable WISC-R profiles are and as to which comparisons are reliable and which are not. It is precisely these questions for which the multivariate reliability index and maximally reliable composite were developed. Conger et al. (1979), using data from the WISC-R manual (Wechsler, 1974) investigated the multivariate reliability and maximally reliable composites for 10 subscales at each of 11 age levels. Analyses were required for each group separately because of differences in the true score covariance matrices of the different age groups. For our purposes we simply need to focus on one age group, the 6½-year-olds.

Wechsler (1974) provides correlation matrices (R_{xx}) among all WISC-R subscales for 200 children in the 6½-year-old age group. In addition, split-half reliability estimates for this group are provided for 10 of the 12 subscales (split-half estimates were not available for Digit Span or Coding). The split-half estimates were considered to be reasonable estimates of reliability because they were based on correlations between half-scales comprised of odd versus even items for tests that have an implicit ordering of items according to difficulty level. The quality of the reliability estimates is critical and is discussed in detail by Conger (1974).

To determine the global index of profile reliability the reliability estimates were substituted into the diagonal of R_{xx} to obtain R_{xx}^* and then Equation 2 was used. The resulting index of profile reliability was .60, indicating that the average comparison of profiles has a moderate reliability. By comparison, the average WISC profile reliability was only .51 (Conger & Conger, 1975).

In addition to computing a global index, maximally reliable composites were derived using Equation 3. The results of this analysis indicated (Fig. 1.1) the presence of one very reliable dimension (.96) and three reasonably reliable dimensions (.81, .76, and .73). All together seven of a possible 10 composites had reliabilities exceeding .50. The nature of the maximally reliable composites can be ascertained by looking at the weights used to form the composite (the pattern coefficients) and at the correlations between the composite score and the subscales themselves (the structure coefficients). The terms *pattern* and *structure* are purposely chosen to be identical with those used in oblique factor analyses because canonical solutions do not result in an orthogonal structure. But the composite scores are, in fact, uncorrelated with one another.

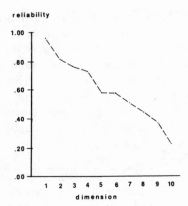

FIG. 1.1.   Reliabilities of maximally
reliable composites.

The pattern and structure coefficients for the four most reliable composites are shown in Table 1.1. The most reliable composite obviously resembles a simple combination of equally weighted subtest scores with the largest ratio of weights being .23 to .09. The structure coefficients are even more uniform, indicating that this composite is approximately equally correlated with all subscales. In this sense it should come as no surprise that the gain in reliability obtained from an optimally derived composite would be comparable to a rationally derived composite in which all subscales were weighted equally (i.e., the profile level or average of subscale scores). The reliability of the rationally determined profile level was computed (by Equation 1 and equals .95. This value obviously is nearly equivalent to the maximum obtainable and furthermore it corresponds exactly to the concept of Full-Scale IQ (with a reliability of .95, Wechsler, 1974).

The patterning of weights for the second most reliable composite overall

TABLE 1.1
Weights and Structure Coefficients:
Four Most Reliable Composites

Scale	w_1	r_1	w_2	r_2	w_3	r_3	w_4	r_4
Information	09	68	06	11	04	03	28	34
Similarities	23	70	92	63	14	08	-63	-31
Arithmetic	14	70	08	09	13	11	66	52
Vocabulary	12	71	13	18	-08	-09	31	30
Comprehension	09	64	06	09	09	11	17	20
Picture Completion	19	69	-18	-15	-93	-62	-35	-21
Picture Arrangement	14	74	-12	-15	-05	-05	06	05
Block Design	16	74	-31	-33	-07	-06	10	07
Object Assembly	12	69	-29	-37	11	11	-22	-20
Mazes	16	65	-36	-34	69	52	-42	-28
composite r_j		.96		.81		.76		.73

indicates a split between the Verbal and Performance subscales. But Similarities has an inordinately high weight in comparison to the other Verbal subscales. The structure coefficients indicate a relatively more uniform weighting for Similarities but not so uniform as to suggest calling this composite a Verbal Scale versus Performance Scale contrast (usually represented as $V_{IQ}-P_{IQ}$). Reliability for a Verbal-Performance composite was computed, however, to determine how different it would be from the second most reliable comparison. The value obtained by using Equation 1 was .76, indicating a moderate gain in reliability if the empirically weighted comparison were used; however, the simplicity of comparing average Verbal and average Performance scores (or Verbal IQ and Performance IQ) may well warrant the loss in reliability. It is also worth noting (Conger et al., 1979) that for only one other age level did such a great disparity exist among the weights or structure coefficients (i.e., age 16½). For every other age (7½ to 15½) the second most reliable composite more closely resembled the standard Verbal-Performance contrast.

The third most reliable composite (Table 1.1) also has an obvious interpretation; it is the difference between the Picture Completion scaled score and the Mazes scaled score. Comparisons between every pair of scaled scores represent a traditional approach to the interpretation of the profiles of the various Wechsler intelligence tests. Tables (for example, Table 12 of the WISC-R manual: Wechsler, 1974) are provided in the form of differences between scaled scores required for claiming that two scaled scores differ at the 15% level of confidence. At least for the 6½-year-olds, there is evidence that one of the 45 possible comparisons (among 10 subscales) is relatively uncorrelated with the overall profile level and the Verbal-Performance difference.

The meaning of the fourth most reliable composite is unclear and it bears no simple resemblance to the scale combinations discussed in the WISC or WISC-R literature. It does, however, help illustrate a potential difficulty inherent in the derivation of maximally reliable composites. The fourth composite, like the first and second, has approximately equivalent weights for Picture Completion and Mazes. By comparison the third composite contrasts these two subscales. This indicates a kind of "factorial complexity" that arises in variance or covariance maximization problems. One dimension is extracted that weights two variables about equally and a subsequent dimension is extracted that contrasts those same two variables.

Psychometricians have long been uncomfortable with this situation and it has led them to seek alternative frameworks for interpreting factor analyses and canonical correlational analyses. The problem with factorially complex solutions is exacerbated further by considering the dependence of the maximization solution on the specific variables included in the study. For example, if the Coding subtest had been substituted for the Mazes subtest the third and fourth most reliable composites would obviously be different. There is thus a problem of *composite invariance* that is not unlike the problem of *factor invariance* (Gorsuch, 1974). In order to overcome this problem and to maximize interpretability, the s "largest" dimensions are rotated, usually by a Varimax rotation (Kaiser, 1958).

Rotated Dimensions

The analysis of the reliability of test batteries or profiles as presented so far has been focused on the global index and the entire set of maximally reliable composites. A profile user on the basis of the magnitude (assuming statistical significance) of the composite score reliabilities may choose to use all, or merely some of the canonical composites. If only the s largest components are retained, then differences among subscale scores or profile elements would be taken in an s-dimensional space with an overall reliability determined by:

$$\rho_s = \frac{1}{s}\sum_{k=1}^{s} \lambda_k .$$

The s retained dimensions would thus constitute the most reliable subspace that could be obtained from s dimensions and a variety of uncorrelated composites could be used to describe this subspace. One set of s composites has already been described, the s most reliable composites; however, these may not always be readily interpretable, as was illustrated in the foregoing.

In the analysis of the WISC-R, the distribution of the roots of the canonical equation (Equation 3) suggested that either four or seven dimensions could be retained depending on what was defined as a satisfactory reliability. If a reliability of .50 were considered adequate then seven dimensions could be retained (with an average reliability of .71), but if .73 were considered adequate then only four should be retained (with an average reliability of .82). In the overall investigation of the WISC-R structure, Conger et al. (1979) were considering 11 age groups rather than just a single age group. They determined that a varimax rotation of seven dimensions provided a better basis for understanding the WISC-R across and within age groups than did the rotation of four, five, or six dimensions.

The varimax rotation of the seven most reliable dimensions for the 6½-year-olds (Table 1.2) resulted in a solution that consists of six "specific" contrasts and one composite contrast. A "specific" contrast was defined by Conger et al. (1979) as a dimension for which one subscale has a very high weight (for example, .90 or above), whereas all other subscales had low weights (for example, .30 to −.30).

For the 6½-year-olds, the specific contrasts are for the subscales of Similarities, Arithmetic, Picture Completion, Picture Arrangement, Block Design, and Mazes. These specifics may at this stage of the analysis be interpreted along the following lines. Each of these six subscales of the WISC-R contains a sufficient amount of reliable but unshared variance to warrant a relatively inde-

TABLE 1.2
Composite Weights for Seven Rotated Dimensions

	INFO	SIM	MATH	VOC	COM	Scale P-COM	P-ARR	B-DES	O-ASS	MAZES	Reliability
w	.33	-.13	.97	.11	-.19	-.12	-.19	-.13	.16	-.18	.72
e	-.08	-.06	-.00	-.15	-.03	-.05	-.14	-.18	.39	.96	.78
i	-.07	-.17	-.19	.52	.78	-.00	.04	-.03	-.55	.25	.64
g	.19	-.10	-.34	.12	-.14	-.23	1.08	-.17	.36	-.31	.62
h	-.09	-.10	-.04	.05	-.08	1.16	-.17	-.16	.09	-.11	.76
t	-.02	1.19	-.14	-.11	-.10	-.09	-.08	-.00	-.03	-.07	.80
s	-.07	.02	-.08	-.26	.04	-.15	-.11	1.32	-.16	-.18	.61

pendent interpretation of scores. This does not mean that the subscales are uncorrelated with one another, however. The independent information in any subscale relative to other subscales may be determined by comparing its reliability to its squared multiple correlation with the remaining variables. In factor analytic terms, the total variance in a variable is often partitioned into three components: the variance shared with other variables (commonality), the reliable variance not shared with other variable (specificity), and the error variance. Conger and Lipshitz (1973) showed that the multivariate reliability index could be expressed as a function of univariate reliabilities (ρ_j's) and shared variances expressed as squared multiple correlations (R_j^2's). The equation is:

$$\rho_p = \frac{1}{K}\sum_j \frac{\rho_j - R_j^2}{1 - R_j^2}.$$

In the specific example being considered, the subscales of Similarities, Arithmetic, Picture Completion, Block Design, and Mazes all had very high reliabilities compared to their squared multiple correlations with the other variables. By comparison, the Information subscale which appears neither as a specific nor a doublet had the lowest reliability, both overall and relative to its shared variance with the remaining subscales. With this in mind, the emergence of the specific contrasts should come as no surprise.

In this overall analysis of the WISC-R, Conger et al. (1979) found that specifics of the aforementioned type emerged at all age levels. They noticed, however, that different subscales appeared at different ages and were systematically related to the amount of specific variance possessed by the subscale. The reader should not, however, gain the impression that every test battery or profile can be satisfactorily reduced to a set of specific contrasts. The WISC-R is a rather unique instrument in that its subscales are highly reliable. The WISC, upon which the WISC-R is based, did not yield a structure comparable to that of the WISC-R. Conger and Conger (1975) did note that the first two maximally reliable composites were similar to profile level and a Verbal–Performance contrast. But the sequence of canonical roots for the $7\frac{1}{2}$-year-olds (the most comparable age group to the WISC-R $6\frac{1}{2}$-year-olds) indicated only five reasonably reliable dimensions rather than seven. Furthermore their rotated solution did not in general indicate the existence of specifics.

Rational Alternatives

In the earlier discussion of the first two maximally reliable composites (unrotated), the notion of a rational composite was introduced. Thus because the pattern and structure coefficients of the most reliable composite were nearly uniform, it was decided to compare its reliability to that of a composite formed by weighting all variables equally. The nearly identical value of the uniformly weighted composite to that of the optimally weighted composite leads to the conclusion that the scales might just as well be equally weighted as optimally weighted. This is reasonable not only from a practical standpoint but also from a statistical one. It has long been argued, for example, that the use of unit or integer weights leads to better cross-validation (Nunnally, 1967). With this basic principle in mind, Conger et al. (1979) decided to compare reliabilities of rationally constructed composites to the reliabilities of the optimally weighted composites.

Two rational composites were actually established for each subscale: a contrast of the subscale score with the average subscale score, and a contrast of the subscale score with either the average verbal subscale score or the average performance subscale score depending on the classification of the subscale. Thus the Similarities subscale, for example, was compared to the average of all subscales by using a weight vector of $(-\frac{1}{10}, \frac{9}{10}, -\frac{1}{10}, -\frac{1}{10}, \ldots)$ and also to the average of all verbal subscales by using a weight vector of

$$(-\tfrac{1}{5}, \tfrac{4}{5}, -\tfrac{1}{5}, -\tfrac{1}{5}, -\tfrac{1}{5}, 0, 0, \ldots).$$

These weight vectors were then used in Equation 1 to determine the reliability of the rationally established composites. Their results indicated that, with only a few minor exceptions, the rational composites contrasting subscale scores with the average subscale score were nearly as reliable as the optimally weighted specifics, whereas the rational composites contrasting a subscale score with its respective verbal or performance subscale average generally had a lower and often unacceptable reliability. The obvious conclusion was a recommendation that clinicians interpret WISC–R profiles by:

1. Comparing profiles on the basis of total IQ.
2. Comparing the Verbal IQ to the Performance IQ.
3. Comparing individual subscale scores to the average score for all scales.

The actual comparison should of course take into account the standard error of measurement of the composite (as described earlier).

Summary

Profiles and test batteries can provide a clinician or researcher with valuable information; however, if consideration is not given to the reliability of the pattern of scores, the clinician or researcher may instead be provided with noise. In order to provide users of profiles with a measure of the degree of confidence they might have in interpreting a profile, an index of profile reliability was developed (ρ_p). This index is of limited value, however, in that it does not specify which profiles are reliable nor does it have a standard error of measurement. Thus, both Bock (1966) and Conger (1974) recommended that profiles be transformed to a set of uncorrelated and sequentially maximally reliable composites. This derived set of composite scores may be represented as a profile and scores can be compared using the simple Cronbach–Gleser approach (1953) rather than the more complex Mahalonobis approach (Overall, 1964). Conger and Conger (1975) also considered the problem of assigning meaning to the maximally reliable composites and found that some were readily interpretable, whereas others were not. Consequently they introduced the idea of rotating the maximally reliable composites to a more readily interpretable structure. In their analysis of the WISC they found that a Varimax rotation of structure coefficients yielded an interpretable set of new composites. Other rotational options have not yet been explored, however. Conger et al. (1979) used all the foregoing steps in their analysis of the WISC–R with satisfactory results. They further found that the optimally weighted rotated composites could be nicely approximated by a set of rationally derived contrasts in which each subscale was contrasted with the average of all subscales.

The foregoing is a brief summary of developments in a multivariate procedure that is still relatively new. There are many implications of this procedure for test theory and for the analysis of multiple measures that have not yet been explored, but two implications have been investigated. Conger and Stallard (1976) demonstrated that if a principal component reduction of fallible measures with arbitrary scale units was desired, and their reliabilities were known, the measures should first be transformed by equating their errors of measurement. The principal components of the transformed measures would then possess the additional property of being the sequentially maximally reliable composites. In a more recent development (Conger, 1980), it has been argued that the various procedures used to analyze congeneric measures (Lord & Novick, 1968) are special cases derivable from a more general multivariate approach to test scores.

There are also limitations to the profile reliability approach, for example, when there is interest in independently interpreting profile characteristics of level, scatter, and shape. But a recent article by Skinner (1978) may contain the key to integrating the analysis of these characteristics and the analysis of profiles as discussed in this chapter.

REFERENCES

Anastasi, A. *Psychological testing.* New York: Macmillan, 1968.

Bock, R. D. Contributions of multivariate experimental designs to educational research. In R. B. Cattell (Ed.), *Handbook of multivariate experimental psychology.* Chicago: Rand McNally, 1966.

Cattell, R. B. r_p and other coefficients of pattern similarity. *Psychometrika,* 1949, *14,* 279–298.

Cohen, J. r_c: A profile similarity coefficient invariant over variable reflection. *Psychological Bulletin,* 1969, *71,* 281–284.

Conger, A. J. Estimating profile reliability and maximally reliable composites. *Multivariate Behavioral Research,* 1974, *9,* 85–104.

Conger, A. J. Maximally reliable composites for unidimensional measures. *Educational and Psychological Measurement,* 1980, *88,* 322-328.

Conger, A. J., & Conger, J. C. Reliable dimensions for WISC profiles. *Educational and Psychological Measurement,* 1975, *35,* 847-863.

Conger, A. J., Conger, J. C., Farrell, A. D., & Ward, D. What can the WISC-R measure? *Applied Psychological Measurement,* 1979, *3,* 421-436.

Conger, A. J., & Lipshitz, R. Measures of reliability for profiles and test batteries. *Psychometrika,* 1973, *38,* 411-427.

Conger, A. J., & Stallard, E. Equivalence among canonical factor analysis, canonical reliability analysis, and principal components analysis: Implications for data reduction of fallible measures. *Educational and Psychological Measurement,* 1976, *36,* 619-626.

Cronbach, L. J., & Gleser, G. C. Assessing similarity between profiles. *Psychological Bulletin,* 1953, *50,* 456-473.

Gaier, E. L., & Lee, M. C. Pattern analysis: The configural approach to predictive measurement. *Psychological Bulletin,* 1953, *50,* 140-148.

Gorsuch, R. L. *Factor analysis.* Philadelphia: W.B. Saunders, 1974.

Guttman, L. A basis for analyzing test retest reliability. *Psychometrika,* 1945, *10,* 255-282.

Harris, C. W. Characteristics of two measures of profile similarity. *Psychometrika,* 1955, *20,* 289-297.

Kaiser, H. F. The varimax criterion for analytic rotation in factor analysis. *Psychometrika,* 1958, *23,* 187-200.

Lord, F. M., & Novick, M. R. *Statistical theories of mental test scores.* Reading, Mass.: Addison-Wesley, 1968.

McNemar, Q. On WAIS difference scores. *Journal of Consulting Psychology,* 1957, *21,* 239-240.

Newmark, C., Conger, A. J., & Faschingbauer, T. The interpretive validity and effective test length functioning of an abbreviated MMPI relative to the standard MMPI. *Journal of Clinical Psychology,* 1976, *32,* 27-32.

Nunnally, J. C. *Psychometric theory.* New York: McGraw-Hill, 1967.

Osgood, C. E., & Suci, G. A measure of relation determined by both mean difference and profile information. *Psychological Bulletin,* 1952, *59,* 251-262.

Overall, J. Note on multivariate methods for profile analysis. *Psychological Bulletin,* 1964, *61,* 195-198.

Robb, G. P., Bernardoni, L. C., & Johnson, R. W. *Assessment of individual mental ability.* Scranton, Pa.: International Text Book Co., 1972.

Sattler, J. M. *Assessment of children's intelligence* (Rev. ed.). Philadelphia: Saunders, 1974.

Skinner, H. A. Differentiating the contribution of elevation, scatter, and shape in profile similarity. *Educational and Psychological Measurement,* 1978, *38,* 297-308.

Tellegen, A., & Briggs, P. F. Old wine in new skins: Grouping Wechsler subtests into new scales. *Journal of Consulting Psychology,* 1967, *31,* 499-506.

Wechsler, D. *Manual for the Wechsler Intelligence Scale for Children—Revised.* New York: The Psychological Corporation, 1974.

Symmetric and Asymmetric Rotations in Canonical Correlation Analysis: New Methods with Drug Variable Examples

2

Peter M. Bentler
George J. Huba
University of California, Los Angeles

Canonical correlation analysis is a procedure for reducing two sets of variables to a smaller set of weighted sums of the original variables, called canonical variates, in order to simplify the total correlations between the two domains under study. For example, when there are 10 variables in one set and eight in another, there are $10 \times 8 = 80$ bivariate correlations between domains. If all variables in each domain are essentially independent of one another and related to only a small number of the variables in the other domain, we would probably have to study all 80 of the cross-domain bivariate correlations in order to understand fully the interrelationships of the sets of variables. When, however, the variables within and across sets are redundant, it is sometimes possible for a small number of canonical variates to summarize all the between-set covariation. That is, we can sometimes transform the original measures in each set into a small number of weighted sums so that the cross-set correlations among the sums will explain all the statistically robust covariation between the original variables in Set 1 and those in Set 2. As a total data analysis method, traditional canonical correlation analysis consists of: (1) testing to see if two domains are significantly correlated; (2) forming weighted sums in each domain in an optimal fashion so that the cross-domain correlations can be explained by as few of these sums as possible; (3) testing to see how many of the weighted linear combinations are necessary and statistically robust.

Of course, the ultimate usefulness of the canonical correlation procedure for summarizing cross-domain covariation hinges on two criteria. It must be ascertained not only how well a small number of canonical variates can summarize statistical association through the canonical correlations, but also how well the variates can be conceptualized and interpreted. Unfortunately, it is often found that canonical variates are statistically adequate but theoretically meaningless. An early suggestion for increasing the theoretical importance of canonical correlation analysis was the interpretation of an alternate "loadings" matrix (Cooley & Lohnes, 1971); as shown in the following, this matrix is the most appropriate set of summary coefficients to interpret. A more recent aid to interpretation has been the suggestion that rigid rotation of the canonical correlation solution may yield a better theoretical summary of the data relationships than was previously possible (Cliff & Krus, 1976). This chapter discusses canonical correlation analysis conceptually, and presents new rotation methods to increase the interpretability and meaningfulness of the results. The mathematics of canonical correlation analysis (without rotation of axes) were first developed by Hotelling (1936) and are well presented in standard texts (Anderson, 1958; Cooley & Lohnes, 1971; Morrison, 1976; Tatsuoka, 1971; Van deGeer, 1971).

The idea of canonical correlation can be grasped most simply with the use of some diagrams that represent original variables and the derived canonical variates. Figure 2.1 presents the interrelations among eight variables prior to any analysis by canonical correlation. As is well known, with eight variables there are $8(8 - 1)/2 = 28$ intercorrelations between different pairs of variables. These are represented by the lines in the figure. The diagram has been labeled to indicate that the eight variables have been partitioned into two sets, here called X and Y, with four variables in each set. The investigator must be able to classify variables unambiguously into one set or the other if the method of canonical correlation is to be fruitfully applied. In the area of adolescents' drug use, for example, a clear distinction can be made between current usage of various drugs and intended future usage of drugs (this is an example we return to later in the chapter), so that the X set may be taken to be current use and the Y set, future use. (Classification into an X and a Y set does not necessarily imply a contrast of independent and dependent variables.) It follows that the observed correlations

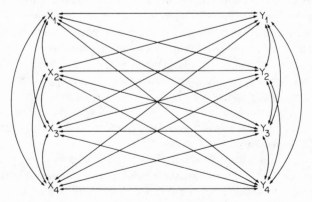

FIG. 2.1.   Relations among observed variables X_1, X_2, X_3, X_4, Y_1, Y_2, Y_3, and Y_4.

among all variables can then be conceived of as: (1) those correlations representing within-set relations; and (2) those correlations representing between-set relations. In Fig. 2.1, the within-set correlations are represented by curved lines, whereas the between-set correlations are shown as straight lines. Canonical correlation analysis takes the within-set correlations (curved lines) as given, and attempts to find a simplifying description of the between-set correlations (straight lines). Thus, in the figure $6 \times 2 = 12$, correlations are not subject to a special analysis, but the 16 between-set correlations are the focus of analysis to yield a simpler form. Although the within-set correlations are crucial to the mathematics of obtaining actual solutions, they can be ignored in a conceptualization of the technique; for purposes of clarity, we do not show the within-set correlations in subsequent figures.

Figure 2.2 shows a description of the variables of Fig. 2.1 using canonical variates; it is apparent in this case that simplification has not been achieved. However, it is important to study the figure to determine what has occurred in the analysis. In the first place, it will be noted that, in addition to the original eight variables, the figure now contains eight new variables subscripted by Latin numerals. These new variables are canonical variates. Each one is a new variable that represents a linear combination of the original variables as indicated by the directional arrows. In particular, X_I is a new variable that represents a linear combination of all the original variables X_1–X_4, as shown by the arrows emanating from the original variables and terminating at X_I. Each arrow represents a weight attached to an original measure to generate the canonical variate. If the variables have been standardized to unit variance, as is usual, these weights are typically in the range from $+1$ to -1. Specifically, the coefficients are the beta weights of ordinary multiple regression, in the prediction of X_I from X_1–X_4. The unusual feature of canonical correlation, however, is that the variates such as X_I are not known before the analysis, but are determined in the analysis itself. For example, if X_1–X_4 represent students' current use of beer, wine, marijuana, and hashish, X_I would represent some new variable that is a composite of the original

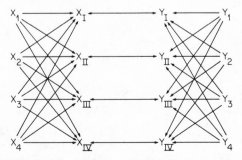

FIG. 2.2.   Relations among observed variables X_1–X_4, Y_1–Y_4 and canonical variates X_I–X_{IV}, Y_I–Y_{IV}: A useless case.

drug use variables. The problem of *interpreting* this new variable is a very real one, and we shortly address this point. But note in the figure that although we started with four X variables we have generated four new, derived canonical variates; the same effect occurs for the Y variables. It is hard—in fact impossible—to speak of simplification here. The figure does represent a fact about canonical analysis: The maximum number of pairs of canonical variates that can be obtained is the minimum of the number of variables in each of the two sets. In this case, each set has four variables, so four is the maximum number of possible variate pairs. If the set Y had only two variables, however, it would not be possible to obtain more than two pairs of variates. Fortunately, there are several statistical criteria for determining the number of statistically robust variates (cf. Mendoza, Markos, & Gonter, 1978, for a Monte Carlo comparison), so it is usually possible to eliminate several variates from consideration.

The fact that the variates in Fig. 2.2 have been labeled with corresponding Latin subscripts is no accident, as a special relationship exists between pairs of variates from the X and Y domains. As seen by the straight lines, again representing correlations, the canonical variates are paired with each other. That is, X_I correlates only with Y_I and not at all with any of the other X or Y variates. There are no lines, or correlations, connecting X_I to any other variate. Unrotated canonical variates are, by definition, uncorrelated within and between sets. Furthermore, the variates are determined under a mathematical constraint that the correlation between the pair X_I, Y_I is not smaller than the correlation between the pair X_{II}, Y_{II}, and so on. In other words, the canonical variates are those derived variates that are uncorrelated within and between sets except that they correlated pairwise in decreasing order of magnitude. The pairwise correlations are called canonical correlations. The variates having the smallest canonical correlations are usually statistically unreliable and discarded.

If only two canonical correlations are statistically significantly different from zero, the figural representation that would be obtained in our example is shown in Fig. 2.3. It is apparent that a great deal of simplification has now been achieved, though we develop further possibilities shortly. We need to reiterate the interpre-

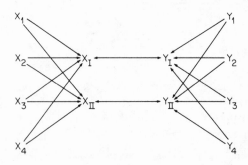

FIG. 2.3. Relations among observed variables and canonical variates expressed via canonical weights.

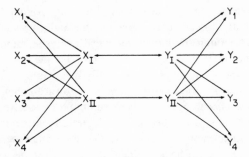

FIG. 2.4.   Relations among observed variables and canonical variates expressed via canonical loadings.

tation of the directional arrows, however. The weights are attached to the original variables to generate the canonical variates. These weights are usually called canonical weights, and their pattern shows how the variables are weighted to form the variates. An equivalent representation of canonical correlation is possible in which the variables are interpreted as functions of the variates. This schema is depicted in Fig. 2.4.

In comparing Fig. 2.4 to Fig. 2.3, it will be noted that the directional arrows have been reversed, whereas the lines representing the canonical correlations have not been changed. The arrows aiming at the observed variables represent a description of the observed variables in terms of the canonical variates. For example, variable X_1 is now interpreted as a linear combination of the variates X_I and X_{II}, and in an actual application the arrows would be replaced by specific numerical weights. The arrows of Fig. 2.4 are called canonical loadings, to distinguish them from canonical weights. As before, these loadings are regression (or beta) coefficients, but they have a further, more illuminating interpretation. Because the canonical variates are uncorrelated, canonical loadings can be interpreted as correlation coefficients between the variables and variates (when both are standardized to unit variance, as is usually the case). In this representation, then, the canonical variates are seen as more basic variables than the observed variables, and they are considered to generate the observed variables.

ROTATION OF CANONICAL VARIATES

A basic feature of canonical correlation analysis as typically conceived lies in the fact that the canonical variates are completely uncorrelated within and between sets, except for the single pairwise linkage of a variate from one set to a variate from another set. In some ways, this lack of linkage makes traditional canonical correlation a simplifying multivariate method. However, a glance at Fig. 2.4

makes it clear that the canonical loadings are not at all simplified; each and every possible linkage between a variable and a variate may be nonzero.[1]

Although traditional canonical analysis, then, may be thought of as an attempted simplification of cross-correlations into a diagonal form, such reduction may not be the most theoretically meaningful one. In psychology we often find that our theories and intuition point toward *complex relationships among simple constructs* rather than the assumption of simple relationships among complex constructs, as embedded within traditional canonical correlation analysis. An alternate method of simplification is to force the matrices of loadings for the X and Y sets to have as many zero elements as possible while maintaining the explanatory power of the solution. Cliff and Krus (1976) present the necessary mathematical proof that this alternate form of simplification can be accomplished if no constraints are placed on the simplicity of the correlations of canonical variates *between sets*. That is, simplification can be applied to the loadings matrix if we are willing to forego diagonal simplicity in the canonical variate correlations, while maintaining the explanatory power of the traditional solution. This alternate simplification can be achieved by a rotation of the original solution. Such simplification is analogous to the case in factor analysis, where one first seeks an optimal reduced-dimensionality solution under certain mathematical constraints and then rotates the loadings to a more theoretically meaningful position.

Actually it is possible to find a way to modify the method of canonical correlation so as to yield simplification in the loadings of the diagrammatic representation. In Fig. 2.4, every variable is considered to be a linear combination of all possible canonical variates in its set; if simplification could be achieved, variables might be combinations of fewer canonical variates. For example, X_1 may be interpreted as a linear function of only one canonical variate rather than two as in the current figure. The simplification of canonical loadings involves rotation of the canonical variates. One could equally well discuss rotating the canonical weights, but we do not feel this approach is usually desirable. Our discussion focuses on the loadings, although the mathematical development at the end of the chapter is more general. Cliff and Krus (1976) also appear to recommend rotation of loadings, though their only example is based on a rotation of weights. Actually, in either case it is the canonical variates themselves that are rotated, but the effect of that rotation is observed in the loadings and weights.

---

[1]For those cases in which it would possible a priori to state that certain weights should be exactly zero, it would be desirable to have a procedure (more direct than the rotation suggested) to determine such a model. Bentler and Wingard (1981) have developed methods of confirmatory canonical correlation analysis, based on the family of covariance structure models encompassed in Bentler's (1976) or Bentler and Weeks' (1979, 1980) general formulations. In the absence of such an analog to confirmatory factor analysis, it might be advisable to use orthogonal confirmatory, least squares alignment ("Procrustean") rotations such as those suggested by Schönemann (1966) and Browne (1972). .

The rotation of canonical variates refers to the process of taking a set of canonical variates (X_I, X_{II}, Y_I, and Y_{II} in Fig. 2.4) and creating new linear combinations of these variates to yield a new set of variates that may be labeled X_{I*}, X_{II*}, Y_{I*}, and Y_{II*}. For example X_{I*} may be a particular linear combination of X_I and X_{II}. (The X's are not used to generate Y's, nor vice versa). These new variates will have new relations both among each other and to the original variables. Let us examine these relations in turn.

It was previously mentioned that canonical variates have the property that they are uncorrelated within and between sets, as shown in Fig. 2.4. It must now be added that these variates—which we shall now call unrotated variates—are the only possible set of variates to have these characteristics! Consequently, any new variates that might be determined through rotation cannot be uncorrelated in the same way. In the most general case, developed elsewhere by the writers, we might consider new variates that are allowed to correlate freely among themselves. However, such generality creates some new problems that are beyond the scope of the current chapter, and so we restrict our discussion to new variates that must remain uncorrelated within sets. The example of Fig. 2.5 will make this concept clear.

The new variates indicated in the figure have stars attached to them to indicate that they are not the same variates as those previously considered. Like the previous variates, however, they can be seen to be uncorrelated within sets. In this case, we see that X_{I*} and X_{II*} are uncorrelated, as also are Y_{I*} and Y_{II*}. There are no lines connecting these variates. In contrast to the unrotated variates, however, the new variates are correlated across the X and Y sets. Cliff and Krus (1976) develop only the case where the correlation between X_{I*} and Y_{II*} is taken to be exactly the same as the correlation between X_{II*} and Y_{i*}. In that specialization, called here the *symmetric* case for obvious reasons, the two dashed lines would take on equal values. Actually, there is no particular reason to assume that these correlations need to be the same. In this chapter we develop, for the first time, the concept of *asymmetric* rotation of canonical variates that have the property that the between-set correlations need not be symmetric. In this case, the two dashed lines would be free to take on different numerical values.

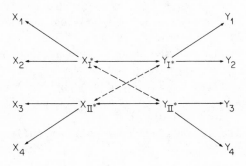

FIG. 2.5. Relations among observed variables and rotated canonical variables.

The new relations between the rotated canonical variates and the original observed variables, represented by the canonical loadings, have now also been modified. In particular, we see a tremendous simplification in this hypothetical example. Each observed variable is no longer represented as a combination of several canonical variates, but rather is generated by only a single variate. In the beer, wine, "pot," "hash" example mentioned previously, Fig. 2.5 would be consistent with an interpretation of X_{I*} as alcohol use and X_{II*} as cannabis use. The missing, absent arrows represent regression weights (or correlations) that are exactly zero. These zero correlations make the figure simple and allow one to interpret the relations between sets X and Y in a particularly simple way. The goal of rotation in canonical correlation is to introduce as many zero or near-zero loadings as possible, while having the cross-variate correlations remain interpretable. The rotation strategies we discuss focus only on the simplification of the loadings and allow the correlations between $X*$ and $Y*$ to be unconstrained. In many practical applications we have found that the off-diagonal correlations between $X*$ and $Y*$ are rarely of sufficient magnitude to merit interpretation.

SYMMETRIC ROTATIONS

In order to implement symmetric simplicity rotations for the loading matrix, one must consider two components. The first is a mathematical criterion of loading simplicity. The mathematical criterion must faithfully represent one's concept of the goal to be attained in the loading matrix. This goal is often considered to be Thurstone's specification of simple structure, a concept derived in factor analysis to indicate criteria for the location of zero loadings in a loading matrix. That is, each variable should be represented in terms of few canonical variates, and each canonical variate should influence only few variables (Comrey, 1973; Harman, 1976; Mulaik, 1972). Two mathematical criteria that quantify this concept easily are varimax (Kaiser, 1958) and orthosim (Bentler, 1977). An equally important, but inexplicably overlooked, ingredient to implementing symmetric rotations involves a choice as to the relative importance to be given to the two sets of variables in determining the final loading solution. We shall develop this concept for the first time, but it helps to have a more concrete idea about canonical correlation analysis and rotation before examining it in detail.

We shall utilize the device of using artificial data to present a canonical correlation analysis. Although artificial data have the drawback of appearing too specialized to generalize to the real world, real data often have the drawback of remaining ambiguous in interpretation because one cannot verify the underlying "truth" one is attempting to reveal through the analysis. Later, of course, we shall turn to real data.

The artificial example was constructed as follows. Three sets of parallel tests

TABLE 2.1
Correlation Coefficients for Artificial Examples

	1	2	3	4	5	6	7	8
1	–	.773	.428	.010	.390	.293	.014	.018
2	.576	–	.104	.320	.501	.376	.018	.023
3	.501	.530	–	.480	.288	.216	.298	.383
4	.052	-.046	-.160	–	.216	.162	.223	.287
5	-.054	.156	-.042	.598	–	.720	.300	.180
6	.176	.163	.062	.535	.539	–	.553	.339
7	.330	.017	.076	-.016	.035	.193	–	.941
8	.155	.108	-.001	-.095	-.015	.035	.658	–
9	.182	.055	.033	.160	.234	.122	.568	.652

Note: Example 1, $N = 50$, is the 9-variable matrix below the diagonal.
Example 2 is the 8-variable matrix above the diagonal.
Diagonal elements $r_{ii} = 1.0$ omitted.

were generated with the equations:

$$z_1 = t_1 + e_1 \qquad z_2 = t_1 + e_2 \qquad z_3 = t_1 + e_3$$
$$z_4 = t_2 + e_4 \qquad z_5 = t_2 + e_5 \qquad z_6 = t_2 + e_6$$
$$z_7 = t_3 + e_7 \qquad z_8 = t_3 + e_8 \qquad z_9 = t_3 + e_9,$$

where $\sigma_{z(i)}(i = 1, 2, \ldots, 9)$ was set at unity and $\sigma_{e(i)}(i = 1, 2, \ldots, 9) = \sigma_{z(i)}(1 - \rho_{zz})^{\frac{1}{2}}$ and $\sigma_{t(i)}$ $(i = 1, 2, \ldots, 9) = \sigma_{z(i)} \rho_{zz}^{\frac{1}{2}}$. True scores ($t$) and error ($e$) were uncorrelated and ρ was set at .5. It is apparent that variables z_1-z_3, z_4-z_6, and z_7-z_9 measure the same underlying quality (t_j) except for errors of measurement. Fifty normally distributed observations for each variable were generated using the APL "?" operator with Gaussian summation to convert uniformly distributed deviates to normally distributed ones. The bottom half of Table 2.1 shows the resulting correlations among the nine variables in this sample.

For the canonical variable problem, variables 1, 4, and 7 were assigned to the X set and variables 2, 3, 5, 6, 8, and 9 were put in the Y set. In other words, the X set consisted of three variables and the Y set of six variables, so that there can be no more than three pairs of canonical variates. The question is: Do the canonical variates correspond in any reasonable way to the three true scores t_1, t_2, and t_3?[2]

The left side of Table 2.2 presents the canonical loadings for the unrotated solution, that is, the loadings as typically reported. These loadings correspond to numerical values of directional arrows as described in Fig. 2.4. The bottom part

---

[2]For the artificial example all three canonical correlations are significant. For the omnibus test, $\chi_{18}^2 = 92.62$. With two roots partialled, $\chi_4^2 = 20.03$, indicating that all three canonical correlations must be considered statistically reliable.

TABLE 2.2
Canonical Solutions for Example 1

Variable	Canonical Loadings					
No.	Unrotated			Rotated ($\alpha = 1/3$)		
Set X	X_I	X_{II}	X_{III}	X_{I*}	X_{II*}	X_{III}
1	-.444	.602	.664	.969	.104	.225
4	.647	-.235	.725	-.036	.996	-.073
7	.391	.918	-.073	.104	.061	.993
Set Y	Y_I	Y_{II}	Y_{III}	Y_{I*}	Y_{II*}	Y_{III*}
2	-.531	.321	.632	.881	.067	-.055
3	-.519	.390	.385	.743	-.118	.057
5	.603	-.191	.592	-.076	.863	-.027
6	.472	.123	.719	.225	.821	.173
8	.308	.853	-.250	.013	-.114	.934
9	.436	.678	.116	.095	.267	.764

Canonical Correlations

	Y_I	Y_{II}	Y_{II}		Y_{I*}	Y_{II*}	Y_{III*}
X_I	.786	0	0	X_{I*}	.695	-.081	-.009
X_{II}	0	.706	0	X_{II*}	-.081	.686	.036
X_{III}	0	0	.605	X_{III*}	-.009	.036	.717

of the left side of Table 2.2 presents the canonical correlations between the corresponding canonical variates of the X and Y sets. These correlations correspond to the between-set lines shown in Fig. 2.4. As would be expected in the unrotated solution, the matrix of cross-correlations is diagonal because only specific pairs of variates are allowed to correlate.

In order to interpret the canonical variates, we examine the patterns of correlations between variables and variates. In the ideal case, we would hope that variables of the X set and variables 2 and 3 of the Y set would be highly correlated with a corresponding X and Y variate, and that all the other variables would be uncorrelated with that pair of variates; similar statements apply to the remaining loadings. However, as may be seen, the unrotated canonical loadings show no correspondence to the underlying structure that generated the data. It should be noted particularly that the first dimension in each domain represents a contrast between the first versus the second and third true variables.

The final, symmetrically rotated solution for this example, obtained using a two-matrix orthosim procedure described later, is shown in the right part of Table 2.2. In contrast to Fig. 2.5, there do not appear to be exact zeros in the loading matrix, which would correspond to missing arrows in a figure. However, it will be noted that there is a clear separation between large loadings and small ones, the latter presumably being larger than zero primarily because of the sampling experiment that was performed. In very large samples one might expect the small values to be still closer to zero, as it can be noted that the pattern of small loadings for a given pair of variates corresponds to all the variables that do not indicate a given "true" variable, whereas the large loadings mirror the artificial structure that was built into the data. Thus, for example, the variates X_{I*} and Y_{I*} are clearly interpretable as the true variable t_1.

The intercorrelations among the canonical variates are presented in the bottom part of Table 2.2. In the symmetrically rotated solution, the correlation matrix is symmetric. Although the unrotated variates have the property of correlating pairwise in sequential, decreasing order, the rotated pairs of parallel variates need show no such order and in general will show less extreme correlations than the unrotated variates. The highest correlation in the rotated solution (here, .717) will rarely be as large as the largest correlation in the unrotated solution (here, .786), whereas the smallest correlation in the diagonal of the rotated correlation matrix (.686) will typically be substantially larger than the smallest unrotated correlation (.605). The off-diagonals of the correlation matrix in this example are quite small, so that the cross-correlations among presumably different variates are very low. Thus the rotation has almost maintained the between-set orthogonality (lack of correlation) traditionally associated with canonical solutions. In our experience, such a result is frequently observed.

We are now ready to return to the neglected problem of determining the relative importance to be attached to simplification in the loading matrices of two sets. In previous descriptions of rotation in canonical correlation analysis (Cliff & Krus, 1976), this issue is not addressed. It is only pointed out that some method must be chosen to simplify the loadings of both sets combined. That is, in Table 2.2 one might desire the solution to determine as many near zero values in the $X*$ and $Y*$ loading matrices as possible, irrespective of whether more such values appear in one matrix or the other. In practice, this is typically achieved by placing the unrotated matrices end to end, thus generating a larger matrix (here, 9 × 3), and submitting this matrix to a standard rotation program such as varimax or orthosim. In many instances such a procedure can be defended because one has no particular reason to be concerned with simplification in one matrix versus simplification in the other matrix. However, it must be recognized that this method implicitly weights each matrix in proportion to the number of variables in the set. For example, in Table 2.2 there are only nine possible loadings that could potentially be made small in the X set, whereas there are 18 loadings that are potentially tiny in the Y set. It could happen, in some examples, that all the simplification occurs in one set and virtually none in the other. Such a phenomenon is sometimes best left not to chance, but rather to the control of the experimenter. If one set of variables were quite well understood to have a simple structure but the other set were quite arbitrary, one might want the simplicity to manifest itself as much as possible in the first matrix but not necessarily at all in the other matrix. If the artificial example consisted of the same X set, but the Y variables were arbitrary criterion variables to be predicted from X, one might wish the smaller loading matrix involving the X variables only to show the best possible simplicity, without potential dilution from the other variables.

In the last section of the chapter we present the mathematics for weighting a simplicity function of the two loading matrices in accord with one's choice. There is a parameter α $(0 \le \alpha \le 1)$ that represents the relative influence one would like the X variables to have in the rotation. In the absence of a specific rationale, α should probably represent the proportion of variables in the X set so that each variable has approximately the same influence on the solution. The solution reported in Table 2.2 used this rationale, with $\alpha = \frac{1}{3}$. Another way to handle this case is to place the matrices end to end, as previously mentioned. In other instances, α might be chosen to be another number such as 1 or 0 at the extremes. The extreme cases, of course, can also be handled by traditional rotation algorithms by using only the X or Y loading matrices as inputs to a rotation algorithm. The resulting rotation matrix would be saved and then applied to the remaining matrix to obtain the complete solution. Although we develop a two-matrix version of orthosim (Bentler, 1977), the concept is equally applicable to other orthogonal rotation criteria such as varimax (Kaiser, 1958).

ASYMMETRIC ROTATIONS

The method of rotating canonical variates asymmetrically is introduced with a second artificial example that corresponds closely to the introductory figures. The upper triangle of Table 2.1 presents the intercorrelations among eight artificial variables. The first four variables were arbitrarily assigned to the X set, and the remaining variables to the Y set. The unrotated canonical solution is presented in the left part of Table 2.3, using the format introduced in Table 2.2. It will be noted that in this artificial example there are only two canonical variates; the remaining variates are, by construction, zero to within rounding error. Consequently, the solution corresponds to that shown in Fig. 2.4. The numbers of Table 2.3 can now be used to describe accurately the arrows and lines of Fig. 2.4. The middle part of Table 2.3 presents the $\alpha = .5$ two-matrix orthosim solution. It may be observed that the solution now mirrors approximately the diagram shown in Fig. 2.5; it would be exact if loadings of .2 or less in absolute value were exactly zero, or if we used the convention of not drawing small loadings in the figure. The value of this contrived example, as well as the previous one, is that it clearly illustrates the extent to which rotation can make the solution more interpretable, and possibly more valid as a representation of the relationships inherent in the data. Although we certainly would not argue that rotation will always make the results more representative of the underlying processes, to the extent to which there are clusters of variables in one domain

TABLE 2.3
Canonical Solutions for Example 2

Canonical Loadings

Variable No.	Unrotated		Rotated Symmetrically		Rotated Asymmetrically	
Set X	X_I	X_{II}	X_{I*}	X_{II*}	X_{I*}	X_{II*}
X_1	.454	−.502	.662	.142	.676	−.030
X_2	.583	−6.44	.850	−.181	.868	−.038
X_3	.520	.562	.093	.760	−.034	.765
X_4	.391	.421	.071	.570	−.025	.574
Set Y	Y_I	Y_{II}	Y_{I*}	Y_{II*}	Y_{I*}	Y_{II*}
Y_1	.721	−.353	.791	.136	.803	.003
Y_2	.540	−.266	.594	.100	.602	.001
Y_3	.313	.628	−.114	.692	.003	.702
Y_4	.401	.807	−.147	.889	.002	.901

Canonical Correlations

	Y_I	Y_{II}		Y_{I*}	Y_{II*}		Y_{I*}	Y_{II*}
X_1	.980	0	X_{I*}	.780	.278	X_{I*}	.743	.053
X_{II}	0	.395	X_{II*}	.278	.595	X_{II*}	.502	.558

related to clusters of variables in the other, the rotation should increase meaningfulness.

In an asymmetric rotation, each of the two unrotated loading matrices for sets X and Y are rotated separately, and the effects of that rotation are traced mathematically to the two loading matrices as well as to the intercorrelations among canonical variates. This procedure was implemented using orthosim for the example, and the results are reported in the last columns of Table 2.3. There are two main features to be noted in these results. First, the near-zero loadings of the symmetric solution are now even closer to zero, and the larger loadings are also larger. The results correspond more closely to Fig. 2.5. In other words, the loading matrices tend to be simpler in form with an asymmetrical rotation, and consequently it is easier to interpret the variables in terms of the canonical variates and vice versa. However, it must be noted that the matrix of correlations among the canonical variates is now asymmetric, meaning that the two off-diagonal correlations are no longer equal. Evidently, X_{II*} correlates more highly with Y_{I*} than does X_{I*} with Y_{II*}. Equally importantly, X_{II*} is now seen to be related almost as highly to the variate Y_{I*} as to its paired variate Y_{II*}. Such a result could have important substantive implications in some examples.

It must be pointed out that the symmetric solution will generally yield off-diagonal correlations that are an approximate weighted average of the correlations observed with the asymmetric solution. Consequently, one can obtain a fairly good idea about the symmetric case from the asymmetric case, but the reverse does not appear to be true. We would propose carrying out the asymmetric rotation first, then using the symmetric method. In general, if the results of the two methods do not differ in an important substantive way from each other, one need only report a single result, but probably that should be an asymmetric one. A general FORTRAN program is available from the authors which does both types of rotations (Huba, Palisoc & Bentler, in press).

CROSS-SET PREDICTION WITH CANONICAL VARIATES

It is sometimes useful to determine the total extent of possible prediction of a canonical variate in one set from the variates in the other set. Such prediction is equivalent to the extent of prediction of the canonical variate from the original variables in the other set, because the intermediate canonical variate is simply a linear combination of the variables. This problem has an obvious solution in the unrotated case, but it is more complex with rotated variates.

When canonical variates remain unrotated, the between-set correlation matrix of the canonical variates is diagonal. As a consequence, prediction of Y_I, say, from all the X variates cannot exceed the squared correlation with its parallel variate X_I. Thus, in the example of Table 2.3, the squared multiple correlation of Y_I from all the X variates is given by $.980^2 = .960$; this value also represents the extent to which one could predict Y_I from the original variables X_1–X_4. Similarly, Y_{II} has a squared multiple correlation of $.395^2 = .156$ on all the X variates or, equivalently, on all the X variables. It will be obvious that these values similarly describe the prediction of the X variates from the Y set, as the problem has a natural symmetry.

Symmetry of prediction is maintained when investigating squared multiple correlations with symmetrically rotated variates. However, computation of the R^2 value itself is somewhat different. It will be remembered from the theory of multiple correlation that when a set of predictors of a criterion variable are all mutually uncorrelated, one can calculate R^2 as a simple sum of the squares of the individual predictor–criterion variables. Because the canonical variates themselves remain uncorrelated after rotation, this formula applies to describe between-set prediction. Thus, using the correlations presented in the middle part of Table 2.3 we obtain as the squared multiple correlation of Y_{I*} from X_{I*} and X_{II*} the value $.685 = .780^2 + .278^2$. Similarly, the R^2 for predicting Y_{II*} from X_{I*} and X_{II*} is given by $.278^2 + .595^2 = .432$. Notice in particular that with symmetric rotation the prediction of X_{I*} from the two Y variates takes on the same value as the prediction of Y_{I*} from the two X variates. Thus symmetry in squared multiple correlations is also maintained with symmetric rotations. This feature is lost with asymmetric rotations.

The computation of R^2 values takes the same form as the previous case in a solution with asymmetrically rotated variates. That is, considering the intercorrelation matrix of the variates as presented in the right part of Table 2.3, the squared multiple correlations for predicting a given criterion is given by the sum of squares in either the row or column that identifies the criterion variate. These R^2 values are thus .803, .314, .553, and .563 for Y_{I*}, Y_{II*}, X_{I*}, and X_{II*}, respectively. Note that the values for the X variates and the Y variates are not the same in this example. However, it may also be noted that the sum of the R^2 values for predicting a given domain from the other are exactly equal. That is, .803 + .314 = .553 + .563 = 1.117 (except for roundoff error). In fact, this sum is an invariant across all the canonical solutions we have been discussing. That is, predictability is the same whether we rotate or not, and, furthermore, it does not matter which rotation we choose.

A CANONICAL ANALYSIS OF ACTUAL AND INTENDED DRUG USE

As an example of the utility of canonical loadings rotation within a representative data set, we have selected a small subsample of data from our ongoing longitudinal study of adolescent drug use. Each of 818 7th–9th grade students from greater Los Angeles completed a questionnaire assessing the frequency of use of 13 psychoactive substances and intentions to use 12 of these substances in the future. Responses to the drug use frequency questions were made on an anchored five-point scale (never tried; only once; a few times; many times; regularly). Intentions to use drugs in the future were coded on another five-point anchored scale (never; don't think so; not sure; probably; yes, for sure).

In our sample of 818 young adolescents, the domains of current and intended drug use were highly related ($\chi^2 = 1788.92$, d.f. = 156, $p < .05$). Inspection of the individual canonical correlations indicated that 11 coefficients were significant ($\chi^2 = 12.98$, d.f. = 6, $p < .05$ with 10 roots partialled; $\chi^2 = .78$, d.f. = 2, $p > .05$ with 11 roots partialled) using the standard stepdown procedure for Bartlett's χ^2 test (cf. Tatsuoka, 1971). Although a large number of dimensions are necessary to span totally the two domains, our inspection of the canonical correlations (.72, .54, .50, .45, .42, .37, .31, .27, .25, .20, .12, .03) led us to retain six dimensions as psychometrically robust for the rotation.[3] The six dimensions were largely in canonical form with several general dimensions and a

---

[3]We have frequently found in large samples that it is necessary to rotate a subset of the original, statistically significant canonical variates. As criteria for the number of variates to retain we have used: (1) an inspection of the roots for a "break" (cf. Cattell, 1966, for a discussion of this rationale for factor analysis); (2) the magnitude of the canonical correlations. In general, we retain for rotation only those pairs of variates with a correlation of .35 or greater. Such a strategy limits the analysis and theoretical interpretation to the *major* sources of cross-domain covariation.

variety of smaller, seemingly redundant general dimensions among the first six in each domain. In general, the unrotated results did not seem to be any more interpretable in terms of existing knowledge about the patterning of adolescent drug use (Kandel, 1978) than random groupings. The six canonical dimensions were then rotated asymmetrically using the orthosim procedure. The resulting rotated canonical loadings are shown in Tables 2.4a and 2.4b; the adjusted canonical variate correlations are given in Table 2.4c.

As may be seen in Table 2.4, the corresponding columns (X_{i*} versus Y_{i*})

TABLE 2.4
Asymmetrically Rotated Canonical Loadings of Current and Intended Drug Use

(a) *Set X: Current Drug Use*

	X_{I*}	X_{II*}	X_{III*}	X_{IV*}	X_{V*}	X_{VI*}
1. Cigarettes	.368	.253	.129	−.064	.773	.020
2. Beer	.217	.827	.141	−.007	.164	.115
3. Wine	.080	.729	.025	.104	.451	−.005
4. Liquor	.253	.766	.040	.060	.282	.112
5. Cocaine	.312	.113	.371	.303	−.201	−.375
6. Tranquilizers	.167	.095	.269	.121	.021	.758
7. Drugstore Medication	.096	.043	.063	.896	.014	.109
8. Heroin	.114	.045	.453	.138	.076	−.028
9. Marijuana	.827	.183	.141	.053	.316	.226
10. Hashish	.609	.159	.313	.097	.113	−.046
11. Inhalants	−.093	.057	.263	.455	.506	.132
12. Hallucinogenics	.105	.039	.413	−.019	.039	.094
13. Amphetamines	.205	.079	.864	.072	.184	.317

(b) *Set Y: Intended Drug Use*

	Y_{I*}	Y_{II*}	Y_{III*}	Y_{IV*}	Y_{V*}	Y_{VI*}
1. Cigarettes	.305	.152	.146	.078	.737	.162
2. Beer	.280	.775	.164	.038	.088	.180
3. Wine	.119	.815	.040	.065	.353	.075
4. Liquor	.193	.783	.060	.041	.149	.066
5. Cocaine	.134	.070	.241	.173	.133	.594
6. Tranquilizers	.138	.067	.577	.279	.134	.169
7. Drugstore Medication	.108	.044	.254	.769	.096	.225
8. Heroin	.156	.078	.112	.249	.143	.289
9. Marijuana	.774	.175	.183	.104	.281	.181
10. Inhalants	−.068	.097	.336	.276	.369	.234
11. Hallucinogenics	.102	.031	.316	.133	.060	.145
12. Amphetamines	.184	.056	.587	.117	.107	.373

(c) *Adjusted canonical correlations*

		Y_{I*}	Y_{II*}	Y_{III*}	Y_{IV*}	Y_{V*}	Y_{VI*}
Drug Use	X_{I*}	.556	−.009	−.035	−.067	.013	.179
	X_{II*}	.138	.568	.008	−.023	.049	.062
	X_{III*}	.022	−.037	.373	−.099	−.008	.268
	X_{IV*}	−.038	.011	.079	.466	−.045	.075
	X_{V*}	.162	.089	.086	.069	.457	.011
	X_{VI*}	.108	.021	.292	.018	−.053	−.260

are quite similar for the pairs of dimensions I*, II*, IV*, and V*. This finding indicates that the structure of actual drug use and intended drug use is about the same for the "soft" and legally available substances that load on these variates. It must be remembered, of course, that we have limited our attention in developing these "structures" to the covariation in common between domains. In contrast, when allowed to seek their own positions of best "within-domain" simplicity, the "hard" drugs that mark dimensions III* and VI* seem to be structured somewhat differently in the domains of actual and intended use. In the actual use domain, X_{III*} has moderately sized loadings for cocaine, tranquilizers, heroin, hashish, hallucinogenics, and a very sizable loading for amphetamines. The corresponding dimension (Y_{III*}) of intended use has a much smaller loading for amphetamine use and a larger loading for tranquilizer use. The pairs of dimensions X_{VI*} and Y_{VI*} are the most strikingly different in the actual and intended use domains in the asymmetric rotation. In the actual use set, X_{VI*} has a very high loading for tranquilizer use and a moderately sized loading for amphetamine use with a moderately sized loading for cocaine use. This dimension, then, seems to indicate a nonpreference for the use of cocaine and a corresponding tendency to use "pills." The corresponding dimension (Y_{VI*}) in the intended use domain has moderate *positive* loadings for cocaine *and* stimulant use.

Examination of the adjusted canonical correlations presented in Table 2.4c indicates that for the first five pairs of canonical variates, there is cross-domain correspondence as judged by the diagonal correlation. The sixth pair of dimensions are minimally correlated. When we examine the off-diagonal correlations, we can see that there is some tendency for current marijuana use to be related to the intended use of such "rush" drugs as cocaine, heroin, and amphetamines (X_{I*} versus Y_{VI*}). Alcohol use is slightly correlated to intended marijuana use (X_{II*} versus Y_{I*}). The use of legally available substances and intended marijuana use is also correlated (X_{V*} versus Y_{I*}). Focusing now on the "hard drug" dimensions III* and VI* in each domain, the current use of hard drugs (X_{III*}) in a general way is related to intended use in the future of both clusters (Y_{III*} and Y_{VI*}), whereas a preference for the "recreational" drug cocaine at the current time (X_{VI*}) is related to a lowered tendency to use hard drugs in general in the future (Y_{III*}), and an increased tendency to use "rush" drugs (Y_{VI*}). Also, individuals who use cocaine at high levels have a lowered tendency to use marijuana in the future (X_{VI*} versus Y_{I*}).

With the exception of the X_{VI*} versus Y_{III*} and X_{III*} versus Y_{VI*} correlations, the adjusted canonical correlation matrix is not decidedly asymmetric. The asymmetry is associated with a change in sign of a major loading (cocaine) on X_{VI*} and Y_{VI*}, and the loadings of variables on X_{III*} and Y_{III*}. Consequently, it seems to us that it is justifiable to attempt to fit a symmetric solution to the data and then determine if the representation of the relationships is about as good as that found for the asymmetric rotation.

The six unrotated canonical dimensions were rerotated using the symmetric two-matrix orthosim with proportional weighting ($\alpha = 12/25$) of the smaller intentions set. The resulting rotated loadings for the two sets are shown in Tables 2.5a and 2.5b, with the adjusted correlations among the canonical variates shown in Table 2.5c. In our interpretation of these symmetric-rotation generated results, we have restricted attention to those loadings with an absolute value in excess of .25. In doing so, we have attempted to take account of the fact that the "near-zero" loadings in a symmetric rotation will not be as small in absolute size

TABLE 5
Symmetrically Rotated Canonical Loadings of Current and Intended Drug Use

(a) *Set X: Current Drug Use*

	X_{I*}	X_{II*}	X_{III*}	X_{IV*}	X_{V*}	X_{VI*}
1. Cigarettes	.429	.237	.140	−.030	.743	.070
2. Beer	.271	.811	.167	−.034	.129	.117
3. Wine	.143	.728	.044	.114	.426	.075
4. Liquor	.323	.757	.092	.059	.235	.067
5. Cocaine	.123	.045	.056	.142	−.141	.678
6. Tranquilizers	.352	.124	.639	.174	−.133	−.321
7. Drugstore Medication	.100	.048	.138	.870	−.069	.192
8. Heroin	.057	.015	.354	.058	.084	.326
9. Marijuana	.870	.141	.194	.044	.231	.149
10. Hashish	.543	.101	.186	.013	.099	.411
11. Inhalants	−.033	.074	.353	.472	.452	.058
12. Hallucinogenics	.088	.019	.383	−.073	.033	.182
13. Amphetamines	.213	.048	.882	−.017	.138	.300

(b) *Set Y: Intended Drug Use*

	Y_{I*}	Y_{II*}	Y_{III*}	Y_{IV*}	Y_{V*}	Y_{VI*}
1. Cigarettes	.249	.156	.118	.058	.776	.086
2. Beer	.218	.792	.150	.060	.144	.164
3. Wine	.045	.812	.003	.063	.385	.040
4. Liquor	.131	.790	.034	.052	.185	.052
5. Cocaine	.100	.077	.259	.175	.216	.566
6. Tranquilizers	.111	.080	.546	.333	.193	.123
7. Drugstore Medication	.083	.039	.177	.781	.170	.224
8. Heroin	.130	.082	.099	.246	.196	.276
9. Marijuana	.737	.218	.176	.113	.355	.160
10. Inhalants	−.106	.086	.301	.288	.412	.177
11. Hallucinogenics	.087	.041	.306	.162	.098	.120
12. Amphetamines	.154	.076	.593	.169	.181	.322

(c) *Correlations Among Symmetrically-Related Variates*

	Y_{I*}	Y_{II*}	Y_{III*}	Y_{IV*}	Y_{V*}	Y_{VI*}
X_{I*}	.569					
X_{II*}	.068	.574				
X_{III*}	.033	.000	.487			
X_{IV*}	−.047	.001	.012	.486		
X_{V*}	.085	.073	.020	.014	.471	
X_{VI*}	.073	.014	.020	−.005	.014	.414

as those obtained in the asymmetric transformation. For the current use domain, we find loadings on the first dimensions for marijuana, hashish, cigarettes, tranquilizers, liquor, and beer. In the intended use domain, marijuana (hashish was not included in the test battery) is the only major loading. Our conclusion from this pair of relationships is that the current use of soft drugs (marijuana in combination with tobacco, liquor, and beer) and some experimentation with hashish, a "harder" form of cannabis preparation, and tranquilizers best predicts intentions to use marijuana in the future. The second dimension in both the current and intended use domains has very large loadings for beer, wine, and liquor. Quite simply the relationship suggests that individuals who have used various forms of alcohol intend to continue their approximate rate of use in the future. The third current use dimension has loadings for the use of tranquilizers, amphetamines, hallucinogenics, heroin, and inhalants. The corresponding dimension in the intended use domain is quite similar with heroin failing to load and cocaine loading in a fairly small manner. Consequently, it appears to us that the third pair of dimensions indicates that current use of "hard," highly illegal drugs is associated with intentions to continue use of these substances. The fourth dimension in the use domain has loadings for the use of drug store medications to get "high" and inhalants, both substances that can be obtained legally by the typical adolescent. Individuals who tend to use these legally obtained substances apparently intend to continue to use them as well as to try tranquilizers. The fifth dimension in the current use domain links cigarette smoking, inhalant use, and wine drinking. The corresponding dimension in the intended use domain links the same three substances and also has a nontrivial loading for marijuana smoking. Apparently, youths high on the use of cigarettes, wine, and inhalants can be expected to try marijuana. The sixth current use dimension has nontrivial positive loadings for the use of cocaine, heroin, hashish, and amphetamines and a negative loading for tranquilizer ingestion. The corresponding intentions dimension has high loadings for the use of cocaine, heroin, and amphetamines. As opposed to the more general pair of dimensions in the two domains linking hard drug use (dimensions X_{III*} and Y_{III*}), this pair of variates links the use of drugs like cocaine, hashish, and heroin purported to produce a "rush" with the continued use of these rush-producing drugs. As opposed to linking current use of hard drugs with intentions to continue using such substances, then, the final pair of dimensions delineates a specific type of drug experience and shows that individuals who use the drugs intend to seek the same future experience.

The intercorrelations among the final, rotated canonical variates are presented in Table 2.5c. Because a symmetric method of rotation was used, only the lower triangle is reported. Note first that the off-diagonals are again very close to zero, indicating that a main feature of unrotated solutions is hardly destroyed. For all practical purposes, the off-diagonals can be considered to be zero. Second, the actual size of the correlations in the diagonal should be considered. They range in value from a low of .414 to a high of .574.

Preference for the symmetric over the asymmetric solution would have to be predicated on several premises. First, one criterion is that the solutions would have to yield substantially different interpretations. In the example relating current drug use to intentions to use drugs, it seems to us that the general conclusions drawn from the two analyses are conceptually, if not strictly mathematically, comparable. In both solutions for this data set we have seen that current drug use and intended use can be formed into dimensions of marijuana, alcohol, legal medication, and cigarette use. These dimensions are found in similar form in both domains in either rotated solution. Furthermore, the diagonal canonical correlations are of about the same magnitude for these variates irrespective of whether the rotation was asymmetric or symmetric. Among these variates the pattern of off-diagonal correlations remains about the same and yields about the same interpretations.

The difference between the asymmetric and symmetric solutions is found in those dimensions that have moderately large loadings for the actual or intended use of such "hard" drugs as cocaine, tranquilizers, amphetamines, and heroin. The general advantage of the asymmetric solution is that it points out the relationship between actual marijuana use and intended cocaine use; the correlations indicate that marijuana users tend to believe they will try cocaine, whereas cocaine users indicate that they will probably cut their marijuana use. This "difference" is predicated on the interpretation of .18 and $-.11$ correlation coefficients in the asymmetric solution (considering also the loading reversal) as opposed to the constrained value of .07 or .03 (using the two dimensions where cocaine use substantially loads) in the symmetric solution. In general, it seems to us that the slightly different pattern of correlations for dimensions III and VI in the asymmetric solution is generally offset by the slightly different pattern of loadings for the dimensions in the symmetric solution.

In general, then, we find that the two different rotated solutions are roughly comparable for interpretation, while recognizing that in certain applications, such as the contrived example of Table 2.3, this result will not necessarily be generalizable.

Our final set of comments about this example concerns the usefulness of either rotated solution in comparison to the unrotated loadings. While we have not presented the unrotated loadings for this example because of space limitations, the resulting coefficients are typical; the columns of the unrotated loadings matrices are frequently indistinguishable from one another, and drugs are not clustered in a way that makes either psychological or pharmacological sense. Either of the rotations serves to separate major classes, and patterns, of drug use into easily discernible form, and the inferences that can be made about the rotated loadings are meaningful within the context of studying the relationships of specific drug use patterns with future use intentions.

To our way of thinking, the current results are consistent with Kandel's (1978) summary of adolescent drug use patterns. Various investigators have repeatedly argued for different factors or stages of drug use roughly corresponding to cigarette smoking, alcohol use, marijuana use, and "hard" drug use. In addition, we have found dimensions roughly corresponding to the attempt to achieve a certain type of drug experience and the use of legally obtained drugs to achieve a "high." Several suggestive results are the apparent stability of current use and intentions for future use as well as the possibility that individuals will move from the use of legally obtained substances to tranquilizer use.

Other applications of canonical correlation rotation have recently been presented in several papers trying to relate adolescent drug use to personality dimensions and peer culture characteristics. Huba, Wingard, and Bentler (1979) present a large problem interrelating 13 drug use variables and 36 indicators of cultural influences. In that paper, the canonical correlation analyses and rotations were calculated for two large samples and the resulting solutions were compared. Congruence coefficients calculated by Huba et al. indicate that the rotated loadings may be considered to be quite stable. Similar results of sample replication have been found by Segal, Huba, and Singer (1980, Chapter 8) in their study of 28 daydreaming measures and 20 personality variables. Wingard, Huba, and Bentler (1979) examine a situation where rotation of the canonical loadings is inappropriate because a large general dimension appears in each domain that is artificially split by the rotation.

CANONICAL CORRELATION IN DATA ANALYSIS

Although we realize that the rotational methods advocated here are new and must be applied to many different data sets before a general strategy can be definitively recommended, there are several guidelines that can be generalized from our experience to the typical application. First, it should be reiterated that several different rotations should be made of the same results in order to examine theoretical meaningfulness. Different numbers of dimensions should be rotated using both asymmetric and symmetric methods. Frequently, it will be desirable to rotate fewer dimensions than are statistically robust. Not all statistically necessary canonical variates will correspond to major psychological constructs, and this state can only be ascertained when different dimensionalities are considered. In many cases the different rotations will yield results that support substantially the same theoretical conclusions. When widely variant interpretations can be made from the different rotations, the multiple interpretations should be reported. Finally, it may be desirable in some instances to translate algebraically the canonical results into alternate forms suggested by Skinner (1978).

Second, there are cases for which a canonical rotation is undesirable. Specifically, when there is a true "general" set of relationships across sets, rotation will tend to split up such a general factor into several dimensions. Such a phenomenon is probably best "discovered" using separate derivation and cross-validation samples (Wingard, Huba, & Bentler, 1979).

Third, the form of rotation used should be consistent with major theories of the phenomenon. This point cannot be stressed too strongly. For instance, in the symmetric rotation there are distinct cases where one would want to weight heavily the simplicity in one domain over the other. An example of this would be when one domain (such as measures of intellectual functioning) has well-known simplicity, whereas the other is a conglomerate of measures collected for their possible relevance to the "simple" domain.

As our previous development as well as the drug use examples have made clear, the method of canonical correlation with dimension rotation has important applications to the analysis of social science data. In all such applications it must be remembered that there is a distinction to be made between the statistical issues raised and solved by the technique, namely, the independence or lack of independence from each other of sets of variates, and the applied, scientific questions of relevance to the particular discipline. In general, statistical measurement and scientific meaningfulness are not equivalent concepts, though, as we hope our illustrative examples have shown, statistical significance is a reasonable requisite to meaningfulness. There is no particular point to keeping or rotating dimensions that have been found to be statistically likely to be drawn from a population in which the particular canonical dimension is null. Although we would always argue that only statistically significant relationships should be rotated, it is possible that not all the statistically significant relationships are important enough to be rotated.

The development of this chapter has been limited to considerations of canonical correlation as an exploratory data analysis method, inasmuch as methods of confirmatory canonical correlation are just being developed (Bentler & Wingard, 1981). They can also be applied most fruitfully to latent variable models (Bentler, 1980). With such methods, the dimensionality of the solution would be set and the loading matrices would have specified elements known or fixed, and the remaining parameters would be estimated. It is probable that confirmatory canonical analysis will make less use of the symmetric and asymmetric rotations that we have introduced here, because the loading matrices will tend to have many fixed zeros.

Canonical correlation analysis can also be used as a generalized form of path analysis, as pointed out by Van de Geer (1971). Stated differently, it is possible to use canonical variates as constructs in a series of multivariate regressions. Although newer methods of causal or structural equation modeling have superseded path analysis, such an application of canonical analysis may still be useful when the newer methods cannot be applied (cf., Bentler, 1980; Bentler & Weeks, 1980).

MATHEMATICAL DEVELOPMENT

We shall define the following matrices, using a notation consistent with our previous development.

X_n and Y_m are $N \times n$ and $N \times m$ matrices of standard scores of N subjects on n variables in set X and m variables in set Y.

W_x and W_y are $n \times r$ and $m \times r$ $(r \leq n \leq m)$ matrices of canonical weights such that $X_r = X_n W_x$ and $Y_r = Y_m W_y$ are standardized canonical variates in unrotated form, with $X_r'X_r/N = Y_r'Y_r/N = I$.

R_{xx}, R_{xy}, R_{yy} are the correlation matrices among variables as indexed by the subscripts.

It follows immediately that the correlation matrices are obtained as

$$R_{xx} = X_n'X_n /N, \quad R_{xy} = X_n'Y_m /N \text{ and } R_{yy} = Y_m'Y_m /N \qquad (1)$$

The correlation matrix of unrotated variates is given by

$$\Lambda = X_r'Y_r /N = W_x'X_n'Y_mW_y /N = W_x'R_{xy}W_y, \qquad (2)$$

which is diagonal and contains values ordered in descending size. The correlations of the observed variables and their own canonical variates is given by

$$
\begin{aligned}
Q_x &= X_n'X_r /N = X_n'X_nW_x /N = R_{xx}W_x \\
Q_y &= Y_n'Y_r /N = Y_n'Y_nW_y /N = R_{yy}W_y.
\end{aligned} \qquad (3)
$$

These are the unrotated canonical loading matrices. The computational procedures for obtaining W_x and W_y to generate Equations 2 and 3 is described in the various multivariate analysis texts previously cited. The computer program BMDP6M (Dixon & Brown, 1977) can also be used to obtain the results.

Consider the $r \times r$ square orthonormal transformation matrices T_x and T_y obtainable from any standard orthogonal rotation method such as varimax or orthosim, applied to either the canonical weights or loadings. As applied to the loadings,

$$P_x = Q_xT_x \text{ and } P_y = Q_yT_y \qquad (4)$$

describe the rotated loading matrices. In view of Equation 3, $P_x = R_{xx}W_xT_x$ and $P_y = R_{yy}W_yT_y$, so that if we define

$$V_x = W_xT_x \text{ and } V_y = W_yT_y, \qquad (5)$$

it is clear that $P_x = R_{xx}V_x$ and $P_y = R_{yy}V_y$ remain loading matrices. It is apparent from Equation 5 that the rotation criterion could be equally well applied to the weights, and the consequences for the loadings be determined through Equation 4. In any case, the effect of the rotation on the canonical variates themselves is to generate

$$X_{r*} = X_rT_x \text{ and } Y_{r*} = Y_rT_y, \qquad (6)$$

the rotated variates. The variates remain independent, as

$$X_{r*}'X_{r*}/N = Y_{r*}'Y_{r*}/N = I, \tag{7}$$

and as $T_x'T_x = I$ and $T_y'T_y = I$. The new variates (Equation 6) have correlations with the variables given by Equation 4, as can be seen by steps of the form Equation 3. However, the between-set correlations of the variates is given by

$$L_{xy} = X_{r*'}Y_{r*}/N = T_x'X_r'Y_rT_y/N = T_x'\Lambda T_y, \tag{8}$$

using Equation 2. This matrix is neither diagonal nor symmetric in general. The squared multiple correlations of the Y_{r*} variables from the X_{r*} variables are given in the diagonal of

$$S_{yy} = L_{xy}'L_{xy}. \tag{9}$$

The corresponding squared multiple correlations of the X_{r*} variables from the Y_{r*} variables are given by

$$S_{xx} = L_{xy}L_{xy}'. \tag{10}$$

It is easily verified that the sums of the squared multiple correlations are equivalent (i.e., $tr\, S_{yy} = tr\, S_{xx}$). Furthermore, those values equal $tr\, \Lambda^2$, the sum of squared multiple correlations of the unrotated canonical variates. This concludes the development of the asymmetric case. For a similar conceptualization in the related domain of interbattery factor analysis, see Hakstian (1977).

To obtain transformed canonical variates in the symmetric case, the steps described in the foregoing are repeated for $T_x = T_y = T$. The redefinition of the rotated loadings (Equation 4) is obvious; similarly for the canonical weights (Equation 5) and the variates themselves (Equation 6). The between-set correlation matrix (Equation 8) is replaced by

$$L = T'\Lambda T, \tag{11}$$

which is obviously symmetric. It immediately follows that $S_{yy} = S_{xx} = S = L'L = LL'$.

To determine the single symmetric rotation matrix T that yields loading simplicity, we define the matrices $C_x = P_x^{(2)}$ and $C_y = P_y^{(2)}$, where the notation $P^{(2)}$ refers to a matrix containing squared elements of P. The two-matrix orthosim rotation that generalizes the rotation of Bentler (1977) is then obtained as the maximizing solution to

$$f = \alpha \log \det (C_x'C_x) + (1 - \alpha) \log (C_y'C_y) - 2\, tr\, M(TT' - I), \tag{12}$$

where α is a known value ($0 < \alpha < 1$), and M is a symmetric matrix of Lagrangian multipliers that assures T is orthogonal and normal. Differentiating Equation 12 with respect to T under Equation 4 with $T_x = T_y = T$ yields

$$\delta f/\delta T = 4\, \text{Vec}\, (\alpha\{Q_x'[P_x*C_x(C_x'C_x)^{-1}]\}$$
$$+ (1 - \alpha)Q_y'[P_y*C_y(C_y'C_y)^{-1}] - MT), \tag{13}$$

where $*$ is the element-wise Hadamard matrix multiplication. The solution for T can be obtained by equating Equation 13 to zero, so that

$$\alpha Q_x'[P_x* \, C_x(C_x'C_x)^{-1}] + (1 - \alpha)Q_y'[P_y*C_y(C_y'C_y)^{-1}] = MT. \quad (14)$$

If the left part of Equation 14 has the Eckart–Young decomposition UDB', where $U'U = I$, $B'B = I$, and D is diagonal, it is seen that

$$M = UDU' \text{ and } T = UB' \quad (15)$$

provide unique solutions to Equation 14. In practice, a trial T^k is utilized to obtain a T^{k+1} through Equations 14 and 15, and the iterative procedure terminates when T has been determined to sufficient accuracy. An alternative two-matrix rotation procedure is presented by Hakstian (1976), but it does not provide an option for differential weighting of the sets of variables. Since the current manuscript was completed (in 1978), we discovered that Scott and Koopman (unpublished) independently proposed an asymmetric rotation method that does not allow differential weighting. It forces the matrix L_{xy} to be as close to diagonal as possible, a feature we do not consider fundamental.

REFERENCES

Anderson, T. W. *An introduction to multivariate statistical analysis.* New York: Wiley, 1958.

Bentler, P. M. Multistructure statistical model applied to factor analysis. *Multivariate Behavioral Research,* 1976, *11,* 3–25.

Bentler, P. M. Factor simplicity index and transformations. *Psychometrika,* 1977, *42,* 277–295.

Bentler, P. M. Multivariate analysis with latent variables: Causal modeling. *Annual Review of Psychology,* 1980, *31,* 419–456.

Bentler, P. M., & Weeks, D. G. Interrelations among models for the analysis of moment structures. *Multivariate Behavioral Research,* 1979, *14,* 169–186.

Bentler, P. M., & Weeks, D. G. Linear structural equations with latent variables. *Psychometrika,* 1980, *45,* 289–308.

Bentler, P. M., & Wingard, J. A. *Canonical correlations with latent variables.* Paper presented at annual meeting of the Psychometric Society, Chapel Hill, N.C., May 1981.

Browne, M. W. Orthogonal rotation to a partially specified target. *British Journal of Mathematical and Statistical Psychology,* 1972, *25,* 115–120.

Cattell, R. B. The scree test for the number of factors. *Multivariate Behavioral Research,* 1966, *1,* 245–276.

Cliff, N. S., & Krus, D. J. Interpretation of canonical analysis: Rotated vs. unrotated solutions. *Psychometrika,* 1976, *41,* 35–42.

Comrey, A. L. *A first course in factor analysis.* New York: Academic, 1973.

Cooley, W. W., & Lohnes, P. R. *Multivariate data analysis.* New York: Wiley, 1971.

Dixon, W. J., & Brown, M. B. *Biomedical Computer Programs P-Series.* Berkeley, Calif.: University of California, 1977.

Hakstian, A. R. Two-matrix orthogonal rotation procedures. *Psychometrika,* 1976, *41,* 267–272.

Hakstian, A. R. Transformation of axes in interbattery factor analysis. *Multivariate Behavioral Research,* 1977, *12,* 159–165.

Harman, H. H. *Modern factor analysis.* Chicago: University of Chicago, 1976.

46 BENTLER and HUBA

Hotelling, H. Relations between two sets of variates. *Biometrika,* 1936, *28,* 321–377.

Huba, G. J., Palisoc, A. L., & Bentler, P. M. ORSIM2: A computer program for symmetric and asymmetric rotation in canonical correlation and interbattery factor analysis. *American Statistician,* in press.

Huba, G. J., Wingard, J. A., & Bentler, P. M. Beginning adolescent drug use and peer and adult interaction patterns. *Journal of Consulting and Clinical Psychology,* 1979, *47,* 265–276.

Kaiser, H. The varimax criterion for analytic rotation in factor analysis. *Psychometrika,* 1958, *23,* 187–200.

Kandel, D. B. Convergences in prospective longitudinal surveys of drug use in normal populations. In D. B. Kandel (Ed.), *Longitudinal research on drug use.* New York: Halsted, 1978.

Mendoza, J. L., Markos, V. H., & Gonter, R. A new perspective on sequential testing procedures in canonical analysis: A Monte Carlo evaluation. *Multivariate Behavioral Research,* 1978, *13,* 371–382.

Morrison, D. F. *Multivariate statistical methods.* New York: McGraw-Hill, 1976.

Mulaik, S. A. *The foundations of factor analysis.* New York: McGraw-Hill, 1972.

Schönemann, P. H. A generalized solution of the orthogonal procrustes problem. *Psychometrika,* 1966, *30,* 1–10.

Segal, B., Huba, G. J., & Singer, J. L. *Drugs, daydreaming, and personality: A study of college youth.* Hillsdale, N.J.: Lawrence Erlbaum Associates, 1980.

Skinner, H. A. The art of exploring predictor-criterion relationships. *Psychological Bulletin,* 1978, *85,* 327–337.

Tatsuoka, M. M. *Multivariate analysis: Techniques for education and psychological research.* New York: Wiley, 1971.

Van de Geer, J. P. *Introduction to multivariate analysis for the social sciences.* San Francisco: Freeman, 1971.

Wingard, J. A., Huba, G. J., & Bentler, P. M. The relationship of personality structure to patterns of adolescent substance use. *Multivariate Behavioral Research,* 1979, *14,* 131–143.

3 Multidimensional Psychophysics

Herbert H. Stenson
University of Illinois at Chicago Circle

Broadly defined, psychophysics is the study of relationships among a set of physically defined variables and a set of variables presumed to be indicators of the psychological counterparts of the physical variables. Under such a definition of psychophysics, much of psychology could be subsumed. Thus, what follows in this chapter should not be taken to be limited to the study of traditional psychophysical variables such as sound or light intensities and their relationship to perceived loudness or brightness. Indeed, the discussion applies to any situation where the degree of match between one set of variables and another set of variables is desired. However, the discussion here centers on the situation where one set of variables is defined and measured by the experimenter, and the other set is quantified output from a subject or group of subjects.

As is well known, most traditional psychophysical studies were limited to the study of relationships between single physical variables and their univariate psychological representation. Interest focused on the proper methods for assessing the psychological variables and on the mathematical form of the psychophysical relation. These problems are not reviewed or dealt with here. Rather, the methods discussed are all based on linear algebra. It is assumed that the methods used to obtain data are appropriate and that any appropriate mathematical transformations of data have been made so as to make linear methods applicable. For example, the logarithms of the raw values of a physical variable might be used as input for the methods discussed here if one favored Fechner's Law. If one favored Steven's Power Law then the logarithms of both the physical and psychological variables might be used as input. Alternatively, if one has no reason to favor a particular transformation, then the linear methods applied to the raw data themselves will give, at least, a first approximation of the psychophysical relationships present in the data.

There exist a variety of ways in which one might study the desired match between physically measured variables and psychologically measured variables. The methods used should be a function of the purpose for which one wants the information and/or the theoretical viewpoint that one espouses. For example, one may wish to predict a psychological variable (Y) from a physical variable (X). That is, given various values of X, what may be predicted (and how much cannot be predicted) about Y? The Stevens and Fechner formulations are in this tradition. Stated differently, we wish to assign errors of prediction to Y, and act as though the measurement of X contained no error. We are then attempting to study the accuracy with which the perceptual process can be predicted from knowledge of the ''true'' state of the environment. However, one might also ask, given Y, what is our best prediction of X: To what degree does perception correctly predict the state of the environment? This formulation is in the tradition of Brunswik (1956), who viewed perception as a process by which we make (fallible) judgments about the world around us. In this case we wish to assign the errors of prediction to the physical variable as predicted from the perceptual variable and act as though the perceptual variable were ''error free.''

The distinction being made here is, of course, the familiar statistical possibility of determining the regression of Y on X, or the regression of X on Y. In the simple bivariate case the distinction is not very important, except from a philosophical point of view, because the two regression coefficients in question are simply related by the ratio of the two variances involved. Also, if the correlation coefficient is used to index the degree of match between X and Y, then, because $r(XY) = r(YX)$, there is no distinction at all in a numerical sense. However, if the physical and the psychological systems are multivariate, then the distinction between which set is to be considered to contain the errors of prediction and which set is the set of ''error-free'' predictor variables is not statistically trivial. One will draw different conclusions about the degree of match between the X and the Y systems depending on one's criterion for a best match. The criterion may imply that error is to be attributed to one or the other of these systems exclusively, or to both simultaneously. Also, the size and interrelationship of the ''regression weights'' obtained will depend not only on the criterion for a match and which system is the predictor system, but on the nature of the restrictions that are or are not placed on the types of linear combinations to be allowed. Thus, a number of different methods exist. Each method leads to a different interpretation of the data, or, alternatively, one's goals in the analysis of the data dictate the method. The interpretive aspects of the multivariate methods to be discussed are the focus of this chapter. However, the methods themselves each are briefly discussed, and a single set of data is analyzed by each method that is presented.

A general view of the problem will be helpful. Suppose that one obtains a matrix of p variables that may be termed physical variables, and another matrix of q variables that may be termed psychological variables. Each variable in both

TABLE 3.1
Representation of Two Data Matrices

Case	Physical Variables							Psychological Variables						
	1	2	3	...	j	...	p	1	2	3	...	j	...	q
1	X_{11}							Y_{11}						
2														
3														
.														
.														
.														
i			X_{ij}							Y_{ij}				
.														
.														
.														
n					X_{np}							Y_{np}		

matrices is measured on n cases. The "cases" will most often be stimulus objects or instances of the same object, but they might also correspond to subjects. The situation is depicted in Table 3.1, where the physical variables are denoted by X and the psychological variables are denoted by Y.

It should be noted that either matrix in Table 3.1 may have one or more variables, and that the number of variables in the two matrices may not be equal (i.e., p is not necessarily equal to q). The general problem to be addressed is how one might obtain a match between the two matrices. This might be done by viewing this as a regression problem in which one matrix contains predictor variables and the other contains criterion variables, or as a correlation problem in which neither matrix has any special status. The latter case conforms to the notion of Canonical Correlation Analysis and is discussed first. Following this, two types of analyses called Orthogonal Procrustes Analysis and Nonorthogonal Procrustes Analysis are discussed. Within each, the physical variables are considered as predictors and the psychological variables as the criteria to be predicted, and then the reverse is done; the psychological variables are used to predict the physical variables.

CANONICAL CORRELATION ANALYSIS

If one is willing to accept linear combinations of both the X and the Y variables as being theoretically appropriate, and if these linear combinations can be given some interpretation, then canonical correlation provides a multidimensional method for psychophysics. Hotelling (1935) developed canonical correlation as a method of obtaining the maximum correlation possible between a single pair of linear combinations of two sets of variables, one member from the set X, and the other from the set Y. This technique was subsequently extended to obtain correlations between successive pairs of linear combinations within the two measurement sets. (Morrison, 1967). Each successive pair of linear combinations is determined so as to maximize the correlation between the X member and the Y member of the pair, subject to the restriction that these new linear combinations be independent of (orthogonal to) both members of all previous pairs of linear combinations. The product–moment correlation coefficients between the successive members of each XY pair are called Canonical Correlation Coefficients, the linear combinations themselves are called Canonical Vectors, and the weights applied to the X and Y variables to obtain the vectors are called Canonical Weights.

Note that neither set of variables is singled out as the "predictor" set, linear combinations of both sets are allowed, and the criterion for match is to maximize the successive canonical correlation coefficients obtained for each successive pair of canonical vectors. The canonical correlation coefficients are symmetric measures of match in that they remain the same regardless of whether either the X or the Y set is thought of as the predictor set, and remain the same if neither is the predictor set.

Table 3.2 shows a subset of the data collected in a study by Stenson (1968). The matrix on the left represents a set of six physical measurements made on each of a set of 20 irregular, closed geometric shapes that included arcs as well as line segments in their perimeters. Turns is the number of "turns" in the perimeter of a shape (i.e., the number of arcs plus the number of angles occuring). Arc % is the percentage of the turns in a shape that are arcs. Cmpct is the area of the shape divided by squared total perimeter length (i.e., the "compactness" or lack of jaggedness). Str % is the percentage of the total perimeter that is composed of line segments. Arc Var is the variance of arc lengths within each shape, and Str Var is the variance in line-segment length within each shape. Each measure shown that was not already a percentage was divided by the maximum value that the measure could logically achieve because of the method of construction of the shapes. For example, the number of turns could be no less than five nor more than 20. Thus, the variable labeled Turns is actually the number of turns minus 5 divided by 20.

The matrix on the right in Table 3.2 shows the coordinates of each of the 20 shapes in a six-dimensional "psychological space" derived from similarity judgments about all 190 pairs of the 20 shapes made by one subject. These six reference axes are rotated output from MDSCAL, the multidimensional scaling program designed by Kruskal (1964). The reference axes shown are the result of rotating the MDSCAL output reference axes to a principal components position. These axes do not have any special psychological significance unless one wishes to assume that principal axes represent the way in which subjects actually process the stimuli, a view discussed later.

TABLE 3.2
Values in Units of .01 for Six Physical Variables
and Six Psychological Variables from Stenson (1968)

		Physical Variables					Psychological Variables					
Shape	Turns	Arc %	Cmpct	Str %	Arc Var	Str Var	P1	P2	P3	P4	P5	P6
1	33	30	17	90	90	57	36	-28	22	-46	-64	12
2	73	31	14	86	93	15	-41	46	06	-41	22	24
3	53	15	18	96	80	23	-37	04	40	02	-62	02
4	60	29	25	79	89	24	-14	-16	-32	13	-44	-71
5	40	91	37	57	93	14	05	02	-24	-74	09	-55
6	93	05	18	99	00	43	-03	20	53	45	-60	56
7	93	74	20	77	88	46	-05	02	01	04	-43	-13
8	60	99	79	24	72	01	62	-34	-08	-30	79	-48
9	73	69	28	76	91	16	-50	-68	-23	04	15	24
10	99	65	33	74	82	09	-07	-29	-66	-06	38	02
11	40	73	55	52	86	08	66	-48	-22	02	01	-40
12	80	06	15	99	00	28	02	85	01	30	-33	-01
13	60	57	25	88	87	39	18	-10	74	-24	-07	09
14	53	08	20	99	00	39	-24	48	51	73	24	26
15	67	27	37	91	56	15	-06	-24	-11	46	45	-31
16	73	69	19	78	89	11	05	-07	-42	-50	06	73
17	60	64	22	67	80	37	-40	-04	17	-52	40	-02
18	99	05	15	99	00	14	-42	47	-17	68	-47	51
19	53	23	41	83	62	11	44	01	-40	11	27	11
20	13	00	70	99	00	91	29	13	20	25	56	-28

Table 3.3 shows the results of a canonical correlation analysis using the two matrices in Table 3.2 as input. The first row of the table shows the canonical correlation coefficients for the six dimensions of each space. The first two are the only ones that are statistically significant; however we shall not rely on statistical significance, but upon interpretability as a criterion here. Notice that the first three coefficients are quite high, indicating a considerable degree of correspondence or "overlap" between the spaces defined by the two sets of six reference axes.

The six rows listed under "Physical Variables" in Table 3.3 show the weights to be applied to each physical variable in order to construct each of the six canonical vectors. Because the weights are only determined up to constants of proportionality, the weights for each row were divided by the largest weight in that row so that the largest weight for each row would be 1.00 for ease of interpretation. The weights to obtain the psychological canonical vectors are shown in the last six rows of the table. They have also been scaled so that the largest weight is 1.00.

The first canonical vector for the physical data, then, is highly correlated (.97) with the first canonical vector in the psychological data. The first row of weights

TABLE 3.3
Results of Canonical Correlation Analysis of Table 3.2 Data

Canonical Correlation Coefficients
for
Canonical Vector Pair

		1	2	3	4	5	6
		.97	.89	.69	.37	.33	.01

Canonical Weights for Physical Variables

Canonical Vector	Turns	Arc %	Cmpct	Str %	Str Var	Arc Var
1	-.41	.27	1.00	-.49	.78	.34
2	.05	.05	1.00	.45	-.21	-.28
3	.39	.25	.64	1.00	.15	-.55
4	-.04	.61	.25	1.00	-.10	.03
5	.71	-.81	1.00	.11	.72	.54
6	-.60	.20	.95	1.00	.02	-.63

Canonical Weights for Psychological Variables

Canonical Vector	P1	P2	P3	P4	P5	P6
1	-.38	1.00	-.13	.99	-.34	.68
2	.88	.18	-.12	1.00	.81	-.10
3	.38	.43	1.00	-.21	-.08	-.47
4	-.11	-.79	.89	.02	.65	1.00
5	.23	1.00	-.31	-.67	.45	.37
6	1.00	-.09	-.21	-.25	-.47	.60

for the physical data indicate that this canonical vector is composed primarily of the degree of compactness (Cmpct) of the shapes along with the degree to which the straight segments involved in a shape are of differing lengths (Str Var). Because the most compact shape possible is a disc, shapes that are high on this canonical vector will have no indentations in their perimeters (i.e., tend toward circularity). They will also have straight lengths that vary in such a way as to maximize the circularity of the shape, given the number of turns that the shape has. Shapes that are low on this canonical vector will tend to be "jagged," having indentations in their perimeters and an abundance of straight segments in the perimeter. Notice that although one can imagine such a variable, this interpretation of the canonical vector leaves much to be desired in terms of simplicity or psychological plausibility. The second canonical vector is a little easier to interpret because it has a large weight for compactness, and none of the other weights are very large with the possible exception of Str %, the percentage of the perimeter that is composed of line segments. Thus, this variable may be interpreted as the degree to which a shape tends toward being a disc. The problem here is that compactness is heavily involved in both of the first two canonical vectors, indicating that these two (orthogonal) variables represent two different kinds of compactness. Likewise, we note that compactness is also heavily involved in the fifth and sixth canonical vectors. Thus, the interpretation of all these variables is highly complex and problematic. One can say, however, that compactness is apparently an important component of whatever it is that the subject is processing when he or she makes similarity judgments about a shape.

The only interpretation that can be made of the weights for the psychological canonical vectors is that none of them except for the third appear to be close to the principal axes of the psychological space, which were the input to the canonical analysis. The third canonical vector has its highest weight for the third dimension of the input data, and all the other weights are quite low. But all the other canonical vectors have high weights for more than one input dimension, indicating that these canonical vectors represent dimensions lying ''between'' the original input dimensions (reference axes) of the space.

Thus we see that although the canonical analysis gives us a good idea of how much overlap there is between the physical and psychological spaces represented, it is not of much value for interpreting the psychological dimensions in terms of composite physical dimensions that have any easy geometric or intuitive properties.

Although the canonical vectors may be difficult to interpret, we may take the following view of what the canonical analysis tells us. If there are one or more pairs of canonical vectors that exhibit high canonical correlations, this means that there are orthogonal axes (the canonical vectors) describing the psychological space that are well represented by the canonical vectors in the physical space. The fact that these physical vectors are difficult to interpret in terms of the physical measures that we have made may be an indication that we have seized on the wrong physical measures to describe the perceptual space being used in a task. With this interpretation, then, a good strategy would be to try to invent new physical variables, each of which adequately represents one of the physical canonical vectors found. The canonical weights for the original physical variables can provide a guide for constructing such new physical measures, by telling us how the old measures are related to a new physical variable that is more psychologically relevant. These new measures can then be entered into a canonical analysis to check their validity as representations of psychological dimensions.

Suppose, however, that we are convinced that the physical variables that we originally measure are, a priori, the variables that we wish to relate to the psychological system. The information that we seek is to what degree each of these variables enters into the perceptual process involved in some particular task, such as the judgment of the similarity within pairs of stimuli, as was done for the data being analyzed here. In this case we should like to find linear combinations of the psychological dimensions that give us the best match for each physical variable as measured. If this were the case for the data in Table 3.2, then we should find a best fitting linear combination of the psychological variables to match each physical variable as it exists, rather than also forming linear combinations of physical variables that must be interpreted. This is the kind of problem that the "Orthogonal Procrustes" routine devised by Schoenemann (1966) was designed to handle.

ORTHOGONAL PROCRUSTES

If one of two matrices is to be transformed so as to provide a "best match" with another matrix, one must determine the conditions for, and the definition of a best match. The matrix that is to be matched, that is, the matrix that is not to be altered in any way, is called the Target Matrix. Let us call this matrix Y and the other matrix X. One requirement that might be desirable in order to match the matrix X to the target matrix Y is to require that the successive sets of weights to be multiplied by the variables (columns) of X be independent of each other (orthogonal). This is functionally equivalent to allowing only orthogonal rotations of the reference axes of X, similar to rotating axes in factor analysis. If this requirement is imposed we then speak of Orthogonal Procrustes as opposed to Nonorthogonal Procrustes, which is discussed later. If we assume then that X and Y contain deviations from column means, we are searching for a transformation matrix T in the equation, $Y = XT + E$, such that the columns of T are orthogonal, and the errors of prediction contained in E are minimal. Minimal is usually taken to mean that the mean, squared element of E is as small as possible.

A lack of a match of X to Y can be due partly to the fact that the variances of the columns of the matrix of predictions of Y may be different from the variances of the corresponding columns of Y itself. To compensate for this we multiply by a contraction (or expansion) constant, c, thus making the equation $Y = cXT + E$. In addition, if X and Y do not contain deviations from column means as data, we may add to the equation a vector of constants, which represent the additive constants necessary to move the origins of the columns of X to match the origins of the columns of Y, so as to eliminate this source of mismatch. The equation then becomes $Y = cXT + D + E$, where D is a matrix in which each row contains the same set of constants that are necessary to adjust the origins of the columns of cXT so as to match the origins of the columns in Y. This elaboration of the Orthogonal Procrustes procedure was proposed by Schoenemann and Carroll (1970) and resulted in a computer program to solve for c, T, D, and E in the equation. The program was called MOTION, and is the computer program used to analyze the data in Table 3.2 by first using the matrix of physical variables as the target matrix, and then using the matrix of psychological variables as the target matrix.

Table 3.4 shows the weights determined by MOTION for forming linear combinations of the psychological variables to obtain the best possible match to

TABLE 3.4
Results of Orthogonal Procrustes Analysis: Target = Physical Data
Weights for Psychological Variables

Physical Variable	P1	P2	P3	P4	P5	P6	r
Turns	1.00	.35	.34	-.38	-.19	-.43	.58
Arc %	.28	-.35	-.08	-.93	1.00	.67	.67
Cmpct	-.67	1.00	.07	-.96	-.67	.49	.83
Str %	.44	-.36	.30	.27	-.63	1.00	.54
Arc Var	.16	1.00	.21	.70	.67	.45	.85
Str Var	-.31	-.17	1.00	-.04	.14	-.12	.51

each of the physical variables. For purposes of interpretation and comparison with the other analyses performed here, each row of weights was divided by the maximum weight in the row, thus producing the data in Table 3.4, where the maximum weight for each row is 1.00.

The mean, squared error in the prediction of the physical variables from the psychological variables was .04, which is acceptably small because the numbers used to measure the physical variables were all between .00 and 1.00. More relevant to our discussion here is the correlation of each of the predicted physical variables with the physical variable being predicted. These correlation coefficients are shown in the last column of Table 3.4. The highest of these is .85 for the physical variable Arc Var, indicating that there is a "direction" in the psychological space, as indicated by the weights in that row, that corresponds quite well with the physical measurement of the variability in arc length within each shape under consideration. This is also true for the physical measurement of compactness, which shows a correlation of .83. The next highest correlation is .67 for the physical variable Arc %, which is a measure of the degree to which the shape in question is composed of arcs as opposed to angles. The remaining correlations are lower and therefore of questionable meaningfulness. One might conclude, then, on the basis of this analysis, that this subject was using primarily a combination of curvedness (Arc %), variability in arc length (Arc Var), and compactness (Cmpct) in making his or her judgments of similarity of pairs of shapes.

Notice that in this analysis we have asked how well we may use linear combinations of psychological variables to predict given physical variables with the constraint that sets of weights for predicting physical variables be mutually independent (orthogonal) and that the error of prediction is attributed to the physical variables. The orthogonality of the transformations of the psychological variables geometrically amounts to a rigid rotation of the reference axes of the psychological space. Because the distances between pairs of points (stimuli) in this space are interpreted as the geometric representations of similarity or dissimilarity within the multidimensional scaling technique used, it would be desirable to use only orthogonal transformations as we desire to maintain this isomorphism between interpoint distance and judged similarity. A rigid rotation of reference axes does not destroy this isomorphism.

Suppose, now, that we had reason to believe that the psychological reference axes were in a meaningful position at the outset of the analysis, and that we wished to leave them undisturbed while finding orthogonal transformations of the physical variables that best predict the psychological variables. In this case we could use the MOTION program with the matrix of psychological variables as the target matrix, and the physical variables as the predictors. Table 3.5 shows the weights for each of the physical variables that accomplish this. Again the weights in each row have been divided by the maximum weight for the row so that the largest weight in each row is 1.00. The mean, squared error of prediction for this analysis was .08, which is small considering that the total variance of all the psychological data was constrained to be 1.00. The last column of Table 3.5 shows the correlation coefficient for each psychological variable. The correlation coefficients for $P2$, $P4$, and $P6$ are quite high. Notice that $P2$ and $P4$ are highly related to Arc %, Cmpct, and Arc Var, a finding reminiscent of the Canonical analysis. $P6$ is related primarily to Str %, indicating that this psychological dimension represents the degree to which the perimeter of a shape is composed of line segments as opposed to arcs.

Recall that the psychological variables shown in Table 3.2 were the principal axes of the psychological space as determined by the MDSCAL program. Arguments made by Rodwan and Hake (1964) suggest that the salient psychological dimensions in a perceptual task are those along which the variance is the greatest, thus facilitating discrimination among stimuli. The principal axes of a space are ordered by the amount of total variance accounted for, with the first axis accounting for the most variance and the last accounting for the least. This argument might lead one to theorize that the principal axes of the psychological space as represented in Table 3.2 are psychologically meaningful, so that one should search for the physical representation of each. The psychological dimensions then could be "named" and interpreted.

TABLE 3.5
Results of Orthogonal Procrustes Analysis: Target = Psychological Data
Weights for Physical Variables

Psychological Variable	Turns	Arc %	Cmpct	Str %	Arc Var	Str Var	r
P1	1.00	-.23	-.48	-.41	.14	.37	.59
P2	.41	.32	.85	.39	1.00	.24	.75
P3	-.29	-.05	-.04	.24	-.15	1.00	.59
P4	-.51	1.00	-.93	-.34	.80	.07	.83
P5	.23	1.00	.60	-.73	-.71	.21	.56
P6	.47	.58	-.38	1.00	-.04	-.15	.67

The analysis presented in Table 3.5 is appropriate for this view. As with the canonical analysis, if the linear combinations of physical variables are difficult to interpret, then we should search for a new, more interpretable variable that best represents a psychological dimension. Notice that we already seem to have good single predictors of $P1$, $P3$, and $P6$ where the highest weights are for Turns, Str Var, and Str %, respectively. The remaining weights for these psychological variables are relatively small. However, the variables $P2$, $P4$, and $P5$ cannot be simply described by single physical variables. Each seems to involve Cmpct and Arc Var, and $P4$ and $P5$ also involve Arcs. Thus, the viewpoint that the principal axes are interpretable and meaningful psychologically receives some support here, and would receive even more if $P2$, $P4$, and $P5$ could be given some simple physical interpretation by the creation of new physical variables to describe them.

In this last analysis, where psychological variables were the target matrix, we restricted the transformations of the physical variables by insisting on orthogonality of the sets of weights. There is not as much reason to impose that restriction here as there was when the psychological variables were the target, as discussed earlier. If we simply find that linear combination of physical variables that gives us the best match to each of the psychological variables without the orthogonality restriction, then we should maximize our match. However, the possible dependencies among sets of weights may make our job of interpreting these linear combinations more difficult. Such an analysis is called a Nonorthogonal Procrustes Analysis.

NONORTHOGONAL PROCRUSTES

This procedure is a search for a set of weights for the variables in one matrix that, when applied, will produce a matrix that best matches another (target) matrix, with no orthogonality restrictions on the sets of weights. The procedure (See, for example, Bargmann, 1960) amounts to computing the weights for the predictor variables by means of an ordinary multiple regression procedure, performing this analysis once for each dependent variable (column) in the target matrix. That is what was done here. Each of the psychological variables (columns) in Table 3.2 was used in turn as the dependent variable in a multiple regression analysis with the physical variables in Table 3.2 as the independent variables.

Table 3.6 shows the multiple regression weights for each of the physical variables, again with the weights in each row divided by the maximum weight for the row for purposes of comparison within and across analyses. The final column of Table 3.6 shows the value of the multiple regression coefficient obtained for each row variable. A comparison of these values of r with those reported in Table 3.5 shows that each of the values of r in Table 3.6 is higher than its counterpart in Table 3.5. This is as it should be because the analysis for the data

TABLE 3.6
Nonorthogonal Procrustes Analysis; Target = Psychological Data
Weights for Physical Variables

Psychological Variable	Turns	Arc %	Cmpct	Str %	Arc Var	Str Var	r
P1	-.31	-.07	1.00	-.44	-.01	.08	.71
P2	.18	.22	1.00	.60	.54	.03	.80
P3	-.40	-.04	1.00	-.59	-.29	.83	.66
P4	.60	.41	1.00	.90	-.44	-.40	.86
P5	-.10	.49	1.00	.76	-.13	-.33	.73
P6	.11	.51	-.42	1.00	-.27	-.22	.70

in Table 3.5 imposed the orthogonality requirement, and the present analysis did not. Thus, we might take the results from the present analysis as indicating an upper limit for the goodness of match of the two matrices when one is taken as a target matrix.

Notice that the maximum weight for each row except the last of Table 3.6 is that for the physical variable Cmpct, indicating that this variable is heavily involved in the perception of shape, a fact that we have already deduced from the canonical analysis. This variable was found by Stenson (1966) to be the best single predictor of ratings of these shapes on a scale of "very simple" to "very complex." Notice, also that each of the physical variables has a reasonably high weight for at least one of the psychological variables, indicating that all of them (or linear combinations of all of them) are probably relevant to the perception of shape.

Problems of interpretation are great with this analysis because of the obviously high correlations among the rows of weights. In the first five rows, Cmpct combines in five different ways with the other variables, each time being the single most important variable. Going back to Table 3.5 we see that, because of the orthogonality, each psychological variable has the maximum weight occuring for a different physical variable, with the exception of P4 and P5, both of which have the maximum weight for Arcs. Notice, however, that the weight for Cmpct is −0.93 for predicting P4, a weight that is close to maximum. Thus, determining the nature of the linear combinations indicated in Table 3.5 would be easier than interpreting those in Table 3.6.

It would be statistically possible, of course, to perform a Nonorthogonal Procrustes Analysis using the physical data as the target matrix as well. This analysis was not performed for these data for the reasons discussed earlier concerning the special significance of interpoint distances in these psychological data.

It can be seen from the various analyses performed here that there is no necessarily "right" way to analyze data in multidimensional psychophysics. Each has its virtues and difficulties. Probably the "cleanest" analysis, statistically, is Canonical Correlation Analysis, because one ends up with two sets of dimensions (Canonical Vectors) that are mutually orthogonal within sets and show in descending order the highest possible linear correlations among pairs of dimensions from the two sets. If theoretical or practical constraints dictate that one or the other of the matrices be treated as a target that is to be matched, then the "cleanest" analysis is Orthogonal Procrustes because of the interpretive advantages of obtaining orthogonal sets of weights. The Nonorthogonal Procrustes Analysis will generally provide a better fit to each variable of a target matrix, but if the interrelationships among the sets of weights are complex, the results may be uninterpretable from a psychophysical point of view.

If one were eclectic, and not wedded to a particular theoretical view that dictated which of the matrices, the psychological data matrix or the physical data matrix, was the dependent variable, then performing a variety of the analyses described here would be helpful, as each can contribute a different view of the nature of the psychophysical relationship.

REFERENCES

Bargmann, R. Review of On the unified factor theory of mind by Yrjo Ahmavaara. *Psychometrika*, 1960, *25*, 105–108.

Brunswik, E. *Perception and the representative design of psychological experiments.* Berkeley: University of California Press, 1956.

Hotelling, H. The most predictable criterion. *Journal of Educational Psychology*, 1935, *26*, 139–142.

Kruskal, J. B. Multidimensional scaling by optimizing goodness of fit to a non-metric hypothesis. *Psychometrika*, 1964, *29*, 1–27.

Morrison, D. F. *Multivariate statistical methods.* New York: McGraw–Hill, 1967.

Rodwan, A. S. & Hake, H. W. The discriminant function as a model for perception. *American Journal of Psychology*, 1964, *77*, 380–392.

Schoenemann, P. H. A generalized solution of the orthogonal procrustes problem. *Psychometrika*, 1966, *31*, 1–10.

Schoenemann, P. H., & Carroll, R. M. Fitting one matrix to another under choice of a similarity transformation and a rigid motion. *Psychometrika*, 1970, *35*, 245–255.

Stenson, H. H. The physical factor structure of random forms and their judged complexity. *Perception and Psychophysics*, 1966, *1*, 303–310.

Stenson, H. H. The psychophysical dimensions of similarity among random shapes. *Perception and Psychophysics*, 1968, *3*, 201–214.

Construal of Social Environments: Multidimensional Models of Interpersonal Perception and Attraction

4

Lawrence E. Jones
University of Illinois at Urbana –Champaign

The general assumption that interpersonal attraction, communication, and behavior are mediated by cognitive representations of self, others, and the relationships between self and others, has guided our research on social perception and interpersonal behavior of groups in natural settings (Davison & Jones, 1976; Jones & Hirschberg, 1975; Jones & Young, 1972). The paradigm developed for this research relies on two- and three-mode multidimensional scaling methods and other multivariate techniques for: (1) quantifying and interpreting the structure of these cognitive representations; (2) isolating and measuring individual differences in interpersonal cognition; (3) predicting interpersonal attraction; and (4) tracking changes in social perception over time.

This chapter summarizes the main features of this paradigm, including the general theoretical assumptions on which it is based, the major classes of variables incorporated, and methods of analysis and interpretation. Finally, some of the advantages and disadvantages of this approach in comparison with other paradigms that have been used to conceptualize and investigate these problems are discussed.

Overview

The proposed paradigm, along with the models and analytic procedures that it incorporates, is compatible with several general theories of interpersonal perception and behavior. It permits precise definition and measurement of the major constructs of these theories. In contrast to the narrow perspectives and other constraints imposed by most other approaches to these problems, the paradigm presented here represents a more versatile, unified, and psychometrically sound approach to investigation of problems in interpersonal perception and attraction. It permits several levels and units of analysis, including some that are not possible with more commonly employed paradigms. A basic assumption is that individual differences in personality and interpersonal perception are central to understanding interpersonal attraction and other types of social experience and behavior. The models employed are multivariate in recognition of the fact that both social stimuli and the processes by which we organize and interpret our experiences of these stimuli are multidimensional. Finally, as the research examples presented illustrate, the proposed models and methods are especially well suited to investigating social experience and behavior using intact, enduring groups functioning in natural settings; the methodology allows longitudinal research in which changes in group members' perceptions, relationships, and the structure of the group per se over time, can be measured and understood.

It is emphasized that the paradigm outlined in the following is not intended as a complete theory, but rather as a framework for asking questions and testing hypotheses about social perception and behavior, organizing the resulting data, and providing precise descriptions of the cognitive structures presumed to mediate interpersonal behavior.

In the next section the general theoretical framework underlying this approach is summarized briefly.

CONSTRUAL OF THE SOCIAL ENVIRONMENT

The basic premise that interpersonal behavior is mediated by structured cognitive representations of self, others, and the situations in which behavior occurs, can be found in several general theories of interpersonal behavior (Foa & Foa, 1974; Jones & Thibaut, 1958; Kelly, 1963; Sullivan, 1953) and in symbolic interactionist theory (McCall, 1974; Mead, 1934). A central assumption in these theories is that social reality for an individual is a product of that individual's experiences in groups and organizations. In the course of social interaction, experiences of self, others, and interaction episodes are symbolized and represented in organized cognitive structures that in turn regulate future interactions (Goffman, 1974). The process of social cognition is assumed to involve classification of perceived events into an organized set of categories according to meaning and (sometimes) magnitude. The categories themselves may be organized hierarchically, dimensionally, or both, depending on their contents. In the class of models that we typically use, these categories can be thought of as regions in an n-dimensional space with category members represented as points in this space. We assume that by this process the social environment acquires meaning, enabling the perceiver to understand the present and to anticipate the future. Interpersonal behavior, including communication and attraction, is assumed to depend directly on the categorical and dimensional structure of the internal representation, and specifically on the location of self and other(s) in the representation.

One of the earliest and clearest statements of this general theoretical position was made by George Kelly (1963): "Life is characterized, not merely by its abstractability along a time line, but more particularly, by the capacity of the living thing to represent its environment. Especially is this true of man who builds construction systems through which to view the real world [p. 43]." Kelly's theory posits that an individual's psychological processes are "channelized" by his structured construct system, and that this system both facilitates and restricts interpersonal behavior. Although the primary focus of the theory is personality dynamics, Kelly's "Commonality Corollary" provides a basis for understanding social behavior: "To the extent that one person employs a construction of experience which is similar to that employed by another, his psychological processes are similar to those of the other person." In other words, the basis for similar or coordinated action is in individuals' similar construals of events, rather than in the distal identity of the events or situations themselves. Thus, Kelly maintained a clear and important distinction between the objective social field (i.e., the distal situation) and the perceived social field (i.e., proximal or internal field).[1] Failure to maintain this distinction between psychological and distal reality has created considerable confusion in some of the modern literature on "interactionism."

We assume, as did Kelly, that the basis for similar action and effective communication in a group, is in actors' similar construals of events and individuals, rather than in the distal identities of social episodes and group members. One implication of this view is that traditional sociometric methods for analysis and representation of group structure, and the theories that rely on such methods, have limited psychological relevance. Likewise, Kelly's Repertory Grid method (Kelly, 1963), and paradigms that rely exclusively on actors' ratings on pre-specified attribute scales (Bales, 1970; Ennis, 1979) cannot provide an adequate understanding of interpersonal behavior in groups and organizations. Also, the unit of analysis is important: Methods that rely exclusively on trait terms, situation labels or vignettes, role descriptions, behavior descriptions, or even factorial combinations of any or all of these, can lead to only very limited understandings of interpersonal perception and behavior. I contend that the most relevant units of analysis are persons per se, studied in the context of the social, family, work, and community groups to which they belong.

---

[1] Comparable distinctions have been made by Sullivan (1953), Magnusson and Endler (1977), and Golding (1978).

A PARADIGM
FOR INVESTIGATING INTERPERSONAL
PERCEPTION, ATTRIBUTION, AND ATTRACTION

The paradigm outlined and illustrated here constitutes a general framework for formulating questions and testing hypotheses about social perception and behavior, using individuals and groups as the units of analysis. The next several sections describe its theoretical basis, methods of analysis and interpretation, and some examples illustrating the types and range of possible applications.

Definitions and Theoretical Basis

The conception of interpersonal perception guiding our work distinguishes between *self* and *other* as alternative points of reference. At a given point in time, each individual in a social field is assumed to have an internal representation of significant others, with self positioned somewhere in the representation or schema. This is his or her own "*social environment.*" The term *social structure* refers to the pattern of this environment (Jones & Young, 1972). Further, we assume that the representation is dimensional with distances among self and others (and distances among others), reflecting important information about interpersonal relationships. Individual and temporal differences in the representations can be at the level of: (1) the number and identities (meanings) of dimensions; (2) relative saliences of dimensions; or (3) the positioning of self and others along one or more dimensions. Interpersonal communication and other types of behavior are assumed to be mediated by these representations, and the structures of individuals' representations are assumed to change as a function of such communication and behavior. The degree of isomorphism among the schemata of individuals in a group is assumed to have important implications for their satisfaction and effectiveness. Moreover, the degree of congruence in individuals' representations of themselves and significant others is assumed to be important for predicting and understanding communication and mutual attraction. Finally, any individual's schema is assumed to serve as the basis for his or her judgments and inferences about both self and others.

Measurement Considerations

The primary unit of analysis employed in our research has been the individual, both as judge and stimulus person. Choice of individuals as stimuli to be judged has important theoretical and methodological benefits. Specifically, it is contended that dimensions and structures derived from generalized similarity judgments about self and others have a special relevance for understanding and predicting interpersonal behavior that is lacking in paradigms based on other units or other measures (e.g., covariances among trait ratings). When asked to make generalized interpersonal similarity judgments, the judge may consider the entire complex of demographic, behavioral, and personality cues that he or she deems relevant for judging that pair of individuals. For each pair judged, it is assumed that a social comparison process (Festinger, 1954) is evoked that is essentially similar to the process typically evoked in actual social situations involving two or more group members. Thus, the observed set of interpersonal similarity relations generated by a particular judge contains a wealth of relevant information about that judge's construal of self and significant others, including implicit information about the "locations" of self, others, and the salient dimensions in which this perceived structure is embedded.

Multidimensional scaling techniques are then applied to recover these dimensions and the locations of self and others along them. The geometric structure derived by multidimensional scaling represents self and others as points, with relationships among points representing perceived relationships among group members; the derived configuration will be referred to as the perceived or implicit social structure of the group. Another important feature of this approach is that it allows a detailed analysis of individual and subgroup differences in construal of a common social situation. The models used permit inferences about individual differences in the number, identities, saliences, and predictive validities of these dimensions. We assume that an adequate account of interpersonal behavior requires that these individual differences be taken into account.

Consistent with the general assumption that cognitive schemata mediate interpersonal behavior, behavioral variables such as communication and interaction frequency, and preferential choice (i.e., attraction responses) are treated as *dependent* variables. Similarly, attributions about self and others, as well as other types of directed,[2] unidimensional judgments are regarded as dependent variables, to be predicted from the derived cognitive representation.

In most groups and organizations, a variety of "objective" information about members is often available (e.g., status, age, seniority, role designation, and other demographic and sociometric variables). Although such variables may be predictive of attraction, satisfaction, and certain interpersonal behaviors, the fact that these predictions may be successful is of limited theoretical interest. Rather, we assume that it is the perceived structure of the group that mediates an individual's attitudes and behaviors toward other members and the group per se. Instead of dwelling on the relationships between objective characteristics of group members, a theoretically more interesting approach treats these variables as antecedents and attempts to model simultaneously the relationships among all three classes of variables.

Figure 4.1 diagrams the proposed theoretical framework. Note that a fourth class of variables, self-report measures of judges' own attitudes, personalities,

---

[2]The term "directed" is used because in attributional judgments the subject is asked to rate stimulus-persons on specific attributes denoted by scale labels or other instructions.

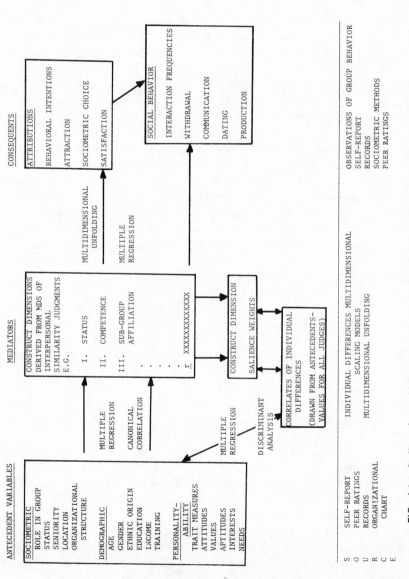

FIG. 4.1. Outline of a multidimensional framework for the investigation of individual differences in interpersonal perception, attraction, and behavior.

66

etc. is included. These are seen as moderators of actors' construals of the group, and are incorporated into our modeling as correlates of model-derived individual difference parameters (e.g., dimension salience weights). Coupled with an appropriate research design and appropriate sampling of judges and stimulus persons, the inclusion of self-ratings and self-report personality measures permits systematic investigation of hypotheses about the relationship between self-perception and construal of others. A general hypothesis of this type predicts that individuals who see themselves as extreme on a relevant dimension will attach more importance to that dimension in judging others (Hirschberg, Jones, & Haggerty, 1978). The present paradigm permits this rather intricate level of analysis and operationalizes the specified constructs in a way that we believe is both theoretically interesting and psychometrically sound. Other examples of such hypotheses are discussed in a later section.

Attraction. In research focusing on the prediction of interpersonal attraction (Davison & Jones, 1976), we have employed modified sociometric and preferential choice procedures, rather than the more global ''liking'' scales typically used in recent attraction research (Byrne, 1971; Clore & Jeffrey, 1972). The item content and response formats have been chosen to reflect domains of interpersonal behavior thought to be important for the group being studied. For example, in our investigation of an ROTC unit, Davison and I constructed two groups of items, one tapping respondents' attraction responses in social situations and the other group concerned with work situations (e.g., formation of squads at summer camp). For each item, the respondent was asked to judge the likelihood that he would choose each of the stimulus persons to engage or participate with him in the specified activity or situation. The resulting data contain more information about the pattern and intensity of subjects' interpersonal preferences than do traditional sociometric nomination data. Moreover, the measurement level of these likelihood estimates is sufficient for analysis with parametric statistical and scaling models, including multidimensional unfolding. Most sociometric data are nominal, restricting the range of models appropriate for analysis and representation of the group structure implicit in these data. In other research (Jones & Hirschberg, 1975; Nygren & Jones, 1977) we have used a paired-comparison format with scales designed to measure both strength and direction of preference. This type of data is sufficiently numerous and ''rich'' that it can be used as a basis for internal unfolding (Coombs, 1964), Thurstone scaling or, after appropriate transformation, multidimensional scaling.

Reliability. Inasmuch as individual differences multidimensional scaling models and, especially, multidimensional unfolding models are sensitive to unreliability in judgments, it is important to provide for assessments of reliability of similarity and preference judgments in the research design. A simple and conservative reliability estimate is given by the correlation between judgments of repeated pairs of representative stimuli (Nygren & Jones, 1977). These estimates may then be used to screen subjects and, further, as a basis for inferring the relative contributions of systematic individual differences and unreliability to total variability in subjects' judgments.

The Structural Model

The desired representation of social structure, and identification of the underlying group members' construal of their social environment, are accomplished by individual differences multidimensional scaling analysis of the set of interpersonal similarities judgments provided by the subjects. The INDSCAL model (Carroll & Chang, 1970) has been used in our research (Davison & Jones, 1976; Jones & Young, 1972) and that of several other researchers using this paradigm (Forgas, 1978; Kuyper, 1980; Shikiar & Coates, 1978). In the representation of the perceived social structure derived by INDSCAL, stimulus persons are represented by points embedded in an r-dimensional space, where distances between points represent perceived similarities–dissimilarities among individuals. The coordinate axes defining this space are assumed to correspond to fundamental attributes underlying interpersonal perception. Also, the analysis derives for each individual judge, a set of weights representing the relative saliences of the r dimensions for that judge. The weights range from 0 to 1. If a particular dimension is not used by a judge in his or her interpersonal similarity judgments, he or she will have a weight of 0 for that dimension. If, on the other hand, a dimension is very important for a judge, the ratio of that dimension's weight relative to his or her other weights will be very large. The matrix of weights summarizes information about differences among judges in a quantitative form that can be related to independently assessed demographic, sociometric, and personality variables (Fig. 4.1).

The input for INDSCAL (and other individual differences scaling models) consists of a set of $n \times n$ (where n is the number of stimulus persons) matrices of interpersonal dissimilarity judgments, with one matrix for each judge. The output consists of: (1) estimates of scale values, x_{jt}, for stimulus persons, each reflecting the amount of attribute t attributed to stimulus person j (the space defined by these is called the aggregate stimulus-person space); and (2) estimates of subject weights, w_{it}, interpreted as reflecting the saliences or importance of the r attributes.[3]

Sampling

Application of the methods outlined here to the study of perception of intact groups or organizations, requires that two groups of individuals be sampled,

---

[3]For a complete description and evaluation of INDSCAL, see Carroll and Chang (1970). Applications to a wide variety of substantive problems are summarized by Wish and Carroll (1974).

stimulus persons and judges. The stimulus persons should consist of a subset of group members chosen to be representative in age, sex, status, role, and other variables thought to be important. If no basis for selection is available, a random sample could be selected. However, it is desirable that the selected stimulus persons be at least moderately well acquainted with one another,[4] and that the entire group of stimulus persons should be known by the remaining members of the group, all of whom would serve as judges. This sampling plan has the important feature that the stimulus persons are also judges, so that their judgments will include ratings about themselves, others, and the relationships between themselves and others. The group of judges may include the entire group or, in large organizations, a representative sample of the members.

Unless it is feasible to designate all group members as stimulus persons, decisions about their number (n) and method of selection are crucial. Because most studies of this type employ paired-comparison designs, and because the number of comparisons increases geometrically with n, it is desirable to keep the number of stimulus persons small to hold judges' interest. On the other hand, n must be sufficiently large to include a representative sample of the group and to result in a stable solution.[5] It is important to realize that in the multiple regression procedures that are used to identify the dimensions resulting from the scaling analysis, the number of stimulus persons (n) *not* the number of judges (N) whose data are being modeled, is the effective sample size for the analysis and the basis for determining degrees of freedom for the associated significance tests. Finally, the selected sample of stimulus persons determines the number and identities of the dimensions resulting from the scaling analyses. Thus, if the selected sample is not representative of the parent group or organization, conclusions about the construct dimensions underlying interpersonal perception within the group will be invalid. The requirement here is completely parallel to that dictating careful selection of test items in factor analytic research on attitudes and abilities.

Prediction of Attributions and Interpersonal Attraction

The individual differences multidimensional scaling analysis of interpersonal similarities judgments by group members results in a geometric representation of the group structure and separate configurations representing each member's

---

[4]In studies where this requirement cannot be met, ratings of familiarity can be collected and used later to screen subjects and/or stimulus persons from further analysis. The ALSCAL program (Takane, Young, & deLeeuw, 1977) permits missing data so that rows and columns corresponding to designated stimulus-persons can be deleted from the data matrices for different judges.

[5]Results of recent Monte Carlo investigations of multidimensional models (Jones & Waddington, 1975; Spence, 1972; Young, 1970) can be used as a guide to determining n, if estimates of solution dimensionality, reliability of judgment, and extent of individual differences can be made ahead of time. In general, the higher the expected dimensionality, the lower the reliability of judgment, and the more diverse the anticipated individual differences, the higher the n.

"view" of the group. A problem addressed by our recent research (Davison & Jones, 1976; Jones & Hirschberg, 1975) concerns the psychological relevance of these derived representations. Specifically, we have been interested in using them to predict: (1) group members' attributions about themselves and others on dimensions such as status and leadership ability; and (2) the strength and valences of interpersonal attraction measured by a modified sociometric choice technique.

Attributions. In this paradigm, the investigators' hypotheses about construct dimensions that should be relevant (or irrelevant) to group members are represented by appropriately designed category rating scales or a set of nominal categories (e.g., male, female). If the construct embodied in the scale is salient for the group or designated subgroup, then ratings of stimulus persons on that scale should be predictable from the MDS-derived configuration. Multiple regression procedures are used to test the hypothesis and to describe the nature of the relationship between the perceived group structure and the construct scale(s). The regression analysis locates a vector corresponding to each scale in the stimulus person space such that projections of points representing stimulus persons on that vector and ratings of those persons are maximally correlated. If the correlation is high, then there is a close relationship between mean ratings on the attribute and projections of points representing stimulus persons; a low correlation indicates that no direction through the space corresponds to the obtained ratings. Thus, the multiple correlation associated with each vector can be considered as an indirect measure of salience of the corresponding attribute for the subgroup or individual whose ratings were used to locate the vector. The location of the vector relative to dimensions of the MDS space and other vectors provide important information for interpreting its meaning for the subject(s).[6] When the construct of interest is represented by nominal rather than ordinal or interval categories, a multiple discriminant analysis (Tatsuoka, 1971), with the MDS solution coordinates matrix as "predictors" and the category memberships of stimulus persons as the "criterion" variable, would be used instead. This analysis locates regions in the MDS space corresponding to the categories of stimulus persons and allows inferences about subgroup differences.

Although this procedure has been employed in a wide variety of investigations as a means of interpreting MDS solutions, its utility for testing hypotheses about individual and subgroup differences in construct salience has not been recognized. Examples of such usage are discussed in a later section.

---

[6]Using this procedure, it is possible to locate vectors for two subgroups of subjects whose attribute scale values refer to the same rating scale, but where the meaning of the scale is different. In a study of black-white differences in face perception (Jones & Hirschberg, 1975), separate scales of face attractiveness were derived for black and white subjects; vectors corresponding to these scales ran in different directions through the (common) MDS derived space. This result reflected the fact that the criteria for judging attractiveness by blacks and whites are systematically different.

Interpersonal Attraction.   The theoretical position adopted in our research assumes that an understanding of the dimensions of interpersonal perception among group members should lead to prediction of the network of attraction bonds among them. Thus, we employ a two-stage modeling procedure in which an MDS-derived stimulus person space is used as a basis for modeling interpersonal attraction. The value of this approach can be appreciated by considering other theories and methods that have been used to investigate attraction.

In their recent review of research on interpersonal attraction, Huston and Levinger (1978) criticized researchers' preoccupation with establishing whether a relationship between similarity and attraction exists. They suggest that instead of being concerned with whether similarity leads to attraction, investigation should focus on: "what kinds of similarity are important, how important they are, and for whom. Studies attempting to determine the role of similarity in the formation of friendship have failed to clarify these issues [p. 136]." I agree with this assessment, but suggest that the problem resides not in researchers' preoccupations but rather in their choice of research paradigms. For example, the widely adopted paradigm devised by Byrne and his associates (Byrne, 1971; Griffitt, 1974) to investigate the attitude similarity-attraction relationship, including both the experimental and correlational "versions," does not permit systematic investigation of the issues identified by Huston and Levinger. Byrne's paradigm requires that the investigator identify the bases of attraction a priori, rather than tapping those attributes underlying attraction responses. Griffitt and Veitch (1974) in their review of field studies investigating the similarity-attraction hypothesis, have blamed the failure to find consistent supporting evidence outside of the laboratory on the methodological weaknesses of profile similarity indices and the irrelevance to any interpersonal behavior of the variables typically assessed. The methodology and models described here: (1) recognize the multidimensional character of the similarity-attraction relationship; (2) allow subjects to describe interpersonal relationships in terms of attributes meaningful to them; (3) assess the relative saliences for individuals of these attributes; (4) provide some insights into the cognitive processes mediating attraction; and (5) avoid the use of profile similarity indices.

Our two-stage model of the similarity-attraction relationship assumes that an individual's attraction responses toward others in a group are based on his or her assessments of others' positions along more basic dimensions of interpersonal perception. In our methodology, these dimensions and group members' positions along them are measured via a multidimensional scaling analysis of interpersonal similarity judgments. Each individual's degree of attraction toward other members is measured, and a generalized multidimensional unfolding analysis (Carroll, 1972) is used to interrelate perceived similarity and attraction. It is noteworthy that this model attempts to account for each group member's attraction responses toward *all* other group members who are included as stimulus persons. The entire network of attraction relations can be represented and summarized geometrically, with stimulus persons represented as points in an r-dimensional space and judges represented by their "ideal points" or vectors through the space, depending on the particular version of the model that is adopted.

Two basic models relating attributes of stimulus persons to attraction are presented here. A more detailed discussion of these and related models is given by Davison and Jones (1976).

Vector Model. This model is basically the same as Anderson's (1971) model relating trait adjectives to overall impressions. It is a linear model in which the attraction judgment for a given stimulus person is represented as a weighted sum of that person's scale values along each dimension of interpersonal perception. If we let p_{ij} be the attraction of subject i toward person j, w_{it} be the weight of dimension t for subject i, and x_{jt} be the scale value for stimulus person j on dimension t, then according to this model, attraction judgments should be of the form:

$$p_{ij} = \sum_{t=1}^{r} w_{it} x_{jt} + c_i \tag{1}$$

where c_i denotes a constant unique to person i. Under this model, attraction is assumed to be linear in the stimulus scale values. Geometrically, this model represents each judge as a vector passing through the origin of a stimulus-person space. Preferences are a function of the projections of the points representing stimulus persons on the vector. The individual's preference function along each dimension is strictly monotonic. For example, if one of the dimensions were status, the higher (or lower) the status of a group member, the more he should be preferred. One might not expect this to be true for all judges. On both theoretical and empirical grounds, it would be expected that some individuals would be most attracted to other group members with status about equivalent to their own. For judges exhibiting this pattern of preferences, the appropriate model is an "ideal point" model (Coombs, 1964) whereby each judge is represented by a point in the stimulus space—his ideal point. The closer another group member is located in the space to the individual's ideal point, the more that person should be preferred.

Ideal Point Model. Work by Byrne (1971) and Anderson (1971) relating attitude and personality measures to interpersonal attraction is consistent with this more general model. Here, subjects' attraction judgments are assumed to be an additive function of the similarity between the subject and the stimulus person. Defining w_{it}, x_{jt}, and c_i as before, and defining x_{it} as subject i's position along dimension t, then the similarity hypothesis suggests that attraction is a linear function of the squared difference between the positions of subject i and person j along each of the r dimensions:

$$p_{ij} = \sum_{t=1}^{r} w_{it} (x_{it} - x_{jt})^2 + c_i. \tag{2}$$

The model embodied in Equation 1 can be fit using linear regression techniques once scale values are known. The parameters of the more general model in Equation 2[7] can also be fit by regression techniques. The PREFMAP program (Carroll, 1972) can be used to estimate parameters of both models, inasmuch as these models are special cases in the hierarchy of generalized unfolding models that are incorporated in the program.

As Davison & Jones (1976) pointed out, because the similarity–attraction hypothesis implicitly assumes that a subject's ideal point corresponds to his or her self-perceived position along each dimension, it predicts that subjects having higher estimated ideals along a dimension of interpersonal perception should rate themselves higher on that variable than persons with lower ideals. In the case where the judge is also a stimulus person, the joint space resulting from the two-stage MDS-unfolding analysis will contain two points for that judge: (1) a point summarizing his or her self-perceived locations along the r dimensions of interpersonal perception; and (2) an implicit ideal point. This feature of the model could be used to test hypotheses about self–ideal self discrepancies as a function of experience in the group, role, or other personality and attitudinal variables. Once again, this represents a level of analysis that is not possible with other paradigms for investigating interpersonal perception and attraction. It is a theoretically interesting level of analysis because it permits formulation and testing of hypotheses about the relationship between self-concept, ideal-self concept, and perception of others.

APPLICATIONS

Studies by Jones and Young (1972), Davidson and Jones (1976), Forgas (1978), Kaman, Shikiar, and Hautaluoma (1979), and Jones and Hirschberg (1975) have used the paradigm discussed previously in studies of social perception and interpersonal attraction. The designs, results, and conclusions of some of these studies will be used to illustrate and highlight important features of the methodology.

---

[7]The model expressed in Equation 2 is usually referred to as the "weighted unfolding (or ideal-point) model," with the w_{it}'s reflecting the salience or importance of the r dimensions in formation of interpersonal preference or attraction. When the w_{it}'s are constrained to be equal, the resulting model is referred to as the "simple unfolding model." PREFMAP permits fitting of the vector model and both the simple and weighted unfolding models. With appropriate goodness-of-fit tests, it is possible to infer which of the three models gives the best account of each judge's attraction judgments.

Social Structure of a Research Group

The longitudinal field experiment conducted by Jones and Young (1972) was designed to: (1) identify dimensions of interpersonal perception for members of a laboratory; (2) test hypotheses about individual and subgroup differences in the salience of these dimensions; and (3) investigate relationships between perceived group structure and interpersonal behavior.

The participants in the study were the faculty, staff, and students of a large laboratory. It was expected that role and status differences among members would be reflected in their perceptions of self and others, and that these differences in construal would moderate interpersonal attraction and behavior in important ways. The "stimulus persons" in this study were a subset of the group, but with the entire group serving as judges. Thus those judges who were also stimulus persons made judgments about others, themselves, and the relationship between themselves and others. Three types of data were collected:

1. *Interpersonal similarities.* Judges were asked to make similarity judgments about all possible pairs of stimulus persons, taking into account "whatever characteristics of the individuals that are relevant." Judgments were made on a 9-point scale ranging from "extremely similar" to "extremely dissimilar."

2. *Unidimensional attribution scales.* Subjects were asked to rate each of the stimulus persons on scales indicating degree of interest in various professional activities, status, life-style, and political orientation. These scales represented our hypotheses about the identities of the dimensions of interpersonal perception. As explained in an earlier section, a central feature of our methodology is the use of multiple regression to systematically relate stimulus-person scale values on these construct scales to the perceived group structure derived from the multidimensional scaling of the interpersonal similarity judgments. Not only does this procedure make interpretation of the dimensions less subjective, but also it allows us to make inferences about the degree to which a given dimension is salient for different subgroups of judges in different situations.[8]

3. *Sociometric choices.* Each subject was asked to choose the two sets of three individuals with whom they associated *least* and *most* frequently: (1) for research advice; and (2) socially. These tasks were intended to tap two important

---

[8]The multiple regression analysis uses scale values of the stimulus persons on the dimensions derived from MDS as predictor variables and scale values on the unidimensional scale as the criterion variable. The weights resulting from this analysis are direction cosines of the vector through the space best representing the scale construct. The multiple correlation (R) measures the goodness-of-fit of the vector in the dimensional space and is the desired measure of salience; a high value of R indicates close agreement between stimulus-person scale values on the unidimensional scale and the projection of the points representing stimulus persons in the MDS space. Comparisons of this salience measure across different groups of stimulus persons, situations, and/or judges requires only that the same rating scale be used, and the assumption that the construct measured by the scale has the same meaning.

domains of interpersonal behavior, social and work-related. The resulting choice data served as dependent variables in analyses designed to relate interpersonal perception and behavior.

Data were collected on two occasions, one year apart, using the same individuals as judges and stimulus persons. A generalization of the INDSCAL model involving parameters for stimuli, judges, and occasions was applied to investigate change in interpersonal perception as a function of seniority and experience.

INDSCAL analyses of the interpersonal similarities data from both years revealed three clear dimensions underlying interpersonal perception, listed in order of overall salience:

1. Status. Individuals with the lowest scale values were first-year graduate students, individuals in the middle were advanced graduate students and assistant professors, and those with the highest scale values were associate and full professors. Correlations between stimulus persons' projections on the dimension and an objective measure of status was .94.

2. Political persuasion. Scale values of individuals on this dimension were highly correlated with perceived position along a left–right or liberal–conservative political spectrum and a measure of orthodoxy of life-style.

3. Professional interests. Individuals' locations on this dimension were predictable from the patterns of their interests in substantive problem areas and methodology. For example, perceived degree of interest in statistical problems correlated −.91 with projections along this dimension.

Multiple regression analyses relating the INDSCAL-derived dimensions to the various unidimensional scales revealed that three subsets of construct vectors closely coincided with the unrotated dimensions. These results supported the assertion that the orientation of the dimensions was meaningful and that the group perceived itself according to the status, professional interests, and political persuasion of its members.

The multiple regression analyses also revealed that Interest in Teaching and Interest in Computer Programming were *not* salient dimensions of construal for the group as a whole; the low multiple correlations obtained for these scales meant that vectors corresponding to these constructs were not locatable in the group stimulus space.

The subject space resulting from the INDSCAL analysis was analyzed to determine if there were consistent points of view in interpersonal construal associated with four role-defined subject groups: New Graduate Students, Graduate Students, Faculty, and Clerical–Secretarial Personnel.[9] Multiple discriminant

---

[9]Geometrically, a distinguishable point of view would be inferred if the set of points representing the group of role encumbents were located in a distinct subregion of the space. When no a priori empirical or theoretical basis for defining groups is available, cluster analytic procedures could be used to determine whether distinguishable groups are present.

analysis using the salience weights as predictor variables and the four groups as "the criterion" variables indicated overall significant differences among the centroids of the groups. Salience of professional interests was the most important variable differentiating the groups, with Graduate Students exhibiting the highest weights and Clerical Workers the lowest weights. Faculty were more status conscious than the other groups; New Graduate Students and Clerical Personnel paid more attention to political persuasion.

A generalization of the INDSCAL model, with data from both years combined, was developed to explore changes in the saliences of the dimensions over time. The subject space resulting from this model contains two points for each subject, representing the relative saliences of the stimulus space dimensions at Time 1 and Time 2. Thus, changes in interpersonal perception over time are reflected by differences in the direction and magnitude of change in weights.

We predicted that temporal stability in interpersonal perception was a function of duration of group membership. The results of the longitudinal analysis demonstrated that Faculty and Advanced Graduate Students exhibited very small changes in dimension salience, whereas New Graduate Students exhibited relatively larger changes, confirming the prediction. Over the one-year period, Political Persuasion became more salient for the new students, and Professional Interests became less salient.

The final objective of our research was to predict interpersonal choice and behavior using what had been learned about the dimensions of interpersonal construal and individual differences in the saliences of these dimensions. A simple model, capitalizing on the fact that a subgroup of judges were stimulus persons with locations in the group stimulus space was devised to generate these predictions. Distances between each judge and the remaining stimulus persons were computed in the relevant subspace. Then, the three stimulus persons closest to the judge and the three farthest from the judge were identified. Finally, these two sets of predicted choices were compared to each judge's actual choices, and the percentage of correctly predicted choices was determined. The accuracy of these predictions ranged from 46% to 62% when the group space (or a subspace) was used as the basis for prediction. Using each judges *own* stimulus space[10] as the basis for prediction increased accuracy by approximately 10%. In the subsequent study by Davison and me, a modified sociometric rating procedure was adopted. As noted in the section on measurement procedures, the data resulting from this task allow for a more elaborate and precise modeling of the perception–attraction relationships.

A final analysis was designed to predict membership on graduate students' thesis and dissertation committees. The one-dimensional subspace defined by the Professional Interests dimension was used to make those predictions. The average distance between each student and the faculty members on his or her commit-

---

[10]The stimulus space for an individual was constructed by applying that individual's salience weights to the coordinates matrix (X) of the group stimulus space.

tee, and the distance to faculty *not* on the committee, were computed. For eight of the nine students, the members of the student's committee were closer to him or her, on the average, than were faculty not on the committee.

Perception of Persons and Social Episodes

In an investigation very similar in design and methodology to that of Jones and Young, Forgas (1978) studied the social environment of a large psychology department at a British university. An interesting additional purpose of Forgas' study was to explore the relationship between social structural variables (formal status and sociometric position) and two aspects of social perception (perception of the group and its "social episodes").

The dimensions of interpersonal perception derived from an INDSCAL analysis of interpersonal similarities were identified as Sociability, Creativity, and Competence; these dimensions were comparable in meaning to those identified by Jones and Young (1972) and Davison and Jones (1976). An analysis of profile distances among social episodes, derived from judgments of the episodes on 11 bipolar scales, resulted in four dimensions: anxiety, involvement, evaluative, and socioemotional task orientation. The role and status positions of group members were related to their perceptions of the episodes; faculty judged episodes in terms of involvement, and students and staff relied most on the socioemotional dimension. Also, a variety of interesting relationships between the perceived characteristics of group members and their perception of episodes was shown. For example, group members who were seen as sociable tended not to discriminate between episodes in terms of whether they were tense-relaxed, pleasant-unpleasant, etc., presumably reflecting their self-confidence and social skills.

Forgas' effort to relate group member characteristics, perceived social structure, and perception of social episodes is a research direction with considerable theoretical interest; this level of analysis ties together some of the central problems in interactionist theory (Magnusson & Endler, 1977) and traditional lines of work on interpersonal perception (Tagiuri & Petrullo, 1958).

By extending the research paradigm to include interpersonal attraction and behavior, such that all three classes of variables (i.e., perceptual, affective, and situational) could be studied together, the resulting scope and level of analysis would approximate that required to formulate a general theory of social cognition and behavior.

Social Structure and Communication

Kaman, Shikiar, and Hautaluoma (1979) conducted a study of a large psychology department using a methodology modeled after that employed in the Jones and Young, and Davison and Jones studies. However, the focus in the Kaman et al. study was on the relationships among organizational roles, perceptual structures, interpersonal communication, and sociometric choice. Two types of communication measures were used: items tapping percentage of total communications falling into nine content categories, (e.g., concerning department policies, research, outside interests); and items reflecting percentage of total communications directed to specific others. The results contained systematic differences in communication content and message recipients as a function of: (1) stimulus persons' sectional affiliations within the department; and (2) saliences of dimensions of interpersonal perception derived from an INDSCAL analysis. The authors suggest that a logical next step in pursuing this line of research would be an exploration of the causal links among role, perceptual structure, and communication constructs. A longitudinal study employing the three-mode model used by Jones and Young would allow inferences about those causal linkages. Also, multidimensional unfolding procedures could be used in such a study to relate the communication variables to perceived group structure.

Other Studies

Other studies of interpersonal perception in natural settings that have used multidimensional scaling to quantify perceived group structure include: Davison and Jones' (1976) study of an ROTC unit; Ennis' (1979) study of a Bales self-analytic group; Shikiar and Coates' (1978) investigation of black and white children's perceptions of role figures; Kuyper's (1980) study of training and feedback on interpersonal perception in small groups; Goldstein, Blackman, and Collins' (1966) study of perception and liking in army squads; Smith, Pedersen, and Lewis' (1966) study of the social structures of two classes of MBA students; Jackson, Messick, and Solleys' (1957) investigation of personality perception in a college fraternity; Stone and Coles' (1971) study of graduate students' perceptions of a psychology faculty; and Lewis, Lissitz, and Jones' (1975) study of change in interpersonal perception in a T-group.

ADVANTAGES AND DISADVANTAGES

The paradigm outlined in this chapter has several important advantages compared to other approaches commonly used to investigate problems in interpersonal perception and group behavior. Also, it has some inherent limitations; some of these are at the level of model assumptions, whereas others can be alleviated by care in research design, model selection, and interpretation of results.

Advantages

1. Generalized Similarities. In studies where it is possible and appropriate to collect pair-wise interpersonal similarities data, the judgmental task is simple, nonreactive, and natural. Important attributes of interpersonal perception, ones that might not be accessible to directed judgment methods (i.e., attribute ratings on unidimensional scales specified by the investigator), are tapped in these similarity judgments. For example, in groups where power struggles or other forms of dissension and conflict are present, members might be reluctant to express their feelings about other members in their ratings of likability. Yet, such evaluations would be expected to be reflected in generalized similarity judgments about pairs of members (e.g., a pair containing a well-liked co-worker and a disliked co-worker would be seen and judged as dissimilar). When both descriptive and affective characteristics of group members are important in group functioning, both should be reflected in interpersonal similarity judgments. Indeed, the same dimension may be descriptive for some judges and evaluative for others. Some of the dimensions underlying perception of political candidates identified in a study by Nygren and Jones (1977) were shown to have such dual significance.

2. *Quantification of Individual Differences.*   Individual difference scaling techniques (e.g., INDSCAL) employed in our paradigm quantify individual differences at the level of dimension saliences. The salience parameters allow inferences about both intra- and interindividual variation in the degree to which judges rely on the derived dimensions in judging themselves and others. These salience weights can then be related to independently assessed attributes of the judges, hypothesized to be predictive of interpersonal perception and preference; these external measures can be demographic characteristics, personality or attitude measures, information about role or prior experience in the group studied, or even information about the judges sociometric "position" in the social structure resulting from the same analysis. For example, in the Jones and Young (1972) study of a research unit, salience of status was found to be closely related to judges' roles, with faculty judgments reflecting much more concern about status than judgments by students or technical-clerical staff. Assessment and identification of individual and subgroup differences at the level of dimension saliences represents a potentially important type and level of analysis. These model-derived salience measures are not plagued by the types of response bias that typically contaminate self-reports about attribute importance, and other measures derived from unidimensional judgment scales. At the same time, hypotheses about the relationship between trait scores derived from conventional self-report or peer rating measures and dimension salience weights derived from similarities may be investigated. For example, our recent work on face perception (Hirschberg et al., 1978) investigated the hypothesis that individuals who saw themselves as very attractive or very unattractive would attach high salience to attractiveness in judging similarities and differences among opposite-sex faces. In the Davison and Jones (1976) study of a military unit, hypotheses about the relationship between members' status in the unit and salience of status in their

construal of others were investigated. We found that members who were seen by themselves and the group as low in status attached relatively high salience to status in judging others.

3. *Longitudinal Analysis.*   The basic paradigm can be extended to investigate longitudinal changes in interpersonal perception. One possible model assumes that the judges use essentially the same dimensions[11] at two (or more) points in time, but that the relative saliences of these dimensions change in different ways for different judges. Carroll & Chang's (1970) INDSCAL program and Takane, Young, & deLeuuw's (1977) ALSCAL program both can be used to fit this more general model. With appropriate normalization of the salience weights, a subject space can be constructed in which subjects' points of view at different times can be represented. This type of three-mode modeling (the modes are stimuli, judges, and time periods) has considerable potential for measuring and understanding changes in perception and structure over time. For example, the method could be used to investigate the effects of changes in group composition, training, policy changes, leadership, or other types of intervention. The methods used would seem to avoid many of the logical and psychometric difficulties usually encountered in the measurement of change.

4. *The Group as a Unit of Analysis.*   The focus of analysis assumed so far has been a single group, as construed by its members, at one or more points in time. The basic paradigm can be extended to allow inferences about interpersonal perception for different groups of respondents who are members of *distinct* groups or organizations. Comparisons of this type are at the level of attribute saliences and involve the use of multiple regression procedures for locating "property vectors" in the group stimulus-person spaces derived by multidimensional scaling. As noted earlier, the R resulting from such an analysis can be thought of as a measure of the degree to which ratings about group members on the specific attribute tapped by a unidimensional rating scale can be predicted or accounted for by the defining dimensions of the group stimulus space.

In the work by Hirschberg and me on black and white women's perceptions of black and white men's faces, group differences in attributions to faces were investigated using this procedure. Vectors corresponding to mean ratings on the scales "Threatening–Nonthreatening" and "Cruel–Kind" were well defined ($R > .9$) directions through the stimulus space for white female subjects, but in the group stimulus space of faces for black females, these attributes did *not* correspond to well-defined vectors, as evidenced by low ($R < .4$) multiple correlations.

---

[11]In fact, the model can handle the case where different subsets of judges rely on different dimensions at different times.

In individual differences multidimensional scaling models, the salience weight parameters refer to the defining dimensions of the group stimulus space. The alternative method of defining and measuring salience just described results in measures of salience for *any* direction(s) through the group stimulus space, rather than just the directions defined by the coordinate axes. This method of measuring salience can be used to investigate differences among groups of judges who are members of different groups and whose ratings refer to members of their respective groups.

An experiment conducted by Kuyper (1980) at the University of Groningen in the Netherlands employed this procedure. Kuyper is studying the effects of different types of training on interpersonal perception and effectiveness in small groups. In his experiment, a group is formed, the members are given a chance to become acquainted, and then rate themselves on interpersonal similarity scales and several specified attributes. Next, the group is given training and performance feedback designed to heighten members' sensitivity to certain attributes of themselves and others. After completion of training, members again rate themselves on interpersonal similarity and the specified attributes. Multidimensional scaling solutions (INDSCAL) are computed using the pre- and posttraining similarities, and property vectors corresponding to the attribute scales are located in the resulting stimulus-person spaces. Both INDSCAL and scale-based salience measures are available from those analyses, allowing a test of the hypothesis for the group. Other groups were run to provide replications and as a basis for investigating the relative effectiveness of other training methods. Because it was possible that the derived dimensions might not be common to the groups, comparisons at the level of INDSCAL salience weights were not feasible. Instead, Kuyper used the attribute-based saliences (i.e., R^2s) derived from multiple regression analyses as the basis for assessing the effects of a particular training method and for making comparisons between different methods and groups.

5. Modeling Similarity-Attraction Relationships. Prediction of interpersonal attraction measures (or other types of sociometric data) is possible within this paradigm by using the dimensions of the group and individual stimulus-person spaces derived by MDS as the basis of external unfolding analyses. As detailed in a previous section, the unfolding or "ideal-point" analysis represents each group member as a point in the stimulus-person space. Under this model, strength of interpersonal attraction is predicted to be an inverse function of distance between the implicit ideal point of an individual and points representing other group members. The joint space resulting from such an analysis represents self, other group members, and implicit ideals as points, allowing tests of hypotheses about attraction, self-concept, and the relationship between self-concept and perception of others. This type of modeling can also be used to predict behavioral dependent variables such as frequency of interaction and sociometric choice.

Ennis (1979) has contrasted our model with two other methods designed to measure group structure: Bales (1979) SYMLOG model and block-model (Arabie, Boorman, & Levitt, 1978) procedures for extracting structure from sociometric observations. He argues that an advantage of the block-model technique resides in its capability to represent the intrinsic asymmetries of interpersonal behavior (e.g., *A* likes *B*, but *B* dislikes *A*). Although it is true that the multidimensional scaling model central to our paradigm does not represent these asymmetries, the two-stage MDS ideal-point model can handle such asymmetries. For example, if we were to hypothesize that high status members would be recipients of relatively more communications or sociometric choices than low status members, the expected pattern of results could be modeled by an external unfolding analysis in which ideal points representing the group members as respondents would be located in a group space derived by multidimensional scaling. The model assumes that frequency of choice is inversely proportional to distances between the ideal point for a respondent and the points representing other group members. A "joint space" derived in this fashion *can* account for asymmetries in interpersonal behavior. Each individual has two locations in the joint space, his or her location as a stimulus person (as perceived) and his or her ideal point (perceiver). In predicting his or her sociometric choices, or communication frequencies with other members, the predicted values are functions of ideal point to other distances. In predicting choices by others, the predicted values are a function of distances between their ideal points and the target person's location as a stimulus person.

Disadvantages and Limitations

1. Heuristic Value. Our approach depends on multidimensional scaling methodology to quantify and represent group structure. The perceptual–judgmental model implicitly assumed is dimensional and continuous. In contrast, the processes involved in person perception are probably more categorical and discontinuous in nature, and ideally should be modeled with procedures that mirror this process. Also, interpersonal perception and attraction reflect an interplay of cognitive, affective, and behavioral influences. Representation of cognitive structure by a static, geometric model tends to draw our attention away from this interactive cycle.

2. Practical Problems. Acquisition of generalized similarity judgments requires a paired-comparison task. Thus, the subjects' judgment task is repetitious and tedious, especially when the number of stimulus persons is large. Sorting procedures, ranking methods, and pair-reduction schemes can be used to increase task interest and efficiency. A related problem occurs when the stimulus materials are lengthy, complex, or unfamiliar (e.g., videotape segments, written descriptions of situations, etc.). The time required for subjects to process and judge pairs of such complex stimuli often exceeds that available, especially in field research.

Another interesting alternative to the paired-comparison task would start with free-response descriptions of the stimulus persons. Similarity measures would be derived from a content analysis and coding of the descriptions. Even though this approach is time-consuming and best suited to idiographic studies, its application to the class of problems considered here would be worthwhile. Rosenberg (1977) has used a similar task in his work on implicit personality theory.

CONCLUSIONS

In interpersonal perception, experiences of self and other(s) are construed along multiple salient dimensions; the structure defined by these dimensions is the basis for specific interpersonal judgments, attraction, and behavior. When asked or required to do so, an individual *can* attend to and make reliable discriminations along other dimensions, but these dimensions are likely to have limited relevance for predicting interpersonal attraction and behavior. Moreover, the fact that an individual can make such judgments tells us nothing about whether he or she routinely *does* use these dimensions. The fact that a covariance structure underlying attribute ratings is orderly and interpretable is no guarantee that the derived structure is psychologically relevant.

Factor analytic studies of the covariation among attribute scale ratings of group members rely on strong assumptions: The scales themselves typically come from the investigator's theories and hunches or from content analyses of protocols, interviews, or naturalistic data. All these sources may miss important attributes and, at best, result in a set of attributes relevant to the *group* studied. There is no reason to believe that the set of attributes derived is relevant to any particular individual. Finally, the dimensional structure derived from covariances among trait ratings may depend on semantic factors or beliefs about trait covariation. When structures are derived from interpersonal similarity judgments with individuals as units of analysis, such an explanation is implausible.

The paradigm I've just described seems to be a powerful and versatile approach to the study and description of social perception and interpersonal attraction. On the idiographic to nomothetic continuum, it represents a hybrid research strategy—one that can provide detailed insights into the structuring of social experience for individuals and at the same time permit detailed comparisons among judges and identification of communalities and differences in their perceptions of the social environment.

ACKNOWLEDGMENT

A preliminary, abbreviated version of this chapter was presented as an invited paper at the Midwestern Psychological Association meeting in Chicago on May 5, 1979.

REFERENCES

Anderson, N. H. Integration theory and attitude change. *Psychological Review*, 1971, *78*, 171-206.

Arabie, P., Boorman, S. A., & Levitt, P. R. Constructing blockmodels: How and why. *Journal of Mathematical Psychology*, 1978, *17*, 21-63.

Bales, R. F. *Personality and interpersonal behavior*. New York: Holt, Rinehart, & Winston, 1970.

Bales, R. F., Cohen, S. P., & Williamson, S. A. *SYMLOG: A system for the multiple level observation of groups*. New York: Free Press, 1979.

Byrne, D. *The attraction paradigm*. New York: Academic Press, 1971.

Carroll, J. D. Individual differences and multidimensional scaling. In R. N. Shepard & S. Nerlove (Eds.), *Multidimensional scaling: Theory and applications in the behavioral sciences* (Vol. 1). New York: Seminary Press, 1972.

Carroll, J. D., & Chang, J. J. Analysis of individual differences in multidimensional scaling via an N-way generalization of "Eckart-Young" decomposition. *Psychometrika*, 1970, *35*, 283-319.

Clore, G. L., & Jeffrey, K. M. Emotional role playing, attitude change, and attraction toward a disabled person. *Journal of Personality and Social Psychology*, 1972, *23*, 105-111.

Coombs, C. H. *A theory of data*. New York: Wiley, 1964.

Davison, M. L., & Jones, L. E. A similarity-attraction model for predicting sociometric choice from perceived group structure. *Journal of Personality and Social Psychology*, 1976, *33*, 601-612.

Ennis, J. G. Blockmodels and spatial representations of group structure: Some comparisons. In H. C. Hudson (Ed.), *Classifying social data*. San Francisco: Jossey-Bass, 1979.

Festinger, L. A theory of social comparison processes. *Human Relations*, 1954, *7*, 117-140.

Foa, V. G., & Foa, E. B. *Societal structures of the mind*. Springfield, Ill.: Charles C Thomas, 1974.

Forgas, J. P. The perception of social episodes: Categorical and dimensional representations in two different social milieus. *Journal of Personality and Social Psychology*, 1976, *33*, 199-209.

Forgas, J. P. Social episodes and social structure in an academic setting: The social environment of an intact group. *Journal of Experimental Social Psychology*, 1978, *14*, 434-448.

Goffman, E. *Frame analysis*. New York: Harper and Row, 1974.

Golding, S. L. Towards a more adequate theory of personality: Psychological organizing principles. In H. London & N. Hirschberg (Eds.), *Strategies of personality research*. Washington, D.C.: Hemisphere Publishing Co. (Wiley), 1978.

Goldstein, K. M., Blackman, S., & Collins, D. J. Relationships between sociometric and multidimensional scaling measures. *Perceptual and Motor Skills*, 1966, *23*, 639-643.

Griffitt, W. Attitude similarity and attraction. In T. L. Huston (Ed.), *Foundations of interpersonal attraction*. New York: Academic Press, 1974.

Griffitt, W., & Veitch, R. Preacquaintance attitude similarity and attraction. *Sociometry*, 1974, *37*, 163-173.

Hirschberg, N., Jones, L. E., & Haggerty, M. Individual differences in face perception. *Journal of Research in Personality*, 1978, *12*, 488-499.

Huston, T. L., & Levinger, G. Interpersonal attraction and relationships. In M. R. Rosenzweig & L. W. Porter (Eds.), *Annual Review of Psychology*. Palo Alto: Annual Reviews Inc., 1978.

Jackson, D. N., Messick, S. J., & Solley, G. M. A multidimensional scaling approach to the perception of personality. *Journal of Psychology*, 1957, *44*, 311-318.

Jones, E. E., & Thibaut, J. W. Interaction goals as bases of inference in interpersonal perception. In R. Tagiuri & L. Petrullo (Eds.), *Person perception and interpersonal behavior*. Stanford: Stanford University Press, 1958.

Jones, L. E., & Hirschberg, N. *What's in a face? Individual differences in face perception*. Paper presented at the American Psychological Association Convention, Chicago, Ill., 1975. (Mimeographed)

Jones, L. E., & Waddington, J. *Sensitivity of INDSCAL to simulated individual differences in dimension usage patterns and judgmental error*. Unpublished manuscript, University of Illinois, 1975.

Jones, L. E., & Young, F. W. Structure of a social environment: Longitudinal individual differences scaling of an intact group. *Journal of Personality and Social Psychology*, 1972, *24*, 108–121.

Kaman, V., Shikiar, R., & Hautaluoma, J. *Perceived social structure, role, and communication patterns in an organization.* Unpublished paper, Colorado State University, 1979.

Kelly, G. H. *A theory of personality: The psychology of personal constructs.* New York: Norton, 1963.

Kuyper, H. *About the Saliency of social comparison dimensions.* Department of Social Psychology. University of Groningen, Netherlands, 1980.

Lewis, P., Lissitz, R. W., & Jones, C. L. Assessment of change in interpersonal perception in a T group using individual differences multidimensional scaling. *Journal of Consulting Psychology*, 1975, *22*, 44–48.

Magnusson, D., & Endler, N. Interactional psychology: Current issues and future prospects. In D. Magnusson & N. Endler, (Eds.), *Personality at the cross-roads: Current issues in interactional psychology.* Hillsdale, N.J.: Larence Erlbaum Associates, 1977.

McCall, G. J. A symbolic interactionist approach to attraction. In T. L. Huston (Ed.), *Foundations of interpersonal attraction.* New York: Academic Press, 1974.

Mead, G. H. *Mind, self and society.* Chicago: University of Chicago Press, 1934.

Nygren, T. E., & Jones, L. E. Individual differences in perception and preferences for political candidates. *Journal of Experimental Social Psychology*, 1977, *13*, 182–197.

Rosenberg, S. New approaches to the analysis of personal constructs in person perception. In J. Cole (Ed.), *Nebraska Symposium on Motivation.* Lincoln: University of Nebraska Press, 1977.

Shikiar, R., & Coates, C. A multidimensional scaling study of person perception in children. *Multivariate Behavioral Research*, 1978, *13*, 363–370.

Smith, K. H., Pedersen, D. M., & Lewis, R. E. Dimensions of interpersonal perception in a meaningful ongoing group. *Perceptual and Motor Skills*, 1966, *22*, 867–880.

Spence, I. An aid to the estimation of dimensionality in nonmetric multidimensional scaling. *University of Western Ontario Research Bulletin* No. 229, 1972.

Stone, L. A., & Coles, G. J. Psychology graduate students' multidimensional perceptions of their psychology faculty. *Acta Psychologica*, 1971, *35*, 364–377.

Sullivan, H. S. *The interpersonal theory of psychiatry.* New York: Norton 1953.

Tagiuri, R., & Petrullo, L. *Person perception and interpersonal behavior.* Stanford: Stanford University Press, 1958.

Takane, Y., Young, F. W., & de Leeuw, J. Nonmetric individual differences multidimensional scaling: An alternating least squares method with optimal scaling features. *Psychometrika*, 1977, *42*, 7–67.

Tatsuoka, M. *Multivariate analysis.* New York: Wiley, 1971.

Wish, M., & Carroll, J. D. Applications of individual differences scaling to studies of human perception and judgment. In E. C. Carterette & M. P. Friedman (Eds.), *Handbook of Perception* (Vol. 2). New York: Academic Press, 1974.

Young, F. W. Nonmetric multidimensional scaling: Recovery of metric information. *Psychometrika*, 1970, *35*, 455–473.

5
The Perception of Crowding: Conceptual Dimensions and Preferences

Janet E. Stockdale
London School of Economics

Denise A. Hale
City of London Polytechnic

The results of the bulk of crowding research over the past decade clearly indicate the need to identify the conceptual dimensions that determine people's perceptions of being crowded. One must distinguish crowding—a perceived and subjective state—from environmental attributes commonly used to describe situations as crowded. This chapter is concerned with the application of multidimensional scaling techniques to the area of subjective crowding and, in particular, it focuses on the relationship between perceptions of similarity and preferential choice among crowded situations.

Despite the consensual view of crowding as an experiential state whose antecedent conditions are not defined solely by high density (Stokols, 1972a) there is wide divergence about what constitutes the necessary and sufficient conditions for inducing the state of feeling crowded (Stockdale, 1978). The essential characteristic of crowding is seen variously as the restriction in the range of behavioral choice induced by the close proximity of others (Proshansky, Ittleson, & Rivlin, 1970), inability to control interactions with others (Zlutnick & Altman, 1972), excessive stimulation from social sources (Desor, 1972), perceived inadequacy of space (Stokols, 1972b), unwanted social interactions (Valins & Baum, 1973), interference and blocking (Sundstrom, 1975), and inability to attain desired levels of privacy (Altman, 1975). An important preliminary step in evaluating these conceptions is to establish how people, as opposed to crowding theorists, construe the experience of being crowded. Only when individuals' conceptions of crowding are known will it be possible to formulate a relationship between individuals' perceptions of crowded situations and the behavioral consequences.

A major implication of recent crowding research is that crowding has multiple determinants and therefore cannot be considered a unidimensional concept. Acceptance of this view raises two questions of theoretical interest and practical importance. First, what dimensions do individuals use in perceiving situations as crowded? Although previous crowding research has suggested a variety of key determinants, there has been no direct evidence that any of these form the basis for an individual's perception of crowding. The second question is whether the major perceptual dimensions are equally salient for all individuals and, if not, are the differences in salience related to personality differences among indivduals? It might be expected, for example, that individuals' scores on variables previously linked to crowding, such as Internality/Externality (Schopler, McCallum, & Rusbult, 1977), preference for privacy (Altman, 1975), and interpersonal space (Cozby, 1973) would be correlated with the weights associated with the perceptual dimensions of crowding.

An individual differences multidimensional scaling analysis (INDSCAL) permits both the identification of dimensions that individuals use in discriminating among a set of subjectively crowded situations and an examination of individual differences in perceptions of crowding. The judgmental model implicit in multidimensional scaling assumes that: (1) the individual conceptualizes the stimuli as though they are points in space; (2) the perceived dissimilarities among the stimuli are psychological distances that are related to the distances among the points that represent them; and (3) the dimensions of the space are the relevant psychological dimensions along which stimuli are judged and compared (Nygren & Jones, 1977). As most multidimensional scaling models require only that subjects provide similarity or difference judgments among stimulus objects, the dimensions that emerge are not a function of the experimenter's preconceptions of what is salient about the stimuli, but are constrained only by the sample of stimulus objects and, perhaps, by the instructions. The identification of the dimensions of subjective crowding allows one to ask a further question: What is the relationship between the dimensions of subjective crowding and individuals' tolerance of crowding as expressed by preference judgments? If one assumes that the dimensions underlying similarity judgments also determine preference, then PREFMAP (Carroll, 1972) can be used to represent the individual and his or her preferences by one of a hierarchy of distance models. PREFMAP provides an external analysis of preferences in which subjects' preferences are related to an a priori set of dimensions obtained, for example, from INDSCAL.

The simplest model of preference is the vector model, the major assumption of which is that if a specified amount of a given characteristic is good, then more of the characteristic must be even better. However, there are many properties for which this relation fails to hold in that too much of the characteristic can be perceived as bad. This concept is central to the unfolding models in which it is assumed that there is some optimal value on a given dimension (or some ideal point in the multidimensional case) where stimulus objects will be most preferred and that they become less preferred as they move away from that optimal value—or ideal point. The simple unfolding model assumes that the same set of stimulus dimensions applies to each subject and individual differences merely result, therefore, from differences in ideal-point location in the n-dimensional space. PREFMAP offers two more general models, a weighted unfolding model, in which individuals are permitted to differ in the importance they attach to a stimulus dimension, and a general unfolding model in which all the assumptions are relaxed. The present study was designed to investigate the applicability of these distance models of preferential choice to subjective crowding.

Conceptual Dimensions of Crowding[1]

In order to report the results of the preference analysis it is necessary to describe briefly how the conceptual dimensions of crowding were obtained in the first stage of this study. This involved the use of INDSCAL to construct an n-dimensional Euclidian stimulus space. Although INDSCAL assumes that all subjects share a common or group space, it allows subjects to weight the dimensions of this space idiosyncratically. Thus INDSCAL takes individual differences into account by computing dimensional saliences or weights for each individual that reflect his or her perception of similarities and differences among stimuli.

A set of 15 descriptions was selected to represent a larger population of situations that induced feelings of crowding. The stimulus set is described in abbreviated form in Table 5.I. Subjects completed three types of task:

1. Similarity ratings and preference judgments. When subjects had familiarized themselves with the set of stimulus descriptions they made judgments of the overall similarity between all possible pairs of descriptions ($n = 105$) on a nine-point scale. In addition, for each pair of stimulus situations subjects indicated which member of the pair they preferred.

2. Unidimensional scale ratings. Subjects rated each of the stimulus descriptions with respect to crowding, associated environmental attributes, and affective reactions, using 18 nine-point scales. The attributes defined by these scales reflected hypotheses about the dimensions of subjective crowding and were selected on the basis of previous research (Rapoport, 1975; Schopler & Stockdale, 1977). Subjects were instructed to respond as they perceived the person in the description to feel.

3. Personality questionnaires and personal space measurement. Prior to completion of the rating tasks an estimate of each subject's personal space was obtained using a direct behavioral measure (Horowitz, Duff, & Stratton, 1965). Following the rating tasks each subject completed the 25-item North Carolina Internality–Externality scale (Schopler, Langmyer, Stokols, & Reisman,

---

[1]Details of this research were previously reported by Stockdale, Wittman, Jones, and Greaves (1979).

TABLE 5.1
Set of Stimulus Descriptions in Abbreviated Form

1.	MOTOR SHOW	many people but in a large area; restricted choice of direction but generally defined and orderly movement.
2.	OXFORD STREET	busy shopping street; movement and purchases impeded by slow moving window-shoppers; annoyance.
3.	HOTEL	hotel room hot and humid, small and oppressive; alone but felt hemmed in.
4.	PUB	with boyfriend in pub; felt oppressed by the number of people and noise and took no part in the conversation so felt separated from friends; had to leave.
5.	WEDDING	family wedding reception "invaded" by friends of groom; did not know them, found them boring and unlikable; resentful.
6.	INTERVIEW	candidate apprehensively waited for university interview; bewildered and confused by college ritual and behavior of students and principal.
7.	TUBE	standing in a rush-hour tube train; oppressively hot and unable to move.
8.	TRAIN	physically cramped and claustrophobic on long train journey; solved by overcoming embarrassment and intertwining arms and legs to get more comfortable.
9.	BOX OFFICE	large crowd pushing toward box office; wanted to retrieve bag and leave but movement nearly impossible; claustrophobic.
10.	PROMS	realization that it would be impossible to leave promenade concert quickly; felt faint due to heat and others pressing against barrier.
11.	FOOTBALL	crushed in football crowd leaving match; feet lifted off the ground and frightened of being trampled.
12.	OFFICE	working in open-plan office; disliked colleagues; felt unable to get away from the presence of others and trapped in a fixed routine.
13.	FLAT	living in a small flat with two small children and husband working at home; expressed hostility, resentment, and lack of privacy.
14.	A-LEVELS	severe, inescapable academic and emotional pressure from examinations and family tension; accentuated by unsympathetic cultural environment.
15.	PRISON	mental and physical constriction; following solitary confinement continually and intrusively questioned by officials in small, cramped cell.

1973) and a 13-item Preference for Privacy questionnaire adapted from two subscales of Marshall's Preference for Privacy Scale (Marshall, 1971).

In the analysis stage the similarity data were used as input to INDSCAL in order to determine the dimensions along which stimuli are judged and compared and to assess individual differences in the importance of each dimension. INDS-CAL solutions based on the dissimilarities matrices for 32 subjects, who displayed satisfactory judgmental consistency, were computed in one to seven dimensions. The four-dimensional solution was selected as the most adequate and parsimonious presentation of the data following consideration of such features of the solutions as the goodness of fit measures, both overall and for individual solutions, and the pattern of salience weights. The identification of the dimensions underlying the perception of crowding was achieved by means of multiple regression analyses, relating unidimensional judgments to the multidimensional configuration. If it is valid to assume that unidimensional judgments are mediated by the judges' multidimensional "map" of the stimuli, then a significant multiple correlation would obtain between the stimulus dimensions of the scaling solution and the scale values of the stimuli on a unidimensional rating scale. Furthermore the closer the vector, representing a unidimensional judgment, to any given dimension, the more important that dimension is in determining the unidimensional judgment. This "property-fitting" process (Rosenberg, 1976) therefore offers a means of identifying or labeling the dimensions derived from a multidimensional scaling analysis.

Although such analyses offered some insight into the identity of the dimensions, a clearer picture emerged when the multiple regression analyses were performed using composite scales derived by combining unidimensional scales with equal weighting. Dimension I was labeled *Interpersonal overload-Interference* and discriminated between situations involving large numbers of people in close physical proximity and those involving minimal interaction with others. Dimension II was labeled *Alienation,* because it differentiated between situations in which feelings of not belonging and uninvolvement were expressed and situations in which such feelings were not salient. However, situations that were judged highly alienating were, in general, instances of "psychological" crowding, whereas those situations lower in alienation were dominated by attributes of the physical environment. Johnson's Hierarchical Clustering Analysis (Diameter Method) confirmed the existence of a qualitative structure. The stimuli clearly divided into two main clusters, which were differentiated by whether feelings of crowding are generated by physical or psychological factors. Those situations that were judged to involve physical crowding were typically short term, secondary environments in which there were a large number of strangers and where crowding was easily attributable to external environmental attributes. In contrast, environments that were characterized by psychological crowding generally contained fewer people in physically smaller settings. The attribution of crowding was meditated not by physical density or number of people, but by the type and amount of involvement with others.

Dimension III was labeled *Anger* versus *Claustrophobia/Helplessness* because it differentiated between situations expressing or resulting in feelings of anger or resentment and those commonly described as "claustrophobic" or "oppressive," which induced feelings of helplessness. Dimension IV was highly correlated with the stress scale and other scales that either expressed negative affect or encompassed feelings or response toward desired but inhibited action. A composite scale based on these ratings resulted in the best fitting vector and Dimension IV was therefore labeled *Stress plus negative affect or behavioral response*.

An individual differences scaling analysis was used in order to examine individual differences in the perception of crowded settings. The salience weight matrix resulting from INDSCAL showed that Dimension I was most salient for 63% (N = 20) of the subjects, Dimension II was most salient for 19% (N = 6), with Dimensions III and IV each being the most salient dimension for 9% (N = 3) of the subjects. Although individuals differed in the importance they attached to the perceptual dimensions, there was no significant difference between the pattern of salience weights for males and females, nor were any of the personality variables measured significantly related to dimension salience.

The results of a multidimensional scaling study by Schopler, Rusbult, & McCallum (1979) lend some support to the generality of the dimensions identified in this study. Using a different scaling procedure, different stimuli, and different subject populations, Schopler et al. identified the dimensions of subjective crowding as physical–psychological, familiar–unfamiliar, and resultant stress. These three dimensions have much in common with Dimensions II and IV identified in the current study.

Preferential Choice among Crowded Situations

The major aim of this research was the prediction of subjects' preferences among crowded situations. The initial analysis of the preference judgments relied on Carroll's (1972) PREFMAP model and was undertaken in order to determine the type of model that would best characterize subjects' preferences. Major attention was devoted to a comparison of the vector preference model and the unfolding or ideal-point model, because, in the case of the two more general models there was some doubt as to their value in view of the large number of parameters involved relative to the number of data points. In the current study, if the vector model were appropriate for any individual, then his or her least preferred situation would be one involving high interpersonal overload/interference, strong feelings of alienation or psychological crowding, strong feelings of anger, and a high level of stress and negative affect. The unfolding model, however, assumes that for each individual an ideal point exists in the four-dimensional space defined by the INDSCAL solution, and that the further a given crowding situation is from an individual's ideal point, the less that situation is preferred.

The preference scale values for each of the 15 stimulus situations were obtained for each subject separately and for the group of 31 subjects who displayed reliable preferences. The 15 preference scale values were obtained in the following way. For each subject a 15 × 15 interstimulus preference matrix was constructed in which the entries indicated the subject's preference for the column over the row stimulus. A matrix entry of *2* indicated that the column stimulus was preferred over the row stimulus, whereas a *1* indicated that the column stimulus was not preferred over the row stimulus. For such a matrix the mean of each of the 15 columns yields the subject's preference scale values for each of the stimuli. For the group analysis the preference scale values for each of the stimuli were averaged across 31 subjects.

The essential question of this research was: Do the dimensions of perceived similarity, derived from INDSCAL, predict the preference judgments? This question was examined using PREFMAP to test the vector and unfolding or ideal-point model for each subject. The input to PREFMAP comprised subjects' preference scale values and the four-dimensional configuration from INDSCAL. The root-mean-squares of the correlations between PREFMAP scale values and the best fitting monotonic function of the preference data were comparatively high, .879 for the vector model and .922 for the ideal-point model. Using a significance level of .05 there was a gain in prediction from the vector model to the ideal-point model for only 13 of the 31 subjects. Athough the vector model provided an adequate fit to the data for all of the sample, other aspects of the data did not support the view that differences in subjects' preferences can be fully accounted for by the multidimensional representation that emerged from the INDSCAL analysis.

First, examination of the direction cosines, which reflect the relative importance of the dimensions in the preference judgments, suggested that Dimension I (Interpersonal overload–Interference) and Dimension IV (Stress plus negative affect and behavioral response) were the only dimensions that were of any relevance in determining preferences. As may be seen in Fig. 5.I the subjects' preference vectors lie in the I/IV plane of the INDSCAL stimulus configuration and these two dimensions appear to be equally important in determining preference. When one examines the I/III plane it may be seen that the majority of subjects' preference vectors lie closer to I than to III (Fig. 5.2). Similarly, consideration of the II/IV plane indicates the importance of Dimension IV relative to Dimension II (Fig. 5.3). Thus Dimensions II and III appear relatively unrelated to preference. In addition, consideration of the nature of crowding led to misgivings about the appropriateness of the basic assumption of PREFMAP that the dimensions defined by INDSCAL also predict subjects' preferences. Although this assumption is intuitively plausible in the case of perceptions and preferences for political candidates (Mauser, 1972; Nygren & Jones, 1977), it is

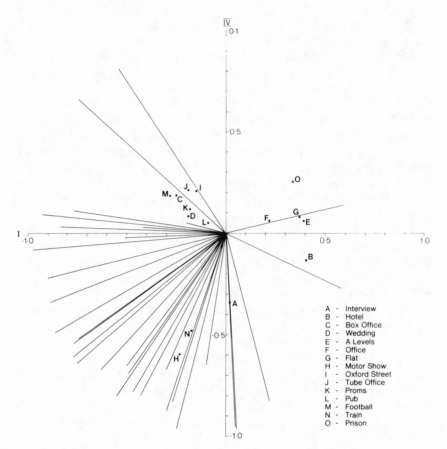

FIG. 5.1. External vector model analysis (PREFMAP) relating subjects preferences to Dimensions I and IV of the four-dimensional stimulus configuration
(INDSCAL).

questionable whether it is justified in the area of crowding. In the case of political
judgments the dimensions that emerge as salient in discrimination among political candidates such as Liberal, Reform-oriented versus Conservative,
non-reform-oriented, and Democrat versus Republican are essentially evaluative
in nature (Nygren & Jones, 1977). As the rationale underlying political judgment
is essentially one of evaluation, it is not surprising that the dimensions characterizing perceived similarity are also those that typically affect preference and
hence determine voting behavior.

Crowding, in contrast, has both situational and evaluative components and, in
making their similarity judgments, subjects appeared to attend to both these
characteristics. However, in making their preference judgments subjects needed
to rely on only the evaluative dimensions of subjective crowding. Both Dimen-

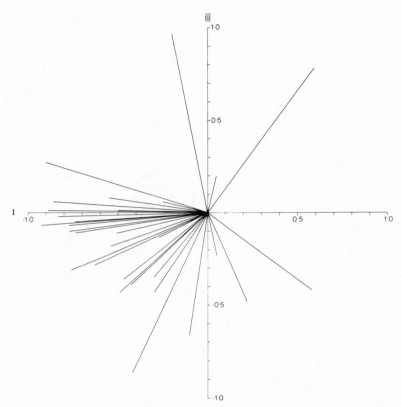

FIG. 5.2. External vector model analysis (PREFMAP) relating subjects preferences to Dimensions I and III of the four-dimensional stimulus configuration
(INDSCAL).

sions I: Interpersonal overload–Interference and IV: Stress plus negative affect
and behavioral response are clear dimensions and reflect an evaluation of the
implications of the crowding. In contrast, Dimension III: Anger versus Claustrophobia derives from the descriptive content of the stimulus descriptions in that
the two poles of the dimension represent alternative behavioral strategies. Furthermore, there is no indication as to which end of this so-called dimension is
more negatively loaded. Similarly, Dimension II is more adequately represented
by a qualitative structure describing the origin of crowding as psychological or
physical.

The PREFMAP analysis thus appeared to indicate that all four dimensions
defined by INDSCAL do not underlie preference. Rather, preference appears to
be based on the two evaluative dimensions of subjective crowding. This result
suggested the need to check the basic assumption of PREFMAP that the dimensions of similarity are common to preference. In order to examine this assump-

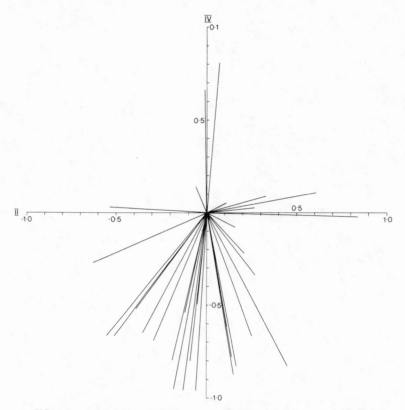

FIG. 5.3. External vector model analysis (PREFMAP) relating subjects preferences to Dimensions II and IV of the four-dimensional stimulus configuration
(INDSCAL).

tion two multiple regression analyses were carried out, one of which was a group
analysis and one of which used individual data. In the group analysis the independent variables were the coordinates of the 15 stimuli on each of the four
INDSCAL dimensions, and the dependent variable was the average preference
scale value for each of the 15 stimuli. In this analysis none of the four INDSCAL
dimensions emerged as significant predictors of average preference. However
Dimension I just failed to attain significance ($p < .057$). In comparable analyses
using individuals' raw preference scale values, Dimension I was a significant
predictor of preference for 10 of the 31 subjects and Dimension IV predicted
preference in another eight cases. Although these data lend some support to the
PREFMAP analysis in indicating the importance of Dimensions I and IV, the
INDSCAL dimensions clearly do not fully explain preference for all subjects.

An obvious question therefore is what other features of crowded situations
determine preference judgments? In order to examine this issue further the prefer-

ence scale values for each subject were correlated with stimulus ratings on each of the 18 unidimensional scales. Of the scales that correlated significantly with preference, the most frequently occurring were: "I feel under stress," "I feel helpless," "I feel anxious," "I feel I want to escape," and "I feel I have too little privacy." These scales correlated with the preferences of at least two-thirds of the sample. Apart from the privacy scale, all these scales define Dimension IV of the INDSCAL solution. Therefore this analysis confirmed the importance of feelings of stress and associated negative implications (Dimension IV). However the scales defining Dimension I emerged as significant correlates for only four subjects. In view of the PREFMAP analysis this result is somewhat surprising. However, it may merely reflect the relatively low correlations between Dimension I and the unidimensional scales used to label that dimension.

An interesting aspect of this analysis is the emergence of privacy as a significant correlate of preference for a majority of the subjects. Altman (1975) makes privacy a key explanatory concept in his analysis of the etiology of crowding. The condition of crowding is seen to arise solely from a failure of boundary control mechanisms that regulate privacy such that the desired level of privacy is not achieved or can be achieved only at high cost. Contrary to this view in our study privacy was not associated with any of the dimensions of subjective crowding, but clearly was associated with preference. These findings indicate that although privacy is not perceived to be a dimension of subjective crowding, it is important in evaluating the implications of social contact and therefore emerges as a correlate of preference.

A further issue examined was the degree of concensus inherent in subjects' preferences. A Principal Component analysis of subjects' preference judgments revealed five factors with eigenvalues greater than unity. Although the loading of two-thirds of the subjects on Factor I indicated the validity of examining the mean preference order, the remaining factors suggested the possibility of individual differences in preference. The question is whether these are related to the measured personality variables. This was examined by means of a series of three multiple regression analyses, in which the subjects' factor scores on the five preference factors were used as predictor variables. Subject preference factors failed to predict either Internality–Externality or Preference for Privacy scores, but were significant predictors ($p < .02$) of personal space scores. This result implies that of the three individual difference measures obtained in this study, personal space alone is a correlate of individual differences in preference. However, it is obvious that in any future study attempting to explore the basis of individual differences in preference, more individual difference measures must be collected. In contrast, examination of the mean preference scale values revealed an interesting relation between the preference order and the categorical structure of the stimulus set. The ordering of the stimulus descriptions in terms of their mean preference scale values is displayed in Fig. 5.4. The most preferred stimulus description was the "Motor Show," which, although it involved a large

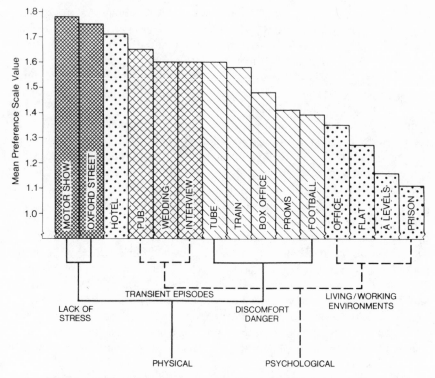

FIG 5.4.   Relation of mean preference scale values of the stimulus descriptions to the categorical structure of INDSCAL Dimension II.

number of people in close physical proximity, also expressed a strong feeling of control and orderliness and was judged to be most extreme in terms of lack of stress. Similarly "Oxford Street," the second most preferred stimulus, was dominated by a purposeful attitude on the part of the actor. These two stimuli represented one stimulus grouping within the physical crowding cluster revealed by the earlier cluster analysis, which showed the categorical structure underlying Dimension II. Both of these stimuli, Motor Show and Oxford Street, were judged to involve physical crowding but, unlike other stimuli in this category, they did not involve anxiety about personal safety and so did not generate high levels of stress.

This match between the two most preferred stimuli and one cluster of the categorical structure stimulated us to look further at the relation between the mean preference order and the total pattern of clustering. A simplified version of the dendrogram representing the clustering pattern is shown at the bottom of Fig. 5.4. As discussed earlier, the clustering analysis indicated a primary division between stimuli involving physical crowding and those characterised by psychological crowding. Within the physical crowding cluster, situations that were characterized by lack of fear were differentiated from situations that evoked anxiety about personal integrity or safety. Within the psychological cluster, descriptions of relatively transient social settings were distinguished from those referring to living and working environments, that is essentially primary environments.

How does this categorical structure relate to preference? Situations involving physical crowding and lack of stress (Motor Show, Oxford Street) are preferred to transient psychological episodes (Pub, Wedding, Interview); physically uncomfortable or even dangerous situations (Tube, Train, Box Office, Proms, Football) are preferred to living and working environments involving psychological crowding (Office, Flat, 'A' levels, Prison). "Hotel" is the odd one out, but throughout, this stimulus description was considered atypical. As an instance of crowding it is unusual in that it involves only one person and although in terms of its perceived characteristics it may belong with other living/working environments it is not surprising that it is preferred to these environments, and to transient psychological and physically uncomfortable situations because of its low level of stress.

This pattern of average preference scale values and its relation to the categorical structure underlying the perception of crowded situations indicates that, although preference is related to perceived stress, it is also related to whether the settings involve physical or psychological crowding and whether they are transient or enduring living and working environments.

Conclusions

Multidimensional scaling and unfolding techniques were employed to identify the dimensions underlying perceptions of crowded settings and to examine how these dimensions are related to preferential choice. A major implication of the results of this study is that the dimensions used by individuals in making similarity judgments among crowded situations are not necessarily those they use in making preference judgments. The multidimensional scaling analysis suggested that individuals' conceptions of crowding may be adequately encompassed by four dimensions and confirms that crowding may not be viewed simply in terms of properties of the physical environment. The first dimension reflected the impact of interpersonal interaction. The second dimension, which reflected the degree of perceived alienation, was adequately represented by a qualitative structure in which crowding was construed in terms of whether the source was physical or psychological. One end of the third dimension was defined by feelings of anger, the other by feelings of claustrophobia and helplessness. The fourth dimension reflected the degree of stress and negative affect experienced, and the extent to which it was resolved.

The model underlying the multidimensional representation of subjective crowding implies that judgments of similarity among crowded settings are based on comparisons of the positions of the settings on these psychological dimensions. Our analysis of individual preferences among the crowded settings, however, raises some doubts about the applicability of a distance model that assumes a communality between the dimensions of similarity and those of preference. The results of the current study suggest that the dimensions of subjective crowding that derive from the descriptive aspect of the crowded situation are relatively unrelated to preference judgments. The overall pattern of results suggests that preference is based on those dimensions and attributes that reflect an evaluative judgment of the negative implications of the crowded setting for the individual.

The importance of the evaluative attributes of stress and privacy can be considered in the context of whether the source of crowding is physical or psychological. The extent to which anxiety about physical safety is aroused appears to be of major importance in assessing the degree of stress in physically crowded situations. In psychological crowding, lack of privacy appears to be the salient stressor that distinguishes transient social settings from primary (i.e., living and working) environments. Such an analysis would account for relative preferences within the two different categories of crowded situations. The overall preference for physical over psychological crowding may very well reflect the superior adaptation to physically crowded settings on the part of London subjects.

The methodology employed in this study represents a different approach to the problem of characterizing crowded situations. Although it offers no way of unequivocally identifying the perceptual dimensions as antecedents, concomitants, or resultants of crowded settings, the dimensions are in no way predetermined or imposed on the subjects, but are directly inferred. Furthermore, the application of this methodology raises intriguing questions concerning the relation between the dimensions underlying perceived similarities and preferences among crowded settings, and individual differences in crowding perception and preference. Future research aimed at answering these questions is a basic step toward providing a comprehensive picture of how people construe their environment and evaluate its implications.

ACKNOWLEDGMENT

This research was supported by a grant to the first author from the Social Science Research Council.

REFERENCES

Altman, I. *The environment and social behavior*. Monterey, Calif.: Brooks Cole, 1975.
Carroll, J. D. Individual differences and multidimensional scaling. In R. N. Shepard, A. K. Romney, & S. B. Nerlove (Eds.), *Multidimensional scaling: Theory and applications in the behavioral sciences* (Vol. 1). New York: Seminar Press, 1972.

Cozby, P. G. Effects of density, activity and personality on environmental preferences. *Journal of Research in Personality*, 1973, *7*, 45-60.

Desor, J. A. Toward a psychological theory of crowding. *Journal of Personality and Social Psychology*, 1972, *21*, 79-83.

Horowitz, M. J., Duff, D. F., & Stratton, L. O. Human spatial behavior. *American Journal of Psychotherapy*, 1965, *19*, 20-28.

Marshall, N. J. *Orientations towards privacy: Environmental and personality components.* Unpublished doctoral dissertation in Psychology, University of California, Berkeley, 1971.

Mauser, G. A. A structural approach to predicting patterns of electoral substitution. In A. K. Romney, R. N. Shepard, & S. B. Nerlove (Eds.), *Multidimensional scaling: Theory and applications in the behavioral sciences* (Vol. 2). New York: Seminar Press, 1972.

Nygren, T. E., & Jones, L. E. Individual differences in perceptions and preferences for political candidates. *Journal of Experimental Social Psychology*, 1977, *13*, 182-197.

Proshansky, H. M., Ittleson, W., & Rivlin, L. G. Freedom of choice and behavior in a physical setting. In H. M. Proshansky, W. H. Ittleson, & L. G. Rivlin (Eds.), *Environmental psychology: Man and his physical setting.* New York: Holt, 1970.

Rapoport, A. Toward a redefinition of density. *Environment and Behavior*, 1975, *7*, 133-158.

Rosenberg, S. New approaches to the analysis of personal constructs in person perception. *Nebraska Symposium on Motivation*, XXIII, 1976.

Schopler, J., McCallum, R., & Rusbult, C. E. *Behavioral interference and internality-externality as determinants of subjective crowding.* Unpublished paper, University of North Carolina, Chapel Hill, 1977.

Schopler, J., Langmyer, D., Stokols, D., & Reisman, S. The North Carolina Internal-External Scale: Validation of the short form. *Research Previews*, 1973, *20*, 3-12.

Schopler, J., Rusbult, C. E., & McCallum, R. Conceptual dimensions of crowding: A multidimensional analysis. In M. R. Gurkaynak & W. A. Lecompte. (Eds.), *Human consequences of crowding.* New York: Plenum Press, 1979.

Schopler, J., & Stockdale, J. E. An interference analysis of crowding. *Environmental Psychology and Non-Verbal Behavior*, 1977, *1*, 81-88.

Stockdale, J. E. Crowding: Determinants and effects. in L. Berkowitz (Ed.), *Advances in experimental social psychology.* New York: Academic Press, 1978.

Stockdale. J. E., Wittman, L. S., Jones, L. E., & Greaves, D. A. A multidimensional analysis of subjective crowding. In H. R. Gurkaynak & W. A. Lecompte (Eds.), *Human consequences of crowding.* New York: Plenum Press, 1979.

Stokols, D. On the distinction between density and crowding: Some implications for further research. *Psychological Review*, 1972, *79*, 275-277. (a)

Stokols, D. A social-psychological model of human crowding phenomena. *American Institute of Planners Journal*, 1972, *38*, 72-83. (b)

Sundstrom, E. Towards an interpersonal model of crowding. *Sociological Symposium*, 1975, *14*, 129-144.

Valins, S., & Baum, A. Residential group size, social interaction and crowding. *Environment and Behavior*, 1973, *5*, 421-429.

Zlutnick, S., & Altman, I. Crowding and human behavior. In J. Wohlwill & D. Carson, (Eds.), *Environment and the social sciences: Perspectives and applications.* Washington, D.C.: American Psychological Association, 1972.

6 Configural Self-Diagnosis

Leland Wilkinson

Bonnie R. Gimbel

David Koepke
University of Illinois at Chicago Circle

> *One of the most important words in the vocabulary of clinicians is the word "pattern." We speak of ourselves as thinking in terms of totalities, organizations, configurations; and we congratulate ourselves for being able to look upon case material in this patterned, non-atomistic way. The question as to how much we really do this, and the further question of how well it pays off in terms of predictive efficiency, is a very complicated one on which neither theoretical nor adequate empirical data as yet exist.*
>
> —Meehl (1950)

At a time when additive linear models dominated psychometrics, Paul Meehl proposed a method of configural scoring of psychometric data to capture "patterned" responses. Meehl believed that certain patterns of responses on individual items of a test might predict a criterion more accurately than additive subscales of the same test. From his own clinical experiences, Meehl believed that this type of scoring would reflect the thinking of the clinician who judged nonpsychometric, or case data. The simplest instance of configural judgments that Meehl (1950) cited was: "the case in which a datum is taken as evidence for a certain hypothesis . . . when seen in a certain context of the evidence, whereas the same datum could be taken as arguing against the very same hypothesis with the context different."

More generally, configurality in judgment implies that the significance (or weight) to the judge of a datum in a set of data depends on the significance of the other data. Chest pain, for example, may signal a heart attack when accompanied by weak pulse and sweating. Chest pain, on the other hand, may indicate only mild heartburn in the presence of nausea and loss of appetite. In terms of overall severity (or morbidity), all these symptoms are relatively mild when considered alone. Only certain combinations of them denote serious illness.

Meehl's attempt to operationalize what has been called intuition arose from his belief that clinical decisions could be improved by formal representation. *Clinical Vs. Statistical Prediction* (1954) presented this point of view and prompted numerous studies on configurality in clinical judgment. Although the book did not tie configurality either to clinical judgment or to a statistical model, many subsequent studies did. Some confusion might have been avoided if Meehl had labeled the two polar facets in the debate as *human* versus *automated* prediction and *configural* versus *additive* combination of cues. Each of these two polar facets has had its own controversy, but the issues are independent. Human judges may act in a configural manner under certain conditions (Einhorn, 1970; Libby, 1976a, 1976b; Payne, 1976; Slovic, 1969; Wiggins & Hoffman, 1968) and additively under other conditions (Green, Carmone, & Wind, 1972; Krantz & Tversky, 1971). Likewise, some automated prediction models may be configural (Hogarth, 1974; Kleinmuntz, 1968; Meehl, 1950) or may be additive (Dawes, 1971; Goldberg, 1970). In our opinion, the first facet, automated versus human prediction, is no longer a matter of controversy. Those who believe that a computer program cannot outwit a skilled diagnostician of psychometric data may wish to bet that a computer cannot beat a grand master at chess. Our concern is rather with the second facet, namely configural versus additive models of judgment. In particular, we are interested in the use of configural models to predict human decisions.

CONFIGURALITY AND MEASUREMENT ARTIFACTS

The configural-additive distinction depends on measurement assumptions. At least two types of additivity can be defined from different assumptions: ordinal and interval. Each implies a different definition of configurality. Assume the following table represents judgments of the severity of medical symptoms A, B, C, and D taken in pairs. Note that any entry of the table can be predicted by the sum of its corresponding marginal values if A = 1, B = 2, C = 3, and D = 4. That is,

$$x_{ij} = x_{i.} + x_{.j}. \tag{1}$$

The dot in the subscript denotes the marginal element. For example, the severity of symptoms A and C when they occur together is 4.

	A	B	C	D
A	2	3	4	5
B	3	4	5	6
C	4	5	6	7
D	5	6	7	8

If this condition holds for all cells in the table, as it does in the example, then the table is additive for the given marginal scale values. Additivity in this sense means that configurality cannot occur for any symptom pairs in the set, since severity is an additive function of each symptom in the pair. Notice further that if symptoms are ordered as they are in the table and if the table is additive, then the marginal values must comprise a unidimensional scale. In this example, the row and column scales are the same, since the row set of symptoms is identical to the column set.

Ordinal and interval additivity refer to the types of permissible transformations of a given data matrix to achieve the condition defined for the preceding table. Each type of additivity defines a class of matrices for which a given transformation type (ordinal, interval) will exist to achieve the additivity condition. Correspondingly, each type defines a class of matrices for which a permissible additivity transformation does not exist. This latter class of matrices is nonadditivie, or configural, within the transformation type.

Ordinal additivity obtains when a monotonic transformation will yield an additive marginal scale. The following table, for example, is ordinally additive and can be transformed into the first table by a monotonic transformation. Another way of saying this is that the row or column elements in this table strictly increase as the marginal indices increase for any row or column.

	A	B	C	D
A	1	2	3	7
B	2	4	5	9
C	3	5	7	10
D	7	9	10	14

Analysis-of-variance models with fan-type or "catalytic" interactions are ordinally additive, since they can be transformed to additivity via monotonic functions. The "configural models" proposed by Einhorn (1970) and Anderson (1972) are ordinally additive for the same reason. Ordinal nonadditivity or ordinal configurality obtains when an ordinal function for transforming a matrix to additive form does not exist. Analysis-of-variance models with crossover interactions are of this form, since only nonmonotonic transformations can produce additivity in the ANOVA table.

Interval aditivity obtains directly for any matrix that fits the additive condition of the first table shown. Any linear transformation of the matrix elements x_{ij} will correspondingly act on the marginal scale values $x_i.$ and $x._j$, preserving the additivity condition. Main effects ANOVA and regression models are intervally additive. The models of Einhorn and Anderson cited previously are intervally configural, as are all ordinally configural models.

Meehl's definition of configurality for continuous functions was of the interval type, as he used partial derivatives of the response surface in the definition. Although this type of configurality "paramorphically" represents the judgment phenomenon described by many clinicians, testing it in empirical studies is problematic. Drifting anchor points, scale nonlinearities, ceiling and floor effects all can produce interval configurality. When significant interactions are found in a data analysis, it is difficult to determine whether they are due to a configural process or to measurement and response function artifacts. Anderson's fundamental measurement is one attempt to circumvent this problem, but it rests on a firm prior belief in the appropriateness of the model. This belief itself depends on prior tests of the model with similar methods, so the inferential process is circular. Also sensitive to these artifacts are Einhorn's configural models, because the location of the measurement scale affects the linearizing transformations used in the analysis. Neither Einhorn (1970, 1971) nor Goldberg (1971) treated the location point as an additional parameter to be estimated in the model. Only systematic violations of ordinal additivity can provide unequivocal evidence of configurality, therefore, since they are invariant with respect to measurement artifacts, nuisance parameters, and monotonic variations in the response function.

MODELS FOR TESTING
ORDINAL CONFIGURALITY

Several nometric methods are available for testing ordinal configurality in judgment. Two principal alternatives are conjoint measurement (Luce & Tukey, 1964; Tversky, 1967) and multidimensional scaling (Guttman, 1968; Kruskal, 1964a, 1964b; Shepard, 1962a, 1962b). Conjoint measurement allows a direct global test of ordinal nonadditivity. Krantz and Tversky (1971) have recommended it for judgments involving multiple cues. Systematic violations of additivity can be detected with this method. Multidimensional scaling and simultaneous conjoint measurement are in fact closely related. Both rely on the same computational algorithms in specific instances. Young (1972) has described a conjoint measurement data analytic system which includes nometric multidimensional scaling as a special case. We have chosen the spatial representation of multidimensional scaling for its ease of interpretation, although our conclusions are consistent with a conjoint measurement model.

Multidimensional scaling offers a graphical method for analyzing configurality. Two approaches to the problem may be taken: external and internal. The external approach involves two stages: (1) multidimensional scaling of ratings of similarity among all possible pairs of cues; and (2) fitting judgments on the criterion to the multidimensional scaling configuration. This procedure thus requires two data collections—one of similarities among the cues and one of judgments on the criterion. Fitting the judgments to the scaling may be accomplished via a vector model (Tucker, 1960) or an unfolding model (Coombs, 1964). In either model, configurality may be represented by cross products of parameters in the equation relating criterion judgments to the configuration. Carroll and Chang (1967) have specified this configural term in Model 1 of their external unfolding procedure. Norman Cliff and Nancy Hirschberg have applied these external methods to a variety of judgments (Cliff, 1972; Cliff & Young, 1968; Wiggins, 1973; Wiggins, Hoffman, & Taber, 1969).

The external method for assessing cue utilization in judgment is essentially indirect. It assumes that cognitive structures underlying similarity ratings are used in judgments on an external criterion. Although this assumption has been substantially supported, counterexamples have been found (Cooper, 1973). A direct test of configurality with multidimensional scaling requires working with the judgments themselves rather than with separately estimated similarities among cues.

For an internal analysis, we have reparameterized the response function. This allows direct scaling of the judgments themselves. We first present an index of interval configurality and then modify it to represent ordinal configurality. This index is computed for all pairs of cues and then used in the multidimensional scaling.

Consider the variation in judgments on paired cues to be represented by the following model:

$$x_{ij} = \mu + \alpha_i + \alpha_j + \gamma_{ij} \tag{2}$$

This model follows analysis-of-variance terminology in which the α's are main effects (Row cue i and Column cue j) and the γ is an interaction term. Each x_{ij} is a judgment on some criterion for the cues represented by Row i and Column j. We assume judgments have been pooled across subjects, so we omit an error term for subjects in the model. Because our hypothesis is a structural one involving many cues, this omission has trivial consequences for the final result.

The similarity in the way pairwise judgments are made on any two cues can be represented by comparing the judgments when each cue is paired with other cues in the set. If two cues interact similarly with other cues, then each should produce a similar judgment when paired with another cue. Cues which are processed configurally should produce different profiles of judgments when paired with other cues. To see this, we must correlate the judgments made on pairs containing cue j with the same cues paired with Cue k. Correlations between Cues j and k have the following form:

$$\rho_{jk} = \frac{\sum_{i=1}^{p} (\alpha_i + \gamma_{ij})(\alpha_i + \gamma_{ik})}{\left[\sum_{i=1}^{p} (\alpha_i + \gamma_{ij})^2 (\alpha_i + \gamma_{ik})^2 \right]^{\frac{1}{2}}}$$

Expanding this formula and dropping terms which are constant across all correlations, we have the following index of similarity:

$$\eta_{jk} = \frac{\sum_{i=1}^{p} (\alpha_i \gamma_{ij} + \alpha_i \gamma_{ik} + \gamma_{ij} \gamma_{ik})}{\left[\sum_{i=1}^{p} (2\alpha_i \gamma_{ij} + \gamma_{jj}^2) \sum_{i=1}^{p} (2\alpha_i \gamma_{ik} + \gamma_{ik}^2) \right]^{\frac{1}{2}}}$$

The total configural variation is included in this measure. The cross product of the interactions is represented by the last term in the numerator. The other two terms in the numerator represent the extent to which the main effects are related to the interactions.

If the matrix of intercorrelations or similarity coefficients is scaled with smallest space analysis or nonmetric multidimensional scaling, the resulting configuration should reveal similarities in the way cues interact with other cues in the pairwise judgments. Because distances are related to cross products of interactions rather than to interactions themselves, the sign of the interactions cannot be inferred from the configuration. Cues which are close together in the configuration interact similarly with other cues and have large positive coefficients of ordinal configurality. Mutually distant cues, on the other hand, interact differently with other cues and have near-zero coefficients of ordinal configurality.

One modification of this model we have made in our analysis is to substitute monotonicity coefficients for correlations (Levy & Guttman, 1975). Although the resulting similarity coefficients still present the configural structure of the judgments, they are unchanged by ordinal transformations of the raw judgments. They allow, in other words, a monotonically invariant measure of profile similarity among cues across pairs, revealing the configurality of the pairwise judgments.

The "null hypothesis" of lack of configurality is specified by the full dimensionality of the space itself. That is, if configurality does not occur in the judgments, then the similarity coefficients will all be large and positive; in this case, for 28 symptoms we should expect a space of no less than 27 dimensions to yield a perfect fit to the data. Practically, we might expect a "good" fit in somewhat fewer dimensions, but certainly not two or three.

SELF-DIAGNOSIS

Of the many cue domains in everyday judgment problems, medical symptoms are especially promising for revealing configural judgments. The American Cancer Society and other health organizations have long publicized that certan combinations of seemingly trivial cues can be serious, for example. Furthermore, medical diagnosis is usually presented as a configural problem in medical school and postgraduate training. Hoffman, Slovic, and Rorer (1968) have demonstrated systematic configural effects in doctors' diagnoses of ulcers and Einhorn (1972) has fit intervally nonadditive models to pathologists' judgments.

We decided to sample symptoms that represent the full range of prevalent illnesses. Fifty diseases common in the United States were selected from Krupp and Chatton (1977). For each disease, accompanying symptoms were tabulated and clustered into similar categories. Each symptom category was labeled in ordinary language and the preliminary list was pretested for recognition by college students. By this method the list of 100 symptoms was reduced to 28 symptoms. This set comprised our experimental cues.

The experiment itself was controlled by a time-sharing computer system, with subjects seated individually at a video terminal. The subjects were 19 male and 28 female undergraduates with an average age of 20 years. They were introduced to the study by the computer program, which printed the following text:

> Welcome. This is a study of how people make decisions about the seriousness of medical symptoms. The computer will be showing you various symptoms, and your job will be to rate them by typing in a number from a rating scale.
>
> For the first part, imagine you go to bed at night healthy. The next morning you wake up with a symptom and you have to decide whether to see the doctor. The computer will print this symptom and then ask you to rate whether you should see the doctor. The form of the rating will be on a 9-point scale from No to Yes.
>
> If you are certain you should not see a doctor, choose a 1. If you are certain you should see a doctor, choose a 9. If you are not certain whether to see a doctor, choose a number between 1 and 9 to represent how uncertain you are. The computer will ask for your rating by typing the following question: Should you see a doctor?

Additional instructions concerned the mechanics of the terminal, data entry, and correcting errors. Subjects were given practice symptoms before beginning the experiment. After rating each of the 28 symptoms on the seriousness scale, the subjects began the second part of the study, which involved syndromes, or groups of symptoms. The instructions were printed as follows:

> Good. Now for the second part. This time you will be asked to make the same type of ratings for syndromes. A syndrome is a group of several symptoms together. For example, a cold syndrome could be fever, stuffy nose, coughing, and sneezing. The rating scales this time will be exactly the same but now you will have to consider a group of symptoms together instead of a single symptom.

For this second part, syndromes of 2 to 4 symptoms were presented randomly for subjects' rating until the session was finished.

Several additional variables were collected by the computer. Response time in seconds was measured for each syndrome. To assess familiarity with the syndromes, subjects were asked, "Do you know a disease which could cause this symptom?". This question had the same nine-point scale for response. Finally, demographic variables were collected at the end of the session.

Because the computer controlled the presentation of syndromes, sequence and pattern effects were randomized. This raises a Brunswickian question, however. Did some of the symptom combinations represent impossible or unbelievable syndromes? The data on this question were mixed. The familiarity scale had a mean of 5 and standard deviation of 3. For a small number of syndromes, subjects were replying with a flat "No." On the other hand, all subjects were debriefed at the end of their sessions. Not a single subject had realized that the syndromes were constructed from randomly selected symptoms. Undoubtedly, the demand characteristics of the experiment (especially the use of a computer) contributed to the perception of the subjects that the diagnostic problem was real, but practically no combination of symptoms in the set presented was medically impossible (even diarrhea and constipation can occur simultaneously). Reaction time and the familiarity scale were only slightly negatively correlated, with mean response delay of 12 seconds and standard deviation of 5 seconds.

The data for all subjects were pooled in a 28 × 28 matrix of mean judgments on all pairs of symptoms. The single symptom judgments and those on syndromes consisting of more than two symptoms were not analyzed for this study. This left 3267 separate judgments that were used to compute the means in the pooled data matrix. Profile similarities were computed on the columns of this matrix using Guttman's coefficient. The similarities were then scaled with KYST (Kruskal, Young, & Seery, 1978).

Figure 6.1 presents the results of this analysis. The stress (Formula 1) for this solution is .19. Spence and Ogilvie (1973) give a stress value of .33 for 28 random points fitted in two dimensions; the critical values in the lower tail of

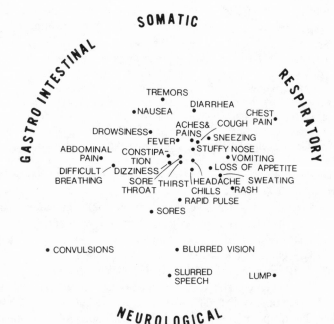

FIG. 6.1.   Spatial configuration of 28 medical symptoms judged in pairs for severity. Sectors of the configuration, labeled at the circumference, represent perceived syndromes.

Levine's (1978) stress distribution are also well above our value. We may plausibly reject the null hypothesis of no configurality.

The structure of the solution is appropriately described by Guttman's radex (Guttman, 1954). Severity of symptoms is represented by distance from the centroid, whereas sectors in the space represent groups of symptoms that interact similarly with other symptoms. In terms of polar coordinates, the radii of symptoms correspond to severity and the angle between two symptoms represents the similarity of their interactions with other symptoms.

That this structure emerged in the analysis reflects the composition of the data. Specifically, weak symptoms generally had positive interactions when paired with strong symptoms and negative interactions when paired with other weak ones. Conversely, strong symptoms usually interacted negatively with strong symptoms and positively with weak ones. This covariation of main effect terms with interactions allowed the main effects to contribute to the overall structure. This source is represented by the first two terms in the numerator of Equation 4. The other source of variation in the configuration is the pure interaction structure. This variation is represented by the last term in the numerator of Equation 4.

The main effect structure is a one-dimensional simplex. It can be obtained: (1) by seriating the 28 × 28 matrix of mean judgments using Euclidean distance instead of monotonicity coefficients; or (2) by examining the marginal means directly; or (3) by looking at means for the judgments of the single symptoms that were collected in the first part of the experiment. All three methods yielded nearly identical results on our data. The Spearman rank order correlation of the main effects with the radii of the symptoms is over .8. The interaction structure, on the other hand, is circular. It can be scaled separately by subtracting the main effects from the judgment matrix and scaling the cross products of the resulting matrix. Combining these two data structures (simplex and circumplex) results in a radex. Note again that the main effects contributed to this structure for this particular data set only because they were not independent of the interactions.

Symptoms that interact similarly with other symptoms (i.e., are roughly exchangeable) might be expected to comprise a syndrome themselves. For example, pairing sneezing with other symptoms produced judgments that were similar to those when cough was paired with the same symptoms. Sneezing and cough may have been evidence to the judges of the same underlying factor, perhaps a head cold. This inference appears supported by the configuration. Various sectors of the space correspond to types of diseases.

The sectors are readily interpretable. Respiratory symptoms (chest pain, sneezing, stuffy nose, cough) are represented in the northeast sector. Somatic symptoms (fever, aches and pains) are in the northern sector. Gastrointestinal symptoms (nausea, constipation, abdominal pain, diarrhea, thirst) are in the northwest sector. Neurological symptoms (convulsions, blurred vision, slurred speech, dizziness) are in the southern sector. Other types of syndromes are represented between and within these general sectors. Flu symptoms (fever, aches and pains, diarrhea, thirst) and cold symptoms (cough, stuffy nose, headache) are represented in the northern sectors.

REAL DISEASES

Do these sectors represent real syndromes, or are they simply conventional wisdom? Is lay diagnosis medical diagnosis? We decided to investigate more formally how this configuration maps real symptoms of real diseases. Taking the original list of diseases from which we had tabulated symptoms, we noted whether or not each of the 28 symptoms occurred for each disease. After eliminating diseases with only one of our 28 symptoms, we compiled a binary matrix of symptom occurrences for 34 different diseases. We computed an inter-correlation matrix to obtain similarities among the diseases. This matrix was then scaled by the same KYST program. Figure 6.2 presents the results.

Figures 6.1 and 6.2 show a remarkable similarity even though the models generating the interpoint distances are different. In Fig. 6.2, main effects are not present, as only co-occurrence of symptoms was included in the correlations. As

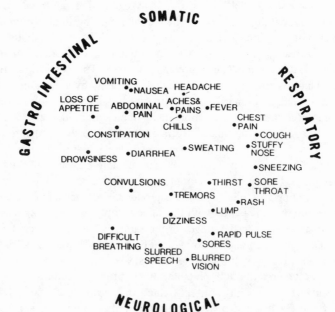

FIG. 6.2. Spatial configuration of 28 medical symptoms derived from co-occurrences among 34 prevalent diseases. Sectors of the configuration, labeled at the circumference, represent real syndromes.

a result, distance from the centroid in Fig. 6.2 does not reflect seriousness. Because symptoms that tend to occur together are near each other in Fig. 6.2, however, the sectors of the figure can be compared to Fig. 6.1. The same sectors—respiratory, somatic, gastrointestional, and neurological—appear in both figures in the same relative positions. Not only are the sectors internally consistent across figures, but they are also related to each other in the same general typology of symptoms.

This global correspondence permits the identification of symptoms that are "out of place" in Fig. 6.1. Vomiting, for example, clearly belongs to the gastrointestinal group of symptoms. Diarrhea, another gastrointestinal symptom, is also somewhat out of place. Like vomiting, it can indicate neurological disorder, so it probably belongs in the lower part of the gastrointestinal sector. Tremors is clearly a neurological symptom belonging in the southern sector. Subjects probably interpreted tremors as trembling or feverish shaking, a somatic symptom. We have not been able to identify why other anomalies occurred in the judgment data, however. Research we are now conducting with medical students and doctors may provide a clue when we have scaled their judgments.

In conclusion, we have been able to reveal systematic patterns of configurality in an ordinary judgment task with a robust, nonmetric data analysis. Unlike ANOVA and regression methods, which are susceptible to measurement artifacts and which can obscure configural patterns even when they exist in the data, our technique provides a plausible fit of a configural model to actual judgment data. There were undoubtedly substantial individual differences in the judgments underlying the pooled data set. Previous research has indicated the importance of these differences in judgment strategies (Wiggins & Hoffman, 1968). In particular, ignoring individual differences can obscure configural effects in the analysis because pooling data favors additive models. Nevertheless, configurality clearly emerged in our global analysis. Encouraged by this, we have decided to reduce our cue set to 20 symptoms and to present subjects with all possible pairs of symptoms. This will allow an analysis of individual differences in configural structures.

ACKNOWLEDGMENTS

This research was supported by funds from the Bio-Medical Research Board of the University of Illinois at Chicago Circle. Nancy Hirschberg, Rowell Huesmann, and Ernie Kent provided useful suggestions for the analysis.

REFERENCES

Anderson, N. H. Looking for configurality in clinical judgment. *Psychological Bulletin*, 1972, 78, 93-102.

Carroll, J. D., & Chang, J. J. *Relating preference data to multidimensional scaling solutions via a generalization of Coombs' unfolding model.* Paper presented at meeting of Psychometric Society, Madison, Wisc., April 1967.

Cliff, N. Consistencies among judgments of adjective combinations. In A. K. Romney, R. N. Shepard, & S. B. Nerlove (Eds.), *Multidimensional scaling: Theory and applications in the behavioral sciences* (Vol. 2). New York: Seminar Press, 1972.

Cliff, N., & Young, F. W. On the relation between unidimensional judgments and multidimensional scaling. *Organizational Behavior and Human Performance*, 1968, *3*, 269-285.

Coombs, C. *A theory of data.* New York: Wiley, 1964.

Cooper, L. G. A multivariate investigation of preferences. *Multivariate Behavioral Research*, 1973, *8*, 253-272.

Dawes, R. M. A case study of graduate admissions: Application of three principles of decision making. *American Psychologist*, 1971, *26*, 180-188.

Einhorn, H. J. The use of nonlinear, noncompensatory models in decision making. *Psychological Bulletin*, 1970, *73*, 221-230.

Einhorn, H. J. Use of nonlinear, noncompensatory models as a function of task and amount of information. *Organizational Behavior and Human Performance*, 1971, *6*, 1-27.

Einhorn, H. J. Expert measurement and mechanical combination. *Organizational Behavior and Human Performance*, 1972, *7*, 86-106.

Goldberg, L. R. Man versus model of man: A rationale, plus some evidence, for a method of improving on clinical inferences. *Psychological Bulletin*, 1970, *6*, 422-432.

Goldberg, L. R. Five models of clinical judgment: An empirical comparison between linear and nonlinear representations of the human inference process. *Organizational Behavior and Human Performance*, 1971, *6*, 458-479.

Green, P. E., Carmone, F. J., & Wind, Y. Subjective evaluation models and conjoint measurement. *Behavioral Science*, 1972, *17*, 288-299.

Guttman, L. A new approach to factor analysis: The radex. In P. F. Lazarsfeld (Ed.), *Mathematical thinking in the social sciences.* Glencoe, Ill.: The Free Press, 1954.

Guttman, L. A general nonmetric technique for finding the smallest coordinate space for a configuration of points. *Psychometrika*, 1968, *33*, 469-506.

Hoffman, P. J., Slovic, P., & Rorer, L. G. An analysis of variance model for the assessment of configural cue utalization in clinical judgment. *Psychological Bulletin*, 1968, *69*, 338-349.

Hogarth, R. M. Process tracing in clinical judgment. *Behavioral Science*, 1974, *19*, 298-313.

Kleinmuntz, B. The processing of clinical information by man and machine. In B. Kleinmuntz (Ed.), *Formal representation in human judgment.* New York: Wiley, 1968.

Krantz, D. H., & Tversky, A. Conjoint measurement analysis of composition rules in psychology. *Psychological Review*, 1971, *78*, 151-169.

Krupp, M. A., & Chatton, M. J. (Eds.). *Current medical diagnosis and treatment 1977.* Los Altos, Calif.: Lange Medical Publishers, 1977.

Kruskal, J. B. Multidimensional scaling by optimizing goodness of fit to a nonmetric hypothesis. *Psychometrika*, 1964, *29*, 1-27. (a)

Kruskal, J. B. Nonmetric multidimensional scaling: A numerical method. *Psychometrika*, 1964, *29*, 115-129. (b)

Kruskal, J. B., Young, F. W., & Seery, J. B. How to use KYST-2, a very flexible program to do multidimensional scaling and unfolding. Murray Hill, N.J.: Bell Laboratories, 1978.

Levine, D. M. A Monte Carlo study of Kruskal's variance based measure on stress. *Psychometrika*, 1978, *43*, 307-315.

Levy, S., & Guttman, L. Structure and dynamics of worries. *Sociometry*, 1975, *38*, 445-473.

Libby, R. Man versus model of man: Some conflicting evidence. *Organizational Behavior and Human Performance*, 1976, *16*, 1-12. (a)

Libby, R. Man versus model of man: The need for a nonlinear model. *Organizational Behavior and Human Performance*, 1976, *16*, 23-26. (b)

Luce, R. D., & Tukey, J. W. Simultaneous conjoint measurements: A new type of fundamental measurement. *Journal of Mathematical Psychology*, 1964, *1*, 1-27.

Meehl, P. E. Configural scoring. *Journal of Consulting Psychology*, 1950, *14*, 165-171.

Meehl, P. E. *Clincial vs. statistical prediction*. Minneapolis: University of Minnesota Press, 1954.

Payne, J. W. Task complexity and contingent processing in decision making: An information search and protocol analysis. *Organizational Behavior and Human Performance*, 1976, *16*, 366-387.

Shepard, R. N. The analysis of proximities: Multidimensional scaling with an unknown distance function. I. *Psychometrika*, 1962, *27*, 125-140. (a)

Shepard, R. N. The analysis of proximities: Multidimensional scaling with an unknown distance function. II. *Psychometrika*, 1962, *27*, 219-246. (b)

Slovic, P. Analyzing the expert judge: A descriptive study of a stockbroker's decision process. *Journal of Applied Psychology*. 1969, *53*, 255-263.

Spence, I., & Ogilvie, J. C. A table of expected stress values for random rankings in nonmetric multidimensional scaling. *Multivariate Behavioral Research*, 1973, *4*, 511-517.

Tucker, L. R. Intra-individual and inter-individual multidimensionality. In H. Gulicksen & S. Messick (Eds.), *Psychological scaling: Theory and application*. New York: Wiley, 1960.

Tversky, A. A general theory of polynomial conjoint measurement. *Journal of Mathematical Psychology*, 1967, *4*, 1-20.

Wiggins, N. Individual differences in human judgments: A multivariate approach. In L. Rappoport & D. A. Summers (Eds.), *Human judgment and social interaction*. New York: Holt, Rinehart. & Winston, 1973.

Wiggins, N., & Hoffman, P. J. Three models of clinical judgment. *Journal of Abnormal Psychology*, 1968, *73*, 70-77.

Wiggins, N., Hoffman, P. J., and Taber, T. Types of judges and cue-utilization in judgments of intelligence. *Journal of Personality and Social Psychology*, 1969, *12*, 52-59.

Young, F. W. A model for polynomial conjoint analysis algorithms. In A. K. Romney, R. N. Shepard, & S. B. Nerlove (Eds.), *Multidimensional scaling: Theory and applications in the behavioral sciences* (Vol. 1). New York: Seminar Press, 1972.

7

The Method of Sorting in Multivariate Research with Applications Selected from Cognitive Psychology and Person Perception

Seymour Rosenberg
Rutgers University

Object sorting has a well-established place as a data-gathering technique for investigating a variety of cognitive, developmental, and perceptual phenomena (Bruner, Goodnow, & Austin, 1956; Rosch, 1977; Vygotsky, 1962; Werner, 1957). The sorting method is a relative newcomer, however, in the multivariate research of these phenomena, where its primary purpose is to provide co-occurrence data from which estimates of psychological distance between the objects can be calculated. The distance measures so obtained are usually intended as input for such multivariate techniques as clustering and multidimensional scaling.

The more traditional and familiar methods for estimating psychological distance are the judgment of pairwise similarities and the method of triads (Torgerson, 1958, pp. 259–268). One of the main advantages of the sorting method is that the subject can make judgments about the entire set of objects in a relatively short time, even when a large number of objects are involved. Consider, for example, the time required for a subject to sort 50 nouns on the basis of their similarity in meaning with that required to judge all their pairwise similarities, that is, to make the 1225 ($n(n-1)/2$) pairwise comparisons. A large number of pairwise comparisons can also severely tax a subject's motivation. The preparation by the investigator of the stimulus materials for the sorting method is also correspondingly simpler than for the more traditional methods.

The sorting method shares with the more traditional methods the advantage of making it unnecessary for either the subject or the investigator to specify any of the dimensions or attributes of the objects that could be used as a basis for the judgments. The identification of underlying dimensions or attributes can take place from the structures obtained from clustering and scaling analyses, leaving a subject's judgments uncontaminated by an investigator's preconceptions.

In spite of its relatively short history of use in multivariate research, useful applications of the sorting method have been made in such diverse areas as subjective meaning (Anglin, 1970; Burton, 1972; Fillenbaum & Rapoport, 1971; Miller, 1967, 1969; Steinberg, 1967), person perception (Friendly & Glucksberg, 1970; Rosenberg, Nelson, & Vivekananthan, 1968; Rosenberg & Olshan, 1970; Sedlak, 1971; Sherman, 1972; Wing & Nelson, 1972), perception of nations and ethnic groups (Jones & Ashmore, 1973; Wish, Deutsch, & Biener, 1972), lay conceptions of psychopathology (Rosenberg & Cohen, 1977), facial affect (Stringer, 1967), and attitudes expressed in editorials (Schmidt, 1972).

The main purposes of the present chapter are: (1) to explicate the basic method of sorting, as well as its variants; and (2) to point up the salient properties both of sorting data and of the multivariate structures obtained from such data. For these purposes, applications from the two substantive areas in which sorting has been used most extensively are described in some detail: subjective meaning and person perception. A final section summarizes a number of empirical comparisons of sorting with other, more traditional data-gathering methods in multivariate research.

SORTING METHODOLOGY AND DISTANCE MEASURES

The basic feature of the sorting method in multivariate research is that subjects are free to partition a set of interrelated objects into categories of their own making. Beyond this common feature, there is considerable variation in the constraints that investigators place on the sorting procedure. In most applications, investigators require that subjects form mutually exclusive categories; on the other hand, there are usually no restrictions on the number of objects that subjects assign to the categories they form. In some applications, subjects are also free to form as many categories as they wish, whereas in other applications, bounds are placed on the number of categories that subjects are permitted to form.

Two other procedural variations have been used in certain special applications of the sorting method.

One is referred to as either the "clustering technique" (Bricker & Pruzansky, 1970; Sherman, 1972) or the "merge method" (Clark, 1968; Drasgow, 1976). In the merge (or clustering) method, subjects first sort the objects into subgroups; subjects are then instructed to merge two of the subgroups that they consider most similar, and this process is repeated until a final group is formed that contains all the objects. Another special type of clustering technique performed by the subjects is the tree construction method used extensively by Fillenbaum and Rapoport (1971) in their study of the subjective lexicon. The tree construction method is an analog of the hierarchical clustering algorithms described by

Johnson (1967). An empirical comparison of the "merge method" with the basic sorting method showed that this variant yields structures very similar to those obtained from the basic sorting method (Drasgow, 1976). Fillenbaum and Rapoport (1971) came to the same conclusion as a result of their empirical comparisons of the tree construction method with basic sorting.

In a second, and quite different, procedural variation, subjects are given several opportunities to sort the same objects, each time on a different basis. Comparisons of this multiple-sort method with the more commonly used single-sort method have yielded some interesting methodological findings, which are reported in the next section (Rosenberg & Kim, 1975).

In all the aforementioned variations, subjects may be instructed to classify the objects on the basis of either their "similarity," their "relatedness," or their "co-occurrence"—depending on the particular application. Thus, in multivariate applications of sorting, subjects are not necessarily limited to forming identity or equivalence categories, as is usually the case for "object sorting" (Bruner et al., 1956, pp. 2-6). For example, in studies of personality perception, subjects are asked to put those traits they perceive to be present in the same individual into the same category—a co-occurrence instruction, essentially.

Several distance measures, based on the subjects' grouping of the objects, have been defined and used by different investigators. A simple measure of distance is one in which a count is made of the number of subjects who do *not* sort any given pair of objects into the same category: the larger the number of subjects in the sample who group two objects together, the smaller the distance between them. Other, more elaborate measures have been defined, one based on information–theoretic principles (Burton, 1972), another referred to as the "δ-measure" that takes into account indirect as well as direct groupings among the objects (Rosenberg, et al., 1968), and still another when the categories are not required to be mutually exclusive (Wing & Nelson, 1972).

One of the more important problems facing the investigator is the choice of an appropriate distance measure to compute from sorting data. This problem has not, as yet, been adequately investigated for sorting data—although it has been extensively examined for data obtained from certain other data-gathering methods (Sneath & Sokal, 1973). A recent study (Drasgow & Jones, 1979) compared a direct distance measure with the "δ-measure" referred to previously, using hypothetical data but, unfortunately, not of the kind obtained from the sorting method.

At this point at least the choice of a distance measure is ad hoc, to some extent. One strategy is the use of two or more distance measures in the multivariate analysis of the set of sorting data. As Sneath and Sokal (1973) have commented, after an extensive discussion of distance measures in the context of numerical taxonomy: "But when all is said and done, the validation of a similarity measure by the scientist working in a given field has so far been primarily empirical, a type of intuitive assessment of similarity [pg. 146]."

APPLICATIONS TO SUBJECTIVE MEANING

Kinship Terminology

The vocabulary of kinship has been of long-standing interest among anthropologists—an interest motivated by the desire to understand the cognitive and social organization of peoples, in this important domain of their culture (Bohannan & Middleton, 1968). One type of semantic analysis, particularly of kinship terms, that has appealed to anthropologists is known as "componential analysis" (Romney & D'Andrade, 1964; Wallace & Atkins, 1960; Wexler & Romney, 1972). Componential analysis is a multidimensional analysis in which the componential structure consists of a number of semantic dimensions with each dimension having a discrete number of values. Examples of such dimensions in kinship terminology include generation, sex, and lineality.

Componential analysis is an a priori structural analysis, and as such may yield different structures in the hands of different theorists. Several empirical studies have demonstrated that the sorting method (Fillenbaum & Rapoport, 1971; Kim, 1973; Steinberg, 1967), as well as other multivariate methods (Romney & D'Andrade, 1964), can provide empirical tests of "the psychological reality" of a kinship structure produced by componential analysis.

In a methodological study of sorting with kinship terms serving as the stimulus materials, Rosenberg and Kim (1975) compared two variants of the sorting method: single-sort, in which each subject was given only one opportunity to sort the terms; and multiple-sort, in which the subject was given several opportunities to sort, each time on a different basis. In both procedures, the subjects were instructed to sort the terms according to their similarity in meaning and were told in advance how many sorts would be permitted. The terms consisted of 15 mutually exclusive kinship terms selected by Wallace and Atkins (1960): *aunt, brother, cousin, daughter, father, granddaughter, grandfather, grandmother, grandson, mother, nephew, niece, sister, son, uncle.*

The sortings of a subsample of 85 female subjects who used the single-sort procedure are reproduced in Table 7.1. The rows and columns in this table have been permuted to reveal certain sorting patterns in the data. Note, for example, that subjects 20 through 31 put grandparents and grandchildren in one category, the other lineal kins (i.e., parents, siblings, children) in a second category, and collateral kins in a third category. Subjects 62 through 79 also put grandparents and grandchildren in one category, but formed two or more categories for other lineal kins and for collateral kins. An entirely different sorting strategy is exhibited by subjects 80 through 85; they put all the male terms in one category, all the female terms in a second category, and *cousin* in a third category.

Table 7.2 summarizes the non-co-occurrences for all pairs of the 15 terms obtained from this subsample of 85 subjects. For example, 11 of the 85 subjects did not put *grandmother* and *grandfather* into the same category. Because the matrix is symmetric, only the lower triangle of the matrix is reproduced. That is,

TABLE 7.1

Sorting of 15 English Kinship Terms by Each of 85 Subjects:
Single-Sort Method
(Data from Rosenberg & Kim, 1975)

	Grandfather	Grandmother	Granddaughter	Grandson	Brother	Sister	Father	Mother	Daughter	Son	Niece	Nephew	Cousin	Aunt	Uncle
1.	B	B	A	A	B	B	B	B	A	A	B	A	B	B	B
2.	X	Y	D	C	C	D	A	B	D	C	C	D	C	B	A
3.	A	A	C	C	C	C	B	B	C	C	C	C	C	B	B
4.	A	A	G	G	F	F	B	B	E	E	E	E	F	B	B
5.	A	A	C	C	E	E	B	B	E	E	C	C	C	B	B
6.	A	A	C	C	E	E	B	B	E	E	C	C	C	B	B
7.	A	A	C	C	E	E	B	B	E	E	C	C	E	B	B
8.	A	A	C	C	B	B	B	B	C	C	C	C	D	D	D
9.	A	A	A	A	B	B	A	A	A	A	C	C	C	C	C
10.	A	A	A	A	A	A	A	A	A	A	C	C	C	C	C
11.	F	E	E	F	A	B	A	B	B	A	D	C	C	C	D
12.	A	B	B	A	D	D	A	B	B	A	C	C	C	C	C
13.	A	B	B	A	D	D	A	B	B	A	C	E	F	E	C
14.	A	B	B	A	A	B	A	B	B	A	C	C	C	C	C
15.	A	A	A	A	C	C	B	B	B	B	C	C	C	C	C
16.	A	A	A	A	B	B	B	B	B	B	B	C	C	C	C
17.	E	E	F	F	B	B	B	B	B	B	D	D	C	C	C
18.	E	E	F	F	B	B	B	B	B	B	D	D	C	C	C
19.	A	A	A	A	B	B	B	B	B	B	D	D	C	C	C
20.	A	A	A	A	B	B	B	B	B	B	C	C	C	C	C
21.	A	A	A	A	B	B	B	B	B	B	C	C	C	C	C
22.	A	A	A	A	B	B	B	B	B	B	C	C	C	C	C
23.	A	A	A	A	B	B	B	B	B	B	C	C	C	C	C
24.	A	A	A	A	B	B	B	B	B	B	C	C	C	C	C
25.	A	A	A	A	B	B	B	B	B	B	C	C	C	C	C
26.	A	A	A	A	B	B	B	B	B	B	C	C	C	C	C
27.	A	A	A	A	B	B	B	B	B	B	C	C	C	C	C
28.	A	A	A	A	B	B	B	B	B	B	C	C	C	C	C
29.	A	A	A	A	B	B	B	B	B	B	C	C	C	C	C
30.	A	A	A	A	B	B	B	B	B	B	C	C	C	C	C
31.	A	A	A	A	B	B	B	B	B	B	C	C	C	C	C
32.	A	A	A	A	B	B	B	B	B	B	C	C	D	C	C
33.	A	A	B	C	C	B	D	E	D	E	F	H	G	F	H
34.	A	A	A	A	C	C	V	X	Y	Z	F	F	F	H	H
35.	A	A	B	E	C	C	D	D	B	E	F	F	G	H	H
36.	A	A	B	B	C	C	D	D	E	E	F	F	F	H	H
37.	A	A	B	B	C	C	D	D	E	E	F	F	G	H	H

(*continued*)

TABLE 7.1—*Continued*

	Grandfather	Grandmother	Granddaughter	Grandson	Brother	Sister	Father	Mother	Daughter	Son	Niece	Nephew	Cousin	Aunt	Uncle
38.	A	A	B	B	C	C	D	D	E	E	F	F	G	H	H
39.	A	A	B	B	C	C	D	D	E	E	F	F	G	H	H
40.	A	A	B	B	C	C	D	D	E	E	F	F	G	H	H
41.	A	A	B	B	C	C	D	D	E	E	F	F	G	H	H
42.	A	A	B	B	C	C	D	D	E	E	F	F	G	H	H
43.	A	A	B	B	C	C	D	D	E	E	F	F	G	H	H
44.	A	A	B	B	C	C	D	D	E	E	F	F	G	H	H
45.	A	A	B	B	C	C	D	D	E	E	F	F	G	H	H
46.	A	A	B	B	B	B	D	D	E	E	C	C	C	C	C
47.	A	A	B	B	C	C	D	D	C	C	F	F	F	H	H
48.	A	A	B	B	C	C	D	D	C	C	F	F	H	H	H
49.	A	A	B	B	C	C	C	C	E	E	F	F	H	H	H
50.	A	A	B	B	C	C	C	C	E	E	F	F	H	H	H
51.	A	A	B	B	C	C	D	D	E	E	F	F	H	H	H
52.	A	A	B	B	C	C	D	D	E	E	F	F	H	H	H
53.	A	A	B	B	C	C	D	D	E	E	F	F	H	H	H
54.	A	A	B	B	C	C	D	D	E	E	F	F	H	H	H
55.	A	A	B	B	C	C	D	D	E	E	F	F	H	H	H
56.	A	A	B	B	C	C	D	D	E	E	F	F	H	H	H
57.	A	A	B	B	C	C	D	D	E	E	F	F	H	H	H
58.	A	A	E	E	D	D	B	B	B	B	C	C	G	C	C
59.	A	A	E	E	D	D	B	B	B	B	C	C	C	C	C
60.	A	A	E	E	D	D	B	B	B	B	F	F	H	H	H
61.	A	A	E	E	D	D	B	B	B	B	F	F	G	H	H
62.	A	A	A	A	D	D	B	B	B	B	F	F	H	H	H
63.	A	A	A	A	D	D	B	B	B	B	F	F	H	H	H
64.	A	A	A	A	D	D	B	B	B	B	F	F	H	H	H
65.	A	A	A	A	D	D	B	B	B	B	F	F	H	H	H
66.	A	A	A	A	D	D	B	B	B	B	F	F	H	H	H
67.	A	A	A	A	D	D	B	B	B	B	C	C	C	C	C
68.	A	A	A	A	D	D	B	B	B	B	C	C	C	C	C
69.	A	A	A	A	D	D	B	B	B	B	C	C	C	C	C
70.	A	A	A	A	D	D	B	B	B	B	C	C	C	C	C
71.	A	A	A	A	D	D	B	B	B	B	C	C	C	C	C
72.	A	A	A	A	D	D	B	B	E	E	C	C	G	C	C
73.	A	A	A	A	D	D	B	B	B	B	C	C	D	C	C
74.	A	A	A	A	D	D	B	B	B	B	C	C	D	C	C
75.	A	A	A	A	D	D	B	B	B	B	C	C	G	C	C
76.	A	A	A	A	D	D	B	B	B	B	C	C	G	C	C
77.	A	A	A	A	D	D	B	B	B	B	C	C	G	C	C
78.	A	A	A	A	D	D	B	B	B	B	C	C	G	C	C
79.	A	A	A	A	D	D	B	B	B	B	C	C	G	C	C

(*continued*)

TABLE 7.1—*Continued*

	Grandfather	Grandmother	Granddaughter	Grandson	Brother	Sister	Father	Mother	Daughter	Son	Niece	Nephew	Cousin	Aunt	Uncle
80.	M	F	F	M	M	F	M	F	F	M	M	F	N	F	M
81.	M	F	F	M	M	F	M	F	F	M	M	F	N	F	M
82.	M	F	F	M	M	F	M	F	F	M	M	F	N	F	M
83.	M	F	F	M	M	F	M	F	F	M	M	F	N	F	M
84.	M	F	F	M	M	F	M	F	F	M	M	F	N	F	M
85.	M	F	F	M	M	F	M	F	F	M	M	F	N	F	M

Note 1:   The horizontal lines divide the subjects into relatively homogeneous subgroups and were obtained from a clustering analysis of intersubject similarities.

Note 2:   The letters within each row identify the categories formed by a given subject. The letters were selected by the author to highlight similarities and differences among the 85 subjects' sortings.

if we denote a typical entry in Table 7.2 as s_{ij}, then $s_{ij} = s_{ji}$, the diagonal entries are zero, that is, $s_{ii} = 0$ for $i = (1,15)$. Miller (1969) has also shown that the entries in such a matrix satisfy the triangular inequality. Thus, the entries in a non-co-occurrence matrix constitute a metric.

Does the sorting method—single versus multiple—produce important variations in the semantic structure of the kinship terms? To answer this question, an INDSCAL analysis (Carroll & Chang, 1970) was performed on the data. Inter-item distances were calculated separately for each of the following six groups:

Male subjects, single-sort;
Female subjects, single-sort;
Male subjects, multiple-sort, first sort;
Female subjects, multiple-sort, first sort;
Male subjects, multiple-sort, second sort;
Female subjects, multiple-sort, second sort.

The three-dimensional configuration produced by the INDSCAL analysis, based on the data from all six groups, is shown in Fig. 7.1. Three dimensions were found to be necessary to represent the data adequately and to demonstrate the differences between single- and multiple-sort methods. No new interpretable dimension emerged in the four-dimensional configuration.

A three-dimensional configuration for any particular group can be obtained by stretching and shrinking the dimensions in Fig. 7.1 in proportion to a set of dimensional weights calculated for that group by INDSCAL. A relatively high

TABLE 7.2
Number of Subjects (Out of 85) Who Did Not Put Any Two Given
Terms into the Same Category: Single-Sort Method
(Data from Rosenberg & Kim, 1975)

	GF	GM	GD	GS	SI	BR	MO	FA	DA	SO	NE	NI	CO	AU	UN
GRANDFATHER	0														
GRANDMOTHER	11	0													
GRANDDAUGHTER	48	38	0												
GRANDSON	38	48	13	0											
SISTER	83	76	73	82	0										
BROTHER	76	83	82	73	10	0									
MOTHER	82	73	74	83	55	63	0								
FATHER	73	82	83	74	63	55	13	0							
DAUGHTER	83	74	69	80	52	61	34	43	0						
SON	74	83	80	69	61	52	43	34	14	0					
NEPHEW	78	84	80	73	81	74	83	77	81	74	0				
NIECE	85	79	72	79	76	83	79	85	74	81	12	0			
COUSIN	84	84	82	81	78	77	84	84	83	82	53	53	0		
AUNT	84	78	79	85	77	83	72	79	79	85	49	42	38	0	
UNCLE	78	84	85	79	83	77	79	72	85	79	42	49	39	10	0

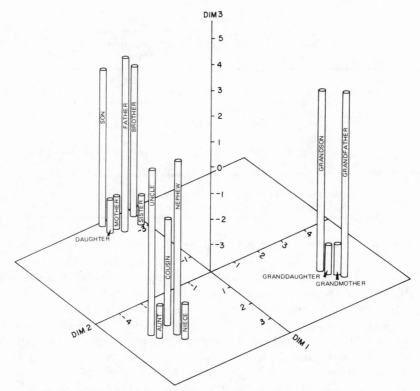

FIG. 7.1. The composite three-dimensional solution of the 15 English kinship terms obtained by INDSCAL analysis. (From Rosenberg & Kim, 1975).

weight on a dimension is usually interpreted to mean that the dimension has relatively high psychological salience for the particular group.

The weights that each group accorded in their sorting to each of the three dimensions in Fig. 7.1 are summarized in Table 7.3. Dimensions 1 and 2 were weighted much more heavily by the single-sort groups than by the multiple-sort groups. Conversely, Dimension 3 was weighted more heavily by the multiple-sort groups. It is clear from Fig. 7.1 that Dimension 3 represents the sex dimension—all the male terms are at the upper extreme of this dimension and all the female terms are at the lower extreme, with *cousin* at an intermediate position.

A perusal of the sorting data indicated that most subjects in each group sorted either on the basis of sex or ignored it completely. Table 7.4 summarizes these proportions. The "Sex Only" column lists the proportion of subjects who partitioned the 15 terms into a male category and a female category, with *cousin* either in a separate category or included with the male or the female terms. The "Mixed" column lists the proportion of subjects who sorted partly on the basis

TABLE 7.3
Weights for Each Group in the Three-Dimensional
Configuration Obtained by the INDSCAL Procedure
(From Rosenberg & Kim, 1975)

	Dimension		
Group	1	2	3
Male Subjects:			
Single-Sort	.54	.57	.25
Multiple-Sort One	.34	.40	.75
Multiple-Sort Two	.30	.22	.83
Female Subjects:			
Single-Sort	.62	.60	.05
Multiple-Sort One	.10	.10	.97
Multiple-Sort Two	.47	.46	.53

of sex and partly on some other basis. There is a difference in the degree to which male and female subjects use sex as a basis for sorting; females tend to ignore sex when only a single sort is permitted and to overemphasize (relative to males) sex in the first of a series of multiple sorts.

The relatively low weights obtained for the sex dimension in the two single-sort groups (male and female subjects) do not necessarily reflect the general salience of this dimension. On the contrary, subjects may tend to ignore a dimension that is extremely obvious (such as sex) when they believe they have only one opportunity to indicate the dimensions in a set of objects.

Shepard (1972) obtained analogous results in a comparison of pairwise judgments of similarity with actual listener confusions among a set of consonant phonemes. He noted that whereas voicing (e.g., t vs. d, f vs. v) is the phonemic feature most easily discriminated by the listeners, this feature tends to be ignored by the subjects who made the pairwise judgments.

TABLE 7.4
Proportion of Subjects Who Sorted the Kinship Terms
Either on the Basis of Sex, or on Another Basis, or Both
(From Rosenberg & Kim, 1975)

	Sorting Basis		
Group	Sex Only	Nonsex	Mixed
Male Subjects:			
Single-Sort	.15	.77	.08
Multiple-Sort One	.35	.56	.09
Multiple-Sort Two	.34	.60	.06
Female Subjects:			
Single-Sort	.07	.86	.07
Multiple-Sort One	.53	.37	.10
Multiple-Sort Two	.21	.65	.14

Two important questions can be raised by the results of the kinship study and those of Shepard (1972).

First, what kinds of stimulus domains are most subject to the judgment bias described above? A tentative answer is that the bias is most pronounced when the stimuli vary on several distinct attributes rather than on continua. Shepard's (1972) explanation of his results is interesting in this connection; he hypothesized that subjects in the phoneme judgment task treated it "as an analogy task rather than a pure similarity task [p. 106]." Whatever the cognitive mechanism, multiattribute domains such as kinship terms and phonemes may easily lend themselves to the inclusion or exclusion by a subject of one or more distinct attributes. In contrast, domains such as trait adjectives cannot be so processed cognitively because similarity among the stimuli is more continuous. This distinction between stimulus domains is akin to one discussed by Torgerson (1965).

Second, what can be done to avoid or overcome this bias?

On the data-gathering side, one possibility is the routine use of a multiple-sort procedure. Because pairwise judgments of similarity are also subject to this bias (Shepard, 1972), a similar suggestion may be made for this method; that is, multiple sets of pairwise judgments should be obtained from the same judges, a feasible procedure only when the number of stimuli is relatively small.

Care must be exercised on the data-analysis side, as well. Whereas multidimensional scaling recovers the sex dimension from single-sort data, hierarchical clustering does not. The hierarchical tree structures obtained from the diameter method (Johnson, 1967; Sneath & Sokal, 1973) are shown in Fig. 7.2. The most important difference among the three trees in Fig. 7.2 is between the single-sort tree and the two multiple-sort trees. The trees for the multiple-sort

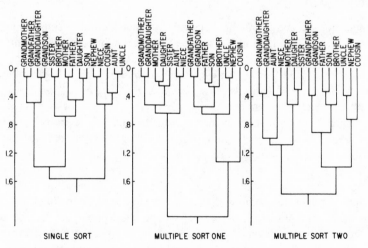

FIG. 7.2.   Hirarchical tree structures of the 15 English kinship terms from each of three sorting conditions. (From Rosenberg & Kim, 1975).

groups incorporate the information about those sorters who used sex as a basis for sorting by containing two parallel sets of clusters—one for male terms and one for female terms. By contrast, the tree for the single-sort group fails to represent the subjects who used sex as a basis for sorting. That is, this tree structure would be exactly the same if no subjects sorted according to sex!

A parallel result was obtained in Shepard's (1972, Fig. 4.22) phonemic data; that is, voicing failed to appear in the hierarchical clustering of the similarity judgments. Thus, an analysis by conventional clustering algorithms may result in the complete loss of certain categorical distinctions among the stimuli.

Two data-analysis methods are currently available that guard against the type of information loss just described. For sorting data, the subjects can be partitioned into "dominant" and "dormant" subgroups and a tree structure obtained for each. Dominant sorters are identified as those judges whose sorts agree most with the tree structure based on the entire sample and dormant sorters as those whose sorts agree least. (For example, subjects 80 through 85 in Table 7.1 who sorted according to sex would be among the dormant sorters.) This is a variant of the dominant–dormant analysis described by Anderberg (1973, pp. 179–180) and by Rosenberg (1977, pp. 239–241). Alternatively, a procedure described by Carroll (1976) may be used to obtain two or more tree structures from a single distance matrix. He showed that with two trees, he was able to extract the sex dimension (as well as the other features of the kinship terms) from the single-sort distance data shown in Table 7.2. (Carroll, 1976, Fig. 10).

Finally, let us turn briefly to the substantive aspects of these kinship data. The INDSCAL analysis provides an empirical test of the validity of certain semantic dimensions postulated by Romney and D'Andrade (1964) and by Wallace and Atkins (1960) in their respective componential analyses of the 15 English kinship terms.

Dimensions 1 and 2 in Fig. 7.1 are best understood by considering them together. Essentially, the following three clusters are differentiated by these two dimensions: the nuclear family (*mother, father, sister, brother, daughter, son*); the collaterals (*aunt, uncle, cousin, niece, nephew*); kins two generations removed from the self (*grandmother, grandfather, granddaughter, grandson*). The latter cluster is in part the "reciprocity" dimension proposed by Romney and D'Andrade (1964). A complete representation of their reciprocity dimension would require two additional groupings: kins one generation removed from self (*father, mother, son, daughter, uncle, aunt, nephew, niece*); kins zero generations removed from self (*brother, sister, cousin*). The ordering of the terms by generation (Wallace & Atkins, 1960) does not appear in this three-dimensional solution. Nor does a generation dimension emerge in the four-dimensional solution of these data. In short, the results support the Romney–D'Andrade model over the Wallace–Atkins model—a conclusion also reached by Fillenbaum and Rapoport (1971) from their empirical study of these kinship terms.

English Nouns

In a study of the subjective organization of verbal concepts, Miller (1969) used the method of sorting to estimate the psychological distances among 48 English nouns. Of the 48 nouns, 24 were names of things and 24 were not. Fifty college students each sorted the 48 nouns according to their "similarity in meaning." The subjects were given a brief definition of each noun taken with minor modification from the *Thorndike Barnhart Beginning Dictionary* (New York: Doubleday, 1964).

The co-occurrence data were subjected to hierarchical clustering using Johnson's (1967) connectedness and diameter methods. The results of these two methods are summarized in Fig. 7.3.

What does the clustering analysis reveal about the subjective organization of these 48 concepts? Because the nouns were deliberately selected so as to include names of things and nonthings, we might see whether the method of sorting (combined with hierarchical clustering) recovers this basic dichotomy in the stimulus objects. Although the first 24 nouns in Fig. 7.3 are object names and the second 24 are not, the tree structure in the connectedness solution has as its first break the five human terms versus the others. Nor does the diameter method confirm the basic distinction between objects and nonobjects, although (as in the connectedness method) objects and nonobjects do not merge at the higher branches of the tree. The complete tree for the diameter method is not shown in Fig. 7.3, but stops at the level where there are five clusters. These five clusters can be more or less interpreted from top to bottom as: (1) names of living things; (2) names of nonliving things; (3) quantitative terms; (4) kinds of social interaction; and (5) psychological (mostly affect) terms.

Unlike the kinship terms, the 48 nouns used by Miller do not seem to have a simple componential structure. Nor do they seem to have a truly hierarchical structure. In a hierarchical system, unlike a dimensional structure, not every item has a value for every dimension. For example, animals may be classified as vertebrates or invertebrates, but plants are neither.

In another study, however, Miller (1968) used names of 20 body parts, whose a priori structure does seem to be hierarchical. The co-occurrence data of these 20 body parts, based on 50 sorters, are shown in Table 7.5. The names of the body parts are arranged in alphabetical order in Table 7.5.

Carroll and Chang (1973) analyzed the co-occurrence data in Table 7.5 with a hierarchical analysis they developed explicitly for structures where some of the objects may occupy nodes of the tree other than at the terminals. The results of their analysis are shown in Fig. 7.4. The tree conforms fairly well to what one might expect as a structural representation of the 20 body parts. (For details of their method, see also Carroll, 1976).

It should be noted that the sorting method is probably not the ideal one when

CONNECTEDNESS METHOD   DIAMETER METHOD

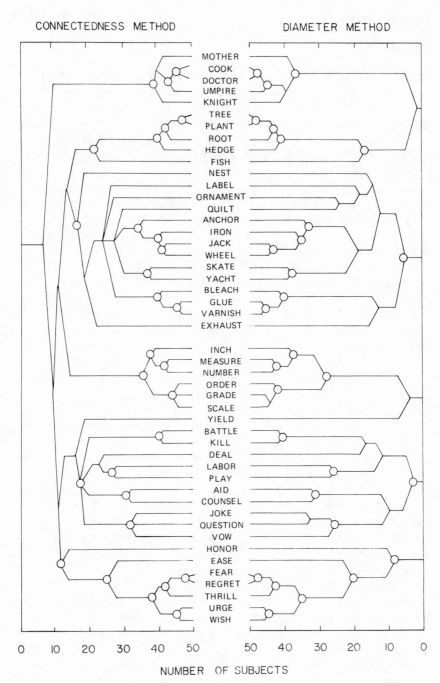

O   IO   20   30   40   50   50   40   30   20   IO   O

NUMBER OF SUBJECTS

FIG. 7.3.   Hierarchical tree structures of 48 English nouns sorted by 50 subjects.
(From Miller, 1969).

TABLE 7.5
Number of Subjects (Out of 50) Who Did Not Put Any Two Given Terms into the Same Category
(Data from Miller, 1968)

	AI	BO	CH'K	CH'S	EA	EL	FA	HA	HE	KN	LE	LI	LU	MO	NE	PA	TH	TO	TR	WA
ARM	0																			
BODY	50	0																		
CHEEK	50	47	0																	
CHEST	46	37	49	0																
EAR	49	49	12	50	0															
ELBOW	08	50	50	50	49	0														
FACE	48	47	08	47	18	48	0													
HAND	14	50	50	50	48	13	48	0												
HEAD	43	45	19	45	18	49	14	46	0											
KNEE	47	50	50	50	49	42	48	46	49	0										
LEG	41	50	50	46	49	47	48	46	43	08	0									
LIP	49	48	05	50	11	49	12	49	18	49	49	0								
LUNG	49	42	48	17	47	48	48	49	48	48	49	47	0							
MOUTH	49	49	07	50	09	49	13	48	19	49	49	02	47	0						
NECK	45	40	39	38	39	47	35	48	31	47	45	38	42	38	0					
PALM	16	48	47	49	49	14	49	04	50	48	48	48	49	49	50	0				
THIGH	45	49	49	48	49	47	50	47	47	05	05	48	49	49	47	47	0			
TOE	47	49	48	50	48	47	50	47	49	11	13	47	48	48	49	46	08	0		
TRUNK	46	28	49	19	50	50	47	50	42	49	45	50	34	50	36	49	47	49	0	
WAIST	45	37	50	26	49	46	47	48	44	47	46	49	37	49	35	49	48	49	23	0

131

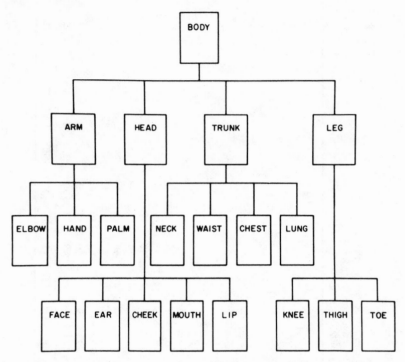

FIG. 7.4.   Hierarchical tree structure of 20 body-parts names sorted by 50 subjects. The data were collected by G. A. Miller (1968) and analyzed with a clustering method developed by Carroll and Chang (1973).

the objects have *part–whole relations,* such as those for body parts, or *asymmetric inclusion relations* (e.g., *living thing, animal, human, child* [Miller, 1967]). A better procedure might be one in which the subjects, themselves, construct a tree structure with some of the objects at the nodes. However, when the investigator is not sure whether such a special hierarchical structure is the appropriate one, the method of Carroll and Chang (1973) does appear to be able to recover such a structure from sorting data.

APPLICATIONS TO PERSONALITY PERCEPTION

In applications of the sorting method to personality perception, subjects are asked to describe each of several persons by sorting a set of trait terms into different groups, each group of terms representing the description of a different person.[1]

---

[1]An alternative sorting procedure might be one in which subjects group trait terms according to their overall judgment of the co-occurrence of the traits in people. However, the sorting of terms that

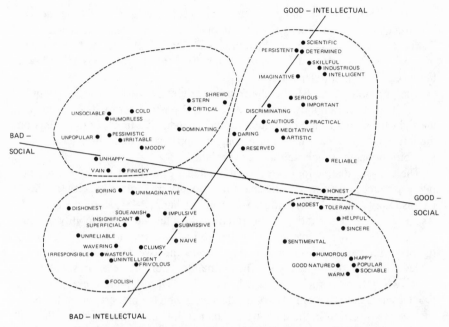

GOOD — INTELLECTUAL

BAD — SOCIAL

GOOD — SOCIAL

BAD — INTELLECTUAL

FIG. 7.5. Two-dimensional configuration of 60 traits showing: (1) four major clusters of the terms derived from a clustering analysis of the sorting data; (2) the best fitting axes of two rated trait properties: intellectual desirability and social desirability. (Adapted from Rosenberg et al., 1968).

Such sortings are very likely to be related to, but conceptually different from a sorting of the trait terms on the basis of their similarity in meaning. For example, *intelligent* and *determined* are not likely to be judged as synonymous, but they are often ascribed to the same individual; *unreliable* and *wavering,* on the other hand, are likely to be judged as more synonymous than *intelligent* and *determined,* and hence are also likely to be attributed to the same individual.

In the first application of the sorting method to a multidimensional analysis of personality perception, subjects described several persons of their own choice by sorting trait adjectives into mutually exclusive groups (Rosenberg et al., 1968). A "miscellaneous" category was provided for those traits that did not seem to the subject "to go together with any others." The traits in the miscellaneous category were each treated as a separate category. The two-dimensional trait configuration obtained in this study is reproduced in Fig. 7.5. Also shown in the figure are two complementary ways of interpreting such a configuration.

result from the description of several real persons, as outlined in the text, seems to be a more naturalistic procedure for this substantive domain. For a review of other "naturalistic" data-gathering methods in the study of personality perception, see Rosenberg and Sedlak (1972) and Rosenberg (1977).

One interpretative method is based on a clustering analysis of the co-occurrence data. The four enclosed sets of terms, each occupying a relatively distinct region of the space, are the four clusters into which a hierarchical clustering analysis (Johnson, 1967, diameter method) partitions the terms at the lower branches of the hierarchical tree.[2]

The psychological basis for the four major clusters in Fig. 7.5 seems quite clear. There are essentially two dichotomies: (1) positive terms (two clusters on the right-hand side of the configuration) versus negative terms (two clusters on the left-hand side); (2) competence content (upper right and lower left) versus sociability content (upper left and lower right).

These basic distinctions were corroborated by an independent set of trait ratings, which were fitted to the space by ordinary multiple-regression methods (Abelson & Sermat, 1962; Miller, Shepard, & Chang, 1964; Rosenberg & Sedlak, 1972). Two trait ratings, one referring to intellectual desirability (good–intellectual versus bad–intellectual) and a second referring to social desirability (good–social versus bad–social) correspond to the two basic dichotomies revealed by the clustering analysis. The optimal location of axes corresponding to these two trait properties is shown in Fig. 7.5. The multiple correlation also provides a quantitative estimate of the degree to which a property actually corresponds to a direction in the trait space. The multiple correlations for intellectual and social desirability are .91 and .95, respectively. These high correlations lend support to the hypothesized interpretation based on the clustering analysis.

This study of personality perception, as well as a number of others using the sorting method (Friendly & Glucksberg, 1970; Rosenberg & Olshan, 1970; Sedlak, 1971) have required that subjects use each trait exactly once in their sorting; that is, the subjects are restricted to forming mutually exclusive categories. A question that arises is whether the resultant structures are distorted by this constraint.

In a study designed to answer this question, Wing and Nelson (1972) used the same 60 traits shown in Fig. 7.5 but permitted subjects to assign each trait to as many persons as they wanted. The distance measure they defined as input for multidimensional scaling took into account the frequency of use of each trait; that is, the more frequently a subject used a particular trait, the less weight any given co-occurrence of the trait with any other contributed to the distance value.

Wing and Nelson (1972) used canonical correlation to compare the configurations obtained from their study with those obtained by Rosenberg et al. (1968). For the two-dimensional configurations, the two canonical correlation coefficients were .96 and .85, suggesting that the two sorting methods yielded highly

---

[2]The partitioning of each of these four major clusters into smaller clusters is not shown in Fig. 7.5 so as not to clutter up the configuration. A configuration in which different levels of the hierarchical clustering are displayed generally resembles a contour map (see, for example, Fillenbaum & Rapoport, 1971; Napior, 1972; Shepard, 1972).

similar configurations. However, the canonical correlations for the three-dimensional configurations were .97, .94, and .58, indicating some discrepancy between the sorting methods in the three-dimensional configuration. Interpreting the three-dimensional configurations obtained from the two sorting methods in terms of the semantic differential, Wing and Nelson (1972) concluded that their method of sorting decreased the orthogonality between potency and activity.

In another study, Davison (1972) also compared trait structures obtained from restricted and unrestricted sorting. In Davison's study, the subjects in the unrestricted sorting condition were permitted to use each trait term up to five times. In both conditions, subjects performed the sorting task three times (multiple sort, essentially) by describing a different set of persons each time. Thirty trait names, selected so as to be uniformly distributed in the two-dimensional space shown in Fig. 7.5, were used as stimuli.

Davison obtained multidimensional configurations (one- through five-dimensional spaces) of the 30 traits from each of the two sets of sorting data. He used canonical correlation to compare these two sets of configurations. The results of the canonical analysis are summarized in Table 7.6.

The table shows that the two sorting methods yielded one significant canonical correlation for the one-, two-, three-, and four-dimensional configurations, and two significant correlations for the five-dimensional configurations. In short, the two methods of sorting apparently yield quite different trait structures. The lack of similarity is particularly striking in view of the fact that canonical analysis permits a nonuniform stretching and shrinking of the dimensions in one configuration to obtain a best fit with a second configuration.

This result is at variance with the Wing and Nelson (1972) finding. There are differences between the two studies in the procedure and trait samples that were used. The two studies also differ in the distance measure that was used as input for multidimensional scaling; whereas Wing and Nelson (1972) adjusted their measure to take into account the frequency of use of each trait, Davison (1972) did not. Which of the differences in design and analysis between the two studies might account for the contradictory findings cannot be ascertained from the

TABLE 7.6
Canonical Correlations Between Multidimensional Configurations
Obtained from Restricted and Unrestricted Sorting Data
(From Davison, 1972)

	1	2	3	4	5
First canonical r	.92*	.94*	.95*	.97*	.97*
Second canonical r		.02	.46	.66	.85*
Third canonical r			.04	.26	.57
Fourth canonical r				.04	.34
Fifth canonical r					.03

$*p < .05$

material available in these two research reports. It should also be noted, in this connection, that Davison compared the two sorting methods with direct similarity judgments, a comparison that is taken up in the next section. Suffice it to say at this point, the restricted sorting yielded a structure quite similar to similarity judgments (at least up through three dimensions), whereas unrestricted sorting did not. The question that this raises is whether the unrestricted sorting data (and their analyses) in Davison's study are somehow a fluke.

EMPIRICAL COMPARISONS OF SORTING WITH OTHER METHODS

We have seen that certain variations in sorting method can produce differences in the resulting structures. The methodological issue to which we turn in this final section of the chapter are the similarities and differences between structures obtained from sorting and those obtained from the more traditional multivariate methods. We will take up four empirical comparisons: one with kinship terms, two with trait terms, and one with facial photographs as the stimulus objects.

In an empirical test of their componential model of kinship terms, Romney and D'Andrade (1964) used the method of triads with eight of the 15 kinship terms discussed earlier in this chapter. Although they were interested in the componential structure of all 15 kinship terms, their triads data were limited to judgments among the seven male terms plus *cousin*. Their rationale for using this reduced set is twofold: (1) the structure for male terms parallels that for female terms; (2) the number of possible triads $[n! \div 3! (n - 3)!]$ for 15 kinship terms is 455, and only 56 for eight terms.

In order to compare the triads method with the sorting method, a Pearson r was computed between the 28 proximities they reported among the eight kinship terms (Romney & D'Andrade, 1964, Table 6) and the corresponding 28 frequencies of non-co-occurrence in Table 7.2 of this chapter. The r between these two sets of data is $-.85$ (the Spearman r is $-.88$). Although a more detailed comparison between the multidimensional structures obtained from the two methods might reveal some subtle differences between them, the magnitude of the overall correlation strongly suggests that they would be quite similar. Also, their use of only the male terms and *cousin* in the triads test precludes a determination of whether the sex dimension is used by subjects who are given the triads method, as was the case with multiple-sort—or tends to be suppressed, as was the case with single-sort.

Two studies in the area of personality perception included direct comparisons of the sorting method with other methods. The first study (Rosenberg & Olshan, 1970) provided a comparison of trait sorting with trait inference, which is essentially an asymmetric pairwise judgment. The second study (Davison, 1972) provided a comparison of each of two trait-sorting methods (restricted and unrestricted) with pairwise co-occurrence judgments.

In the Rosenberg and Olshan (1970) study, subjects sorted a set of 60 trait adjectives gleaned from an earlier study by Peabody (1967). Peabody's subjects had made trait inferences among these trait terms. The trait-inference approach is a widely used method in person perception and appears in several different formats. The format used by Peabody (1967) is illustrated with the following example:

A person is *cautious*. To what extent is he likely to be:

bold	___:	___:	___:	___:	___:	___:	___: *timid?*
inhibited	___:	___:	___:	___:	___:	___:	___: *uninhibited?*
self-controlled	___:	___:	___:	___:	___:	___:	___: *impulsive?*
serious	___:	___:	___:	___:	___:	___:	___: *frivolous?*
gay	___:	___:	___:	___:	___:	___:	___: *grim?*

and so on.

Using Peabody's trait-inference data, Rosenberg and Olshan (1970) calculated a profile distance for each pair of traits. That is, for any two traits, i and j, in the sentence stem "A person is _____", the subjects' mean rating of i was subtracted from their mean rating of j on each of the bipolar scales; each difference was then squared, and the sum of the squared differences was used as a measure of the dissimilarity of i and j, that is, as the input measure for multidimensional scaling.

Rosenberg and Olshan (1970) used a canonical analysis to compare the three-dimensional solution obtained from Peabody's trait-inference data with that obtained from their sorting data. Canonical correlations between the two spaces were .96, .93, and .90. The magnitude of these correlations attest to the utility of the sorting method as an equivalent alternative to the traditional trait-inference method for obtaining multidimensional trait structures.

In the Davison (1972) study, cited earlier for its empirical comparison of restricted and unrestricted sorting, these two sorting methods were also compared with pairwise co-occurrence judgments. Subjects assigned to do the pairwise judgments received a list of all possible pairs of the 30 trait names used as the stimuli in Davison's study. For each pair of terms, the subjects were asked to estimate the proportion of people who would possess both traits. This procedure essentially parallels the method of pairwise similarity judgments, but with a co-occurrence instruction.

Davison obtained multidimensional configurations (one through five dimensions) of the 30 traits from the aggregated pairwise judgments of his sample of subjects. He compared these five configurations with those obtained from each of the two sorting methods, using canonical analysis. The results of these analyses are summarized in Table 7.7.

First, the table shows that restricted sorting yields structures much more similar to the pairwise judgments than does unrestricted sorting. As already noted in the previous section, there is some question about whether Davison's unrestricted sorting data might be aberrant in some way.

TABLE 7.7
Canonical Correlations Between Multidimensional Configurations
Obtained from Pairwise Similarity Judgments and A. Restricted Sorting,
B. Unrestricted Sorting
(From Davison, 1972)

Part A: Pairwise judgments versus restricted sorting					
	1	2	3	4	5
First canonical r	.95*	.97*	.98*	.98*	.99*
Second canonical r		.70*	.81*	.87*	.89*
Third canonical r			.53*	.75*	.82*
Fourth canonical r				.01	.24
Fifth canonical r					.08
Part B: Pairwise judgments versus unrestricted sorting					
	1	2	3	4	5
First canonical r	.87*	.90*	.91*	.93*	.95*
Second canonical r		.04	.13	.27	.40
Third canonical r			.04	.14	.19
Fourth canonical r				.04	.14
Fifth canonical r					.14

*$p < .05$

Turning, then, to the relation between restricted sorting and pairwise judgments, we note that the two sets of resulting structures are similar up through three dimensions. However, the magnitude of the canonical r's, particularly the second and third ones, are not as large as those obtained by Rosenberg and Olshan (1970) in their comparison of sorting and trait inference. The lack of relationship in Davison's data beyond three dimensions may reflect the possibility that genuine differences in structure are produced in higher dimensionality by the two methods, or simply that the additional dimensionality in one or both sets of structures is noise.

The final study to be taken up in this section involved the use of photographs of faces as stimuli (Drasgow, 1976). This investigator asked his subjects to sort the photographs of 60 faces (30 white males and 30 black males) into groups "such that all the faces within a group are similar to each other and dissimilar to faces in any other group."

Three different subsets of these 60 faces had previously been scaled by Jones and Wiggins (1975), using pairwise similarity judgments. Drasgow (1976) compared each of the three multidimensional configurations based on the pairwise judgments with a six-dimensional configuration obtained from the sorting data. His method of analysis was directed at the question of the degree to which a multidimensional structure based on sorting predicts one based on the pairwise judgments. To answer this question, Drasgow computed a multiple correlation for each dimension in the Jones and Wiggins configurations with the six dimen-

TABLE 7.8
Multiple Correlations Obtained by Predicting Configurations Based on
Pairwise Similarity Judgments with a Configuration Based on Sorting Data
(From Drasgow, 1976)

Dimension No. in MDS based on pairwise judgments.	Subset of 18 Faces	Subset of 19 White Faces	Subset of 19 Black Faces
I	.95*	.56	.87*
II	.54	.83*	.91*
III	.88*	.92*	.63
IV	.91*	.82*	.69
V	.40	.52	.74
VI	.62	–	–

*p < .05

sions in the sorting configuration serving as the independent dimensions. The results are summarized in Table 7.8.

In general, two to three dimensions in the configurations based on pairwise judgments are highly predictable from sorting—in all cases, the more salient of the dimensions underlying the pairwise judgments. This mode of analysis casts the pairwise judgments as "criterial," so that dimensions that might emerge from sorting but not pairwise judgments are not detected. Using other analyses, Drasgow noted that one of the dimensions that appeared in the sorting data, but not the pairwise judgment data, was evaluation.

There is as yet a paucity of studies that compare sorting with other data-gathering methods and the studies summarized in this section comprise most of extant ones. Although small in number, the studies reviewed above span a wide range of stimulus domains and all of them point to the same conclusion. There is a substantial commonality between a structure obtained from sorting with one obtained from one of the more traditional methods. The differences that do exist between data-gathering methods may be due to the ability of one method to capture a dimension (or two) not captured by the other. It seems clear, particularly from one of Drasgow's (1976) findings cited previously, that a traditional multivariate method such as pairwise judgments is not necessarily more comprehensive than sorting in tapping all the dimensions underlying the perception of a stimulus domain.

CONCLUDING REMARKS

The applications of sorting reviewed in this chapter demonstrate that this method can produce highly meaningful data for clustering and multidimensional scaling. Moreover, the variants of sorting that were described would seem to provide the researcher with a choice that is particularly suitable to the substantive domain under investigation. As we also saw, however, sorting is not the ideal data-gathering tool for all possible structures. Nor is it suggested that sorting completely replace the more traditional multivariate methods, because it would be unrealistic to expect any particular data-gathering method to extract all the psychological structure implicit in a set of stimulus objects.

The method of sorting undoubtedly owes a share of its initial popularity to the simplicity with which it can be employed, particularly for the multivariate analysis of relatively large numbers of objects. Sustained interest in the method, however, is likely to rest on the continued demonstration of its ability to generate data that are as rich as those provided by other, more laborious methods. Finally, the method of sorting complements in multivariate research the well-established method of object sorting used in the study of cognition and perception.

ACKNOWLEDGMENTS

This chapter was written during the author's 1978 sabbatical sponsored by the Rutgers University Faculty Academic Study Program. The writing of this chapter was also supported, in part, by NSF Grant BNS 76-10675 and BNS 79-06853.

REFERENCES

Abelson, R. P., & Sermat, V. Multidimensional scaling of facial expressions. *Journal of Experimental Psychology,* 1962, *63,* 546–554.

Anderberg, M. R. *Clustering analysis for applications.* New York: Academic Press, 1973.

Anglin, J. M. *The growth of word meaning.* Cambridge, Mass.: MIT Press, 1970.

Bohannan, P., & Middleton, J. (Eds.). *Kinship and social organization.* Garden City, N.Y.: Natural History Press, 1968.

Bricker, P. E., & Pruzansky, S. *A comparison of sorting and pairwise similarity judgment techniques for scaling auditory stimuli.* Unpublished research report, Bell Telephone Labs, Murray Hill, N.J., 1970.

Bruner, J. S., Goodnow, J. J., & Austin, G. A. *A study of thinking.* New York: Wiley, 1956.

Burton, M. Semantic dimensions of occupation names. In A. K. Romney, R. N. Shepard, & S. Nerlove (Eds.), *Multidimensional scaling: Theory and applications in the behavioral sciences* (Vol. 2). New York: Seminar Press, 1972.

Carroll, J. D. Spatial, non-spatial and hybrid models for scaling. *Psychometrika,* 1976, *41,* 439–464.

Carroll, J. D., & Chang, J. J. Analysis of individual differences in multidimensional scaling via an *N*-way generalization of "Eckart-Young" decomposition. *Psychometrika,* 1970, *35,* 283–319.

Carroll, J. D., & Chang, J. J. A method for fitting a class of hierarchical tree structure models to dissimilarities data and its applications to some "body parts" data of Miller's. *Proceedings of the 81st Annual Convention of the American Psychological Association,* 1973, *8,* 1097–1098. (Summary)

Clark, H. H. On the use and meaning of prepositions. *Journal of Verbal Learning and Verbal Behavior,* 1968, *7,* 421–431.

Davison, M. L. *An empirical comparison of card sorting and paired comparisons judgments as methods for gathering data in a multidimensional scaling study: An exploratory study.* Unpublished master's thesis, University of Illinois, 1972.

Drasgow, F. *Subjective grouping as a method for the multidimensional scaling of faces.* Unpublished master's thesis, University of Illinois, 1976.

Drasgow, F., & Jones, L. E. Multidimensional scaling of derived dissimilarities. *Multivariate Behavioral Research,* 1979, *14,* 227–244.

Fillenbaum, S., & Rapoport, A. *Structure in the subjective lexicon.* New York: Academic Press, 1971.

Friendly, M., & Glucksberg, S. On description of subcultural lexicons: A multidimensional approach. *Journal of Personality and Social Psychology,* 1970, *14,* 55–65.

Johnson, S. C. Hierarchical clustering schemes. *Psychometrika,* 1967, *32,* 241–254.

Jones, L. E., & Wiggins, N. *What's in a face? Individual differences in facial perception.* Paper presented at meeting of the American Psychological Associaton, Chicago, 1975.

Jones, R. A., & Ashmore, R. D. The structure of intergroup perception: Categories and dimensions in views of ethnic groups and adjectives used in stereotype research. *Journal of Personality and Social Psychology,* 1973, *25,* 428–489.

Kim, M. *The meaning of kinship terms: A psychological approach.* Unpublished master's thesis, 1973.

Miller, G. A. Psycholinguistic approaches to the study of communication. In D. L. Arm (Ed.), *Journeys into science: Small steps—great strides.* Albuquerque: University of New Mexico Press, 1967.

Miller, G. A. Alegebraic models in psycholinguistics. In C. A. J. Vlek (Ed.), *Algebraic models in psychology.* Proceedings of the NUFFIC International Summer Session at "Het Oude Hof," The Hague, 1968.

Miller, G. A. A psychological method to investigate verbal concepts. *Journal of Mathematical Psychology,* 1969, *6,* 169–191.

Miller, J. E., Shepard, R. N., & Chang, J. J. An analytic approach to the interpretation of multidimensional scaling solutions. *American Psychologist,* 1964, *19,* 579–580. (Abstract)

Napior, D. Nonmetric multidimensional techniques for summated ratings. In R. N. Shepard, A. K. Romney, & S. B. Nerlove (Eds.), *Multidimensional scaling: Theory and applications in the behavioral sciences* (Vol. 1). New York: Seminar Press, 1972.

Peabody, D. Trait inferences: Evaluative and descriptive aspects. *Journal of Personality and Social Psychology,* 1967, *7*(4, Whole No. 644).

Romney, A. K., & D'Andrade, R. G. Cognitive aspects of English kin terms. *American Anthropologist,* 1964, *66,* No. 3, part 2 (special publication), 146–170.

Rosch, E. Human categorization. In N. Warren (Ed.), *Advances in cross-cultural psychology* (Vol. 1). London: Academic Press, 1977.

Rosenberg, S. New approaches to the analysis of personal constructs in person perception. In *Nebraska Symposium on Motivation* (Vol. 24). Lincoln: University of Nebraska Press, 1977.

Rosenberg, S., & Cohen, B. D. A method for the study of lay conceptions of psychopathology: A free-response approach. *American Journal of Community Psychology,* 1977, *5,* 177–193.

Rosenberg, S., & Kim, M. J. The method of sorting as a data-gathering procedure in multivariate research. *Multivariate Behavioral Research,* 1975, *10,* 489–502.

Rosenberg, S., Nelson, C., & Vivekananthan, P. S. A multidimensional approach to the structure of personality impressions. *Journal of Personality and Social Psychology,* 1968, *9,* 283–294.

Rosenberg, S., & Olshan, K. Evaluative and descriptive aspects in personality perception. *Journal of Personality and Social Psychology,* 1970, *16,* 619–626.

Rosenberg, S., & Sedlak, A. Structural representations of implicit personality theory. In L. Berkowitz (Ed.), *Advances in experimental social psychology* (Vol. 6). New York: Academic Press, 1972.

Schmidt, C. F. Multidimensional scaling analysis of the printed media's explanations of the riots of the summer of 1967. *Journal of Personality and Social Psychology,* 1972, *24,* 59-67.

Sedlak, A. *A multidimensional study of the structure of personality descriptions.* Unpublished master's thesis, Rutgers University, 1971.

Shepard, R. N. Psychological representation of speech sounds. In E. E. David & P. B. Denes (Eds.), *Human communication: A unified view,* New York: McGraw-Hill, 1972.

Sherman, R. Individual differences in perceived trait relationships as a function of dimensional salience. *Multivariate Behavioral Research,* 1972, *7,* 109-129.

Sneath, P. H. A., & Sokal, R. R. *Numerical taxonomy.* San Francisco: Freeman, 1973.

Steinberg, D. D. The word sort: An instrument for semantic analysis. *Psychonomic Science,* 1967, *12,* 541-542.

Stringer, P. Cluster analysis of non-verbal judgments of facial expressions. *The British Journal of Mathematical and Statistical Psychology,* 1967, *20,* 71-79.

Torgerson, W. S. *Theory and methods of scaling.* New York: Wiley, 1958.

Torgerson, W. S. Multidimensional scaling of similarity, *Psychometrika,* 1965, *30,* 379-393.

Vygotsky, L. S. *Thought and language.* New York: Wiley, 1962.

Wallace, A. F. C., & Atkins, J. The meaning of kinship terms. *American Anthropologist,* 1960, *62,* 58-80.

Werner, H. *Comparative psychology of mental development.* New York: International Universities Press, 1957.

Wexler, K. N., & Romney, A. K. Individual variations in cognitive structures. In A. K. Romney, R. N. Shepard, & S. B. Nerlove (Eds.), *Multdimensional scaling: Theory and applications in the behavioral sciences* (Vol. 2). New York: Seminar Press, 1972.

Wing, H., & Nelson, C. The perception of personality through trait sorting: A comparison of trait sampling techniques. *Multivariate Behavioral Research,* 1972, *7,* 269-274.

Wish, M., Deutsch, M., & Biener, L. Differences in perceived similarity of nations. In A. K. Romney, R. N. Shepard, & S. Nerlove (Eds.), *Multidimensional scaling: Theory and applications in the behavioral sciences.* (Vol. 2). New York: Seminar Press, 1972.

8
Attraction
and Conversational Style

Gerald L. Clore
Stuart M. Itkin
University of Illinois Champaign

We once met a person who talked about herself incessantly. She was bright, friendly, and attractive, but she was not liked by others as much as her considerable assets would have led one to expect. We attributed this regrettable truth to her tendency to fill conversations with details about her own thoughts, feelings, and activities, rarely pausing to ask anyone about themselves. The experiment discussed here (Clore, Itkin, & McGuire, 1980) was designed in part with her in mind.

At the time the research was conducted, a number of students and colleagues were interested in behavior modification. Moreover, we had written often about the importance of rewards in attraction. The project, then, began with the question—can one modify another person's conversational behavior to make that person more rewarding and hence more liked? Accordingly, we arranged a series of two-person conversations in which the participants were instructed to adopt different strategies.

Although the project began as a behavioristically oriented study, by the time we reached the data analysis stage, the focus had changed. In the process of listening to the taped conversations and coding them, we were impressed by the richly joined nature of conversations. The term *richly joined* is borrowed from Heider (who in turn borrowed it from Ashby's 1960 book, *Design for a Brain*). Explaining the term, Heider (1967) writes: "In opposition to the environment of solid, everyday things . . . our social environment . . . is usually a system that is richly-joined. In a group of people the change of a single variable, e.g., one person behaving in a certain way, may very well bring about changes in every one of the other members of the group, and, what is more, not the same change in each one [pp. 25–26]." Heider goes on to argue that despite this complexity, the meaning of everyday social events is easily grasped by the participants. This is true because our thought systems are as richly joined as the social event. Unfortunately the results of psychological research rarely offer us the same clear understanding that our everyday perception does. One reason is that the most commonly used techniques for data analysis allow us to represent social events in only a piecemeal and oversimplified fashion. The events analyzed here, for example, were a series of conversations, each involving two persons who took different conversational roles. We felt that the analyses of these data only at the level of single behaviors and single roles in isolation did not capture their richly joined nature. Therefore, we have reanalyzed Clore, Itkin, & McGuire's (1980) data in a three-mode factor analysis (Tucker, 1964, 1966).

Three-mode factor analysis provided an attractive alternative because it allowed us to study whole conversations as well as individual roles and behaviors. Applied to these data, the three-mode technique detected homogeneous types of conversations that were defined in terms of the dimensions of conversational behavior displayed by each partner. The goal of the analyses reported here, then, was to ask what conversation types emerged, what styles defined them, and what affective concomitants they showed.

Previous Research

The research literature on conversations is a large and diverse one belonging to no single discipline or theoretical point of view. Among the more common topics are studies of the effects of verbal style on perceptions of leaders (Bales, 1970) and therapists (Kleinke & Tully, 1979). The aspects of conversations that stimulate personal self-disclosure have also been a very popular topic (Jourard & Jaffee, 1970). The literature includes papers reporting the development of different scoring systems for verbal behavior (Bales, 1970; Borgatta & Crowther, 1965, Gottman, Markman, & Notarius, 1977; Whalen, 1969) and nonverbal behavior (Duncan & Fiske, 1977; Hall, 1963; Mehrabian, 1972). There are also a number of psychologists, sociologists, and others engaged in the microanalysis of stages within conversations. Schegloff (1968), for example, has studied sequencing in conversational openings, and Duncan and Niederehe (1974) treat the ways in which auditors signal their readiness to take a speaking turn.

More relevant to our current focus are studies of interpersonal attraction and conversational style. For example, Jourard (1971) maintained that intimate self-disclosure fosters liking, and some research has supported that hypothesis (Jourard & Friedman, 1970; Worthy, Gary, & Kahn, 1969). Other investigators, however, have reported either no relationship between disclosure and attraction (Derlega, Walmer, & Furman, 1973; Ehrlich & Graeven, 1971) or a curvilinear relationship (Cozby, 1972). Presumably whether self-disclosure leads to liking depends on the level of disclosure involved and its perceived appropriateness in the particular social situation studied.

Another variable studied in relation to attraction has been overall activity level. Fiske (1974), for example, found at least preliminary evidence that observers assign positive traits to more active participants in conversations. Others have reported a curvilinear relationship. Bales (1970), for example, found that the most liked group members were not the first but the second or third most frequent initiators of interaction. His observation was tested by Stang (1973) and also by Kleinke, Kahn, and Tully (1976), who found that observers were most attracted to persons who talked an intermediate amount. These studies are relevant to the present experiment where we studied the effects of talking a lot about one's self versus asking one's partners about themselves.

A somewhat offbeat contribution to this literature was made by John Kenneth Galbraith (1962) who published a tongue in cheek story entitled "The McLandress Dimension." In the story, McLandress was a social scientist who had discovered an important social dimension and began making systematic measurements of public figures. The dimension was the amount of time in a person's conversation between self-references. A 60-minute McLandress coefficient, for example, would indicate that one's thoughts were diverted from one's self for intervals averaging an hour. The lowest value, a McLandress coefficient of only 3 seconds, was allegedly posted by Richard Nixon.

Although not exactly representative of the psychological research literature on conversations, Galbraith's dimension bears some similarity to the categories of "personal" and "impersonal self-disclosure," used in the study by Clore, Itkin, & McGuire (1980) to be discussed here. Together these two categories referred to the number of clauses (in a 5-minute conversation) involving a first-person pronoun. As indicated earlier, the project was inspired by an acquaintance whose conversations were single-mindedly about herself. The experiment was an attempt to study in a systematic way the effects of variations in self-reference versus question asking on attraction.

THE EXPERIMENT

Conversations

The data for the analyses reported in this chapter were from 36 undergraduate women who were paired off at random to get acquainted. They had a series of 5-minute conversations with different partners.

Prior to some of these conversations they received a page of instructions that asked them to adopt one of two strategies. They were either to find out as much as they could about their partners by asking questions (Q partners) or to impart as much information about themselves as possible (I partners). The instructions emphasized that the goal was simply for participants to have an enjoyable and informative conversation, and that they should attempt to carry out their instructions only as the natural flow of the conversation allowed them to do so. Participants were unaware of what instructions their partners had.

In the conversations included in the three-mode analysis, the two partners always had different instructions; that is, an *I* partner always conversed with a *Q* partner. Each subject served once in each role; therefore, each had one conversation in which she was oriented toward asking questions of her partner, who talked about herself, and a second conversation in which she was oriented toward talking about herself with a partner who asked questions. These two types of conversations were among a total of six in which each subject participated. The other four consisted of two natural or uninstructed conversations (which we shall refer to again) and two in which both partners were instructed either to talk about themselves or to ask questions.

Attraction Measure

After each conversation, participants were asked to respond to six seven-place scales. A factor analysis suggested that four of these formed an attraction factor: (1) how willing they were to accept the other person as a possible roommate; (2) how much they enjoyed the conversation; (3) how much they felt the other person enjoyed the conversation; and (4) in general, how much they liked the other person. The sum of these items constituted the attraction measure.

Coding Conversational Style

The study was primarily concerned with the effect on attraction of telling about one's self versus asking about one's partner, but the coding system included 10 categories of verbal behavior. Some of the categories were adapted from the systems used by Linquist and Rappaport (1973) and Whalen (1969) in studies of self-disclosure. Unlike their coding schemes, however, this one was not an exhaustive system. Only utterances that fit scoring categories of interest were scored. The 10 conversation categories counted were: (1) Similarity Statements; (2) Dissimilarity Statements; (3) Positive Responses; (4) Negative Responses; (5) Personal Self-Disclosure; (6) Impersonal Self-Disclosures; (7) Affective Expressions; (8) Questions; (9) Positive Self-References; (10) Negative Self-References. The categories are defined with examples in Table 8.1.

Two coders scored each partner's utterances independently and without knowledge of the instructional conditions in which their subjects served. They were instructed to code each independent clause that fit the categories. Rather than transcribe the conversations, scorers coded conversations as the tape recorder proceeded at its normal pace. Scorers were, however, free to call for as many replays of parts of the tape as they needed.

One consequence of coding the conversations directly from the tapes rather than transcribing them first was an inevitable decrease in interrater reliability. In addition to the effects of disagreements about the proper categorization of a given

TABLE 8.1
Categories of Conversational Behavior
(from Clore, Itkin, & McGuire, Note 1)

Category	Criteria and Examples
1. Similarity Statements	Agreements, similar experiences, indications of feeling the same or different about a person, event, or idea. "I live in a dorm" (when partner has already indicated she lives in a dorm), "I don't like him either," "me too."
2. Dissimilarity Statements	Disagreements, statements of oppositeness, differentness, or having had a contrary experience. "No, that's not really true," "I've never been there," "I don't know him."
3. Positive Responses	Any positive response not scored as similarity. Includes brief conversational facilitators such as "Yeah," "Really?", "Outta sight!", "Sure." Statements of understanding such as "I see." Also laughter when appropriate.
4. Negative Responses	Any negative response not scored as Dissimilarity. Includes failures to answer a question, silence where a response is called for, indications of disbelief or of not getting the speaker's point. "I don't see what you mean," "Well, sort of," or "Well, I suppose" (indicating only marginal assent).
5. Personal Self-Disclosures	Information or feelings that are nonpublic and are not ordinarily volunteered. Should be interpersonal in nature or of some psychological significance, thus, "I like psychology" is not disclosing. Examples might include, "I'm a status-seeker like a lot of people," "I might try homosexuality," "I can't get along with my roommate." Includes disclosures about others close to speaker, "My sister dates a married man."
6. Impersonal Self-Disclosures	Biographical information about oneself that is readily volunteered by most people. Must be focused on the person who speaks them. "My parents are from Peoria," "I think the snow is going to melt." Impersonal disclosures that do not include self-references are not scored. All self-referent statements are in either #6 or #5.
7. Affective Expressions	Statements concerning emotions, evaluative statements with definite feeling. "It was terrible," "I hate introductory psychology," "They loved it." Statements without emotional words are not scored. Affective statements including a personal referent to the speaker are scored as #5 or #6 as well as #7.
8. Questions	Any questions ("What is your name?" "What's yours?" "Why?" "Don't you think so?") except rhetorical ones not intended to be answered. Some rhetorical examples are: "You know what I mean?", "Is that a face?".
9. Positive Self-References	Statements conferring status on self or associates. "I have been drunk every night for a week," "My boyfriend is a law student," "I'm going to Ft. Lauderdale over Easter."
10. Negative Self-References	Statements indicating shortcomings ("I don't date."), problems ("I get anxious on tests"), excuses ("I really don't know anything about politics"), but not simple statements of fact without a self-effacing emphasis ("I'm a freshman"). Any example of #9 or #10 must also be scored as either #5 or #6.

clause, reliability suffered whenever judges differed in the number of clauses into which they divided a given utterance.

Interrater reliabilities calculated separately on the totals of each of the 10 categories ranged from $r = .44$ (for negative self-references) to $r = .78$ (for questions) with a mean of $r = .60$. The final counts used for each category were the average of the counts given by the two scorers. The stability of the data analyzed, therefore, was higher than the reliabilities suggest.

RESULTS

The analyses to be discussed were focused on three different kinds of questions: (1) the three-mode factor analysis looked at differences among types of conversations, and two sets of regression analysis considered; (2) the importance of the behavior of the person rated versus the behavior of the rater herself; and (3) the role of individual differences among persons in their natural conversational styles. We discuss the three-mode analysis first. It was especially useful as a way of representing individual differences in conversational style. To apply the three-mode model to this conversation data, however, required a couple of variations on the usual procedure. The variations, as we shall see, were: (1) to leave one of the three modes unfactored; and (2) to add the attraction variable as an extra unfactored dimension in one mode of the core matrix.

Three-Mode Factor Analysis

Three-mode factor analysis (Tucker, 1964; 1966) involves a principal components analysis for the data in each mode. In general, decisions about the number of components to be retained and the appropriate rotation for each mode are handled exactly as in the more familiar one-mode case. Once these operations are complete, the core matrix is computed and rotated. The core matrix is a matrix of factor loadings that provides a succinct description of the interaction of the factors from the three modes. The loadings from the three-mode core matrix might be thought of as serving the same function as the means from a three-way analysis of variance—both provide the user with a description of how the three source variables interact. In our case we wanted the analysis to reduce the total sample of conversations to a small number of "prototypical conversations" or conversation factors. These "prototypical conversations" would then represent (through their interaction with behavior and role factors) the distinctive styles that occurred in the conversations.

The analysis began with a matrix of data arrayed as conversations ($i = 36$) × roles of participant ($j = 2$) × conversational behaviors ($k = 10$). The 10 behavior categories were first standardized around their respective means. The data were further standardized over conversation and role. A three-mode factor analysis (Tucker, 1966) was performed on this matrix, and the principal eigenvectors for the conversation and behavior modes were examined.

The Conversation Mode (i)

In the usual case, subjects make up the individual differences (i) mode of a three-mode analysis. The strategy of using conversations rather than subjects in the individual differences mode was chosen to obtain a sufficiently large sample of independent observations for analysis. A plot of the eigenvalues suggested a five-factor solution, which accounted for 60% of the variance. To maximize interpretability, the five conversation factors were subjected to a varimax rotation (Kaiser, 1958).

The Role Mode (j)

The data for the three-mode analysis were conversations in which subjects had identifiable and distinct roles. These included two sets totaling 36 conversations in which one subject was instructed to talk about herself (I) and one was instructed to ask questions (Q). Because only these two roles were included, the j mode was not factored.

Having role as a variable allowed us to think of subjects as crossed with conversations rather than as nested within conversations, as would otherwise have been the case. Also, most correlational procedures, including factor analysis, require one to specify which entry goes in the x column and which in the y column. Without identifiable roles, there would have been no way to make that specification. An arbitrary assignment could be employed, but the results could be understood only relative to that assignment.

The Behavior Mode (k)

The 10 behavior coding scores, obtained by classifying what the participants said, made up the behavior (k) mode. A plot of the eigenvalues suggested retaining four or five factors. Solutions of from three through six factors were considered, and ultimately a varimax rotation (Kaiser, 1958) of the four-factor solution was chosen on the ground of apparent psychological meaningfulness. The four factors accounted for 61% of the variance. The loadings of the 10 conversational behavior variables on the varimax-rotated factors are shown in Table 8.2. We labeled the factors on the basis of the pattern of high loadings.

Factor 1 was labeled *Punishment,* because only the "negative responses" category loaded highly on it. Factor 2 was labeled *Reward,* and the categories loading highly were "similarity statements," "positive responses," and "negative self-references." Factor 3 was labeled *Personal Differentiation.* A pattern of

TABLE 8.2
Principal Components Analysis of Conversational Behavior Mode
(Showing Loadings over .30) after Varimax Rotation

	Components			
	1	*2*	*3*	*4*
				Self-References versus
			Personal	*Questions*
Behavior	*Punishment*	*Reward*	*Differentiation*	*(I vs. Q)=*
Negative Responses	.91			
Positive Responses		.43		
Similarity Statements		.71		
Dissimilarity Statements			.76	
Negative Self-References		.47	-.38	
Positive Self-References				.35
Personal Self-Disclosures			.51	.31
Impersonal Self-Disclosures				.49
Affective Expressions				.45
Questions				-.43

positive loadings for "dissimilarity statements" and "personal self-disclosures" along with a negative loading for "negative self-references" seemed to describe a concern for differentiating oneself from the partner and disclosing personal material without being self-effacing. Factor 4 was called *Self-References versus Questions*. "Impersonal self-disclosures," "affective expressions," "positive self-references," and "personal self-disclosures" all loaded positively, whereas "questions" loaded negatively. Thus, positive values on Factor 4 indicated relatively more self-references, and negative values indicated relatively more questions. The four conversational behavior factors, then, were referred to as "Punishment," "Reward," "Personal Differentiation," and "Self-references versus Questions."

The Core Matrix with Attraction Added

The rotated core matrix[1] is based on the five rotated conversation factors and the four rotated behavior factors. Role of participant *j* was not factored. In order to

---

[1]Tucker (1966) states that the relationship between the raw data matrix and the core matrix is as shown in Equation 1.

$$_mC_{pq} = [I(I^1I)^{-1}]^1{}_i R_{jk}[K(K^1K)^{-1}J(J^1J)^{-1}]$$

where

   C is the core matrix ($m \times p \times q$)
   R is the raw data matrix ($i \times j \times k$)

relate attraction to conversational style, attraction scores were first zero centered around the scale midpoint and then were added to the core matrix as a fifth factor in the behavior mode k.[2] The final core matrix appears in Table 8.3.

Prototypical Conversations

The individual differences factors in three-mode studies are often called "idealized" or "prototypical individuals." The individual differences factors in the present study were referred to as "prototypical conversations." The five prototypical conversations are shown in the core matrix defined in terms of the role variable and their distinctive patterns of behavior. The interpretation of the core matrix that follows is based on a visual comparison of the relative sizes of the loadings in the prototypical conversations from Table 8.3.

Conversation 1 (Punishment).   The most distinctive stylistic feature of this *conversation* type is that the partners traded punishments with each other (Factor 1). In no other conversation do we find any substantial loadings on the Punishment factor. Perhaps as a consequence, this was the only conversation type in which the partners strongly disliked each other (Attraction factor).

Conversation 2 (Moderation).   The most distinctive aspect of Conversation Type 2 is its undistinctiveness. The loadings of both partners were middle-ranked on most of the factors, including how much they liked each other. In addition, more than their counterparts in other conversations, the Q partner avoided giving punishing responses (Factor 1) to the answers she got from her partner, and the I partner avoided being personal and self-differentiating (Factor 3) in what she said.

I is the matrix of conversation mode eigenvectors ($i \times m$)
J is the matrix of role mode eigenvectors ($j \times p$)
K is the matrix of behavior mode eigenvectors ($k \times q$)

The matrices I and k in Equation 1 are represented by the matrix of rotated conversation vectors (36×5) and the matrix of rotated behavior vectors (10×4), respectively. Because the J mode (roles) was left unfactored, matrix J is an identity matrix of Rank 2. Because both matrices I and K are orthonormal, the rotated core matrix can be more simply expressed as in Equation 2.

$$_m C_{pq} = I^1{}_i R_{jk}\, K \tag{2}$$

[2] Attraction scores were added to the raw data matrix, R, as an eleventh behavior, defining a new matrix, S, ($36 \times 2 \times 11$). A new (11×5) matrix, B, was defined by augmenting a column vector and a row vector to the matrix K such that the ($k + 1$), ($q + 1$) element was 1, and all other elements in row ($k + 1$) and column ($q + 1$) were 0. By substituting the matrices S and B into Equation 2, a rotated core matrix D was computed, which contained attraction as an additional factor in the k mode, as described in Equation 3.

$$_m D_{pq+1} = {}_m I^1_i \cdot {}_i S_{jk+1} \cdot {}_{k+1} B_{q+1} \tag{3}$$

TABLE 8.3
Core Matrix
from a Three-Mode Factor Analysis of Conversations, Roles, and Behaviors

		Behaviors				Attraction
		1	*2*	*3*	*4* Self-reference	*5* Rating*
Prototypical				*Personal*	*versus*	*Received*
Conversations	*Roles*	*Punishment*	*Reward*	*Differentiation*	*Questions*	*by Subject*
1 Punishing	I	6.07	-.78	1.35	-.04	-9.88
	Q	1.83	-.67	-.84	-.52	-8.06
2 Moderation	I	.94	3.46	-1.70	4.37	-.67
	Q	-1.57	1.04	-.63	-1.15	1.89
3 Personally	I	.10	-.47	7.29	3.71	-4.40
Differentiating	Q	-1.12	-1.63	2.21	-1.63	.85
4 Role equality	I	.81	-1.63	1.16	-.60	9.10
and Reward	Q	-.40	6.41	3.17	.07	3.31
5 Role defined	I	.35	-2.18	-.53	8.48	-.47
	Q	-1.23	1.86	-.66	-6.35	8.98

*Note: The attraction loadings that appear in a particular row refer to the ratings
received by that person. The same loading also refers to the ratings *given* by
that person's partner. Thus, the ratings in the *I*-partner's row were given by
the corresponding *Q*-partner and vice versa.

Conversation 3 (Personal Differentiation).   The most noticeable aspect of
Conservation type 3 is that the partners (especially the I partner) were high on
Personal Differentiation (Factor 3). This pattern (involving personal disclosures,
dissimilarity statements, and avoidance of negative self-references) did not result
in liking: the I partner was the second most disliked partner.

Conversation 4 (Role Equality and Reward).   Participants in Conversation
Type 4 did not take defined roles (Factor 4). Compared to other participants with
instructions to talk about herself, the *I* partner asked lots of questions. She scored
further toward the question-asking pole than any other *I* partner and was also the
most liked *I* partner. Perhaps as a consequence, the *Q* partner got to talk more
about herself than any other *Q* partner and liked this conversation most. She also
gave more rewarding responses than anyone else in the study and was well liked
in return. The combination of equality in conversational roles and the *Q* partner
being very rewarding was apparently a successful one; this was the only conversation type resulting in mutual attraction.

Conversation 5 (Role-defined).   Partners in this conversation type took the
most highly discrepant roles with respect to asking questions and telling about
themselves. They also gave each other the most discrepant attraction ratings. The
I partner, who was reacted to more or less neutrally, talked about herself more
than anyone else and gave fewer rewarding responses than anyone else. The *Q*

partner was the most liked person in the Q role and asked many more questions than any other subject. In addition, she avoided being punishing and was moderately rewarding in her responses.

Conclusions

These characterizations should give some idea of the homogeneous conversational types that occurred. With respect to the issue of speaking about self versus asking questions, prototypical Conversations 4 and 5 were the most informative. In Conversation 4, the partners did not take different roles. The person who had received self-reference instructions but who instead tended toward asking questions received the highest attraction ratings, and the person who gave that high rating was the Q partner who most got a chance to talk about herself. The participants in Conversation 5, by contrast, took strongly polarized roles, and the attraction ratings were similarly polarized. The Question asker was liked by the I partner, who got to talk a great deal about herself; but the Question asker, who hardly got to talk about herself at all, was neutral or mildly negative toward the I partner.

With respect to a general view of attraction, a summary of the most salient loadings from the core matrix indicates that: (1) the most punishing partner received the lowest attraction ratings; and (2) the most rewarding partner received high attraction ratings. (3) In the case of both Q partners and I partners, those who asked more questions than anyone else in their respective roles were also the most liked partners. This pattern suggests, as hypothesized by Clore, Itkin, and McGuire, (1980), that asking questions is an attractive conversational style.

ATTRACTION RATINGS GIVEN VERSUS RECEIVED

In their treatment of the conversations, Clore, Itkin, and McGuire pointed out an interesting feature of the data. They noted that one can correlate the attraction ratings with either of two sets of behaviors: they can be correlated with the behavior of the person receiving them (the *ratings received* data set) and they can be correlated with the behavior of the person giving them (the *ratings given* data set). These two ways of looking at the same ratings turn out to be useful, because they highlight different aspects of the attraction process.

Table 8.4 shows the weights obtained by Clore, Itkin, and McGuire (1980) from a series of multiple regression analyses predicting the attraction ratings given and received by the subjects in each conversational role. The results point to several conclusions relevant to information from the core matrix. Two of the four multiple regression equations yielded significant predictions of attraction ratings, one involving ratings received ($R = .50$, $F(4, 31) = 2.63$, $p = .05$) and

TABLE 8.4
Multiple Regression Analysis Predicting Attraction Ratings
Given and Received from Conversational Behavior
(from Clore, Itkin, & McGuire, 1980)

	Standardized Regression Weights Predicting:			
Behavior Factor	I's rating of A from Q's behavior	Q's rating of I from I's behavior	Q's rating of I from Q's behavior	I's rating of Q from I's behavior
1 Punishment	-.10	-.41**	.10	-.14
2 Reward	-.07	.00	.24	.10
3 Personal Differentiation	.26	.05	-.11	-.04
4 Self-References vs. Questions	-.16	-.29*	.44**	-.11
Multiple R predicting:	.32	.50**	.52**	.23
	ratings received		ratings given	

**p < .05
*p < .10

one involving ratings given ($R = .52$, $F(4, 31) = 2.80$, $p < .05$). Within these, the significant predictive variables (from the behavior mode of the three-mode analysis) included Punishments for ratings received [$B = .41$, $t(31) = 2.59$, $p < .05$] and Self-references for ratings given [$B = .44$, $t(31) = 2.84$, $p < .05$].

One interpretation of these weights would be that women were disliked (ratings received) when they responded to their partner in a punishing fashion, and that women liked their partners (ratings given) to the extent that they got a chance to talk about themselves. An additional factor that tended to lead to attraction (ratings received) was the extent to which women asked questions [$B = -.29$, $t(31) = 1.85$, $p < .10$].

From these predictor variables the prescription for becoming likable would be *to ask questions, (so that one's conversational partner gets to talk about herself) and to respond in a manner that is not punishing.* This interpretation of the results is especially compatible with the Reinforcement–Affect model of attraction (Clore & Byrne, 1974) and with the original hypothesis of the study.

The Effect of Conversational Role

A curious fact about the results in Table 8.4 is that attraction ratings were predictable only when made by the Q partner and not when made by the I partner. Q partners disliked I partners when they did not get to talk much about themselves and when I partners either responded in a punishing manner or talked too much about themselves. However, there was no such predictability of the ratings made by I partners.

In order to take a closer look, a graph was made of the relationship between scores on the Self-references versus Questions factor and attraction for each partner. The left panel of Fig. 1 shows the conversations categorized into four groups according to whether Q's attraction to her partner was greater or less than one standard deviation above or below the neutral point. The right panel shows the same groupings when based on I's attraction ratings. The ordinate in each case shows the respective Self-references versus Questions factor scores for each partner.

As shown in the left panel of the figure, extreme role separation on the Self-references versus Questions factor was associated with extreme dislike. This is seen in the left-hand panel where the diverging lines indicating extreme role adoption are seen for the most disliked conversation (- -).

The question of interest is why only Q-partners' attraction ratings showed strong relationships with the Self-references versus Questions factor. The answer lies partly in the effects of our instructions and partly in the notion that there is an optimal level of self-reference in conversations.

Instructions. First we compared the factor scores of the two instructional groups on the Self-references versus Questions factor. Nine I partners (compared to only two Q partners) scored more than a standard deviation above the midpoint of the factor in the self-reference direction. Conversely, 11 Q partners (but only two I partners) talked so little about themselves that they scored more than a standard deviation below the midpoint of the factor in the question-asking direc-

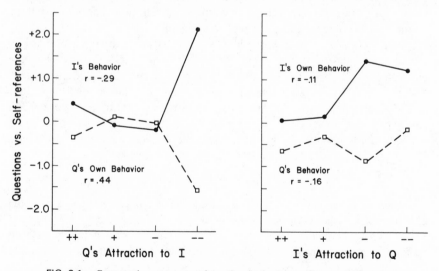

FIG. 8.1. Conversations are grouped (on the abscissa) according to whether attraction ratings given by Q-partners (left) and I-partners (right) were more or less than one standard deviation above or below the midpoint. The ordinate in both cases shows the respective Self-references versus Questions factor scores for each partner (From Clore, Itkin, & McGuire, 1980).

tion. The instructions, therefore, were quite effective; *I* partners were much more likely to be extreme in one direction and *Q* partners to be extreme in the other.

Optimality. The second ingredient in the explanation is the concept of optimality. At the beginning of the chapter we mentioned Galbreith's idea of the McLandress dimension. Implicit was the assumption that there is in public encounters an optimal level of self-preoccupation. The same truth seems to hold in these data: *There is an optimal level of self-reference in conversation below which the speaker will be unhappy and above which the listener will be unhappy.* This generalization explains the relationship pictured in the left panel of Fig. 8.1, in which conversations are grouped according to how much *Q* partners liked them. It shows that *Q* partners reacted with strong dislike when they (as speakers) heard more than they cared to about their partners. Because the instructions were effective, *Q* partners often found themselves in conversations where their role was unrewarding.

The pattern leading to dislike in the left panel of Fig. 8.1 (showing the ratings made by *Q* partners) is not seen in the right panel (showing the ratings made by *I* partners) for the following reason: *I* partners were not in the same predicament as *Q* partners because they were encouraged by the instructions to talk about themselves. They were, therefore, generally well above the minimum level of self-references necessary for their own satisfaction. Moreover, because *Q* partners were encouraged to ask questions rather than talk themselves, they were well below the maximum level of self-references that would have bored the *I* partner. Hence, when ratings were made by *I* partners, neither the *Q* partners, nor the *I* partners, Self-reference scores predicted attraction.

The pattern of the four relationships is explained, then, by the action of two factors: (1) a general desire to express oneself some minimum amount in the conversations; and (2) the fact that the instructions produced different distributions of scores on the Self-references versus Questions factor. As Clore, Itkin, and McGuire, point out, the same behavior is represented in the right and left panels of Fig. 8.1, but the points of view differ. The *I* partner was presumably not particularly bothered by her own self-preoccupation nor by the *Q*-partner's inability to get a word in. The effect of a given class of behavior on attraction depends on whose it is.

Causality. As can be seen in Fig. 8.1, the scores of the two partners on the Self-references versus Questions factor are inversely related ($r = -.58$, $p < .01$). To a remarkable extent, the *I*-partner's behavior appears in this figure to be a mirror image of the *Q*-partner's behavior. In other words, for the *I* partner to talk about herself depended in part on being asked questions by the *Q* partner, which may in turn have depended on the *I*-partner's responding with self-references.

With respect to the mirror-image aspect, the figure nicely illustrates what might be called the "embeddedness" of each partner's behavior. We can see that the conversations were "interpersonal" events in the sense in which Carson (1969), Leary (1957), or Sullivan (1953) use the term; each person's behavior depended on the other person's in a reciprocal system. It is not possible therefore to determine whether Q disliked her partner because she did not get to talk enough about herself or because her I partner bored her by talking too much about herself. Regardless of which of these views one prefers, both assume that variations in behavior caused variation in liking.

The opposite conclusion, that attraction caused behavior, also seems tenable at first. Perhaps attraction judgments were made implicitly in the first moments of the conversation so that conversational style reflected that prior liking rather than causing subsequent liking. If that were the case, however, one would have to conlcude that when Q partners initially disliked I partners, they expressed their dislike by asking questions of the I partner, who responded by talking about herself. This is clearly a less plausible scenario than the one based on the assumption that behavior caused liking.

INDIVIDUAL DIFFERENCES IN NATURAL STYLE

Recall that this project was inspired by an acquaintance who talked too much about herself. The instructions to ask questions were intended to modify the base rate of questions subjects asked and to make them more likable. Thus far we have described the conversation types that occurred and asked which behaviors were associated with attraction, but we still have not determined whether subjects' compliance with our instructions influenced how likable they were. To answer that question we again conducted multiple regression analyses predicting attraction from scores on the four factors of conversational behavior from the three-mode analysis. In this analysis, howerver, we included factor scores representing the natural conversational styles of the participants as obtained in the two uninstructed or base rate conversations.

As indicated earlier, each subject participated in other conversations in addition to the two included in the three-mode analysis. Two of these were intended to capture their natural styles. Thus, the predictors in these regression analyses were as follows: (1) *natural style* (mean scores from the two base-rate conversations on each of the four behavior factors; (2) *change* (scores in the instructed conversation minus the mean scores of the two base-rate conversations); and (3) the *interaction* between natural style and change.

Two multiple regression analyses were conducted, one for attraction ratings received in the I conversation and one for attraction ratings received in the Q conversation. Although the number of subjects is quite small for such an analysis, the multiple correlation for the Q conversations was significant ($R = .76$, $F(12, 22) = 2.55$, $p < .05$).

As can be seen in Table 8.5, the significant predictors included the natural style and interaction terms for the Self-references versus Questions factor. The negative beta weight for the natural style indicates that Q partners were liked to the extent that their natural style was to ask questions (negative values on the Self-references versus Questions factor indicated a tendency toward asking questions). But it is the significant weight for the interaction between the natural style and change that addresses the question of interest. The negative weight indicates that increases in question asking were related to high attraction ratings only for women whose natural style was to talk about themselves. For women who already asked questions naturally, the increase in question asking was related to low ratings. Thus, despite the fact that women with natural question-asking styles more liked overall, those with this style who also responded to the instructions by increasing their rate of question asking were not liked.

Whether instructions to ask questions in conversations is likely to benefit someone appears, therefore, to depend on that person's natural style. For the person who already asks questions, the instruction was counterproductive (although perhaps the suggestion would rarely be made to such a person). For persons like the self-absorbed acquaintance who stimulated our interest in the experiment, on the other hand, the instruction might well be beneficial.

TABLE 8.5

Beta Weights from Multiple Regression Analyses Predicting Attractiveness in Instructed Conversations from Natural Styles and Changes in Style

| | Criteria: | |
Predictors: Behavioral Factor Scores	Attractiveness in Self-reference Role (I)	Attractiveness in Question-asking Role (Q)
Natural Style		
Punishment	.12	-.05
Reward	.01	.33
Personal Differentiation	-.23	-.02
Self-references vs. Questions	-.24	-.53*
Change		
Punishment	-.11	-.10
Reward	-.14	-.45
Personal Differentiation	-.29	.15
Self-references vs. Questions	-.49*	-.31
Interaction (Natural Style x Change)		
Punishment	-.40	.02
Reward	-.06	.18
Personal Differentiation	-.14	.63**
Self-references vs. Questions	.14	-.45*
Multiple R	.64	.76*

$*p < .05$
$**p < .01$

The only other significant variable in the prediction of the Q-partner's attractiveness was the interaction term for the Personal Differentiation factor. The positive sign indicates that subjects were liked more to the extent that they accentuated their natural disclosure tendencies. This relationship indicates that increases in personal self-disclosure (that happened to be stimulated by the question-asking instruction) led to liking only when it was consistent with a subject's natural style. This complex relationship between self-disclosure and liking is consistent with the mixed results from other studies cited earlier in the chapter (Cozby, 1972; Derlega, Walmer, & Furman, 1973; Jourard & Friedman, 1970).

The multiple correlation predicting attraction received by the I partner was not significant, but a sizable (and significant) beta weight can be seen for changes in self-references. Consistent with our earlier analyses, it appears that the I partners who changed in the direction of making the most self-references tended not to be liked.

CONCLUSIONS

We began the chapter with a brief account of an acquaintance whose conversations contained an extraordinary number of self-references. The research was conceived as a sort of therapy analogue to see whether simply instructing participants to adopt certain conversational styles could alter their behavior and affect their attractiveness. The instructions were quite successful in changing behavior, and the hypothesis that question asking would be a rewarding style leading to attraction was supported.

The relationship between asking questions and being liked was not, however, as simple and straightforward as we had supposed. Too much of a good thing led to reversals of the relationship when participants who were naturally prone to ask questions responded to instructions by increasing their inquisitiveness beyond the optimal level.

The concept of an optimal level for certain behaviors was also useful in understanding the relationship between self-references and attraction. Within normal limits the frequency of self-references was not strongly related to liking, but when partners with instructions to talk about themselves became highly self-absorbed, they received low ratings from their question-asking partners because the partners did not get a chance to talk enough about themselves to keep the conversation enjoyable.

Our instructions seem to have produced unnaturally extreme levels of self-reference in some conversations. On the other hand, a number of other investigators of conversations have also suggested that the most liked members of groups are often not the members who are most active (Bales, 1970; Kleinke, Kahn, & Tully, 1976; Stang, 1973).

As it turned out, variations in attraction ratings depended as much on what the rater herself got an opportunity to say as on what the partner said. This finding is consistent with a conception of attraction that emphasizes the role of the affective experience of the perceiver (Clore & Byrne, 1974; Griffitt & Veitch, 1971; Kerber, 1978) rather than the role of perceived attributes of stimulus persons (Fishbein & Ajzen, 1975). In this regard, the findings are analogous to the results of a study by Werner and Latané (1974) on attraction among rats. They report a variety of attempts to change the characteristics of stimulus rats to discover the secret of their attractiveness. They shaved them to change their texture, perfumed them to change their smell, and anesthetized them to make them motionless. They concluded, however, that the stimulus rat was attractive not because of any particular attribute but because it afforded a chance for the responding rat to engage in snuggling, a highly enjoyable behavior among rats.

In this chapter we have reported both descriptive and hypothesis-testing analyses. The three-mode factor analysis offered a description of the distinctive conversation types that occurred, and the regression analyses allowed us to test hypotheses about the role of variations in the target person's natural conversational style and about the relative roles of the target persons's behavior and the rater's own behavior in attraction. Our experience with these data suggest to us that some such combination of techniques is required if psychologists are to meet the demands of ecologically oriented research (Gibbs, 1979) on such richly joined social events as conversations.

ACKNOWLEDGMENTS

The research discussed in this chapter was supported by Grant #MH14510 from the National Institute of Mental Health and by a grant from the University of Illinois Research Board. Thanks are due to Dr. Howard McGuire for running the experiment, to John Cottingham, Barbara Farrell, Howard McGuire, and Steve Tovian for coding the conversations, and to Judy DeLoache and Larry Jones for comments on the manuscript.

REFERENCES

Ashby, W. R. *Design for a brain.* New York: Wiley, 1960.
Bales, R. F. *Personality and interpersonal behavior.* New York: Holt, Rinehart, & Winston, 1970.
Borgatta, E. F., & Crowther, B. *A workbook for the study of social interaction processes.* Chicago: Rand McNally, 1965.
Carson, R. C. *Interaction concepts of personality.* Chicago: Aldine, 1969.
Clore, G. L., & Byrne, D. A reinforcement–affect model of attraction. In T. L. Huston (Ed.), *Foundations of interpersonal attraction.* New York: Academic Press, 1974.
Clore, G. L., Itkin, S. M., & McGuire, H. *Attraction in conversations.* Unpublished paper, University of Illinois at Urbana–Champaign, 1980.
Cozby, P. C. Self-disclosure, reciprocity and liking. *Sociometry,* 1972, *35,* 151–160.

Derlega, V. J., Walmer, J., & Furman, F. Mutual disclosure in social interactions. *Journal of Social Psychology*, 1973, *90*, 159-160.

Duncan, S., Jr., & Fiske, D. W. *Face-to-face interaction: Research, methods, and theory*. Hillsdale, N.J.: Lawrence Erlbaum Assoc., 1977.

Duncan, S., & Niederehe, G. On signalling that it's your turn to speak. *Journal of Experimental Social Psychology*, 1974, *10*, 234-247.

Ehrlich, H. J., & Graeven, D. B. Reciprocal self-disclosure in a dyad. *Journal of Experimental Social Psychology*, 1971, *7*, 389-400.

Fishbein, M., & Ajzen, I. *Belief, attitude, intention, and behavior: An introduction to theory and research*. Reading, Mass.: Addison-Wesley, 1975.

Fiske, D. W. Personal communication. November 11, 1974.

Galbraith, J. K. *The McLandress dimension*. New York: Houghton-Mifflin, 1962.

Gibbs, J. C. The meaning of ecologically oriented inquiry in contemporary psychology. *American Psychologist*, 1979, *34*, 127-140.

Gottman, J., Markman, H., & Notarius, C. The topography of marital conflict: A sequential analysis of verbal and nonverbal behavior. *Journal of Marriage and the Family*, 1977, Autumn, 461-477.

Griffitt, W., & Veitch, R. Hot and crowded: Influences of population density and temperature on interpersonal affective behavior. *Journal of Personality and Social Psychology*, 1971, *17*, 92-98.

Hall, E. T. A system for the notation of proxemic behavior. *American Anthropologist*, 1963, *65*, 1003-1026.

Heider, F. On social cognition. *American Psychologist*. 1967, *22*, 25-31.

Jourard, S. M. *The transparent self* (2nd ed.). New York: Van Nostrand, 1971.

Jourard, S. M., & Friedman, R. Experimenter-subject "distance" and self-disclosure. *Journal of Personality and Social Psychology*, 1970, *25*, 278-282.

Jourard, S. M., & Jaffee, P. E. Influence of an interviewer's disclosure on the self-disclosing behavior of interviewees. *Journal of Counseling Psychology*, 1970, *17*, 252-257.

Kaiser, H. F. The varimax criterion for analytic rotation in factor analysis. *Journal of Personality*, 1958, *23*, 187-200.

Kerber, K. W. *Affective implications, intentionality, and interpersonal attraction in dyadic situations*. Unpublished doctoral dissertation, University of Illinois at Urbana-Champaign, 1978.

Kleinke, C. L., Kahn, M. L., & Tully, T. B. *First impressions of talking rates in opposite-sex and same-sex interactions*. Paper presented at the Western Psychological Association, Los Angeles, April 1976.

Kleinke, C. L., & Tully, T. B. Influence of talking level on perceptions of counselors. *Counseling Psychology*, 1979, *26*, 23-29.

Leary, T. *Interpersonal diagnosis of personality*. New York: Ronald Press, 1957.

Lindquist, C. U., & Rappaport, J. Selection of college student therapeutic agents: Further analysis of the "Group Assessment of Interpersonal Traits" technique. *Journal of Consulting and Clinical Psychology*, 1973, *41*, 316.

Mehrabian, A. *Nonverbal communication*. Chicago: Aldine Atherton, 1972.

Schegloff, E. Sequencing in conversational openings. *American Anthropologist*, 1968, *70*, 1075-1095.

Stang, D. J. Effect of interaction rate on ratings of leadership and liking. *Journal of Personality and Social Psychology*, 1973, *27*, 405-408.

Sullivan, H. S. *The interpersonal theory of psychiatry*. New York: Norton, 1953.

Tucker, L. R. The extension of factor analysis to three dimensional matrices. In N. Fredricksen (Ed.), *Contributions to mathematical psychology*. New York: Holt, Rinehart, & Winston, 1964.

Tucker, L. R. Some mathematical notes on three-mode factor analysis. *Psychometrika*, 1966, *31*, 279-311.

Werner, C., & Latané, B. Interaction motivates attraction. *Journal of Personality and Social Psychology*, 1974, *29*, 328–334.

Whalen, C. J. Effects of a model and instructions on group verbal behavior. *Journal of Consulting and Clinical Psychology*, 1969, *33*, 509.

Worthy, M., Gary, A. L., & Kahn, G. M. Self-disclosure as an exchange process. *Journal of Personality and Social Psychology*, 1969, *13*, 59–63.

9 Interpersonal Construal: An Individual Differences Framework

Stephen L. Golding

Keith Valone

Sharon W. Foster
University of Illinois Champaign

Interpersonal behavior must be given meaning (construed) in order to be anything more than a series of events in the physical world. A critical issue in all approaches to understanding interpersonal interactions is the *extent* and *nature* of individual differences in such construal processes. Unfortunately, there have been no attempts to develop a general theoretical framework for articulating the various points in the interpersonal construal process at which individual differences may occur; rather, researchers in different areas have either developed their own particular manner of conceptualizing individual differences at a single point in the construal process or else have not formally addressed the issue. Additionally, serious methodological and design problems either limit or preclude the discovery of theoretically relevant individual differences in interpersonal construal.

These issues are the focus of the present chapter. In the following section a framework is developed in which interpersonal construal is conceptualized as at least a three-stage process, at any point of which individual differences might occur. In subsequent sections, methodological and design problems characterizing much of the research relevant to the investigation of individual differences at each of these three stages are discussed, and recently completed studies of our own are used to illustrate some ways in which these difficulties might be circumvented. Finally, definitional ambiguities in this literature with respect to what it means to have hypothesized, found, or failed to find individual differences are discussed, followed by a short review of recommendations for future research.

A Framework for Conceptualizing Individual Differences in Interpersonal Construal

It is widely assumed that interpersonal construal is a dynamic process in which an individual actively interprets and imposes meaning upon selected stimuli in a relatively characteristic fashion (Carson, 1969; Kelly, 1955; Neisser, 1967, 1976; Schneider, Hastorf, & Ellsworth, 1979; Sullivan, 1953). Within this framework, an individual's interpersonal behavior may be conceptualized as primarily serving to act on the environment in such a manner as to produce new stimuli that are subsequently construed; these new construals in turn determine further behaviors that serve to produce additional stimuli to be construed. The entire process, thus conceptualized, continues in an endless cycle (Golding, 1978; Neisser, 1976; Powers, 1973, 1978).

The construal process itself may be conceptualized as consisting of at least three interaction stages hereafter called *cue selection, encoding,* and *representation.* In the cue-selection stage, certain stimuli about another person are actively attended to or selected from the large number of cues potentially available. Cues thereby selected must be processed according to the construer's interpersonal interaction goals or purposes in the *encoding* stage. The output of this stage is a *representation;* that is, the cue is engendered with connotative or affective meanings and possibly combined with other relevant information concurrently generated or retrieved from memory. This internal representation may be linguistic in form or, alternatively, may consist of affective states, images, and so forth.

Individuals may be seen to differ from one another at any or all of these stages. Thus, two individuals presented with the "objectively" identical interpersonal transaction may attend to very different cues about the other person, may encode the same cue according to widely divergent goals, and/or may represent the same output in radically different ways.

This conceptualization of interpersonal construal is used in subsequent sections as an organizational framework for discussing existing research on individual differences, as well as to highlight relevant aspects of our own research. Before proceeding to these sections, however, a brief "context-setting" overview of the methodologies used in our studies is provided.

Methodological Overview

The three studies reported in this chapter employ three-mode factor analysis (Tucker, 1966) as the basic data reduction and interpretation technique. In general, three-way data matrices (in the present studies consisting of interpersonal cues × attributes × subjects) may be analyzed by the three-mode procedure such that a separate factor matrix is calculated for each of the modes (cues, attributes, and persons). Additionally, a "core" matrix is generated that yields weights representing the interrelations among the factors from each of the separate modes. The person, attribute, or cue modes may be rotated independently by graphical or analytic procedures; such rotations also require a counter-rotation of the core matrix. Conversely, "simple structure" can be sought in the core matrix itself, which would then require counter-rotation of the appropriate individual modes. When appropriately rescaled, entries in the rotated core matrix may be interpreted relative to the original metric on which subjects' ratings were based. Typically, the presence of individual differences in subjects' judgments is inferred if an inspection of the eigenvalues for the persons mode indicates that more than one factor should be retained. Explicit computational details of the procedures used in the present studies may be found in Tucker (1966, 1972), N. Wiggins (1973), and Levin (1965).

Study I (Valone & Golding, In Preparation). Thirty-nine heterosexually anxious males identified using Arkowitz, Lichtenstein, McGovern, and Hines' (1975) criteria served as subjects in this study, which investigated the relationship between psychological dysfunction and interpersonal construal style. Subjects saw what they thought was a live interaction between the female confederate and another subject (actually a male confederate) on a videomonitor. In fact, subjects were shown a videotape in which the female confederate successively enacted 11 nonverbal behaviors selected for their connotations of warmth or coldness in heterosexual interactions (Clore, Hirschberg, & Itkin, 1975). No sound accompanied the videotape in order to increase the saliency of the nonverbal cues. In order to maximize self-involvement in these tasks, subjects were led to believe that they too would be subsequently role-playing a date with the same woman. Under different conditions, the videotape was replayed and stopped, either by the experimenter at preset points, or by the subject whenever he felt the female confederate was communicating her feelings. Each time the subject (experimenter) stopped the videotape, the subject rated how he thought the female confederate was feeling toward him on 18 bipolar scales selected from Wish, Deutsch, and Kaplan (1976). Subjects also completed a number of personological measures consisting of self-ratings of heterosexual and social anxiety, and reactions to the female confederate.

The nonverbal behavior cues by bipolar attributes by subjects matrix of metaperspective ratings (Laing, Phillipson, & Lee, 1966) was then analyzed by means of a three-mode factor analysis in order to determine whether individual differences in connotative implication strategies were related to heterosexual anxiety. The three-mode factor procedure utilized in this study (and Study II) inserted communalities consisting of estimated reliable sums of squares prior to analysis. Two dimensions were retained for each of the behaviors, scales, and persons modes. Rotation of the factors in the behaviors mode recovered a Warm and Involved factor (marked by "grins at him" and 'moves toward him'') and a Cold and Aloof factor (marked by "moves away from him" and "plays with her split ends''). Rotation in the attribute space resulted in two factors, Hostile versus Friendly (marked by "hostile–friendly" and "unfair–fair") and Intense versus Superficial (marked by "intense-superficial feelings toward you" and "formal-informal"). The personological correlates were regressed onto the unrotated dimensions of the persons space; two theoretically and statistically significant correlates (dating frequency and desirability of confederate as date) were chosen as rotational directions (Golding, 1977; Tucker, 1972).

Study II (Foster & Golding, In Preparation). This study investigated the hypothesis that interpersonal dominance is multidimensional in nature and that individuals differ in connotative implications drawn about the cues indicative of such dimensions. Forty-five male and 45 female undergraduates rated 15 cues of interpersonal dominance on 14 bipolar attribute scales in a standard trait implication task. The cue set was rationally chosen from a larger set nominated by subjects in a pilot study. The attribute scales represented markers of the Evaluation, Potency, and Activity dimensions of the semantic differential (Osgood, Suci, & Tannenbaum, 1957), and single "feminine-masculine" and "submissive-dominant" scales. Additionally, subjects were administered personological measures consisting primarily of self-reported personal needs as measured by subscales of Jackson's (1976) Personality Research Form.

The resulting cues by attributes by subjects data matrix was subjected to a three-mode factor analysis; three dimensions were retained for the cue and attribute modes, while four were retained for the persons mode. The rotated factors of the cue space were labeled Pure Leadership (marked by "is a good leader" and "concern for others"), Interpersonally Domineering (e.g., "monopolizes conversation" and 'draws attention to self"), and Task Orientation (e.g., "prefers work over people" and "directive"). The rotated dimensions of the attribute space were interpreted in terms of the semantic differential, resulting in clear Evaluation ("pleasant-unpleasant" and "good-bad") and Potency ("sturdy-delicate" and "strong-weak") dimensions, and a weaker Activity dimension (marked by scales such as "vivid-muted" and "submissive-dominant"). The core matrix was rotated internally to an approximation of simple structure, primarily because the regression of outside correlates onto dimensions of the subject space was largely unsuccessful.

Study III (Golding, In Preparation). This study attempted to expand constructively on the individual differences in construal style discovered in Golding (1977). Subjects in two large samples ($N = 139$ and 156 respectively) rated 10 transcribed conflictual interactions drawn from Knudson, Sommers, and Golding's (1980) work on dyadic perception. The husband and wife of each vignette were rated on six parallel scales of interpersonal style; additionally, their relationship style was rated on seven scales (Leary, 1957; Norman & Goldberg, 1966; Wish et al., 1976). In addition, subjects rated themselves on a variety of scales and personality measures (see Table 9.4), as well as rating their direct and metaperspective perceptions of significant relationships (Laing et al., 1966).

Direct perspectives ("I see my relationship with X as . . .") and metaperspectives ("I think X sees my relationship with him/her as . . .") were gathered with respect to mother, father, and same and opposite sex peers on multiple scales of interpersonal style (a la Leary, Norman, Wish, etc.). Separate three-mode analyses were performed on the data from each sample. In both analyses, three dimensions were retained in the persons space, two in the vignette (cue) space, and three in the attribute space. Rotated factors in the attribute space reflected Wife's Disaffiliation and Husband's Disaffiliation ("friendly–hostile," "cooperative–uncooperative") and Relationship Dishonesty ("relationship honesty–dishonesty"). Rotated factors in the vignette (cue) space reflected dimensions of Normal and Dysfunctional conflict (see Golding, in preparation). Although it had been intended to use outside correlates to rotate the persons space, special problems having to do with replication (see subsequent discussion) led to a compromise of rotating the core matrix itself to an internal position approximating simple structure, in a manner similar to Study II.

Individual Differences in Cue Selection and Utilization

On experiential grounds, it is clear that individuals differ widely in cues to which they attend. Unfortunately, most of the research related to this issue, by employing factorial research designs that require the stimuli presented to be constant across subjects, precludes a true study of cue selection. This research strategy is counterfactual because individuals are not allowed to attend to different subsets of stimuli, as they do in naturalistic interpersonal settings, and because no two individuals elicit the same behavior from another person or situation (Mischel, 1977; Raush, 1977; Wachtel, 1977). For example, Wiggins, Hoffman, and Taber (1969) presented subjects with cue profiles and demonstrated individual differences in cues used for judging intelligence that were related to personality variables and subject's own intelligence. Hamilton and Gifford (1970), using a similar technique, uncovered interesting cue utilization differences in judgements of liberalism–conservativism, but did not relate these differences to personality or demographic correlates. Although such studies are impressive in various ways, they do not directly investigate cue selection in representative judgement situations. Thus, we do, especially in academia, make judgements of how "smart" or "informed" or "creative" our students and colleagues are, but it is doubtful that we do so on grounds of how often they study or what their high school grades were. Some of us, at least, are more likely to attend to cues such as whether or not an idea is expressed well, or is "novel," or whether precise language is used, or common words mispronounced.

Although our Study II presented all subjects with the same cue set, it nevertheless demonstrates two important points about individual differences in cue selection. First of all, subjects helped to generate the larger cue set, thereby providing a degree of ecological representativeness in the specification of the cue domain.

Furthermore, although dominance is a major factor in interpersonal measurement (Benjamin, 1974; Carson, 1969; Leary, 1957), it was anticipated that subjects would use different cues in inferring its presence, although it normally appears as a single variable in most studies. Inspection of Table 9.1, which presents the factor structure of the cue space in Study II, suggests that the obtained dimensions reflect psychologically meaningful differences in subjects' views of the *cues indicative of dominance.* The first cue dimension (*Pure Leadership*) has a pattern of loadings suggestive of a blend of Leary's (1957) "Managerial" and "Responsibility" octants (e.g., is a good leader, concern for others, high status, responsible, and work over people). Cue dimension II, *Interpersonally Domineering,* is marked by cues such as monopolizes conversation, draws attention to self, intrusive, and controlling, and seems very much like Leary's "Competitive–Narcissistic" octant, where "dominance" is perceived as interpersonally managing or perhaps self-aggrandizing. Dimension III is loaded positively by "prefers work over people," "controlling," "directive," and negatively by "concern for others," and suggests a pattern of construal of a dominant person as one whose primary concern was work and impersonal directiveness. In line with previous research (Fiedler, 1967), this dimension was interpreted as *Task Orientation.* One should note that similar differentiations among dominant

TABLE 9.1
Rotated Cue Space (Study II)[a]

Cues	Cue Dimensions		
	I	II	III
	Pure Leadership	Interpersonally Domineering	Task Orientation
Directive	11	18	37
Good leader	48	06	-12
Concern for others	48	-33	-51
High status	36	09	-06
Work over people	-43	03	80
Responsible	35	-08	-01
Controlling	-08	45	57
Thinks for self	25	-10	07
Draws attention to self	03	54	-11
Highly evaluative	04	05	24
Self-confident	32	-02	06
Courage of own convictions	24	02	15
Monopolizes conversation	07	61	15
Wise	33	21	-12
Intrusive	-11	47	26

[a]Rotational procedure was Tucker's "least squares hyperplane," an oblique analytic technique that rationally approximates simple structure. Decimal points are omitted.

interpersonal orientations are made in Benjamin's (1974, 1979) system of classification.

Even though subjects generated the cues analyzed in Study II in response to questions about how "dominant people" behaved in various situations that were indicative of their "dominance," it is clear that *dominance is a superordinate construct* and is not a "cue" in the normal sense of that word. Trait implication experiments that ask subjects to relate "dominance" to some other personality trait descriptor (e.g., "friendliness") are thus quite likely to tap *nothing but* normative semantic implications (Block, Weiss, & Thane, 1979; Fiske, 1978; Lamiell, Foss, & Cavenee, 1980; Shweder, 1978). They certainly have little to do with interpersonal construal, because they demonstrate only the *contextless structure among linguistic descriptors,* having precluded all steps of selection, attention, encoding, and representation.

The importance of cue selection is demonstrated in other ways by studies I, II, and III, as well as in the prior work of Golding (1977). Most work in the area of individual differences has been more like a methodological "show and tell" than a use of these multivariate methodologies to begin testing theoretical assumptions or postulates (see Schneider et al., 1979, for a similar point). With few exceptions (e.g., Wiggins, Wiggins, & Conger, 1968), multivariate studies have been long on methodology and short on theory. Our studies in this area are properly seen as second generation attempts to use this methodology in the service of theory. Thus, Study I (Valone & Golding, in preparation) attempts to begin testing an interpersonal construal model of psychological dysfunction by looking for individually different styles of cue selection, connotative implication, and trait inference in contrasted groups of heterosexually anxious and nonanxious males. The existence of an admittedly sketchy theory (Arkowitz, 1977; Curran, 1977; Valone & Golding, in preparation) permitted us to target cues of interpersonal warmth and aloofness. Such a theoretically guided rationale is of tremendous value, not only to determine subject and cue selection, but also attribute selection (i.e., upon which attribute scales shall we ask subjects to *represent* their construals?). In Study I, we had the prior work of Wish (1976) and the long history of work on interpersonal behavior (for reviews, see Benjamin, 1974; Carson, 1969; Golding & Knudson, 1975; Swensen, 1973; J. Wiggins, 1979) to guide our selection. The same was true in Study III and in Golding (1977). In Study II, we used the commonly accepted tripartite (Evaluation, Potency, Activity) view of semantic space (Osgood et al., 1957), knowing in advance that it would only crudely approximate any given individual's semantic space (Rosenberg, 1979; Wiggins & Fishbein, 1969). The importance of "theory-guided" stimulus selection and ecological design is of heightened importance in these multivariate designs because the multiple domains (subjects, cues, attributes, settings) interact with each other. To the extent that one forces subjects to represent and describe their construals in inappropriate, artificial, or irrelevant ways (Bem & Allen, 1974; Koltuv, 1962; Rosenberg, 1977), one not only compromises the internal validity of one's experiment, but one also loses important data and theory-building opportunities.

In Study III, the conflict vignettes were chosen from a conveniently available domain (the actual transcripts of Knudson et al., 1980), but not according to any compelling theoretical rationale. The resulting cue space, though highly replicable, is not easily interpretable. (This difficulty arises for the same reason as in persons-space rotations, because unless objects [subjects] cluster, or have some preexisting, relatively known structure, rotations become psychologically arbitrary. This point is well recognized in multidimensional scaling, where one really does not seek to discover object [cue] dimensions; rather, one builds them into the stimuli to be judged. In a parallel fashion, one must have some rationale for selecting certain cues, or let the subjects do it themselves. One loses on both counts if one constrains subjects' judgements, and has little rationale for doing so.) In contrast, Golding (1977) selected and constructed interpersonal vignettes on an explicit basis drawn from the work of Leary (1957) and Lorr and Suziedelis (1969; see also Golding & Knudson, 1975), and was thus able to interpret individual differences in reference to a well-articulated and meaningful stimulus domain. Our Study II (Foster & Golding, in preparation) represents a compromise strategy (pilot subject cue generation, experimenter rational selection) that was successful in obtaining a meaningful cue and attribute space, but would have been more so had we more explicitly built a cue space around theory-dictated dimensions. There is, of course, a trade-off relationship between research done under the *context of discovery* as opposed to the *context of justification* (Reichenbach, 1938).

A line of work on unitizing the stream of behavior begun by Dickman (1963), and now used extensively by Newtson (1976), has important implications for the study of cue selection. Whereas most of this work focuses on the effects of task or instruction set on how subjects unitize or "chunk" incoming information (Cohen & Ebbesen, 1979; Newtson & Engquist, 1976), our own research bears more directly on the cue-selection issue, and how this might relate to important individual differences.

Trierweiler, Golding, and Valone (in preparation), for example, are analyzing data from Study I and from Trierweiler and Golding (in preparation) in terms of individual differences in "stopping points." Heterosexually anxious males are expected to identify different "cues" than nonanxious males, who are expected to be relatively more "consensual" with one another. In a somewhat different vein, Cohen and Ebbesen (1979) showed that subjects instructed to remember details segmented a videotape more than subjects who were told to form impressions of the actor, and Wilder (1978) found that subjects used more segments when the actor's behavior was unpredictable or changed in the direction of unpredictability (as would be predicted by most theories of attention). Such results must be viewed with caution, however, as current work by Trierweiler and Golding (in preparation) demonstrates. They have found that the effect reported by Cohen and Ebbesen (1979) depends on type of target and type of encoding strategy. If subjects are asked to segment when one psychologically meaningful unit ends and another begins, they segment differently than when asked to break the tape up into units based on what "happens" on the tape. But, this effect interacts with whether or not subjects are given memory or impression sets (a la Cohen and Ebbesen) and whether the target behavior judged is a simple action sequence or portrays a realistic interpersonal sequence. Furthermore, Cohen and Ebbesen demonstrate that the location of breakpoints depends on processing purpose (memory versus impression), but Trierweiler and Golding show that this effect is, in fact, highly dependent on a variety of experimental conditions. Their results bring into question whether or not the concept of a "unit," based in the objective structure of the stimulus materials alone, is a meaningful concept. There is a wide range of individual differences present in such segmenting data, even when all subjects have received the same task instructions and judge the same target (which themselves create substantial main effects).

Individual Differences in Encoding Strategies

In the cognitive literature, encoding strategies (Baddeley, 1978; Bower, 1975; Craik & Lockhart, 1972) typically are provided by the experimenter and are operationally synonymous with task instruction (see Wyer & Srull, 1979, for an extensive review in the area of memory for social information). For example, in Rogers' work (Kuiper & Rogers, 1979; Rogers, 1977; Rogers, Kuiper, & Kirker, 1977), subjects were asked to judge personality trait descriptors according to whether or not they were long words, had specific meaning, described the experimenter, or described the subject him/herself. The *tasks* or *information-processing purposes* are the experimenter's way of manipulating encoding strategies. (In the pioneering work of Craik and his colleagues [Craik & Lockhart, 1972; Craik & Tulving, 1975] the encoding strategies studied were more circumscribed, usually referring to various characteristics of words [i.e., structural, lexical, phonemic, or semantic].) We assume that in the real world of social interaction and interpersonal perception, encoding strategies also operate. *It is clear, however, that such strategies are "self-selected" as a function of both the external situations to which the individual exposes himself and as a function of internal styles, habits, traits, or psychological organizing principles* (Golding, 1978). Furthermore, they most likely concern "psychological tasks" other than "is this word descriptive of me?" In fact, we know little about the *domain of encoding strategies* normally used in interpersonal construal, nor do we have much empirical data on the question of the nature of individual differences in encoding strategies.

Nevertheless, we do suppose that there are wide-ranging individual differences in such encoding strategies. It is not clear what these naturalistically occurring encoding strategies will look like. *Interaction goals* such as forming an impression of a person or trying to "understand" his or her behavior are certainly one class of encoding strategies. In Jones and Thibaut (1958), for example, these are referred to as "causal–genetic" sets. *Motivational goals* (Jones and Thibaut's "value maintenance set") that reflect the pursuit of positive and self-confirming experiences, are also likely candidates. Thus, evaluating an interaction in terms of its possible threat value to one's self-esteem, or its potential to result in self-gratifying or actualizing experience, or the likelihood that it will result in a successful sexual encounter, may all be considered as possible encoding strategies. In fact, such global concepts as goal, intention, motive, and purpose are intimately involved in encoding strategies because they all speak to the fact that information, interpersonal and otherwise, is processed for a purpose (Neisser, 1976).

Research on interpersonal perception that presents a subject with precoded, nicely packaged stimuli, such as trait descriptors (e.g., "John is a competitive person"), not only masks the *selective aspects* of attentional strategies; it also masks the *encoding* aspects because we also *tell* our subject how to deal with the information ("If John is an assertive person, how likely is he also to be an intelligent person?" or "Would a woman who is domineering be the sort of person with whom you would like to solve anagrams?"). Theorists of a social learning orientation (Bandura, 1977; Kanfer & Hagerman, 1979; Mischel, 1973) have long emphasized the importance of encoding strategies (under the heading, for example, of "cognitive transformations") in the maintenance and control of behavior. Their research demonstrations of the importance of such transformations (Mischel, Ebbesen, & Zeiss, 1972) emphasize *experimenter-controlled* encoding strategies. To our knowledge, they have not taken the logical next step of assessing individual differences in encoding strategies, whether these are under situational or personal control, or some complex interaction of both (Golding, 1978).

Individual Differences in Representation

In one form or another, this question forms the background of most empirical studies of interpersonal perception. It was most clearly stated in George Kelly's (1955) Individuality Corollary: "Persons differ from each other in their construction of events [p. 55]." Although Kelly's system emphasizes *linguistic* descriptors (honest–dishonest) and assumes dichotomous construct dimensions, it nevertheless was a pioneering approach. Individuals may differ with respect to whether or not construals are represented as dimensions or categories, how many different dimensions (or categories) are used, and how they covary with each other. More importantly, perhaps, is the *form* of the representation, that is, whether construals are based on *description* ("He's a person who is punching me"), *trait descriptors* ("He's aggressive"), *intentional judgements* ("He wants to hurt me''), *purpose* (''He's trying to humiliate me''), *affective states and connotative judgements* (''This hurts,'' ''I'm angry,'' ''He's a bad person''), or *trait implications* (''He is aggressive and also, perhaps, unpredictable'').

Koltuv (1962) found evidence that the number of dimensions and the co-variance structure of trait-based dimensions might depend on the nature of the target construed, particularly the degree of familiarity between the rater and the ratee (but see Norman & Goldberg, 1966, and Passini & Norman, 1966). By implication, raters might also have *different* dimensions or categories by which they construed the same event (e.g., Dornbusch, Hastorf, Richardson, Muzzy, & Vreeland, 1965). This theme of differences in category (dimension) usage and structure has resulted in several research traditions, most of which focus on individual differences in "implicit personality theories," connotative impli-cation structures, and category (dimension) type, and utilized a variety of multivariate modes (Schneider, 1973; Schneider et al., 1979; Wiggins, 1973).

In methodological/statistical terms, the representation issue is partially recog-nized in the points of view (POV), individual differences in multidimensional scaling (INDSCAL), and three-mode factor analysis (3MFA) models (Carroll & Chang, 1970; Tucker, 1966, 1972; Tucker & Messick, 1963; Wiggins, 1973). In both INDSCAL and 3MFA, one may derive individual "saliency" or factor weights that correspond, in general, to an individual's *degree of usage* of a *common set* of dimensions. Because the models are based on an Eckart-Young decomposition (1936), we know that they give preference to large, commonly used dimensions because this would maximally account for variance. In the POV model, a more individualistic representation of the dimensions of similarity spaces is possible, but one suspects that the Eckart-Young procedure will lead to a subordination of individual points of view unless one is in a "substantial minority." This matter has been preliminarily addressed by Jones and Wadington (1976) and could be fruitfully investigated by more elaborate Monte Carolo procedures that expand on the definition of what an "individual dif-ference" means (see the following).

Regardless of the sensitivity of statistical methodologies, however, the ex-perimental designs themselves have precluded the emergence of *mode of repre-sentation* as a discoverable phenomenon. Whether or not the categories used for description are experimenter or subject provided, it has been assumed that the form of representation is linguistic. This is evident from the fact that well over 95% of the available studies present stimuli as *words* to subjects. Important exceptions are Hirschberg and Jones' work with faces, Hirschberg's work with body types (Wiggins et al., 1968) and our Study I. Even though multidimen-sional scaling strategies that require only global similarity/dissimilarity judge-ments are frequently justified by their apparent nonreliance on preexisting experimenter-derived verbal categories, it is important to note that in interpreting the resulting configurations, experimenters rely heavily on correlations between an object's coordinates in such a multidimensional similarity space and its mean values on linguistic description scales (so-called unidimensional correlates, see Rosenberg & Sedlak, 1972).

Although a variety of cognitive psychologists (Posner & Snyder, 1975; Wickens, 1972) have proposed that emotional memory for an event may be stored separately from other details of the event, we know of no serious program of research, *using naturalistic stimuli,* that has investigated the form of memorial and conscious representation of interpersonal events (but see Anderson, 1978; Carlston, 1979; Kintsch, 1974; Kosslyn, 1976).

Our own research reported in this chapter touches on this issue in the traditional manner. All three studies employed experimenter-provided attribute scales. In our concluding section, we allude to some interview-based, traditional experimental, and discourse analytic methods that may be helpful in breaking ground in the area of individual differences in representation. Presently, however, we discuss the representation issue in reference to our own data on individual differences in connotative implication. The results of two interrelated research programs, the influence of *category relevance* (as determined by free versus experimenter-provided attribution/representation scales) and the issue of *category type* (i.e., are interpersonal perceptions, even if processed linguistically, represented as trait descriptors, scene memories, or behavioral instances?) are also briefly discussed.

Representation as Connotative Implications.   The main studies in this area have directly assessed individual differences in the construal (along interpersonal or semantic dimensions) of interpersonal stimuli (our studies I, II and III, as well as Golding, 1977). Other studies may be seen as relevant, but they are not reviewed in detail here because their focus is usually more abstract and linguistic. Thus, Walters and Jackson (1966), Pedersen (1965), and Sherman (1972) studied trait–trait inference networks; Wiggins and Wiggins (1969) and Beck, Ward-Hull, and McLear (1976) scaled somatic stimuli; Posavac (1971) studied preference for socially desirable behaviors; and Messick and Kogan (1966) studied dimensions of roles. Wish's studies (Wish, 1976; Wish et al., 1976) are closer in interpersonal focus, but they are primarily concerned with the rather abstract similarity of various interpersonal relationships (e.g., "how similar is the relationship between husband and wife to the relationship between guard and prisoner?").

For illustrative purposes, we concentrate on the individual differences uncovered in our Study I, referring the interested reader to Foster and Golding (in preparation), Golding (in preparation), and Golding (1977) for further examples. Table 9.2 presents the core matrices of four "idealized individuals" (Tucker, 1966; N. Wiggins, 1973) selected to represent various regions of the two-dimensional persons space (derived and rotated by procedures discussed previously). Points were chosen to represent an "individual" at the centroid of the persons space, two "ecologically" representative individuals whose projections

TABLE 9.2
Personal Core Matrices for Four Idealized Individuals
(Study I)

Idealized Individual	Warm and Involved Behaviors		Cold and Aloof Behaviors	
	Hostile Versus Friendly	Intense Versus Superficial	Hostile Versus Friendly	Intense Versus Superrficial
Centroid	0.57	0.18	-0.45	0.09
Dimension I	1.09	0.34	-1.14	0.19
Lower Axis	0.12	-0.01	-1.42	0.08
Dimension II/Upper Axis	1.05	0.39	0.39	0.11

are markers of Dimensions I and II (projections on opposing dimensions take the correlation [0.38] between dimensions as rotated into account), and one "individual" who represents the extreme lower part of the main axis of the scatter plot of person coefficients. (The "Dimension II" individual's point was so near to the upper extreme of the main axis that it is used for both purposes.) The entries in Table 9.2 may be interpreted as *idealized ratings* (regressed toward the mean by error) that would be given on the original -3 to $+3$ scales by individuals at that point in the persons space with respect to the two behavior factors (Warm and Involved and Cold and Aloof) and the two scales factors (Hostile versus Friendly and Intense versus Superficial).

Because the person dimensions were rotated to personologically meaningful positions, the interpersonal construal style of each of these "individuals" can be related to how frequently he has dated in the last month (Person Dimension I) and how close the female confederate is to his concept of an "ideal" date (Person Dimension II). Several interesting differences in connotative implication strategies emerge from comparing the personal core matrices for the representative individuals. The "Dimension I" individual (who has had few or no dates in the last month and who sees the woman in the videotape as somewhat approximating his concept of an ideal date) is best characterized as drawing more extreme connotative implications than the centroid individual on the Hostile versus Friendly dimension when she is engaged in either behavior type.

The "upper-axis"/"Dimension II" individual (who has not dated frequently in the last month and who sees the woman as very closely approximating his concept of an ideal date) construes her as feeling friendly toward him regardless of what she does. This connotative implication strategy contrasts with the centroid individual, who construes the woman as feeling less intensely friendly when engaged in Warm and Involved behaviors and who construes her as feeling moderately hostile when engaged in Cold and Aloof behaviors. There is a slight tendency for both Dimension I and II individuals to construe the woman as feeling more superficial when engaged in the Warm and Involved behaviors than does the centroid individual.

The "lower axis" individual (who has dated frequently in the last month and who sees the woman as quite distant from his concept of an ideal date) contrasts with the centroid individual in that he does not draw any connotative implications about the woman's feelings toward him when engaged in Warm and Involved behaviors, whereas the centroid individual construes these same behaviors as indicating a friendly feeling toward him. Additionally, the "lower-axis" individual construes the woman as feeling extremely hostile toward him when engaged in the Cold and Aloof behaviors, whereas the centroid individual construes these behaviors in much more moderate terms. An even more striking contrast emerges when comparing the connotative implication strategies of the "upper-axis" individual and the "lower-axis" individual. The former individual construes all the nonverbal behaviors as indicating that the woman is feeling friendly to very friendly toward him; the latter individual construes these *same* behaviors as indicating that the woman is feeling anything from indifference toward him to extreme hostility toward him.

Thus, marked individual differences in connotative implication strategies are demonstrated in Study I, and these individual differences are meaningfully related to the dating frequency of the construer as well as to how closely the woman fits his concept of an ideal date. It is interesting to note that individual differences among the various representative individuals emerge primarily with respect to the Hostile versus Friendly dimension. All individuals construed the woman as feeling either moderately superficial or indifferent toward them, regardless of the type of behavior she was engaged in, suggesting that although this dimension was a factor of the attribute space, it was not seen as particularly relevant in construing the woman's intentions toward the subject.

Category Relevance and Category Type.   When subjects are required to make judgments about others on experimenter-provided attributional scales or categories, highly relevant dimensions or categories may be underrepresented or altogether absent, thereby forcing subjects to make their judgments on bases that are irrelevant or meaningless to them for interpersonal perception purposes (Bem & Allen, 1974; Dornbusch et al., 1965; Gibbs, 1979; Kelly, 1955; Koltuv, 1962; MacLeod, 1947; Rosenberg, 1977; Rosenberg & Sedlak, 1972; Schneider, 1973).

Early attempts to address this problem employed a free-response technique in which subjects were simply asked to describe other individuals, either verbally or in writing. These protocols were then content analyzed using coding schemes derived from experimenters' subjective impressions of the major dimensions used by subjects in their descriptions of others. Beach and Wertheimer (1961), in one of the first studies employing free-response techniques, demonstrated that subjects differed on the dimensions used in their descriptions of others; furthermore, the salience of a given dimension depended on the particular stimulus person being described. Yarrow and Campbell (1963) found that children's peer descriptions emphasized social interaction and evaluation. Individual differences related to the perceiver's age, sex, and style of interpersonal behavior emerged in both the content and the organization of children's descriptions. In another study, children's free-response peer descriptions (Dornbusch et al., 1965) demonstrated the active involvement of the individual perceiver in constructing his or her own representation of his or her interpersonal world. Although this early work did not reveal any theoretically consistent patterns, it did provide us with a clear indication that we could not assume that trait descriptors were the natural units of interpersonal perception. Moreover, it was likely that units and categories themselves were not consensual.

Modern variations in this strategy for free-response analysis of descriptive speech have been applied to children's construal of self (Bannister & Agnew, 1977) and others (Livesley & Bromley, 1973), college students' descriptions of peers (Fiske & Cox, 1979; Ostrom, 1975; Schneider, 1977), married couples' descriptions of their experiences during conflictual and nonconflictual interactions (Knudson et al., 1980), and longitudinal analyses of category change (Peevers & Secord, 1973; Scarlett, Press, & Crockett, 1971). This strategy has a serious flaw, however, in that the free-response material, no matter how naturalistic, must be scaled, scored, or categorized in some fashion. Most investigators have used categories that bear only a minimal relationship to the subject's interpersonal frame of reference as he or she generated the materials. Thus, Ostrom (1975) categorized the content of descriptive speech as traits (or habits), physical and biological characteristics, behaviors (and activities), attitudes and beliefs, and a mixed group of socioeconomic characteristics. Most other descriptive category schemes have been similarly based on "word class" differences. Important exceptions to this are Knudson et al. (1980), who applied an empirically based "interpersonal circumplex" structure based on Sullivan (1953) and Leary (1957); and Scarlett et al. (1971), who categorized description by a system based on Werner's developmental theory. In general, however, the coding schemes used in these few studies have been related neither to any theoretical conceptualization of interpersonal construal, nor to any scheme for allowing subjects to categorize their own descriptors.

An important exception in a closely related area is the extensive work of Rosenberg on the dimensionality of implicit theories of personality. In a long series (Jones & Rosenberg, 1974; Jones, Sensenig, & Haley, 1974; Kingsley, 1978; Kim & Rosenberg, 1978; Rosenberg, 1977, 1979; Rosenberg & Sedlak, 1972), Rosenberg and his co-workers have demonstrated, using a variety of free-response, constrained, partially constrained, and computer-interactive methodologies, that most subjects share a large common dimension of Evaluation, but differ markedly in what behaviors and/or feelings are relevant to that dimension. Moreover, subjects differ markedly in the remaining dimensions and covariance structures that characterize their implicit personality theories. Most significantly, the orthogonal, three-dimensional Evaluation, Potency, Activity model of semantic space (Osgood et al., 1957) characterized subject's implicit personality theories only when subjects' responses were aggregated.

Taken together, the studies referred to in this section lead clearly to the broad conclusion that, if one's goal is to unfold the processes by which the physical world of "behaviors" is translated into the interpersonal world of "experience," then one must pursue the question of individual differences in representation. The dimensions or categories that one uses to represent, experientially, the actors and interactions of our personal worlds, are fundamental to an understanding of the construal process.

The Definitional Problem in Individual Differences

There are no commonly agreed upon strategies for defining individual differences. Inspection of the literature yields these divergent working definitions of what it means to have "discovered" individual differences:

1. The discovery of different numbers of dimensions for members of contrasted groups in principal components analyses of Role Construct Repertory Grids; or differences between contrasted groups in structural characteristics of Repertory Grids, usually accomplished via nonparametric analyses. Correlations with outside personality measurements are unnecessary to assert individual differences.

2. More than one dimension emerging in an INDSCAL, POV, or 3MFA analysis as a function of some statistical or conceptual "goodness of fit" criterion (e.g., eigenvalue descent, stress values, etc.). Again, investigators are usually willing to discuss/interpret "subject factors," "subject dimensions," or "idealized subjects" without reference to outside personality or demographic correlates. When such correlates are present, they are capitalized on without concern for literal or constructive replication (Lykken, 1968).

3. The existence of empirically or visually detectable clusters in the person spaces generated by INDSCAL, POV, or 3MFA.

4. The existence of significant personality or demographic correlates of subject projections in person spaces derived from INDSCAL, POV, or 3MFA, chosen on the basis of some theoretical rationale, the number of factors decision having been previously or concurrently made on statistical/conceptual grounds.

5. Combination strategies and the use of literal and constructive replications as a criterion for interpreting (or not interpreting) individual differences (as in the case of Study III, discussed in detail later).

Each approach has drawbacks that are infrequently acknowledged or discussed. Strategy (1) makes the least conceptual sense, because, even if the statistical criterion for deciding on the number of dimensions to retain is psychologically meaningful, the number of dimensions in the REP grids analyzed is artifactually a function of context effects and the degree of heterogeneity of the roles and scales chosen. Strategies (2) and (3) are the most commonly employed, but as our Study III suggests, empirically risky. Fundamentally, they fail to take a coherent stance on the issues of what, theoretically, constitutes an individual difference. Studies by Wiggins and Blackburn (1976), Posavac (1971), Pedersen (1965), Sherman (1972), Wish (1976), and Walters and Jackson (1966) have used analytic rotations, rotations to subject cluster centroids, or no rotations, in determining the orientation of axes (and hence the psychological-theoretical meaning) in their studies' subject spaces. This is a critical problem because, unlike most object spaces we subject to such rotations, we have no hypotheses about the nature of the individual differences we seek to study empirically. In short, we're usually on a fishing expedition, *without replication*. Analytic interpretations of simple structure, or visual rotations to clusters, rarely work in the pursuit of individual differences, primarily because, unless we have selected our subjects on a priori grounds, their distribution in the unrotated subject spaces is rather uniform. Thus, in most of the empirical data to which we have had access, graphic displays of subject projections tend to look like ellipsoids in all but the first dimension. Especially in analyses using POV or 3MFA, the first unrotated subject dimension tends to recapture subjects' scale usage characteristics or their resemblance to the group centroid, whereas the higher dimensions, plotted pairwise, give elliptical plots, without any "lumpiness."

Because subjects tend not to fall into homogenous types or categories, their projections on the subject dimensions tend to be quasi-normally distributed. The problem is not whether or not one can interpret a subregion of the space legitimately only if it falls near a real individual (Cliff, 1968; Wiggins, 1973) but rather, what subregion, if any, makes sense to interpret. Unless subjects are chosen by some a priori contrasted groups strategy (e.g., Study I; Wiggins & Blackburn, 1976), they are unlikely to fall "lumpily" into the subject space. Further, "simple structure" analytic rotations of individuals are somewhat arbitrary and assume that subjects ought to be relatively pure representatives of given construal styles. The rotational problem in POV and especially 3MFA is severe if one cannot rely on outside correlates. Analytic rotations such as binormamin (Wiggins & Blackburn, 1976) or varimax have little conceptual meaning when applied to persons spaces and one must have a compelling reason for deviating from the unrotated, "variance maximizing" orientation of axes. Clusters rarely exist in subject spaces, and the investigator who is careful enough to try different clustering algorithms will find they often are capable of locating different clusters, even when none are obviously present (Anderberg, 1973; Golding, 1975b). Advocates of INDSCAL claim that its placement of axes is optimal and unique, but the criterion is based on the Eckart-Young procedure, and is inherently statistical, not psychological.

The importance of this rotational ambiguity (Mulaik, 1972) becomes apparent when one regresses some outside correlates onto an unrotated subject space, and then rotates that space by *any* orthogonal rotation. It is a matter of *mathematical necessity* that the size of the multiple regression coefficient (R) will remain constant, but the beta weights will change as a function of the transformation. If there are significant outside correlates, but one was unfortunate enough not to include them in the analysis, it is clear that one would be guessing (and most likely, wrongly) about a psychological meaningful location for the axes by use of analytic rotational criteria. If one did include all likely outside correlates, but found that none or very few of them related to one's subject space, one would of course be unable to use them as rotational directions to determine which of the (infinitely rotatable) subject spaces to interpret. Moreover, it always would be possible that one had chosen correlates inappropriately or unwisely. Only if one finds significant and replicable correlates of subject projections does one have a theoretical leg on which to stand (unless one is lucky enough to have natural clusters). In such a case, the significant outside correlates provide a rationale for meaningful rotation, in that one can use the matrix of unstandardized beta weights as a set of direction numbers to rotate to a position that maximizes the association between dimension projections and outside correlate scores. This technique has been successfully applied by Golding (1977) and our Study I. Unhappily, however, no study (save perhaps for Walters & Jackson, 1966, and our Study III) has attempted any sort of replication.

Study III was intended as a constructive replication of Golding (1977). The details of the structure of the vignette and attribute spaces do not concern us here; it is suffiient to say that the structures in these spaces were highly replicable, congruence coefficients (Harman, 1967) ranging from .936 to .997 in the vignette space, and from .973 to .995 in the attribute space. Moreover, the absolute factor-loading discrepancies between corresponding entries averaged .056 in the vignette space and .025 in the attribute space. It was clear that the vignette and scale spaces replicated quite well.

Replication in the subject space was altogether another matter. Because we did not define replication in the sense of test–retest reliability, we cannot compare the dimensions of subject's rating judgements at two points in time. We intended to replicate indvidual differences in two ways: first, by showing that the core matrices from Sample A and Sample B were within an orthogonal rotation of each other; and secondly, by showing that the person dimensions in Samples A and B had the same outside correlates and same pattern of beta weights vis-à-vis those correlates. Tables 9.3 and 9.4 display the appropriate data. First, as may be seen in Table 9.3, the core matrices are approximately in line with each other, after orthogonal rotation. With the exception of a single entry (I, I, II, sample B), the two matrices average a discrepancy of .062 (the value rises to only .102 if it is included). Moreover, the congruency coefficients (calculated by interrelating Person dimension entries over Vignette × Attribute dimension entries) range

TABLE 9.3
Core Matrices from Samples A and B, Study III[a,b]

Vignette (Cue) Dimension	Attribute (Scale) Dimension	Sample A Person Dimension			Sample B Person Dimension		
		I	II	III	I	II	III
I	I	37	-07	14	36	-06	15
	II	27	-10	-14	57	00	-13
	III	-31	-28	-15	-25	-09	01
II	I	-05	-22	00	07	-18	-01
	II	-24	-25	-07	-27	-16	-04
	III	-10	-11	-02	-19	-09	-03

[a]Decimal points omitted. Sample A was rotated to Sample B by means of an orthogonal procrustes procedure. Both matrices have been separately counter-rotated by the transformation matrices applied to the cue and attribute spaces, and rescaled by the procedure outlined by Tucker (1966).

[b]These matrices have not yet been rotated by any of the strategies outlined elsewhere in this chapter. It is precisely at this point that an investigator must use outside correlates, find clusters, or rotate by internal analytic procedures to solve the final step of the three-mode problem.

from .774 (Person Dimension III) to .917 (Person Dimension II). The basic Vignette and Attribute Core matrices thus appear replicated. Now look at Table 9.4, which presents only a condensed portion of the available personological correlates. Whereas inspection of either Sample A or Sample B would lead one to conclude that the individual differences uncovered were only moderately related to personality measures, comparison of the entries for the two samples is devastating. Remember that the multiple correlation coefficients are invariant with respect to orthogonal transformations. We had expected that the unrotated core matrices would be within an orthogonal rotation of each other, requiring counter-rotation of the persons spaces. It is irrelevant for our present purposes whether one inspects the significant correlates of either the rotated or unrotated spaces, as long as the rotations were orthogonal. Detailed study of Table 9.4 reveals that one can in no sense claim that the individual differences "replicate"; they most decidedly do not.[1] The critical reader may wonder whether the two samples are reasonably representative of the same population; the answer to this question is a definite "yes." With the exception of age (Sample B's subjects

[1]There is a paradoxical sense in which the individual differences do "replicate." For many of the correlates, significance is not obtained in either sample. In addition, in those cases where significance is obtained in one sample, but not in the other, the difference between the obtained multiple correlations is not statistically significant. The major conclusion to be drawn from this analysis is that individual differences are not well predicted from the subject spaces, and even when some correlate is related to the subject space of one sample it tends not to be related in the other sample.

TABLE 9.4
Prediction of Outside Correlates from Person Space Dimensions, Study III

Type of Correlate	Multiple Correlation	
Direct Perspective of Significant	Sample *A*	Sample *B*
Relationships[a]	*N* = 139	*N* = 156
Parental Affiliation	.21	.16
Parental Power	.18	.25**
Peer Affiliation	.07	.23*
Peer Power	.18	.15
Metaperspective of Significant Relationships[b]		
Anxiousness	.06	.22
Affiliation	.29**	.23*
Dominance	.12	.15
Direct Perspective on Self[c]		
Dominance	.12	.20
Affiliation	.27**	.09
Anxiousness	.07	.32***
Demographics		
Age	.22	.05
Sex	.17	.19
Personality Scales		
Personal Research Form [d]		
Affiliation	.21	.13
Aggression	.11	.08
Cognitive Structure	.07	.31**
Defendence	.19	.09
Dominance	.16	.10
Succorance	.22	.04
Desirability	.18	.15
Snyder's Self-Monitoring Scale[e]	.14	.24*
Marlowe-Crowne Social Desirability[f]	.16	.33***
Machiavellianism[g]	.18	.12

Note: *p* <.05
       **p* <.01
      ****p* <.001

[a]Second-order components of direct perspective ratings reflecting both target (*Peers*, e.g., same and opposite sex, and *Parents*, e.g., Mother and Father) and scale (*Affiliativeness*, e.g., friendly-hostile, emotionally close-distant, and *Power*, e.g., democratic-autocratic, equal-unequal power).

[b]Second-order components of metaperspective ratings reflecting scales (*Affiliativeness*, e.g., good natured-irritable, cooperative-uncooperative; *Anxiousness*, e.g., calm-anxious, composed-excitable; and *Dominance*, e.g., dominant-submissive, talkative-silent). Targets (Mother, Father, same and opposite sex peer) did not emerge as a second-order factor.

[c]Components of direct self-ratings are *Dominance* (dominant-submissive, silent-talkative); *Affiliation* (good natured-irritable, cooperative-uncooperative); and *Anxiousness* (calm-anxious, composed-excitable).

[d]Jackson (1967)

[e]Snyder (1974)

[f]Crowne and Marlowe (1964)

[g]Christie and Geis (1970)

were slightly older), the means, standard deviations, and intervariable covariance structures were virtually identical (Golding, in preparation).

The implications are quite troublesome. Currently, a partial replication of Golding's (1977) study of construal styles is under analysis (Cherney & Golding, in preparation), and we are keeping our fingers crossed. Nevertheless, we will assume that "Lady Luck" has not been simply capricious with us. If one had completed the study with either Sample A or Sample B alone, one would have had reasonably interpretable vignette and attribute spaces, and a sufficient number of "correlates" to guide rotation and interpretation of the person space, although one would have been privately a little disappointed at the low level of correlation, and a bit suspicious of the experiment-wise error rate (the few significant correlates compared to the number tested) Having collected both Sample A and Sample B, however, one must confront the discrepancy.

No multivariate individual differences study has ever been "replicated," in either the sense of the same subjects at two points in time, different subjects at the (approximate) same point in time (our Study III), or different subjects with conceptually equivalent (but literally different) judgment tasks and outside variable measures (e.g., different, hopefully convergent, indices of dominance). The findings of the present study may simply reflect unknown differences in our Samples A and B. Data for the two samples were obtained three months apart, although the fact that subjects in the two samples are virtually identical on many personality and rating task variables makes this an unlikely explanation. Two classes of explanation remain. In the first place, although individual differences in interpersonal construal may be related to personality correlates, the range of such differences and correlates in typical college volunteer of psychology course subjects may be overly restricted (homogeneous), leading to great instability, much like the classic restriction of range effect on both reliability and validity. A detailed examination of the means and standard deviations of our Study III's personality correlates (Golding, in preparation) lends some support to this interpretation. Study I (Valone & Golding, in preparation) used a contrasted groups strategy and discovered more significant correlates of their person dimensions than did Study II (Foster & Golding, in preparation), which, like Study III, selected subjects at random from a subject pool. Somewhat relatedly, Wiggins and Blackburn (1976) used fraternities of a contrasted sort, but they did not define individual differences via personality correlates, relying instead upon an oblique analytic rotation (binormamin) of their person space.

A related explanation is that individual differences in interpersonal construal are of a dimensional nature (and hence don't "cluster" or "type" themselves), but they are not related to traditional personality measures, for a variety of conceptual and methodological reasons (Block, 1977; Golding, 1978; Mischel, 1977). They may simply be inappropriate because most self-report measurement techniques sample *behavioral, attitudinal,* and *content* manifestations of traits, and differences in construal may not be simply related to such variables in a consistent or replicable pattern. For example, Golding (1977) successfully related Machiavellianism to overattribution of hostility and dishonesty, and this makes theoretical sense. However, this finding is not replicated in our Study III, and this may *in part* be because the *belief-based* items of the Machiavellianism scale may not be as *directly* (strongly?) related to the nature of interpersonal construal as they are to other beliefs or belief-based actions. It would be overly simplistic to assume that perceptions, cognitions, beliefs, construals, and behaviors are in one-to-one, "knee-jerk," correspondence (e.g., an aggressive person *always* sees others as threatening, believes violence and threat deserves retaliation in kind, knows a lot of violent behavior skills, and is especially sensitive to nonverbal cues of danger and threat!). The measures may be inappropriate, especially as our "theories" about what individual differences in construal are like are pretty simplistic.

A second class of explanation relates to the methods of analysis and design. As detailed in the next section, our tasks may not generate sufficient self-involvement, or be "experimentally realistic" (Aronson & Carlsmith, 1968), yielding nothing more than "good, normative" subject behavior (Argyris, 1968; Kelman, 1967; Runkel & McGrath, 1972). Methodologically, the statistical procedures (INDSCAL, POV, 3MFA) may tend to discover only the most straightforward and mundane sorts of individual differences, and these may not be what we had in mind or were expecting to relate to personality correlates, theoretically appropriate or not. Thus, if one looks carefully at the individual differences in construal and judgment reported thus far in the literature, most "subject types," "dimensions," or "idealized individuals" differ from each other primarily in terms of relatively simple scale usage tendencies, our Study I notwithstanding. Thus, differences in "elevation" and "scatter" are more usual than more complex or configural pattern or profile differences (a point quite similar to the lack of meaningfully patterned person-by-situation interactions—see Golding, 1975a). Indeed, there is a pressing need to examine these methodologies to determine their power or sensitivity to detect different kinds of individual differences (like sprayed or crossed interactions in the analysis of variance). What we have in mind here is a Monte Carlo type study in which the implicit or explicit definitions of individual differences contained in a variety of theoretical accounts of such differences would be translated in "model" data matrices, and then perturbed by varying magnitudes of error in order to discover to which *kinds of individual differences* the models are varyingly sensitive. Jones and Wadington (1976) have demonstrated that INDSCAL is quite sensitive to common dimensional usage, even with considerable error variance, but their definitions of individual differences (whether or not a subject *uses* a dimension) are not the kind usually implied in work on interpersonal construal (How often, to what extent, in what direction, and under what interpersonal stimulus conditions does one use a dimension?). As noted previously, the work in this area is quite "short" in theory, and one of the most glaring areas is the definition of just what an individual difference means (Golding, 1978).

Realistic Representativeness in the Study of Interpersonal Construal

It is not surprising that the individual differences that emerge in most studies of interpersonal construal are only modest in size and may not be easily replicable. The experimental tasks used in most studies demand that our subjects engage in highly artificial, uninvolving relationships with "interpersonal stimuli." Our subjects' "real" construal styles are overpowered by the normative demand characteristics of the experimental tasks. For example, in work on individual differences in so-called "implicit theories of personality" (Schneider, 1973), we typically present subjects with pairs of trait descriptors (such as "shy" and "intelligent") and ask them to rate the degree to which one attribute implies the other. We do this because we are interested in how individuals represent the dimensionality and structure of their interpersonal experience. When data are collected over many such pairs, a subject's attributional or trait-implicative network emerges, but rarely are the individual differences obtained from such a task overwhelmingly strong. This should not surprise us or lead us to reject the "individuality corollary," because the demand characteristics of the task pull for our generally compliant subjects to respond in normative ways according to the basic structure of the language that they all more or less share. Our goal in doing such experiments has been to delineate individual differences in subjective event structure, but the nature of the laboratory task precludes the possibility of such a result. The task demands heighten the operation of normative cognitive operations (e.g., to what extent does the person descriptor, "kind," imply the person descriptor, "honest," for people in general?), and so we will discover meaningful individual differences in experiential structure only to the extent that they occur in such a rational and logical manner. We do not believe that the flow of social information processing and inference occurs in such a rational manner, with words and the cultural lexicon of semantic implication as the basic process. Rather, construal seems to occur rather rapidly and automatically within an affective or emotionally connected frame of reference. There is now a reasonable body of literature within cognitive psychology to corroborate the assumption that the *affective implications* (presumably for the "self") of incoming stimuli are processed and acted upon rather more rapidly than is typically assumed by a depth of processing model (Baddeley, 1978; Craik & Lockhart, 1972; Craik & Tulving, 1975). Although this work has been done primarily with the all-too-familiar descriptive adjective or category noun (Allport, 1977; Marcel & Patterson, 1978), it holds considerable promise because such early pre- or partial processing would be consistent with the theoretical assumption that affective state serves as the primary reference signal (Powers, 1973) for the operation of the self-system in general and conscious experience in particular (similar to Sullivan's idea that the self-system regulates the affective quality of moment-to-moment experience). If the overall system does function on an emotional, affective, or feeling-toned basis, then we need to know more about the rules of inference that govern emotional and experiential representations. The rules and representational forms discovered are unlikely to have anything to do with the judged semantic similarity of "kind" and "honest."

Instead of studying the central aspects of information processing with respect to the selection, encoding, and representation of interpersonal events, we may simply be observing the operation of a verbal output process, highly conditioned by normative linguistic rules and role expectations. To further constrain the validity of such procedures, it is not unreasonably to suppose that significant self-involvement is a necessary condition for the constellation of important individual differences. Looking for the categories, dimensionality, and structure of experiential event processing in linguistic implications in an artificial context is quite likely to mislead us.

We stress the phrase "realistic representativeness" because all experimental study requires a reasoned compromise between naturalism and experimental control (Cairns, 1979; Runkel & McGrath, 1972). We believe that significant self-involvement of the subject is critical for individual differences in construal to occur at all. In Study I, we explicitly manipulated our subjects' expectancies in order to engender their construal task with personal meaning. Each subject met the woman confederate and anticipated role-playing a date with her. In Study III, we used actual transcripts of marital conflicts as stimuli, but the relative size of the first eigenvalue for the persons space (Golding, in preparation) suggests that the "consensus" was quite strong. We had hoped that subject involvement would be even higher than in Golding (1977), where subjects made judgements of interpersonal vignettes stated in the abstract. It is clear, however, that subjects were not as involved as they might have been. When we heighten the saliency of the "subject role," we decrease our power to discover important individual differences. The problem, succinctly stated, is one of *realistic representativeness.*

Significant self-involvement need not mean *mundane realism* (Aronson & Carlsmith, 1968). Subjects can get actively involved in making judgments about videotaped marital interactions when they are *personally invested* in the experimental task. In Trierweiler and Golding (in preparation) and Valone and Golding (in preparation), for example, subjects are variously instructed to stop the tape when they have observed what they consider to be a significant event. Obviously, the procedure is artificial, and so any results it produces must be "triangulated in logical space" (Cronbach & Meehl, 1955) and subjected to constructive replication. Thus, for example, if a subject "segments" at various locations, he or she should not only remember the action or meaning at that point better in experimental recognition tasks (Newtson & Engquist, 1976), but should also show free recall differences at a later time.

Indeed, studies of memory for interpersonal events may be a crude way to get at selection, encoding, and representational differences. The problem with a "naturalistic memory" study, however, is obvious: Different people by definition are exposed to different stimuli. Furthermore, simple recall data of this sort confound selection, encoding, memory structure, retrieval, and output variables (Loftus & Loftus, 1976). Thus, when we probe memory in one way or another we may get different answers (Loftus & Palmer, 1974), and it is not clear whether any obtained differences are a function of encoding or reencoding.

Nevertheless, creative designs can begin to attack these problems. For example, we think it wise to investigate memory for interpersonal events in a group setting. An obvious advantage is the realistic self-involvement of subjects, particularly as a function of group task (problem solving, self-disclosure, acquaintance making, etc.). An even more important advantage is the possibility of consensus versus individual differences. All members have had the same *approximate* opportunity to process the same information, though from different perspectives. The kind of information recalled, the order, its clustering if any, and its "distortions" across people and time, will all serve as important sources of data about interpersonal construal. Additionally, careful attention to the form, mode, content, and metacommunicative aspects of recalled interpersonal events (Carswell & Rommetveit, 1971; Giles & Powesland, 1975; Labov & Fanshel, 1977; Stiles, 1978; Wold, 1978) holds great promise for those of us interested in how individuals make sense of their interpersonal worlds. When describing social interactions that we have experienced, we all seem to focus on somewhat different aspects. It would clearly be profitable to investigate the meaning of such differences. The content categories (physical appearance, trait descriptors, demographic characteristics) and the affective tones (good–bad, pleasant–unpleasant) that are recalled are certainly of interest; also important are subtler aspects of the recalled communication, such as what is presumed about the other's intentions, the direction in which "distortion" or other elaboration takes place, and other metacommunicative aspects (Watzlawick, Beavin, & Jackson, 1967).

Experimental designs, such as the three-mode analyses reported here, have tremendous power and ought to be used to corroborate the results from research employing other designs. Further, we should seek appropriate convergence using a variety of naturalistic, contrived, and controlled designs. The task is no longer one of "demonstrating" individual differences; rather, we need to delineate clearly our subjects' selection, encoding, and representational processes and relate these to meaningful conceptions of human development, dysfunction, and change.

ACKNOWLEDGMENTS

Part of this chapter was prepared under the auspices of a Public Health Service research fellowship, MH 05885, from the National Institute of Mental Health.

The advice and guidance of Ledyard Tucker is gratefully acknowledged. Nancy

Hirschberg, who encouraged us to expand our work in this area, was an uncommon friend whose untimely death is not easily comprehended.

Ms. Foster is currently at the Department of Psychiatry and Psychology, University of Wisconsin Medical School, Madison.

REFERENCES

Allport, D. A. On knowing the meaning of words we are unable to report: The effects of visual masking. In S. Dornic (Ed.), *Attention and performance* (Vol. 6). Hillsdale, N.J.: Lawrence Erlbaum Associates, 1977.

Anderberg, M. R. *Cluster analysis for applications.* New York: Academic Press, 1973.

Anderson, J. R. Arguments concerning representations for mental imagery. *Psychological Review,* 1978, *85,* 249–277.

Argyris, C. Some unintended consequences of vigorous research. *Psychological Bulletin,* 1968, *70,* 185–197.

Arkowitz, H. Measurement and modification of minimal dating behavior. In M. Hersen, R. Eisler, & P. Miller (Eds.), *Progress in behavior modification* (Vol. 5). New York: Academic Press, 1977.

Arkowitz, H., Lichtenstein, E., McGovern, K., & Hines, P. The behavioral assessment of social competence in males. *Behavior Therapy,* 1975, *6,* 3–13.

Aronson, E., & Carlsmith, J. M. Experimentation in social psychology. In G. Lindzey & E. Aronson (Eds.), *Handbook of social psychology* (Vol. 2). Reading, Mass.: Addison–Wesley, 1968.

Baddeley, A. D. The trouble with levels: A reexamination of Craik and Lockhart's framework for memory research. *Psychological Review,* 1978, *85,* 139–152.

Bandura, A. *Social learning theory.* Englewood Cliffs, N.J.: Prentice–Hall, 1977.

Bannister, D., & Agnew, J. The child's construing of self. In J. K. Cole & A. W. Landfield (Eds.), *Nebraska Symposium on Motivation* (Vol. 24). Lincoln: University of Nebraska Press, 1977.

Beach, L., & Wertheimer, M. A free-response approach to the study of person cognition. *Journal of Abnormal and Social Psychology,* 1961, *62,* 367–374.

Beck, S. B., Ward-Hull, C. I., & McLear, P. M. Variables related to women's somatic preferences of the male and female body. *Journal of Personality and Social Psychology,* 1976, *34,* 1200–1210.

Bem, D. J., & Allen, A. On predicting some of the people some of the time: The search for cross-situational consistencies in behavior. *Psychological Review,* 1974, *81,* 506–520.

Benjamin, L. S. Structural analysis of social behavior. *Psychological Review,* 1974, *81,* 392–425.

Benjamin, L. S. Use of structural analysis of social behavior (SASB) and Markov chains to study dyadic interactions. *Journal of Abnormal Psychology,* 1979, *88,* 303–319.

Block, J. Advancing the psychology of personality: Paradigmatic shift or improving the quality of research? In D. Magnusson & N. S. Endler (Eds.), *Personality at the crossroads: Current issues in interactional psychology.* Hillsdale, N.J.: Lawrence Erlbaum Associates, 1977.

Block, J., Weiss, D., & Thane, A. How relevant is a semantic similarity interpretation of personality ratings? *Journal of Personality and Social Psychology,* 1979, in press.

Bower, G. H. Cognitive psychology: An introduction. In W. K. Estes (Ed.), *Handbook of learning and cognitive processes* (Vol. 1). Hillsdale, N.J.: Lawrence Erlbaum Associates, 1975.

Cairns, R. B. (Ed.). *The analysis of social interactions.* Hillsdale, N.J.: Lawrence Erlbaum Associates, 1979.

Carlston, D. E. Dual processes in impression formation. In R. Hastie, E. B. Ebbesen, T. M. Ostrom, R. S. Wyer, D. L. Hamilton, & D. E. Carlston (Eds.), *Person memory and encoding processes.* Hillsdale, N.J.: Lawrence Erlbaum Associates, 1979, in press.

Carroll, J. D., & Chang, J. J. Analysis of individual differences in multidimensional scaling via an N-way generalization of "Eckart-Young" decomposition. *Psychometrika,* 1970, *35,* 283–319.

Carswell, E. A., & Rommetveit, R. (Eds.). *Social contexts of messages.* London: Academic Press, 1971.

Carson, R. C. *Interaction concepts of personality.* Chicago: Aldine, 1969.

Cherney, R., & Golding, S. L. *The multivariate structure of interpersonal attributions.* Manuscript in preparation, University of Illinois, Champaign, Illinois.

Christie, R., & Geis, F. L. *Studies in Machiavellianism.* New York: Academic Press, 1970.

Cliff, N. The "idealized individual" interpretation of individual differences in multidimensional scaling. *Psychometrika,* 1968, *33,* 225–232.

Clore, G. L., Hirschberg, N., & Itkin, S. Judging attraction from nonverbal behavior: The gain phenomenon. *Journal of Consulting and Clinical Psychology,* 1975, *43,* 491–497.

Cohen, C. E., & Ebbesen, E. B. Observational goals and schema activation: A theoretical framework for behavior perception. *Journal of Experimental Social Psychology,* 1979, in press.

Craik, F. I. M., & Lockhart, R. S. Levels of processing: A framework for memory research. *Journal of Verbal Learning and Verbal Behavior,* 1972, *11,* 681–684.

Craik, F. I. M., & Tulving, E. Depth of processing and the retention of words in episodic memory. *Journal of Experimental Psychology: General,* 1975, *104,* 268–294.

Cronbach, L. J., & Meehl, P. E. Construct validity in psychological tests. *Psychological Bulletin,* 1955, *52,* 281–302.

Crowne, D. P., & Marlowe, D. J. *The approval motive.* New York: Wiley, 1964.

Curran, J. P. Skills training as an approach to the treatment of heterosexual–social anxiety: A review. *Psychological Bulletin,* 1977, *84,* 140–157.

Dickman, H. R. The perception of behavioral units. In R. G. Barker (Ed.), *The stream of behavior.* New York: Appleton–Century–Crofts, 1963.

Dornbusch, S. M., Hastorf, A. H., Richardson, S. A., Muzzy, R. E., & Vreeland, R. S. The perceiver and the perceived: Their relative influence on the categories of interpersonal perception. *Journal of Personality and Social Psychology,* 1965, *1,* 434–440.

Eckart, C., & Young, G. The approximation of one matrix by another of lower rank. *Psychometrika,* 1936, *1,* 211–218.

Fiedler, F. E. *A theory of leadership effectiveness.* New York: McGraw–Hill, 1967.

Fiske, D. W. *Red capes, red herrings, and red flags.* Paper presented at the 86th annual convention of the American Psychological Association, Toronto, 1978.

Fiske, S. T., & Cox, M. G. Person concepts: The effect of target familiarity and descriptive purpose on the process of describing others. *Journal of Personality,* 1979, *47,* 136–161.

Foster, S. W., & Golding, S. L. *Individual differences in the perception of dominance.* Manuscript in preparation, University of Illinois, Champaign, Illinois.

Gibbs, J. C. The meaning of ecologically oriented inquiry in contemporary psychology. *American Psychologist,* 1979, *34,* 127–140.

Giles, H., & Powesland, P. F. *Speech style and social evaluation.* London: Academic Press, 1975.

Golding, S. L. Flies in the ointment: Methodological problems in the analysis of the percentage of variance due to persons and situations. *Psychological Bulletin,* 1975, *82,* 278–288. (a)

Golding. S. L. *Individual differences in the construal of interpersonal interactions.* Paper presented at the Symposium on Interactional Psychology, Stockholm, Sweden, 1975. (b)

Golding, S. L. Individual differences in the construal of interpersonal interactions. In D. Magnusson & N. Endler (Eds.), *Personality at the crossroads: Current issues in interactional psychology.* Hillsdale, N.J.: Lawrence Erlbaum Assoc., 1977.

Golding, S. L. Toward a more adequate theory of personality: Psychological organizing principles. In H. London & N. Hirschberg (Eds.), *Personality: A new look at metatheories.* Washington: Hemisphere Press, 1978.

Golding, S. L. *The problem of replication in individual differences in social perception.* Manuscript in preparation, University of Illinois, Champaign, Illinois.

Golding, S. L., & Knudson, R. M. Multivariable–multimethod convergence in the domain of interpersonal behavior. *Multivariate Behavioral Research,* 1975, *10,* 425–443.

Hamilton, D. C., & Gifford, R. K. Influence of implicit personality theories on cue utilization in interpersonal judgment. *Proceedings of the 78th Annual Convention of the American Psychological Association,* 1970, *5,* 415–416.

Harman, H. H. *Modern factor analysis* (2nd ed., rev.). Chicago: University of Chicago Press, 1967.

Jackson, D. N. *Personality research form manual.* Goshen, N.Y.: Research Psychologists Press, 1967.

Jones, E. E., & Thibaut, J. W. Interaction goals as bases of inference in interpersonal peception. In R. Tagiuri & L. Petrullo (Eds.), *Person perception and interpersonal behavior.* Stanford, Calif.: Stanford University Press, 1958.

Jones, R. A., & Rosenberg, S. Structural representations of naturalistic descriptions of personality. *Multivariate Behavioral Research,* 1974, *9,* 217–230.

Jones, R. A., Sensenig, J., & Haley, J. V. Self-descriptions: Configurations of content and order effects. *Journal of Personality and Social Psychology,* 1974, *30,* 36–45.

Jones, L., & Wadington, J. *Sensitivity of INDSCAL to simulated individual differences in dimensional usage patterns and judgmental error.* Unpublished manuscript, University of Illinois, Champaign, Illinois (1976).

Kanfer, F., & Hagerman, S. *The role of self-regulation in depression.* Paper presented at NIMH Conference on Research Recommendations for the Behavioral Treatment of Depression, Pittsburgh, 1979.

Kelly, G. A. *A theory of personality: The psychology of personal constructs.* New York: Norton, 1955.

Kelman, H. C. Human use of human subjects. *Psychological Bulletin,* 1967, *67,* 1–11.

Kim, M. J., & Rosenberg, S. *Evaluation, potency, and activity (EPA): Dimensions of implicit personality theory.* Paper presented at the 86th annual convention of the American Psychological Association, Toronto, 1978.

Kingsley, S. J. *Implicit self-theory.* Unpublished doctoral dissertation, Rutgers University, 1978.

Kintsch, W. *The representation of meaning in memory.* Hillsdale, N.J.: Lawrence Erlbaum Associates, 1974.

Knudson, R., Sommers, A., & Golding, S. Interpersonal perception and mode of resolution in marital conflict. *Journal of Personality and Social Psychology,* 1980, *38,* 751–753.

Koltuv, B. Some characteristics of intrajudge trait intercorrelations. *Psychological Monograph,* 1962, *76*(33, Whole No. 552).

Kosslyn, S. M. Can imagery be distinguished from other forms of internal representation? Evidence from studies of information retrieval time. *Memory & Cognition,* 1976, *4,* 291–297.

Kuiper, N. A., & Rogers, T. B. Encoding of personal information: Self–other differences. *Journal of Personality and Social Psychology,* 1979, *37,* 499–514.

Labov, W., & Fanshel, D. *Therapeutic discourse: Psychotherapy as conversation.* New York: Academic Press, 1977.

Laing, R. D., Phillipson, H., & Lee, A. R. *Interpersonal perception.* New York: Springer, 1966.

Lamiell, J., Foss, M., & Cavenee, P. On the relationship between conceptual schemes and behavior reports: A closer look. *Journal of Personality,* 1980, *48,* 54–73.

Leary, T. *Interpersonal diagnosis of personality.* New York: Ronald Press, 1957.

Levin, J. Three-mode factor analysis. *Psychological Bulletin,* 1965, *64,* 442–452.

Livesley, W. J., & Bromley, D. B. *Person perception in childhood and adolescence.* London: Wiley, 1973.

Loftus, E. F., & Palmer, J. C. Reconstruction of automobile destruction: An example of the interaction between language and memory. *Journal of Verbal Learning and Verbal Behavior,* 1974, *13,* 585–589.

Loftus, G. R., & Loftus, E. F. *Human memory: The processing of information.* Hillsdale, N.J.: Lawrence Erlbaum Associates, 1976.

Lorr, M., & Suziedelis, A. Modes of interpersonal behavior. *British Journal of Social and Clinical Psychology,* 1969, *8,* 124–132.

Lykken, D. T. Statistical significance in psychological research. *Psychological Bulletin,* 1968, *70,* 151–159.

MacLeod, R. B. The phenomenological approach to social psychology. *Psychological Review,* 1947, *54,* 193–210.

Marcel, A. J., & Patterson, K. E. Word recognition and production: Reciprocity in clinical and normal studies. In J. Requin (Ed.), *Attention and performance* (Vol. 7). Hillsdale, N.J.: Lawrence Erlbaum Associates, 1978.

Messick, S., & Kogan, N. Personality consistencies in judgment: Dimensions of role constructs. *Multivariate Behavioral Research,* 1966, *1,* 165–175.

Mischel, W. Toward a cognitive social learning reconceptualization of personality. *Psychological Review,* 1973, *80,* 252–283.

Mischel, W. The interaction of person and situation. In D. Magnusson & N. S. Endler (Eds.), *Personality at the crossroads: Current issues in interactional psychology.* Hillsdale, N.J.: Lawrence Erlbaum Associates, 1977.

Mischel, W., Ebbesen, E. B., & Zeiss, A. R. Cognitive and attentional mechanisms in delay of gratification. *Journal of Personality and Social Psychology,* 1972, *21,* 204–218.

Mulaik, S. A. *The foundation of factor analysis.* New York: McGraw–Hill, 1972.

Neisser, U. *Cognitive psychology.* New York: Appleton–Century–Crofts, 1967.

Neisser, U. *Cognition and reality.* San Francisco: Freeman, 1976.

Newtson, D. Foundations of attribution: The perception of ongoing behavior. In J. Harvey, W. Ickes, & R. Kidd (Eds), *New directions in attribution research* (Vol. 1). Hillsdale, N.J.: Lawrence Erlbaum Associates, 1976.

Newtson, D., & Engquist, G. The perceptual organization of ongoing behavior. *Journal of Experimental Social Psychology,* 1976, *12,* 436–450.

Norman, W. T., & Goldberg, L. R. Raters, ratees, and randomness in personality structure. *Journal of Personality and Social Psychology,* 1966, *4,* 681–691.

Osgood, C. E., Suci, G. J., & Tannenbaum, P. H. *The measurement of meaning.* Urbana: University of Illinois Press, 1957.

Passini, F. T., & Norman, W. T. A universal conception of personality structure? *Journal of Personality and Social Psychology,* 1966, *4,* 44–49.

Pedersen, D. M. The measurement of individual differences in perceived personality-trait relationships and their relation to certain determinants. *Journal of Social Psychology,* 1965, *65,* 233–258.

Peevers, B. H., & Secord, P. F. Developmental changes in attribution of descriptive concepts to persons. *Journal of Personality and Social Psychology,* 1973, *27,* 120–128.

Posavac, E. J. Dimensions of trait preferences and personality type. *Journal of Personality and Social Psychology,* 1971, *19,* 274–281.

Posner, M. I., & Snyder, C. R. R. Attention and cognitive control. In R. Solso (Ed.), *Information processing and cognition.* Hillsdale, N.J.: Lawrence Erlbaum Associates, 1975.

Powers, W. T. *Behavior: The control of perception.* Chicago: Aldine, 1973.

Powers, W. T. Quantitative analysis of purposive systems: Some spadework at the foundations of scientific psychology. *Psychological Review,* 1978, *85,* 417–435.

Raush, H. L. Paradox levels, and junctures in person–situation systems. In D. Magnusson & N. S. Endler (Eds.), *Personality at the crossroads: Current issues in interactional psychology.* Hillsdale, N.J.: Lawrence Erlbaum Associates, 1977.

Reichenbach, H. *Experience and prediction.* Chicago: University of Chicago Press, 1938.

Rogers, T. B. Self-reference in memory: Recognition of personality items. *Journal of Research in Personality,* 1977, *11,* 295–305.

Rogers, T. B., Kuiper, N. A., & Kirker, W. S. Self-reference and the encoding of personal information. *Journal of Personality and Social Psychology,* 1977, *35,* 677–688.

Rosenberg, S. New approaches to the analysis of personal constructs in person perception. In J. Cole

(Ed.), *Nebraska Symposium on Motivation* (Vol. 24). Lincoln: University of Nebraska Press, 1977.

Rosenberg, S. *An individual differences model for representing the structure of implicit personality theory.* Paper presented at the 87th annual convention of the American Psychological Association, New York City, 1979.

Rosenberg, S., & Sedlak, A. Structural representations of implicit personality theory. In L. Berkowitz (Ed.), *Advances in experimental social psychology* (Vol. 6). New York: Academic Press, 1972.

Runkel, P. J., & McGrath, J. E. *Research on human behavior: A systematic guide to method.* New York: Holt, Rinehart, & Winston, 1972.

Scarlett, H. H., Press, A. N., & Crockett, W. H. Children's descriptions of peers: A Wernerian developmental analysis. *Child Development,* 1971, *42,* 439-453.

Schneider, D. J. Implicit personality theory: A review. *Psychological Bulletin,* 1973, *79,* 294-309.

Schneider, D. J. *Situational and stimulus factors in free descriptions of people.* Paper presented at the annual convention of the American Psychological Association, San Francisco, 1977.

Schneider, D. J., Hastorf, A. H., & Ellsworth, P. C. *Person perception* (2nd ed.). Reading, Mass.: Addison-Wesley, 1979.

Sherman, R. C. Individual differences in perceived trait relationships as a function of dimensional salience. *Multivariate Behavioral Research,* 1972, *7,* 109-129.

Shweder, R. *Fact and artifact in personality assessment: The influence of conceptual schemata on individual differences judgment.* Paper presented at the 86th annual convention of the American Psychological Association, Toronto, 1978.

Snyder, M. Self-monitoring of expressive behavior. *Journal of Personality and Social Psychology,* 1974, *30,* 526-537.

Stiles, W. B. Verbal response modes and dimensions of interpersonal roles: A method of discourse analysis. *Journal of Personality and Social Psychology,* 1978, *36,* 693-703.

Sullivan, H. S. *The interpersonal theory of psychiatry.* New York: Norton, 1953.

Swensen, C. H. *Introduction to interpersonal relations.* Glenview, Ill.: Scott, Foresman, 1973.

Trierweiler, S. J., & Golding, S. L. *The effects of encoding strategies, purpose, and target on the unitization and representation of social events.* Manuscript in preparation, University of Illinois, Champaign, Illinois.

Trierweiler, S. J., Golding, S. L., & Valone, K. *Individual differences in the unitization of social information.* Manuscript in preparation, University of Illinois, Champaign, Illinois.

Tucker, L. R. Some mathematical notes on three-mode factor analysis. *Psychometrika,* 1966, *31,* 279-311.

Tucker, L. R. Relations between multidimensional scaling and three-mode factor analysis. *Psychometrika,* 1972, *37,* 3-27.

Tucker, L. R., & Messick, S. An individual differences model for multidimensional scaling. *Psychometrika,* 1963, *28,* 333-367.

Valone, K., & Golding, S. L. *Interpersonal construal and interpersonal dysfunction: Heterosexual social anxiety in males.* Manuscript in preparation, University of Illinois, Champaign, Illinois.

Wachtel, P. Interaction cycles, unconscious processes, and the person-situation issue. In D. Magnusson & N. Endler (Eds.), *Personality at the crossroads: Current issues in interactional psychology.* Hillsdale, N.J.: Lawrence Erlbaum Associates, 1977.

Walters, H. A., & Jackson, D. N. Group and individual regularities in trait inference: A multidimensional scaling analysis. *Multivariate Behavioral Research,* 1966, *1,* 145-163.

Watzlawick, P., Beavin, J., & Jackson, D. *Pragmatics of human communication.* New York: Norton, 1967.

Wickens, D. D. Characteristics of word encoding. In A. W. Melton & E. Martin (Eds.), *Coding processes in human memory.* Washington, D.C.: Winston, 1972.

Wiggins, J. S. A psychological taxonomy of trait-descriptive terms: The interpersonal domain. *Journal of Personality and Social Psychology,* 1979, *37,* 395-412.

Wiggins, J. S., Wiggins, N., & Conger, J. C. Correlates of heterosexual somatic preference. *Journal of Personality and Social Psychology*, 1968, *10*, 82–90.

Wiggins, N. Individual differences in human judgments: A multivariate approach. In C. Rappaport & D. A. Summers (Eds.), *Human judgment and social interaction*. New York: Holt, Rinehart, and Winston, 1973.

Wiggins, N. H., & Blackburn, M.. Implicit theories of personality: An individual differences approach. *Multivariate Behavioral Research*, 1976, *11*, 267–285.

Wiggins, N., & Fishbein, M. Dimensions of semantic space: A problem of individual differences. In J. R. Snider & C. E. Osgood (Eds.), *The semantic differential technique: A book of readings*. Chicago: Aldine, 1969.

Wiggins, N., Hoffman, P. J., & Taber, T. Types of judges and cue utilization in judgments of intelligence. *Journal of Personality and Social Psychology*, 1969. *12*, 52–59.

Wiggins, N., & Wiggins, J. S. A typological analysis of male preferences for female body types. *Multivariate Behavioral Research*, 1969, *4*, 89–102.

Wilder, D. A. Effect of predictability on units of perception and attribution. *Personality and Social Psychology Bulletin*, 1978, *4*, 281–284.

Wish, M. Comparisons among multidimensional structures of interpersonal relations. *Multivariate Behavioral Research*, 1976, *11*, 297–324.

Wish, M., Deutsch, M., & Kaplan, S. J. Perceived dimensions of interpersonal relations. *Journal of Personality and Social Psychology*, 1976, *33*, 409–420.

Wold, A. H. *Decoding oral language*. London: Academic Press, 1978.

Wyer, R. S., & Srull, T. K. The processing of social stimulus information. In R. Hastie, E. B. Ebbesen, T. M. Ostrom, R. S. Wyer, D. L. Hamilton, & D. E. Carlston (Eds.), *Person memory and encoding processes*. Hillsdale, N.J.: Lawrence Erlbaum Associates, 1979, in press.

Yarrow, M. R., & Campbell, J. D. Person perception in children. *Merrill-Palmer Quarterly*, 1963, *9*, 57–72.

10 A Structural Equation Model of Impression Formation

Lynn Smith-Lovin
University of South Carolina

David R. Heise
University of North Carolina

This chapter has two goals. First, it illustrates how theoretical ideas can be combined with psychological data in structural equation models. We show how to use a computer program, LISREL (Jöreskog & Sörbom, 1978), that allows the analysis of complex structural models. Our second goal is to show how structural equation models can further understanding of social cognition. We want to explore how people process information when they form impressions. To accomplish these objectives, the chapter briefly reviews the previous work that has been done on social cognition, concentrating on those studies that used data similar to ours. We then develop a theoretical model of how information about social events is processed when subjects are exposed to a short event description. The LISREL program is described, and we show how to represent our theoretical model with the program. Finally, the procedures for data collection are described, and we present the results of our analyses.

IMPRESSION FORMATION

Social psychologists usually assume that people use information about others to form impressions of them. Research on these processes is closely linked to work on attitude balance theory, attitude change dynamics, and the literature on attribution. Impression formation can be studied using a model in which nouns that identify actor–persons and object–persons are linked with verbs that describe some interpersonal behavior. Because the nouns and verbs are associated with specific, measurable attitudes or affective meanings, the event description can be

195

presented to subjects to study the impressions they form about the people and the behavior involved in the simple event.

Gollob (1968) first developed an experimental paradigm to specify reactions to such events. He generated sets of simple sentences by combining actors that were either positively or negatively evaluated with object–persons that were either positive or negative. He linked the actor and the object with either a positive or negative behavior. For example, a sentence with a negative actor, a positive behavior, and a positive object–person would be ''the cruel man helps the child.'' Gollob then attempted to predict the subjects' evaluative (good–bad) ratings of the actor within the context of each event–sentence.

Gollob found that the in-context impressions could be predicted very accurately as a function of the original attitudes associated with the actor (A), the behavior (B), and the object (O) in the sentence.[1] Eighty-six percent of the variance in the in-context impressions was explained by a simple regression model containing terms for the out-of-context variables—the original attitude toward the actor, the original attitude toward the behavior, and the product of the original attitudes toward the behavior and toward the object. (The multiplicative interaction represents a balance effect—doing good unto good or bad unto bad enhances the evaluation of an actor.)

Later studies by Gollob, Heise, and their associates (Gollob & Rossman, 1973; Heise 1969a, 1970, 1978, 1979; Heise & Smith-Lovin, 1981) have replicated Gollob's original findings. The following formula from Gollob (1968) can be used to predit in-context evaluations of an actor from out-of-context evaluations on seven-point scales:

$$A_e' = -.26 + .39 \, A_e + .48 \, B_e + .25 \, B_e O_e. \tag{1}$$

The effects described by this prediction formula can be applied interpretively to specific interpersonal events. For instance, the average out-of-context evaluative rating of a Child is 1.9 (quite good), of Pestering someone is -1.8 (quite bad), and of a Schoolgirl is 1.2 (slightly good—ratings and scales taken from Heise, 1978). A Child who has Pestered a Schoolgirl is viewed somewhat negatively, however; the rating of the Child (actor) within the context of this event is -0.92 (as compared with a 1.9 rating before the event). The formula indicates that this difference is a consequence of having engaged in a negative, irritating behavior and, especially, of having directed this negative act at someone who is basically a good, pleasant person.

Heise has expanded this impression formation paradigm to study changes in

---

[1]Gollob (1968) originally used the notation SVO to symbolize the subject, verb, and object of the event-sentence. More recently Heise and his associates (Heise, 1977, 1978; 1979; Heise & Smith-Lovin, 1981; Smith-Lovin, 1979) have used the ABO notation to emphasize the social nature of the described events.

impressions of potency (powerfulness versus weakness) and activity (liveliness versus quietness). Heise's studies also examined how events change impressions of object-persons and behaviors as well as impressions of actors.

The most recent studies (Gollob & Rossman, 1973; Heise, 1978; Heise & Smith-Lovin, 1981) have examined cross-dimensional effects in impression formation (e.g., effects of behavior potency on the evaluation of the actor). At least one significant cross-dimensional effect has been found in each prediction formula. For example, Heise and Smith-Lovin (1981) showed that the evaluation of an actor after an event can be predicted more accurately with the following equation, which includes effects from evaluation (e), potency (p), and activity (a) dimensions:

$$A'_e = .03 + .40 A_e - .13 A_p + .49 B_e - .34 B_a + .20 B_e O_e \qquad .(2)$$

The effects of evaluation are very similar to those from studies that have explored only within-dimension effects (Gollob, 1968; Heise, 1969a, 1970). But now we see that powerful actors (high A_p) are evaluated somewhat more negatively when they engage in interpersonal behaviors, and that very active or frantic behaviors (high B_a) reflect badly on the actor.

Regression equations from earlier studies such as (1) and (2) summarize the total effects of the attitudes toward the event elements (A, B, and O) on the outcomes after the event. In the present analysis, we explore the possibility that these effects are not direct influences. Instead, a model is developed that treats impression formation as a feedback process. We suggest that a subject's out-of-context attitudes toward the event elements (obtained before an event is considered) set the initial attitudes or meanings within the context of the event description. Then, the impressions of (or feelings toward) each event element affects feelings toward the other elements until a stable final outcome is reached. In other words, the affective meanings or attitudes toward the actor, behavior, and object influence each other in indirect ways, as the meanings are modified by the context of the event description.

To illustrate the idea of impression formation as a feedback process, consider Heise's (1969a) finding that the object of a negative action is evaluated more negatively because he has been victimized (an effect of B_e on O'_e). This finding seems rather counter-intuitive as a direct effect. Why should we think less of someone who has *received* a negative action? It makes more sense to posit a feedback model that allows the attitudes toward event elements to affect one another. It may be the case that a negative behavior reflects badly on the *actor* within the event, and *then* the evaluation of the actor affects the attitude toward the object-person (i.e., the object-person must not be very nice, if he was associating with such a nasty person, the actor). Therefore, instead of having a direct effect of behavior evaluation (B_e) on object-person evaluation (O'_e) negative behaviors may operate through actor evaluation (A'_e) to injure the reputation of the object-person.

THE MODEL

A model including the types of indirect feedback effects described in the foregoing can be displayed conveniently using a path diagram (Fig. 10.1). Lowercase letters indicate observed variables, and uppercase letters indicate latent variables. The letters A, B, and O refer to the actor, behavior, and object-person; the subscripts e, p, and a refer to evaluation, potency, and activity. Primed variables (e.g., A'_e) are impressions produced by an event; unprimed variables (e.g., A_e) indicate impressions of the actor, behavior, or object in isolation.

The model has nine outcome variables—the evaluation, potency, and activity ratings of actor, behavior, and object. It has 10 predictor variables, including $B_e O_e$, which is created by multiplying the evaluation of the behavior and the evaluation of the object. Impressions of actor, behavior, and object out of context are not influenced by the feelings resulting from exposure to an event description, so the nine out-of-context impressions and the $B_e O_e$ interaction are exogenous variables. These original impressions of an element directly affect only the postevent feelings toward that same element; cross-element effects occur indirectly. For example, the out-of-context evaluation of a behavior (B_e) can only affect evaluation of that behavior within the context of an event (B'_e), which in turn may influence evaluation of the actor (A'_e) or object-person (O'_e) in the event. This theoretical restriction allows the prior impressions of actor, behavior, and object (the unprimed variables) to be used as instruments for disentangling relationships among the endogenous variables, the in-context impressions (see Heise, 1975, Chapter 5, for a discussion of instrumental variables). For example, the fact that B_e affects only B'_e directly allows us to estimate the effects of B'_e on the other primed variables: A'_e, A'_p, A'_a, O'_e, etc. We allow impression formation processes to involve cross-element effects but not intraelement effects. For example, O'_e is not allowed to affect O'_p and O'_a, but it may influence B'_e, (which then influences O'_p).

THE LISREL PROGRAM

Structural equation modeling is a methodology that permits theoretical knowledge and empirical information to be combined in order to estimate parameters of large causal systems. Parameter estimates for structural equation models can be obtained from computer program LISREL, developed by K. G. Jöreskog (Jöreskog, 1969, 1970; Jöreskog, Gruvaeus, & Vanthillo, 1970; Jöreskog & Sörbom, 1978). A typical LISREL model incorporates a measurement model, which relates latent constructs to observed measures of these constructs, and a structural model that specifies the causal relationship among latent variables.

The LISREL approach has several advantages when compared with other approaches. First, we can examine theoretical systems that include a large

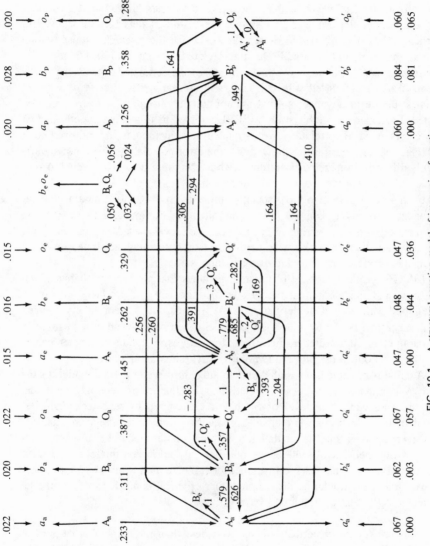

FIG. 10.1. A structural equation model of impression formation.

number of variables and relationships. For example, the impression-formation problem addressed in this chapter involves nine dependent variables, which have many interrelationships. Estimating the parameters of such a large, complex model is very difficult without a program like LISREL. Secondly, LISREL can use information that we have about the errors in our variables while it is estimating the structural parameters. In simple regression models like those used in earlier studies (Gollob, 1968; Heise, 1969a, 1970), the researcher must assume that all the errors in the variables are uncorrelated with one another. In addition, the independent variables must have no error if the estimated regression coefficients are to be unbiased. LISREL allows the researcher to specify a measurement structure in advance, so that assumptions about correlated errors can be tested. For example, in this study LISREL allowed us to test the hypothesis that the errors were uncorrelated. We estimated several models that allowed such correlations, and our results showed that the error correlations were not significantly different from zero. Therefore, we have set these parameters equal to zero for the model that we use as an illustration here.

In this study, we also have specific information about the amount of measurement error in our data (see discussion following). Using LISREL, we can set the measurement error variances at predetermined levels based on other analyses; the program then uses this information to compute more accurate, unbiased estimates of the effects in which we are interested.

LISREL produces the set of parameter values that are most probable, given the data and the theoretical model specification (i.e., it produces maximum likelihood estimates of model parameters). It constructs a theoretical variance–covariance matrix (Σ) by applying the model specifications and initial estimates of parameters, and searchers iteratively for new estimates of parameter values that best reproduce the observed variance–covariance matrix, S.

A chi-square value is computed to help judge how well the final model fits the data. When the chi-squre is small relative to the degrees of freedom, the model fits the data well. The level of fit that is considered to be "acceptable" is problematic. Ideally, a very small chi-square value is possible. In practice, however, a model that fits the data too well will contain a number of parameters that are not theoretically interesting but that only allow the model to represent sampling errors in the observed variance–covariance matrix. Unless a researcher is working with population data, some other criterion is needed for defining an acceptable fit. Three alternatives have been suggested:

1. A chi-square value that is equal to or less than the number of degrees of freedom may be considered a reasonable fit (Jöreskog 1969). In fact, for exploratory purposes any chi-square less than five times the degrees of freedom may be acceptable.[2]

---

[2]Because the chi-square value is a function of both the degrees of freedom *and* the number of observations, it may seem unreasonable that this ratio could be used to evaluate models at any sample

2. Lawley and Maxwell (1971) suggest accepting models when the probability of the chi-square value is greater than or equal to .10. Others have used probability values of .05 or .15.

3. If a researcher is attempting to improve fit by removing constraints on a model's parameters, Sörbom (1975) proposes accepting the more parsimonious model when the difference in chi-square values produced by the two models is no longer significant. This criterion may be used when comparing models, because the difference in chi-square values also is chi-square distributed. The number of degrees of freedom for the comparison is equal to the difference in degrees of freedom for the two models.

Saris, de Piper, and Zegwaart (1979) apply each of these criteria and discuss differences in results. Obviously these are only rough guidelines. Theory and the plausibility of the estimates play an important role in evaluating a model.

In specifying a model for the LISREL program, any particular parameter may be treated in one of three ways: (1) as known a priori on theoretical or empirical grounds and therefore assigned a fixed value; (2) as unknown, but constrained to be equal to one or more other parameters; or (3) as an unknown quantity to be freely estimated by the program. Eight sets of parameters have to be considered in using LISREL, each set corresponding to an input matrix in setting up a problem.

The Θ_δ matrix is the variance–covariance matrix of the errors in measurement for the exogenous indicators. The Θ_ϵ matrix represents the same information for the endogenous indicators. In either case, the matrix diagonal defines the error variances of indicators. If the indicators were scales with known reliabilities, fixed values could be input as the diagonal entries in Θ_δ or Θ_ϵ. If errors in indicators are independent and random, then the off-diagonal elements of the Θ matrices are zero.

The Λ_x matrix represents the factor pattern for the indicators of exogenous variables. It shows which hypothesized latent variables influence each observed indicator. The corresponding factor matrix for the y indicators is Λ_y. Some elements in Λ_x and Λ_y always will be fixed, usually at zero or one. For example, if y_1 and y_2 are indicators of N_1, and y_3 and y_4 are indicators of N_2, then the parameters connecting the latent variable N_2 to y_1 and y_2 are set to zero on the theoretical grounds that their indicators measure only N_1, the construct that they are supposed to measure. Fixing a parameter equal to zero in a LISREL model is

---

size. It is appropriate, however, because the model's deviations from the observed variance–covariance matrix are a much more serious problem if the sample size is large. When the N is small, the matrix contains relatively large amounts of sampling error. The researcher does not want to fit this sampling error with his or her theoretical model. On the other hand, when the sample is large and the variances and covariances are very stable, deviations of the model from the observed interrelationships are more likely to be the result of theoretical misspecification. The use of a ratio of chi-square to degrees of freedom requires a theoretical model to fit a variance–covariance matrix from a large data set more closely than a matrix from a small data set.

equivalent to excluding the variable from the equation in regression or factor analysis. In models where only one indicator is available for each latent variable, the unobserved variables are considered to be the same as the observed indicators. In this case the Λ_x and Λ_y matrices will be fixed equal to an identity matrix.

The Φ matrix contains the variances and covariances of the latent exogenous variables. Usually these parameters are estimated by the program. However, if only one reliable indicator measures each unobserved variable, the Φ matrix is fixed equal to the observed variances and covariances of the indicators.

The structural coefficients relating the latent exogenous variables to the dependent variables are contained in the Γ matrix. If causal effects are eliminated on a theoretical basis, the corresponding parameters are fixed at zero. Again, fixing a parameter equal to zero is equivalent to excluding it from the equation.

The β matrix specifies the causal relationships among the latent endogenous variables. The diagonal entries in β will be 1.0 in most cases (unless a scale transformation in a latent variable is desired). The off-diagonal elements will be freely estimated unless there is theoretical knowledge which eliminates the possibility of particular effects.

The Ψ matrix contains the variances and covariances of unspecified determinants of the endogenous variables. The diagonal values indicate the size of the unexplained variances.

Specifying each parameter in each of the aforementioned eight matrices as fixed, constrained, or free defines a theoretical model. The parameter estimates that are obtained with LISREL provide the best fit to the data *given* that theoretical model. As a detailed example, the following description shows how the impression-formation model diagrammed in Fig. 10.1 is transformed into a set of LISREL matrices.

For our model, the Θ_δ matrix is 10 × 10 (because there are 10 observed exogenous variables) with all its values fixed. The diagonal values are the estimates of error variances (described in the following). The off-diagonal values are all 0.0, because measurement errors were found to be uncorrelated.

The Θ_ϵ matrix is a 9 × 9 matrix with the same structure as Θ_δ.

The Λ_x matrix is a 10 × 10 matrix because there are 10 observed indicators for the 10 latent independent variables. Fixing all off-diagonal elements at 0.0 represents our assumption that measurements are not contaminated by the other dimensions (e.g., ratings of evaluation are not contaminated by potency and activity). A long tradition of research on the semantic differential (summarized by Osgood, 1962, and Heise, 1969b) supports this assumption; correlations among the three dimensions are close to zero in most studies (see Heise 1978, 1979, for a discussion of dimensional independence in ratings of social identities and interpersonal behaviors). The diagonal values of the Λ_x matrix are fixed at 1.0 to set the latent variables to the same scales as their indicators.

The Λ_y matrix (9 × 9) has a structure parallel to that of Λ_x.

The Φ matrix (10×10) is set equal to the observed covariances and variances of the exogenous variables, as there is only one indicator for each latent exogenous variable. If we had multiple indicators of one or more latent concept, the LISREL program could freely estimate the variance–covariance matrix of the exogenous latent factors.

The $9 \times 10 \; \Gamma$ matrix shows relations of the nine endogenous variables to the 10 exogeneous variables. Because of the assumption that prior impressions of an element directly affect feelings only for that same element, most entries in Γ are set equal to 0.0 (Table 10.1). For example, whereas the coefficient for A_e to A_e' is to be estimated freely, the effects from A_e to A_p', A_a', B_e', B_p', etc, are set to 0.0. Initially, the column of effects associated with $B_e O_e$ was completely free, permitting this variable to affect any of the endogenous variables directly. However, a first estimation revealed that only four of these effects were statistically significant. The small, nonsignificant effects were set equal to zero for the estimation presented here.

The β matrix (9×9) also contains both free and fixed values. Within-element, cross-dimensional effects (e.g. the effect of O_e' on O_p' and O_a') are fixed to 0.0 (Table 10.2). All cross-element parameters were left free initially, as none of these effects could be theoretically eliminated. Again, a first estimation revealed that some of these parameters actually are small and nonsignificant, and these parameters were set equal to 0.0 for the reestimation considered here.

The $9 \times 9 \; \Psi$ matrix's diagonal is left free to estimate the variances-of-disturbance terms. The off-diagonal elements are fixed at 0.0, representing the finding that there were no correlations among the disturbances. (After the initial

TABLE 10.1

The Matrix Containing Estimates of the Relations of the In-context Ratings to the Ratings of the Social Identities and Behaviors in Isolation

Endogeneous, In-context Variable:	Out-of-Context, Exogenous Variable:									
	A_e	A_p	A_a	B_e	B_p	B_a	O_e	O_p	O_a	$B_e O_e$
A_e'	0.145	0.0	0.0	0.0	0.0	0.0	0.0	0.0	0.0	0.050
A_p'	0.0	0.256	0.0	0.0	0.0	0.0	0.0	0.0	0.0	0.024
A_a'	0.0	0.0	0.233	0.0	0.0	0.0	0.0	0.0	0.0	0.0
B_e'	0.0	0.0	0.0	0.262	0.0	0.0	0.0	0.0	0.0	0.032
B_p'	0.0	0.0	0.0	0.0	0.358	0.0	0.0	0.0	0.0	0.056
B_a'	0.0	0.0	0.0	0.0	0.0	0.311	0.0	0.0	0.0	0.0
O_e'	0.0	0.0	0.0	0.0	0.0	0.0	0.320	0.0	0.0	0.0
O_p'	0.0	0.0	0.0	0.0	0.0	0.0	0.0	0.288	0.0	0.0
O_a'	0.0	0.0	0.0	0.0	0.0	0.0	0.0	0.0	0.387	0.0

Abbreviations: A: actor; B: behavior; O: object; E: evaluation; p: potency; a: activity.

TABLE 10.2

The   Matrix Containing Estimates of the Relations Among the In-Context, Endogenous Ratings of Evaluation, Potency, and Activity

		Causal Variables:								
		A'_e	A'_p	A'_a	B'_e	B'_p	B'_a	O'_e	O'_p	O'_a
Dependent Variables:	A'_e	1.0	0.0	0.0	0.685	0.164	-0.283	0.169	0.059	0.059
	A'_p	0.0	1.0	0.0	0.0	0.949	-0.260	0.0	0.0	0.0
	A'_a	0.0	0.0	1.0	-0.204	0.410	0.626	0.0	0.044	0.0
	B'_e	0.779	0.0	0.102	1.0	0.0	0.0	0.282	0.0	0.0
	B'_p	0.306	0.0	0.256	0.0	1.0	0.0	-0.294	0.0	0.0
	B'_a	0.064	-0.164	0.579	0.0	0.0	1.0	0.0	0.0	0.0
	O'_e	0.391	0.0	0.0	0.0	0.0	0.0	1.0	0.0	0.0
	O'_p	0.641	0.0	0.0	-0.281	0.0	0.109	0.0	1.0	0.0
	O'_a	0.393	0.0	0.0	-0.244	0.0	0.357	0.0	0.0	1.0
Unspecified Sources (Error)		0.0	0.0	0.0	0.044	0.065	0.003	0.036	0.065	0.057

Abbreviations: A: actor; B: behavior; O: object-person; e: evaluation; p: potency a: activity

estimation of the model, it became apparent that no disturbance terms were needed for the impressions of the actor (A'_e, A'_p, and A'_a; accordingly, these have been fixed at 0.0.) In Fig. 10.1, the disturbances of the endogenous variables have been deleted for graphic clarity; the unexplained variance in each latent endogenous term is shown in the bottom row of the figure.

Heise's (1978, 1979; Heise & Smith-Lovin 1981) data are used for the analyses here. The data collection procedures, stimuli, and data are very similar to those used in earlier impression formation research (Gollob, 1968; Heise, 1969a, 1970). In particular, notice that the *event* is the unit of analysis, rather than the individual subject's ratings. In the following, we outline the stimuli construction, the measurement scales, data collection procedures, scaling analyses, and the estimation of error variances for this study. More information about these topics is contained in Heise (1978).

Stimuli

The event stimuli for this study were constructed using social identities and interpersonal behaviors chosen from a dictionary of 1250 concepts with their average EPA (evaluation, potency, and activity) ratings (Heise, 1978). Identities and behaviors were chosen to represent nine EPA profiles (see the left-hand column of Table 10.3). For example, *hero* is an identity that most undergraduates

TABLE 10.3
Words Used to Construct Stimulus Sentence With
Mean Evaluation, Potency, and Activity Profiles

Profile Type (EPA)		Identities				Behaviors		
		E	P	A		E	P	A
A (+ + +)	Athlete	0.9	1.8	2.2	Convince	0.7	2.0	1.1
	Champion	1.0	2.5	2.2	Protect	2.7	2.6	1.1
	Hero	1.9	2.3	2.1				
	Winner	1.1	1.6	1.7				
B (+ + -)	Boss	0.6	1.4	0.9	Contemplate	0.9	1.2	-0.1
	Judge	1.1	1.8	-0.3	Soothe	2.6	2.1	0.1
	Sheriff	0.9	1.3	0.3				
C (+ - +)	Child	1.1	-0.6	2.7	Amuse	2.2	1.1	1.8
	Infant	1.4	-1.5	2.3	Play with	2.1	0.9	1.8
	Schoolgirl	1.2	-0.5	1.5	Tickle	0.8	0.3	1.7
D (+ - -)	Cripple	0.4	-0.8	-1.3	Indulge	0.4	0.1	0.4
	Invalid	0.5	-1.3	-1.9	Serve	1.5	0.4	0.2
	Underdog	0.7	-0.7	0.3				
E (- + +)	Outlaw	-2.1	0.7	1.5	Attack	-2.3	0.0	1.6
	Roughneck	-1.5	0.8	1.6	Defy	-1.0	0.6	1.1
					Sock	-1.9	-0.4	1.3
F (- + -)	Disciplinarian	0.6	1.2	0.0	Grieve for	0.7	1.1	-0.6
	Orge	-2.5	0.9	0.3	Oppress	-2.6	0.3	0.2
	Warden	0.4	1.1	-0.1	Silence	-0.5	0.8	0.2
G (- - +)	Blabbermouth	-1.6	-1.5	1.0	Laugh at	-1.4	-1.1	0.9
	Gambler	-0.5	-0.4	1.6	Pester	-2.0	-1.1	0.9
	Maniac	-2.6	-0.6	1.3				
H (- - -)	Alcoholic	-1.4	-1.9	-1.2	Avoid	-1.2	-1.4	-0.2
	Beggar	-0.5	-1.5	-1.4	Betray	-2.8	-2.1	-0.2
	Coward	-1.5	-2.3	-1.0	Ignore	-1.8	-1.1	-0.7
O (0 0 0)	Boarder	0.4	-0.2	-0.4	Observe	0.4	0.3	-0.2
	Stranger	0.3	-0.2	-0.3	Tap	0.1	0.1	0.1
					Watch	0.2	0.1	-0.2

rate highly on evaluation, potency, and activity. Therefore, *hero* is used in some event descriptions where an *A*-profile (+ + +) identity is needed. In general, identities and behaviors were chosen so that they could be used to create a relatively large number of events (i.e., the identities would be reasonable interaction partners for a variety of others, and the behaviors could be reasonably enacted in a variety of roles).

Identities with certain EPA profiles were very difficult to find in the U.S. undergraduate culture. For example, the *F* profile (− + +) is represented by the identities *disciplinarian, ogre,* and *warden,* even though both *disciplinarian* and *warden* are slightly positive in evaluation. Bad, powerful but quiet roles are uncommon. Our inability to find identities and behaviors that perfectly represent each EPA profile would only create problems for the analyses if it produced low variance or high colinearity in the measures used. An inspection of the results here indicates that this is not the case.

The identities and behaviors that were chosen (Table 10.3) were then combined into sentences describing social events according to the 8 × 8 Latin square design shown in Table 10.4. Behavior EPA profiles and object–person EPA profiles are orthogonal (every behavior profile occurs with every object profile), whereas each actor profile appears once in every row and column of the square. This design minimizes the covariances among event elments. Thus, it enhances our ability to estimate linear effects and the behavior–object multiplicative interaction.

Each cell in Table 10.4 corresponds to a stimulus sentence. For example, a sentence representing the pattern *FHE* (the 8,5 entry in the square) would be "the warden (− + −) betrayed (− − −) the outlaw (− + +)." Obviously, several different event descriptions could have been created to represent each cell of Table 10.4, as there were several identities and behaviors that matched each profile. For example, another sentence representing the *FHE* pattern would be "the disciplinarian (− + −) avoided (− − −) the roughneck (− + +)." In general, event descriptions that were both reasonable (in the matching of interaction partners and behaviors) and interesting were chosen. The 70 event sentences

TABLE 10.4
Paradigm for Design of Stimulus Sentences

Verb Profile				Object Profile				
	A	B	C	D	E	F	G	H
A	C,A	D	E	F	G	H	A	B
B	D	E	F	G	H	A	B	C
C	E	F	G	H	A	B	C	D
D	F	G	H	A	B	C	D	E
E	G	H	A	B	C	D	E	F
F	H	A	B	C	D	E	F	G
G	A	B	C	D	S	F	G	H
H	B	C	D	E	F	G	H	A,H

Note: Each cell corresponds to a sentence. The EPA profile for the sentence Subject is is indicated within the cell; the profile for the Verb is shown as the row label; and the profile for the Object is given as the column label. Two sentences were created for two of the cells, as shown. Four additional sentences involved all-neutral profiles (*Q*) for the subjects, verbs, and/or objects: two *000*, one *DOA*, and one *EOH*.

Key (the three signs refer to high or low values on evaluation, potency, and activity, respectively):

A + + +	E - + +
B + + -	F - + -
C + - +	G - - +
D + - -	H - - -

used in this study are listed in the Appendix at the end of this chapter, along with the in-context ratings of the three event elements on the EPA dimensions. (The ratings shown combine male and female data.)

Ratings of the out-of-context impressions were obtained by presenting identities with an article (e.g., "a *schoolgirl*") and behaviors in an infinitive form (e.g., "to *avoid* someone"). The mean ratings of the out-of-context impressions are presented in Table 10.3. The in-context impressions were obtained by presenting a stimulus sentence and underlining the component to be rated (e.g., "The *schoolgirl* convinced the champion"). The mean in-context ratings for each actor, behavior, and object–person are presented in the Appendix.

Semantic differential scales were grouped below each stimulus, and five stimuli were rated on a page. A box containing a question mark was set next to each stimulus, to be used by subjects who did not know the meaning of a word.

Measurement

Semantic differential ratings were obtained on machine-readable forms using three scales to measure the dimensions: evaluation, potency, and activity. Each scale had nine rating positions with the adverbial anchors "infinitely," "extremely," "quite," and "slightly," on either side and "neither or neutral" in the middle. The "infinitely" category was an innovation in semantic differential technology that helped minimize ceiling–floor effects in ratings. The poles of the scales were defined by clusters of adjectives known from previous work to be associated with the semantic differential dimensions: *evaluation*—good, helpful, nice, sweet versus bad, unhelpful, awful, sour; *potency*—strong, powerful, big, deep versus weak, powerless, little, shallow; *activity*—hurried, alive, noisy, fiery, young versus slow, dead, quiet, stiff, old. The order of presentation of the three rating scales (evaluation, potency, and activity) and the orientation of each scale (left or right) were varied. More details on the scales, including validity assessments, are presented by Heise (1978) and Smith-Lovin (1979).

Data Collection

Subjects were students in introductory sociology classes at the University of North Carolina. Out-of-context ratings were obtained from all subjects; ratings of the identities and behaviors in the context of the event were obtained from three subsamples, with each subsample rating a different third of the actors, behaviors, and object–persons. The subsamples each contained 26 subjects, 13 males and 13 females. The three forms were distributed randomly in each class.

Each rating booklet consisted of a cover sheet, an instruction page for the out-of-context ratings, 11 pages containing out-of-context stimuli and semantic differential scales, an instruction page for the in-context ratings, 14 pages containing event sentences and semantic differential scales, and a final section containing the questionnaire for another study. After the booklets were distributed, instructions were presented verbally. Subjects were told that the project was attempting to develop "mathematical formulas that do a good job of describing how we react to events and how we develop ideas for new events." They were asked to record how they felt about different kinds of people, different kinds of behaviors, and different kinds of events. After being offered an opportunity to leave if they did not wish to participate, subjects were instructed meticulously in the use of the three semantic differential scales and presented with examples of completed ratings.

All subjects completed the rating task in the 1½-hour period allowed, except one who finished after an additional 15 minutes.

Preliminary Analyses

Cliff (1972) has shown that metric imprecision in equal-interval scoring of semantic differential scales can interfere with estimation of parameters in mathematical models. Preliminary analyses here confirmed Cliff's finding of more parsimonious models with proper scaling—fewer interactions were contained in models developed using a refined metric than in those using assumed-interval scaling. Therefore, a derived metric was used here, developing by applying the successive-intervals scaling procedure to ratings of 650 social identities and 600 interpersonal behaviors by 311 college undergraduates—the data for the dictionary of semantic differential profiles mentioned previously.[3] The values for coding rating positions are presented in Heise (1978, Table 4.7).

Mean ratings on the evaluation, potency, and activity dimensions were calculated for each of the stimuli using the derived metric. These means are

---

[3]The method of successive intervals as specified by Diederich, Messick, and Tucker (1957) was used to scale the data, employing a program prepared in 1972 by Gary Cox at the Thurstone Psychometric Laboratory, University of North Carolina, Chapel Hill. The procedure assumes that ratings of stimuli on a given scale are normally distributed, though the means and the variances of ratings vary for different stimuli. In an iterative process, category boundaries are adjusted until the normality assumption is maximally fulfilled for all stimuli. The final results reported by the program are optimized values for the boundaries between rating positions. The program also provides scale values for stimuli; these are not used here. Because the midpoint and range of the final scale are set arbitrarily in the program, results were standardized with regression formulas so that the boundary values from all analyses correspond as closely as possible to the boundary values of an assumed-interval scale $(-3.5, -2.5, -1.5, -0.5, 0.5, 1.5, 2.5, 3.5)$. The results of the analyses for the EPA (evaluation, potency, and activity) scales are summarized in Heise (1978: Tables 4.3, 4.4, and 4.5). An analysis of variance was also conducted to address the question of whether or not scale metric is influenced by type of stimuli (noun or verb) or by orientation of scale (left or right). The metrics of evaluation, potency, and activity scales all are influenced to a slight degree by type of stimulus and by scale orientation (see a detailed description of these results in Heise, 1978, pp. 70–79). Therefore, the scales in this study have been adjusted very slightly to correct for the changes in the metric according to stimulus type and scale orientation.

presented in Table 10.3 and in the Appendix. Means within the male and female subsamples also were calculated in order to conduct tests for sex differences.[4]

The Variance–Covariance Matrix

The variance–covariance matrix used to estimate the parameters is presented in Table 10.5. This is the S matrix mentioned previously; it is compared to the theoretical variance–covariance matrix, Σ (which is generated by the parameter estimates), in order to evaluate the model's fit. The S matrix shows the relations among the *observed* variables, indicated in Fig. 10.1 by small letters.

For these impression-formation data, the variance–covariance matrix has several unusual properties that merit some discussion. For our data, the unit of analysis is the *event*, and each variance and covariance is based on the 70 event observations. Each data point for these statistics is a mean rating—an arithmetic average of the ratings of several subjects (26 subjects for each of the in-context ratings and 78 subjects for the out-of-context ratings, as all subjects rated all the out-of-context stimuli but only one of the three subsamples rated each in-context stimulus). Using the event as the unit of analysis is unusual. Normally, the number of observations (N) in a LISREL analysis would be the numbers of *individuals* from whom responses were obtained (e.g., in a social survey).

A second unusual feature of the variance–covariance matrix is that the data points involved in the computation of the matrix entries sometimes involve different subject pools. For example, all the out-of-context ratings were completed by all 78 subjects, so each of the data points for the calculation of these variances and covariances is a mean over 78 ratings. On the other hand, the variances and covariances of the in-context elements involve means calculated over a one-third subsample of the subjects. This could create problems for two reasons: (1) the means over the smaller subsamples are less stable (i.e., have more "error") than the means calculated from the entire sample; and (2) the different subsamples could use the ratings scales differently or have different attitudes toward the identities and behaviors, making the means from the different subgroups incomparable.

The first problem cannot confound our LISREL results, although it would be serious if ordinary regression were used. LISREL allows us to input the estimates of the error variances, which we base on the known reliability of the scales *and* the number of ratings involved in calculating each mean (see description of error estimation that follows). Therefore, LISREL "knows" which variances and covariances are based on less stable means (or data points) and can take this fact into account when producing its estimates.

---

[4]No sex differences were found in these impression-formation models (Heise & Smith-Lovin, 1981).

TABLE 10.5
Variance-Covariance Matrix of Observable Variables (S Matrix)

	a_e	a_p	a_a	b_e	b_p	b_a	o_e	o_p	o_a	$b_e o_e$	a'_e	a'_p	a'_a	b'_e	b'_p	b'_a	o'_e	o'_p	o'_a
a_e	1.679																		
a_p	0.657	1.742																	
a_a	0.122	0.828	1.727																
b_e	-0.245	-0.094	-0.065	2.767															
b_p	-0.080	-0.002	0.111	1.742	1.507														
b_a	0.001	0.063	0.094	0.293	0.242	0.556													
o_e	-0.042	-0.061	0.019	0.157	0.061	-0.021	1.413												
o_p	0.378	0.113	0.164	0.178	0.146	0.033	0.596	2.034											
o_a	0.268	0.205	0.071	-0.024	0.005	0.066	0.187	0.814	1.771										
$b_e o_e$	-0.513	-0.066	-0.191	-0.339	-0.274	0.169	-0.087	-0.212	-0.245	4.544									
a'_e	0.385	0.036	-0.059	1.178	0.786	0.019	-0.041	0.191	0.084	0.467	1.067								
a'_p	0.103	0.515	0.320	0.632	0.629	0.074	-0.160	0.004	-0.005	0.345	0.524	0.671							
a'_a	0.076	0.292	0.743	-0.001	0.189	0.253	-0.032	0.111	-0.030	0.055	0.024	0.236	0.530						
b'_e	0.129	-0.037	-0.022	1.517	1.026	0.083	-0.124	0.092	0.019	0.420	1.098	0.600	0.045	1.288					
b'_p	0.023	0.169	0.226	0.829	0.799	0.144	-0.125	0.112	0.064	0.211	0.561	0.549	0.229	0.697	0.622				
b'_a	0.066	0.143	0.405	-0.055	0.090	0.294	-0.017	0.128	0.020	0.098	-0.040	0.085	0.326	-0.015	0.120	0.326			
o'_e	0.068	-0.032	-0.035	0.506	0.320	0.017	0.449	0.247	0.154	0.211	0.387	0.139	0.013	0.380	0.175	-0.017	0.379		
o'_p	0.288	0.062	0.009	0.375	0.226	0.067	0.162	0.692	0.348	0.196	0.420	0.177	0.038	0.376	0.201	0.020	0.219	0.487	
o'_a	0.197	0.131	0.109	0.101	0.093	0.139	0.110	0.276	0.734	0.057	0.164	0.102	0.075	0.135	0.123	0.090	0.144	0.223	0.475

The second problem could not be corrected routinely in a LISREL analysis; it involves the possibility of nonrandom errors or subject differences. Therefore, we have explored in great detail the possibility that groups might differ in either their attitudes or their use of the rating scales. These results are discussed in Heise (1978, 1979); to summarize, the affective meanings of social identities and behaviors are largely shared, and subjects tend to use the semantic differential scales in similar ways. Furthermore, the small differences that have been found are not related to significant social or psychological factors. Therefore, it appears that we are justified in assuming that the three subsamples are not significantly different from one another, given that the subjects were randomly assigned to these subsamples.

Estimation of Error Variances

Because the data presented here were mean ratings by a number of subjects, the error could be estimated independently, then entered as fixed information for the structural equation procedure to use. Variances for measurement errors were estimated from standard errors of mean ratings, using pooled data on 650 identities and 600 behaviors (Heise, 1978). In the case of the independent variables, each observed value is a mean calculated over 78 respondents, so the variance of the mean (i.e., its error variance) is the within-concept rating variance (estimated from the pooled data) divided by 78. For ratings after the event presentation, division is by 26—the number of subjects that made each in-context rating.

The error term for the $B_e O_e$ interaction cannot be calculated in this way, but it could be estimated using a formula proposed by Bohrnstedt and Marwell (1978, Equation 19). The error variance of this product term was estimated at .010; this value was not significantly different from zero, so the $B_e O_e$ variable is considered to have no error in our analyses here.

RESULTS

The maximum likelihood estimates of parameters in our final structural model are presented in Tables 10.1 and 10.2. (Measurement models are not shown, as they are entirely fixed.) The results also are presented in graphic form as Fig. 10.1.

The probability associated with the chi-square value of 204.2 is .0006. Thus, portions of the observed variances and covariances still are unexplained. However, the ratio of chi-square to degrees of freedom in this solution is 2.08, indicating a fairly good fit. Another way of evaluating fit is to examine differences between observed variances and covariances and those reproduced using the parameter estimates. In this analysis, all but three of these residuals are below .130, and exceptions all involve one variable, A_p. Residuals of this size are not unusual given our small sample of events ($N = 70$) and the highly constrained specification of our model. After discussing our results, we propose strategies for improving the model in later studies.

Comparability to Earlier Studies

The LISREL program produces a matrix of reduced-form coefficients for the estimated model; these coefficients are given in Table 10.6. (Reduced-form coefficients evaluate the overall effects of the exogenous variables on each endogenous variable—any relationships among endogenous variables are ignored.)

The reduced-form coefficients in Table 10.6 allow us to check our present results to see if they are consistent with earlier studies. Because these coefficients represent total effects, they are comparable to the regression equations produced by other researchers. The values in one column of Table 10.6 represent the coefficients for one equation (e.g., the first column is the equation coefficients for predicting A'_e from A_e, A_p, etc.). The equation constants were calculated from the LISREL results and the means of the variables.

To illustrate the comparability of the reduced-form equations from the LISREL analysis and the results from earlier research, consider the A'_e results. The equation from Table 10.6 (ignoring coefficients that are not significantly different from zero) is:

$$A'_e = -.094 + .351\,A_e + .425\,B_e - .233\,B_a + .203\,B_e O_e. \tag{3}$$

These coefficients are quite similar to those in Equations 1 and 2 (from Gollob, 1968; Heise & Smith-Lovin, 1981).[5] The only difference in the pattern of results is that the A_p effect in the Heise and Smith-Lovin equation (our Equation 2) was not found in the current results. This is consistent with our examination of the residuals—recall that all the major residuals involved actor potency. We discuss these deviations from a good fit later; at this point we simply wish to illustrate the general similarity between the reduced-form equations from our model in Fig. 10.1 and the regression results of earlier studies. We now turn to the feedback model.

Impressions of Actors

The estimates of the direct effects (as specified in Fig. 10.1) are found in Tables 10.1 and 10.2. Again, equations can be constructed by multiplying the estimated coefficient by the variable with which it is associated. For example, the equation

---

[5]Although the coefficients are not identical, this is not disturbing, because all the impression-formation studies involved small samples of events. Estimates are expected to contain sizable amounts of sampling error. The more relevant comparison is whether or not the same coefficients are significantly different from zero in each study, and perhaps whether or not the coefficients for a given term are roughly the same magnitude. Although we report coefficients to three decimal places, this is not meant to imply that the estimates are this precise; it is merely a convention when reporting structural equation results.

TABLE 10.6
Coefficients for Impression Formation Equations
(Reduced Form of the Model in Fig. 10.1)

from:	A_e'	A_p'	A_a'	B_e'	B_p'	B_a'	O_e'	O_p'	O_a'
	Columns Contain Coefficients for Predicting								
Constant	-.094	-.139	.077	-.136	-.036	.267	-.069	-.430	-.113
A_e	.351	.060	-.010	.234	.065	.007	.137	.160	.083
A_p	.031	.268	-.050	.016	-.007	-.071	.012	.008	-.017
A_a	-.035	.034	.415	.019	.100	.233	-.014	-.003	.065
B_e	.425	.062	-.113	.535	.052	-.049	.166	.117	.018
B_p	.162	.401	.191	.128	.437	.055	.063	.074	.052
B_a	-.233	-.089	.372	-.118	.051	.526	-.091	-.059	.126
O_e	-.059	-.108	-.016	-.134	-.112	.005	.306	.000	.012
O_p	.039	.009	.021	.028	.013	.013	.015	.306	.013
O_a	.056	.009	-.002	.037	.010	.001	.022	.025	.400
B_eO_e	.203	.117	.008	.169	.097	-.002	.079	.083	.037

for predicting A_e' involves the following terms:

$$A_e' = .145\, A_e + .059\, B_eO_e + .685\, B_e' - .283\, B_a' + .169\, O_e'$$
$$+ .059\, O_p' + .059\, O_a' \tag{4}$$

The first two coefficients are found in Table 10.1; the others are from Table 10.2.

The A_e effect is basically a stability effect. It indicates that actors who occupy positively evaluated identities tend to maintain at least some of that positivity even after the event has influenced the meanings and impressions associated with the event elements.

The B_eO_e effect on A_e' is considerably smaller in the feedback model than in the regression (or total effects) models. This does not mean, however, that attitudinal balance is less important. Because of the potential for feedback among event elements, A_e' is affected by B_eO_e both directly *and* through its effects on B_e' and B_p'. Therefore, people who act in appropriate ways toward others seem more positive after the event is observed both because they have acted correctly *and* because their actions seem nicer and more powerful as a result of the event.

The effects of B_e', B_p', and B_a' indicate that actors are more positively evaluated when their actions seem nice (positively evaluated), strong, and quiet within the context of the event. Notice that these are the effects of *primed,* in-context variables. Because behaviors can acquire different evaluations, potencies, and activities within an event (depending on toward whom the act is directed and who does it), these effects must be interpreted differently than the total effects in Table 10.6 (and earlier research). For example, *helping* is a nice, powerful, and lively behavior, but it is seen as even more positive and strong if it is directed at a deserving, weak person (Equation 7). It is this evaluation within the context of the event that is the causal variable in our feedback model (Fig.

10.1). Behaviors that seem irritating, harassing, or aggressive in an event (low B_e', and high B_a') lower our evaluation of the actor.

Finally, actors are evaluated more positively if they are involved in an event with people who are nice, powerful, and lively (high O_e', O_p', and O_a'). This effect is quite intuitive and is more striking in our feedback results than in earlier regression studies.

The following equation describes the direct effects on an actor's potency within an event (again, the first two coefficients are from Table 10.1, the others from Table 10.2):

$$A_p' = .256 \, A_p + .024 \, B_e O_e + .949 \, B_p' - .283 \, B_a' \tag{5}$$

Aside from the stability effect of A_p, we see that impressions of the actor's powerfulness within the context of an event are enhanced by the appropriateness of his or her actions (as summarized by the $B_e O_e$ balance term) and by the impression of the behavior itself within the context of the event. Acts that seem powerful and quiet (high B_p' and low B_a') make the actor seem more potent. These are usually behaviors that involve soothing, calming, or controlling another person.

The impressions of an actor's activity or liveliness after an event also are determined primarily by the impressions of his behavior, as can be seen in the equation derived from Tables 10.1 and 10.2:

$$A_a' = .233 \, A_a - .204 \, B_e' + .410 \, B_p' + .626 \, B_a' \tag{6}$$

Aside from the stability effect of A_a, the perceived liveliness of the actor is increased if his or her behavior in the event is negatively evaluated, powerful, and active. Such actions are those that appear to be aggressive or threatening within the interaction described by the event. Notice that the appropriateness of the behavior ($B_e O_e$) will indirectly affect actor activity, because it affects B_e' and B_p'—inappropriate acts are more likely to be seen as immoral or aggressive within the context of the event and therefore will affect the activity of the actor.

Impressions of Behaviors

The equation predicting the direct effects on the evaluation of a behavior within the context of an event is:

$$B_e' = .262 \, B_e + .032 \, B_e O_e + .779 \, A_e' + .102 \, A_a' + .282 \, O_e'. \tag{7}$$

Acts appear more praiseworthy than usual if they are performed by a positively evaluated, lively actor—for example, an immature person (*baby, child, tot, youngster*) or an intimate (*friend, lover, pal*). Behaviors also are evaluated more positively if they are appropriate (the $B_e O_e$ effect), and if they are directed at nice people (high O_e').

The equation for predicting the potency of a behavior within the event is:

$$B'_p = .358\ B_p + .056\ B_e O_e + .306\ A'O'_e + .256\ A'_a - .294 \tag{8}$$

An act's perceived power is among the most stable elements in an event (the coefficient for B_p is relatively high). However, an act can be strengthened somewhat by being directed at a stigmatized person (low O'_e), particularly when a harmful act matches the object's negative evaluation (the $B_e O_e$ effect). An act seems to have less than usual impact or potency when directed at a highly evaluated person (high O'_e), particularly if the act is harmful and thereby inconsistent with the receiver's evaluation. Acts also seem more potent when performed by good, lively actors (high A'_e and A'_a).

The equation for predicting behavior activity within the context of an event is:

$$B'_a = .311\ B_a + .064\ A'_e - .164\ A'_p + .579\ A'_a \tag{9}$$

Other than the B_a stability effect, the perceived liveliness of the behavior is influenced only by the impressions of the actor. The perception of the object-person only influences behavior liveliness indirectly, through its effects on A'_e and A'_a. Behaviors are seen as more lively if they are carried out by nice, weak, lively actors (high A'_e, low A'_p, and high A'_a), Immature people, female identities, and amateurs usually have this profile. Any element of the event that tends to make the actor look immature or amateurish will also influence indirectly the impression formed of the behavior.

Impressions of Object-Persons

The impressions formed by object-persons are considerably simpler than those of actors and behaviors. For example, the evaluation of the object is directly affected by only one factor, other than the stability effect:

$$O'_e = .320\ O_e + .391\ A'_e. \tag{10}$$

Object-persons who are acted on by positively evaluated people are viewed more positively because of the association. Because the actor's evaluation (A'_e) is determined by so many factors (Equation 4), the evaluation of the object is actually influenced by a large number of factors indirectly. For example, objects of extremely negative acts will tend to be evaluated more negatively; such a victim is not rated more negatively because he or she is the object of an immoral act, however. Instead, he or she is rated lower on evaluation (and potency and activity) because he or she has associated with the type of person who would have committed such an offense. Thus, the feedback model of impression formation leads us to a new understanding of the "derogation of the victim" phenomenon: It is simply a generalization of the fact that we tend to evaluate people on the basis of those with whom they associate.

The formulas showing the direct effects on object potency and object activity are very similar to each other:

$$O_p' = .288 \ O_p + .641 \ A_e' - .281 \ B_e' + .109 \ B_a'; \tag{11}$$

$$O_a' = .387 \ O_a + .393 \ A_e' - .244 \ B_e' + .357 \ B_a'. \tag{12}$$

Both the perceptions of an object–person's potency and activity are based on a stability effect (of O_p and O_a, respectively), on the evaluation of the actor within the context of the event (A_e'), and on the evaluation and the activity of the act $(B_e'$ and $B_a')$. Those who interact with positively evaluated or esteemed others have their power and liveliness enhanced. Those who are acted on by stigmatized (low evaluation) others are perceived as less powerful and lively. Those who have received acts that seem somewhat negative and lively are also perceived as more powerful and lively.

CONCLUSIONS

Overall, the estimated model does provide support for viewing impression-formation processes as a feedback system in which short-term affective reactions are Markovian in nature, with only current impressions affecting future outcomes. We have shown that such a model can largely account for the patterns of variances and covariances observed empirically.

Because all the residuals involve A_p, it seems likely that either the measurement of the actor's potency is distorted in some way or that some of the causal effects to or from A_p are misspecified. If a theorist wished to alter the model to improve fit, several strategies for revision are available (Byron, 1972; Sörbom, 1975; Saris et al., 1979). The most useful strategy involves examining the first-order partial derivatives associated with each constrained parameter and freeing those parameters associated with large derivatives (Saris et al., 1979). (These values are reported in the LISREL output.) The new model and its chi-square value could then be compared to the earlier run to determine whether or not the improvement was significant. In this impression-formation example, however, the fit is already quite adequate. Fitting the model to such a small sample without additional theoretical knowledge would not be advisable. Instead, this model should be tested and refined with a larger data base.

Although the parameter estimates presented here are exploratory, some of the patterns deserve comment. For example, the impressions formed about an object–person are relatively unconnected to the other event elements. On the evaluation dimension, the postevent view of the object is directly affected by just a single in-context variable (ignoring the direct stability effect from the original, exogenous object impression). Specifically, almost all effects on the object's evaluation and potency are mediated through the evaluation of the actor. This pattern is quite different from that observed in the reduced form (Columns 7 and 8 of Table 10.6) and in ordinary regression analyses of impression formation (Heise, 1970; Heise & Smith-Lovin, 1981) where the evaluation of the behavior has a major effect. The results here emphasize the impact that behavior evaluation and potency have on actor evaluation; the object's potency and activity are influenced by the prestige or evaluation of his or her interaction partner and therefore indirectly by what the interaction partner does. As described earlier, this interpretation leads to a new understanding of the "derogation of the victim" phenomena (i.e., the tendency for the objects of negative acts to be rated more negatively than the objects of positive acts).

It is also interesting that the object–person's potency and activity do not have a significant effect on any other postevent impressions. Again, this differs from the pattern obtained using direct-effect model specifications (Heise, 1978; Heise & Smith-Lovin, 1981). In these earlier analyses, object potency and activity had an impact on actor evaluation and on behavior impressions.

The relatively unconnected position of the postevent object impressions might allow experimental studies examining the theoretical assumptions involved in the model specification. For example, the feedback aspect of the structural model might be tested experimentally by selecting event stimuli that would cause very little shift in the evaluation of the actor but major changes in other event elements (e.g., A_p' and A_a'). Under such conditions, the impressions of the object's evaluation and potency should reach stability quite soon relatively to the other postevent impressions. Allowing subjects to provide time-varying ratings of event elements might provide a way to test predicted increments in postevent impressions.

A different test of the theoretical specification of the model will be possible on another corpus of events. Because many of the possible effects in the β matrix were found to be small and nonsignificant, these parmeters have been set to zero for reestimation. This "trimmed" model may now be estimated on a new data set. Because the model will now be overidentified, it would be possible to free some of the parameters that were theoretically set equal to zero in this specification (for example, the effect from the exogenous variable A_p to O_e'). Therefore, the new estimation will provide evidence whether or not the theoretical assumptions used to specify the original model are consistent with covariance patterns in multiple data sets.

Other questions also must be addressed by analyses using a larger corpus of events. The disturbance terms for impressions of the behavior and the object indicate that the determinants of these variables have not been exhausted. Probably more interaction terms (such as the $B_e O_p$ effect noted by Gollob & Rossman, 1973) need to be included. A study using a corpus of 515 events is currently exploring this possibility.

APPENDIX 1

Event Sentences and the Mean Ratings of In Context Actor, Behavior and
Object-Persons on the Evaluation, Potency and Activity Dimensions

	ACTOR	BEHAVIOR	OBJECT-PERSON	A'_e	A'_p	A'_a	B'_e	B'_p	B'_a	O'_e	O'_p	O'_a
1.	Child	Ignore	Judge	-0.6	-0.8	0.7	-1.1	-0.5	0.6	0.0	0.2	-0.5
2.	Schoolgirl	Tickle	Gambler	0.1	-0.2	1.4	0.3	0.0	1.1	-0.2	-0.6	1.0
3.	Sheriff	Attack	Cripple	-2.6	-1.1	1.1	-3.0	-0.6	1.1	-0.4	-2.2	-0.9
4.	Ogre	Contemplate	Schoolgirl	-1.3	0.7	-0.2	0.5	0.4	0.7	0.5	-1.2	0.9
5.	Maniac	Play With	Infant	-0.0	-0.4	-0.1	0.5	0.4	0.7	0.5	-1.2	0.9
6.	Warden	Betray	Outlaw	-0.6	0.0	-0.2	-1.2	-0.9	-0.3	-0.3	-0.7	0.2
7.	Alcoholic	Protect	Disciplinarian	0.8	0.5	0.0	1.2	1.1	0.5	0.5	0.1	-0.5
8.	Disciplinarian	Sock	Coward	-0.9	0.4	0.6	-1.1	0.1	1.2	-1.1	-1.2	-0.1
9.	Champion	Indulge	Underdog	0.7	0.9	0.7	0.1	0.2	0.2	0.6	-0.0	0.1
10.	Roughneck	Laugh At	Outlaw	-0.7	0.1	0.8	-0.8	-0.2	0.6	-0.7	-0.3	0.2
11.	Cripple	Protect	Judge	1.9	0.7	0.5	1.6	1.5	0.5	1.2	-0.1	-0.4
12.	Winner	Laugh At	Champion	-0.8	-0.4	1.3	-1.3	-1.0	1.1	0.2	0.3	-0.0
13.	Athlete	Contemplate	Disciplinarian	0.5	0.9	0.4	0.3	0.4	-0.1	0.2	0.7	-0.3
14.	Invalid	Indulge	Blabbermouth	0.6	-0.4	-0.9	0.3	-0.2	-0.1	-0.4	-0.3	0.6
15.	Maniac	Silence	Coward	-0.8	0.4	1.0	-0.4	0.5	0.5	-0.8	-1.7	-1.2
16.	Judge	Avoid	Champion	-0.2	-0.6	-0.9	-0.7	-0.9	-0.4	-0.2	0.2	0.5
17.	Outlaw	Soothe	Sheriff	0.7	0.7	0.4	1.0	1.0	0.3	-0.0	-0.6	-0.6
18.	Beggar	Indulge	Child	0.2	-0.4	-0.1	0.1	-0.2	-0.4	0.6	-0.4	0.3
19.	Schoolgirl	Grieve For	Cripple	1.6	0.5	0.3	1.8	0.7	0.6	0.7	-0.9	-0.8
20.	Gambler	Protect	Outlaw	-0.3	0.1	0.8	-0.5	0.9	0.4	-1.0	-0.6	-0.2
21.	Roughneck	Silence	Disciplinarian	-1.6	0.5	1.0	-1.0	0.4	0.9	-0.4	-0.6	-0.1
22.	Alcoholic	Betray	Gambler	-1.2	-1.3	-0.8	-1.7	-1.3	0.0	-0.4	-1.2	-0.2

No.												
23.	Schoolgirl	Contemplate	Coward	0.8	-0.0	0.6	0.3	0.3	0.3	0.3	0.6	1.1
24.	Warden	Indulge	Athlete	0.2	0.2	-0.2	-0.4	0.3	0.2	-0.5	-0.6	-0.8
25.	Hero	Opress	Boss	-0.6	0.7	1.0	-1.0	0.5	0.9	0.4	-1.3	0.3
26.	Invalid	Ignore	Infant	-0.8	-1.3	-1.5	-1.3	-1.0	-1.3	0.6	-0.8	-0.8
27.	Blabbermouth	Soothe	Cripple	1.1	0.8	0.9	2.1	1.2	0.1	-0.8	0.2	0.9
28.	Child	Defy	Roughneck	0.5	0.6	1.4	0.7	1.4	1.7	-0.3	-0.2	-0.3
29.	Orge	Laugh At	Disciplinarian	-1.6	0.4	0.8	-1.4	0.2	0.5	-0.7	-0.8	0.6
30.	Athlete	Protect	Maniac	0.9	1.4	1.4	1.1	1.2	0.6	0.0	-0.7	-0.6
31.	Cripple	Amuse	Beggar	0.9	-0.2	0.0	0.9	0.1	0.6	-0.4	-0.5	1.0
32.	Gambler	Sock	Winner	-1.6	-0.9	0.6	-1.9	-0.7	1.2	0.2	-0.6	-0.5
33.	Sheriff	Laugh At	Judge	-0.8	-0.3	0.6	-0.9	-0.4	1.1	1.9	-0.1	1.4
34.	Roughneck	Protect	Infant	2.1	1.7	1.1	2.2	2.0	0.8	-0.7	-1.3	-0.7
35.	Alcoholic	Tickle	Invalid	-0.8	-1.1	-0.1	-0.5	-0.4	0.7	-0.3	-0.4	-0.1
36.	Cripple	Grieve For	Outlaw	0.7	-0.8	-0.9	1.4	0.5	-0.1	-0.1	-0.9	-0.4
37.	Blabbermouth	Ignore	Disciplinarian	-0.9	-1.1	0.6	-1.7	-1.0	0.4	-0.4	-0.5	0.0
38.	Judge	Contemplate	Gambler	1.0	0.2	-0.6	1.0	1.0	0.0	-0.8	-1.3	-1.3
39.	Outlaw	Indulge	Beggar	-0.2	0.5	0.8	-0.2	0.1	0.1	0.1	-0.6	0.2
40.	Alcoholic	Silence	Champion	-0.7	-0.3	0.0	-0.9	0.2	0.4	1.0	0.3	0.5
41.	Schoolgirl	Convince	Champion	1.1	0.6	1.5	0.8	1.2	1.1	0.8	0.4	0.5
42.	Warden	Amuse	Sheriff	0.8	0.7	0.4	1.0	0.4	0.6	-1.0	0.4	0.9
43.	Athlete	Sock	Child	-2.7	-1.2	0.8	-2.5	-1.1	1.6	-0.4	-2.0	-0.7
44.	Cripple	Laugh At	Underdog	-1.1	-1.5	-0.3	-1.8	-1.7	-0.3	-0.3	-0.7	0.2
45.	Coward	Soothe	Roughneck	0.6	0.3	-0.4	1.4	0.9	-0.2	0.4	-0.3	0.1
46.	Schoolgirl	Serve	Disciplinarian	1.2	-0.1	0.6	1.4	0.0	0.5	-0.3	0.4	0.5
47.	Warden	Silence	Blabbermouth	0.7	1.7	0.6	0.6	1.2	0.4	-0.3	-0.7	0.5
48.	Hero	Ignore	Coward	-0.1	0.3	0.6	-0.7	-0.2	0.0	-1.0	-1.4	-1.1

(continued)

APPENDIX 1—Continued

	ACTOR	BEHAVIOR	OBJECT-PERSON	A'_e	A'_p	A'_a	B'_e	B'_p	B'_a	O'_e	O'_p	O'_a
49.	Underdog	Contemplate	Champion	0.8	0.1	0.1	0.5	0.3	0.0	0.4	0.7	0.8
50.	Gambler	Indulge	Judge	-0.7	-0.2	0.5	-1.0	-0.1	0.4	-0.3	-0.5	-0.5
51.	Judge	Silence	Schoolgirl	-0.0	1.2	-0.2	-0.0	0.9	-0.0	-0.0	-0.8	0.9
52.	Outlaw	Ignore	Invalid	-1.9	-0.6	0.0	-1.6	-0.7	-0.0	-0.1	-1.8	-1.4
53.	Sheriff	Protect	Beggar	1.7	1.9	0.6	1.8	1.5	0.8	0.6	-0.4	-0.7
54.	Underdog	Attack	Ogre	0.8	1.1	1.5	0.2	1.0	1.4	-0.9	0.5	0.6
55.	Blabbermouth	Pester	Gambler	-1.0	-1.0	1.0	-1.4	-0.8	1.0	-0.2	-0.4	0.2
56.	Outlaw	Amuse	Champion	0.5	-0.0	0.8	0.9	0.7	1.2	0.2	0.5	0.3
57.	Beggar	Defy	Sheriff	-1.1	-0.0	0.0	-0.9	0.3	0.4	-0.5	-0.0	-0.6
58.	Child	Pester	Schoolgirl	-0.9	-0.8	1.8	-1.3	-0.5	1.1	0.2	-0.0	1.1
59.	Blabbermouth	Convince	Invalid	-0.5	-0.2	0.9	-0.6	0.1	0.9	0.0	-1.1	-0.9
60.	Judge	Indulge	Outlaw	-0.3	-0.2	-0.3	-0.4	-0.2	0.1	-1.0	-0.4	-0.5
61.	Sheriff	Amuse	Warden	0.8	0.4	0.3	1.2	0.5	1.2	0.7	0.3	0.0
62.	Outlaw	Sock	Blabbermouth	-1.1	0.7	1.4	-0.5	0.7	1.2	-0.5	-1.0	0.5
63.	Boarder	Watch	Stranger	0.3	-0.1	-0.2	0.3	-0.1	-0.6	0.1	-0.1	-0.5
64.	Athlete	Tickle	Roughneck	0.2	0.7	1.0	0.6	0.4	1.4	-0.3	-0.2	0.6
65.	Beggar	Pester	Alcoholic	-1.3	-1.3	-1.0	-1.2	-1.1	-0.1	-0.8	-0.8	-0.9
66.	Champion	Convince	Athlete	1.3	1.5	1.6	1.2	1.1	0.9	1.1	1.0	1.4
67.	Stranger	Tap	Boarder	0.1	0.1	0.3	-0.1	0.1	-0.2	0.4	-0.2	-0.2
68.	Alcoholic	Avoid	Beggar	-0.8	-1.2	-1.0	-0.8	-1.3	-0.1	-0.4	-1.2	-0.9
69.	Cripple	Watch	Winner	0.7	-1.1	-1.1	0.4	-0.1	-0.2	1.0	1.2	1.1
70.	Outlaw	Observe	Coward	-0.5	0.3	0.4	-0.0	-0.1	-0.2	-1.2	-1.6	-0.6

REFERENCES

Bohrnstedt, G. W., & Marwell, G. The reliability of products of two random variables. In K. F. Schuessler (Ed.), *Sociological methodology 1978*. San Francisco: Jossey-Bass, 1978.

Byron, R. P. Testing for misspecification in econometric systems using full information systems. *International Econometric Review*, 1972, *13*, 745-56.

Cliff, N. Consistencies among judgments of adjective combinations. In A. K. Romney, R. N. Shepard, & S. B. Nerlove (Eds.), *Multidimensional scaling: Theory and applications in the behavioral sicences* (Vol. 2). New York: Seminar Press, 1972.

Diedrich, G. W., Messick, S. J., & Tucker L. R. A general least squares solution for successive intervals. *Psychometrika*, 1957, *22*, 159-173.

Gollob, H. F. Impression formation and word combination in sentences. *Journal of Personality and Social Psychology*, 1968, *10*, 341-353.

Gollob, H. F., & Rossman, B. B. Judgments of an actor's 'power and ability to influence others'. *Journal of Experimental Social Psychology*, 1973, *9*, 391-406.

Heise, D. R. Affective dynamics in simple sentences. *Journal of Personality and Social Psychology*, 1969, *11*, 204-213. (a)

Heise, D. R. Some methodological issues in semantic differential research, *Psychological Bulletin*, 1969, *72*, 406-22. (b)

Heise, D. R. Potency dynamics in simple sentences. *Journal of Personality and Social Psychology*, 1970, *16*, 48-54.

Heise, D. R. Causal analysis. New York: Wiley-Interscience, 1975.

Heise, D. R. Social action as the control of affect. *Behavioral Science*, 1977, *22*, 163-177.

Heise, D. R. *Computer-assisted analysis of social action: Use of Program INTERACT and SURVEY, UNC 75*. Institute for Research in Social Science, Technical Paper No. 5. University of North Carolina, Chapel Hill. N.C., 1978.

Heise, D. R. *Understanding events: Affect and the construction of social action*. New York: Cambridge University Press, 1979.

Heise, D. R., and Smith-Lovin, L. *Impressions of goodness, powerfulness and liveliness from discerned social events*. Social Psychology Quarterly 1981. *44*, 131-145.

Jöreskog, K. G. A general approach to confirmatory maximum likelihood factor analysis,'' *Psychometrika*, 1969, *34*, 183-202.

Jöreskog, K. G. A general method for the analysis of covariance structures. *Biometrika*, 1970, *57*, 239-251.

Jöreskog, K. G., Gruvaeus, G. T., & Vanthillo, M. *ACOVS—A general computer program for the analysis of covariance structures*. Research Bulletin 70-15. Princeton, N.J.: Educational Testing Service, 1970.

Jöreskog, K. G., & Sörbom, D. *LISREL IV: Analysis of linear structural relationships by method of maximum likelihood*. Chicago: National Educational Resources, Inc., 1978.

Lawley, D. N., & Maxwell, A. E. *Factor analysis as a statistical method*. London: Butterworths Inc., 1971.

Osgood, C. E. Studies of the generality of affective meaning systems. *American Psychologist*, 1962, *17*, 10-28.

Smith-Lovin, L. Behavior settings and reactions to social scenarios. *Social Psychology Quarterly* 1979, *42*, 31-42.

Saris, W. E., de Piper, W. M., & Zegwaart, P. Detection of specification errors in linear structural equation models. In K. F. Schuessler (Ed.), *Sociological methodology 1979*. San Francisco: Jossey-Bass, 1979.

Sörbom, D. Detection of correlated errors in longitudinal data. *British Journal of Mathematical and Statistical Psychology*. 1975, *28*, 138-151.

11 The Hierarchial Factor Model and General Intelligence

Lloyd G. Humphreys
University of Illinois, Urbana –Champaign

In the years since the publication of the Primary Mental Abilities monograph (Thurstone, 1938) psychometrists and factor analysts have tended to lose sight of the general factor in intelligence. This has been more true of research workers in the United States than in the United Kingdom, where Burt (1941) and Vernon (1950) retained the construct of general intelligence while accepting group factors as well. In contrast to this disregard or even disrepute of the construct among research persons working in the domain of human abilities, the dominant point of view among clinical psychologists (Wechsler, 1971) has been quite different. Clinicians have retained the use of intelligence tests for the very good reason that an IQ or its deviation equivalent constitutes an important piece of information about a child or adult. It is more important than the variation in the profile of scores on a battery of primary ability tests.

THE FACTORIAL BASIS FOR GENERAL INTELLIGENCE

The Basic Evidence. The fundamental basis for a general factor in human cognitive functioning is the size of the *smallest* correlations among a wide variety of tests administered in a wide range of human talent. We can look at some of these small correlations in data from Project Talent. Ninth-grade boys and girls represented very nearly the full range of talent in 1960 when Project Talent was initiated. The tests administered also represented a wide range of intellectual functions. Intercorrelations presented in an early publication (Flanagan et al., 1964) were based on more than 3900 boys and almost 3900 girls.

Although the Project Talent tests do not cover all conceivable tests of information, aptitude, etc., the wide coverage allows a test of the hypothesis of generality in the cognitive domain. Inspection of the tables of intercorrelations in question reveals mostly positive correlations of rather substantial size. There are only a small number of near-zero or even negative correlations. The location of these essentially zero correlations is revealing. They are connected with two of three scoring schemes for highly speeded tests containing very easy items. This finding is illustrated in Table 11.1, which contains intercorrelations for both boys and girls of six measures that are not ordinarily considered to be highly loaded on the general factor, including one of the highly speeded tests, Clerical Checking. The mean correlation with eight tests that would be considered good measures of the general factor is also included for each of the six initially selected.

It is seen that the only negative correlations in these subsets from the larger matrices are with two of the three scoring formulas for Clerical Checking. There is also a clear progression from the formula score that penalizes errors to the one that is the number of items attempted. Generality does not extend to mere speed of performance. There must be a small element of problem solving involved even if it is as simple as being correct when checking a name as same or different from a standard.

The generality extends to measures of rote memory, a speeded test of accuracy in simple numerical operations, and to information about either farming (for boys) or home economics (for girls). Note in this regard that the criterion tests of general intelligence cover a rather wide gamut of content and operations: Vocabulary, Reading Comprehension, Creativity, Arithmetic Reasoning, Abstract Reasoning, Visualization in Three Dimensions, English, and Introductory Mathematics. Note also that correlations with a composite of the preceding tests, which would more closely parallel a test of general intelligence than any one of the components, would be substantially higher than the means. A hypothesis that the generality in cognitive functioning extends to tests having right answers and in which some premium is placed on obtaining the right answer is a reasonable one. A test of black urban argot administered in either a black or white sample would be expected to have positive correlations with these eight measures.

TABLE 11.1
Intercorrelations of Selected Measures from Project Talent
Boys are Above, Girls Below, the Diagonal

	1	2	3	4	5	6	7
1. Clerical Checking, R − 3W		510	111	322	197	170	241
2. Clerical Checking, R.	679		911	-086	107	-004	019
3. Clerical Checking, R + W	386	939		-254	029	-085	-094
4. Numerical Operations	286	049	-072		237	282	343
5. Memory for Words	190	088	022	295		294	383
6. Farming/Home Economics	181	021	-059	303	282		464
7. Measures of g	231	046	-050	351	390	449	

TABLE 11.2

Schematic Tables of Intercorrelations Each Defining Two Common Factors

| | Matrix A | | | | Matrix B | | |
	1	2	3	4	1	2	3	4
1.		90	00	00		90	75	75
2.	90		00	00	90		75	75
3.	00	00		.90	75	75		90
4.	00	00	90		75	75	90	

Models of Factor Rotation. The neglect of the general factor in human abilities in the United States has arisen from the popularity of the group factor model and the almost universal restrictions of that model to factors in the first order only. Investigators who prefer orthogonal rotations hide the general factor in the predominance of small positive loadings of measures that are supposedly in the hyperplane. Investigators who prefer oblique rotations reveal the general factor in the intercorrelations of their factors, but these correlations are typically not interpreted.

These problems are highlighted by the comparison of the two matrices in Table 11.2. Each matrix defines two common factors, no more, no less, but there is a great deal of difference in the psychological significance of the two patterns of correlations. Whether the two factors are rotated orthogonally or obliquely, the differences between variables 1 and 2, on the one hand, and 3 and 4, on the other, are the significant findings in matrix *A*, whereas the communality among the four variables is the significant finding in matrix *B*. If all measures in Project Talent had their correlations corrected for attenuation, and if measures of two group factors were compared with each other pair by pair, the correlations would in general look more like those of matrix *B* than matrix *A*.

The communality among psychological measures of cognitive functioning is best portrayed by a hierarchial model of human abilities. Factors are extracted in more than one order and factors in all orders are transformed into a hierarchial, orthogonal structure in a single order by means of the Schmid–Leiman transformation (1957). Although there are certain difficulties with the hierarchial model in terms of its fit to empirical findings (Humphreys, 1962), these difficulties are not with the general factor. The smaller group factors do not break out of the larger group factors as clearly as one would like.

Table 11.3 contains centroid factor loadings for matrix *B* of Table 11.2 along with orthogonal, oblique, and hierarchial rotations. Although these matrices represent a very simple situation consisting of only four variables and two factors, they serve to highlight the different rotational models. The dramatic decrease in the size of the loadings on the group factors from either the orthogonal or oblique rotations to the hierarchial is typical of what happens in actual data. In a wide range of talent the column of general factor loadings not only accounts for

TABLE 11.3
Unnotated and Rotated Factors in Matrix B

	Unnotated		Orthogonal		Oblique*		Hierarchical		
	I	II	I	II	I	II	"g"	I	II
1.	908	276	837	447	949	000	865	390	000
2.	908	276	837	447	949	000	865	390	000
3.	908	-276	447	837	000	949	865	000	390
4.	908	-276	447	837	000	949	865	000	390

*The correlation between the oblique factors is .831.

much more variance than the group factors, but within any row of the hierarchial matrix the general factor loading is likely to be the largest.

COMPUTATIONAL METHODS

It is important to start with a sound research design whenever a factor analysis is planned, but it is especially important to do so when the design requires factoring beyond the first order. Second-order factors as a minimum are required when one wishes to use the hierarchial model. The general factor cannot be equated with the first principal component and only in rare circumstances can a rotated first-order factor be equated with the general factor in human abilities. The latter can occur only when there are both cognitive and noncognitive variables in the analysis.

Design of the Study. A great deal of factor analytic work is done with intercorrelations of the variables based on too few observations. There is no absolute rule, and there is also trade-off with other parameters of the design, but N should be as large as possible. The investigator might well place confidence limits around correlations of the various sizes expected using several levels of N before making a decision concerning the size of the sample needed.

The number of variables (n) in the analysis relative to the size of N is also critical. It is well known that one capitalizes on chance as the number of predictors approaches the number of observations in multiple regression. There is a related phenomenon in factor analysis. The score matrix should depart from squareness as much as possible. The ratio of N to n is typically too small in published studies.

The number of factors (m) one plans to rotate and to interpret is also a critical parameter. It is relatively easy to capitalize on chance in selecting the number of factors to rotate and in the placement of the rotated axes when there are only one or two ''markers'' for a given factor. The presence of four markers may not always be essential, but it is a recommended minimum for a well-designed analysis. (See Humphreys, Ilgen, McGrath, & Montanelli, 1969, for a discussion of the effects of varying N, n, and m.)

A fourth important parameter is communality. Tucker, Koopman, and Linn (1969) have shown that one can locate a known factor structure in a sample more accurately when the variables have high communality. A necessary but not a sufficient condition for high communality is, of course, high reliability. Deliberate use of "hyperplane stuff" should be avoided. Note that it is legitimate to discard variables having low communalities from a prospective factor analysis merely from inspection of the matrix of correlations.

Unfortunately there is little lost and a good deal to be gained, except scientifically, when studies that depart radically from these recommendations are designed. The investigator who proceeds with small N, small communalities, large n, and large m is able to confirm any hypothesis, and his or her ability to formulate hypotheses about his or her factors is limited only by imagination. There is usually, also, no difficulty in publishing these studies.

Factor Analysis Methods.   The method of factor extraction is also important. The initial decision is whether one wants components or common factors. The two models should not be confused. Component analysis involves the entire variance, either raw score or standardized, of each of the variables, whereas common factor analysis involves only the common variance. The preferred method of extracting common factors is the principal components or principal axes method, with estimates of communalities in the principal diagonal of the correlation matrix. Under many circumstances the use of squared multiple correlations in the diagonal is recommended. It is becoming more and more evident, incidentally, that principal components with squared multiples in the diagonal is a more robust technique than the seemingly more elegant and more time-consuming maximum likelihood method (Hymphreys & Montanelli, 1975; Tucker, 1978).[1]

The decision concerning the number of components to rotate can be made by using breaks in the curve of the eigenvalues in conjunction with the application of the "parallel analysis" criterion (Montanelli & Humphreys, 1976). The use of the "roots greater than 1.00" rule based on *component* analysis is not recommended. With respect to the parallel analysis criterion present evidence indicates that one can discard very small factors, even though they might be replicable in the sampling sense, on psychological grounds, without disturbing the structure of the larger factors. On the other hand, anyone who consistently rotates and interprets more factors than indicated by this criterion is probably capitalizing on chance to such an extent that the factors are largely imaginary.

---

[1]Correlation matrices can readily be constructed that involve only two factors but that define three factors when the maximum likelihood criterion is used. The problem appears to be general among methods that require a rescaling based on the inverse of the uniqueness matrix.

Because the hierarchial model requires factoring in more than one order, the investigator must use an oblique rotational program for the first-order factors. The writer has been using binormamin (Kaiser & Dickman, 1959) although he makes no claim that it is optimal. He also frequently obtains a varimax rotational solution for purposes of comparison. If essentially the same factors are found in both sets of rotations, he has a greater feeling of cofidence in the oblique solution. It must be admitted, however, that this feeling of confidence springs from intuition and not from research findings.

Higher-order factoring follows the same procedures outlined for first-order factoring. If there is only one second-order factor or if there are two or more orthogonal second-order factors, factoring stops and the Schmid–Leiman transformation is applied. If there are three or more oblique second-order factors, factoring proceeds into the third order. If there are two oblique second-order factors, the study should be redesigned, as the one correlation between the two factors cannot determine uniquely two separate factor loadings in the third-order.

When the factoring has stopped, a matrix of factor loadings in the highest order is formed to which a diagonal matrix of uniqueness coefficients obtained in that order is attached. This matrix is premultiplied by the matrix of oblique factor loadings (not the reference vector coefficients) from the preceding order to form an orthogonal matrix having as many columns as factors in the two orders combined and as many rows as variables in the preceding order. If factoring has been done in more than two orders, a second transformation following the same procedure is applied. Note that a new diagonal matrix of uniqueness coefficients is required from this stage. The final result is an orthogonal matrix having as many columns as the number of factors in all orders combined and as many rows as the original number of variables. Factors in the highest order will be the broadest factors; factors in the first order will be the narrowest. There is no problem in defining or understanding a higher-order factor when this rotational model is followed. The procedures are usually quite simple. In many correlation matrices of ability measures, only one factor need be extracted at the second order. Only in large correlation matrices in which the investigator has included many sets of highly similar measures will the general factor be located in the third order.

Evaluating the Importance of First-Order Factors.   It is possible for an investigator to evaluate readily the amount of information lost by interpreting only the first-order factors. In a fashion analogous to the use and interpretation of partial correlations one can determine the contribution to the original R matrix of the first-order factors with the higher-order factors held constant and of the higher-order factors with the first-order factors held constant (Hymphreys, Tucker, & Dachler, 1970). In a wide range of talent one finds that higher-order factors make by far the larger contribution to the intercorrelations of cognitive variables. When this procedure is used with the oblique factor matrix in Table

11.3, for example, the contribution of the first-order factors is small (.15) and is made to only the two highest correlations, whereas the contribution of the higher-order factor is .75 and is made to each of the six correlations.

RELATED CONCEPTS

There are two concepts related to the general factor in intelligence that can be placed in perspective at this time. One is the concept of differential validity of predictors for various criteria.[2] The other is the differentiation between fluid and crystallized general ability originated by Cattell (1971).

Predictive Validities.   When one turns from the intercorrelations of tests to correlations of tests with socially relevant criteria, one again is impressed with the importance of the general factor. In samples of adequate size any cognitive test is related to any proficiency criterion with a cognitive component. That some industrial psychologists who had looked at too many validity coefficients based on small N's convinced the Equal Employment Opportunity Commission that test validities were highly labile would be laughable if the consequences had not been so serious. Because test validities were supposedly sensitive to small changes in conditions, the requirement became one of validating tests anew in each job, location, time period, type of industry, etc. In point of fact, however, the problem is to find tests that have differential validity from one criterion to another. The possibility of differential validity requires sizable group factors that are differentially related to the various criteria. After almost 7 years of trying to achieve a useful degree of differentiation in the early and middle 1950s, I reached the conclusion that it was possible to distinguish between mechanical and clerical criteria with two broad clusters of tests, but that finer discrimination in a wide range of talent was highly problematic. I have also had occasion recently to review current military personnel research reports and have not been able to observe any appreciable advance in that regard. Differential classification of pilots and navigators in World War II, although made easier by the restriction of range of talent on the general factor, was based on very similar clusters of cognitive tests.

Fluid and Crystallized Intelligence.   Cattell has an incomplete hierarchial model. His fluid and crystallized intelligence factors, along with several others,

---

[2]Differential validity has been misused in recent years for comparisons of validities of tests for different subgroups of a population (e.g., blacks and whites). Such comparisons require analyses of standard errors of estimate, slopes of regression lines, and intercepts of regression lines. The older and correct use of the term can be illustrated by two tests and two criteria; Test 1 is more highly correlated with Criterion 1 than Criterion 2, whereas the reverse is true for Test 2. These differences must also be stable from the sampling point of view and sufficiently large to have a practical impact on selection and classification, or guidance of examinees.

were originally defined by factoring in the second order. Once defined, however, it is possible to do research on these factors by a careful selection of marker variables so that factors that are typically found in the second order in a more complete selection of tests can appear in the first order. Cattell's second-order factors are also given the symbol g, along with an appropriate subscript. He faces a logical dilemma here in designating each of several coordinate factors as general factors.

The second-order factors are themselves positively intercorrelated and will define a single factor in the next higher order. The appropriate designation for this higher-order factor would be the general factor. In the complete hierarchial model, fluid and crystallized intelligence, along with the other second-order factors, become major group factors and the smaller group factors that typically appear in the first order become minor group factors. Whether measures of so-called fluid intelligence would have the highest loadings on the general factor is not presently known.

There is no problem in higher-order factoring of piling unknowns on top of unknowns when the results are reported in terms of the hierarchial model. Second-order factors need not be defined by first-order factors that are themselves subjectively interpreted, and third-order factors need not be defined by second-order factors that are themselves once removed from the original variables. In the hierarchial model all factors are defined by the original variables, and interpretations become more rather than less tenuous as one moves from the general factor through major group factors to minor group factors. This reverses the usual conception concerning higher-order factors. The common factor methodology as it has been developed extracts the least important factors first—and mistakenly calls them primary—and the most important factor or factors last. It is the general factor that is primary.

APPLICATIONS OF THE HIERARCHIAL MODEL

Examples of the use of the hierarchial model in the factor analytic literature are rare. As described earlier, when an investigator presents and interprets the "primary" factors there is seemingly no reason to look at second-order factors or even to interpret the intercorrelations of the first-order factors. The computational model was described by Schmid and Leiman in 1957; it was discussed by Humphreys (1962) a few years later; it thereupon disappeared from the literature until recently. This seems to say a good deal about the effect of at least one divisional presidential address!

Factor Differentiation.   Atkin, Bray, Davison, Herzberger, Humphreys, and Selzer (1977a) presented their evidence for factor differentiation during development in terms of both first-order oblique factors and of orthogonal hierarchial factors. It is instructive to compare the group factor loadings in the two ways of describing the same data. The intercorrelations of the first-order factors, ranging in number from two at Grade 5 to five at Grade 11, are so high that seemingly large, important first-order factors almost disappear following the orthogonal transformation. The arbitrary example used in Tables 11.2 and 11.3 is really quite realistic.

Factor differentiation in a wide range of talent during the period of development from Grade 5 to Grade 11 is slow and something less than dramatic in amount. In a sample of college undergraduates who are both older and more restricted in range of talent than public school students, there is clearcut differentiation of verbal and quantitative abilities. Among 5th-graders there is hardly any differentiation of these abilities, and the distinction develops very gradually in the ensuing 6 years. The general factor, which shrinks in size from the 5th grade to college, is affected much more by the range of talent than by the differentiation of group factors.

FACTORING LONGITUDINAL DATA

Atkin et al. (1977a) had data for 16 cognitive tests, each administered during the 5th, 7th, 9th, and 11th grades, but reported their factor analyses of the 16 variables separately at each grade level because they had no methodology at that time appropriate for the larger matrices of variables and occasions. Because the intercorrelations of each test over four occasions form a simplex matrix, one cannot obtain meaningful common factors from the complete matrix based on both test and occasions following standard common factor methodology (See Humphreys, 1960, for a discussion of this problem.) With the finding of a highly significant, highly stable cross-lagged difference between a measure of aural comprehension and the remaining variables (Atkin et al., 1977b), the problem of fitting a meaningful common factor model to the intercorrelations became a matter of interest. The direction of the cross-lagged difference, incidentally, was that individual differences on the Listening test anticipated individual differences generally on the other tests in the set.

In order to simplify the problem, Humphreys and Parsons (1978) elected to work with only two occasions: Grade 5 and Grade 11. The process of fitting a model to the data required the use of Jöreskog's restricted maximum likelihood factor analytic procedure (1970). A reasonably good fit descriptively was obtained after allowing all factors having the same identification at both grade levels to be correlated less than unity over the 6-year interval. This does not necessarily mean that factors were functionally different at the two grade levels. A more probable explanation is that the correlations between factor scores were less than unity, which was handled by the model as if the factors were less than perfectly correlated. A typical level of correlation between factors at the two occasions is slightly more than .8. The explanation phrased in terms of change in rank order of factor scores requires nothing more than an assumption that individual growth curves differ. These differences may be either genetic or environmental in origin, or both.

The principle source in common factor terms for the fact that individual differences in aural comprehension anticipate individual differences in other cognitive functions measured visually is in the factor loadings of Listening on the two general factors in the model. Listening at Grade 5 is intermediate in the space defined by the positively correlated general factors, whereas Listening at Grade 11 lies outside the space though close to the general factor at Grade 11. A measure of aural comprehension in Grade 5 is apparently anticipating developmental changes on the general factor measured by tests requiring visual comprehension.

Partially Out Intelligence.   Humphreys and Parson (1977) have shown how an investigator can hold constant the trait of general intelligence while examining the relationship between other variables by means of the hierarchial model. In an adequately designed factor analysis that uses appropriate methodology the general factor can be equated with the construct of general intelligence. Loadings of all variables in the analysis on the orthogonal group factors represent correlations with constructs that are independent of general intelligence (i.e., general intelligence is partialled out of relationships among variables described by group factors). In contrast, the typical procedure involves the selection of a particular fallible measure of intelligence and enters the correlations among the measures being analyzed in the formula for a partial correlation. This usual procedure errs in two ways. The measure of intelligence held constant includes in its variance measurement error. True score variance is not removed by this procedure. In contrast, factors are error free. Measures of intelligence also differ from each other more than one would expect on the basis of their respective reliabilities. Any test of intelligence is also fallible in terms of validity. Holding constant fallible test scores cannot control hypothetical trait variance.

Piagetian Cognitive Development.   The generality in cognitive functioning can also be observed in the relationship between standard tests of intelligence and performance on typical Piagetian tasks. Although the correlation between any one Piagetian task and total score on an intelligence test is far below unity, the same observation can also be made about intelligence test items and total score on the intelligence test. In a recent factor analysis in which we applied the hierarchial model to variables including the Wechsler subtests, three standard academic achievement tests, and 27 Piagetian tasks, the principal factor loading for most of the Piagetian tasks as well as for the intelligence and achievement tests was on the general factor (Humphreys & Parsons, 1979). Furthermore, several of the individual Piagetian conservation tasks had general factor loadings as high or higher than the highest of the Wechsler subtests. As a final step we correlated unit-weighted composites of the Piagetian tasks, on the one hand, and the Wechsler and achievement tests, on the other. The correlation was .88 and involved no capitalization on chance. As a matter of fact the Piagetian composite was less reliable and less valid than it could become because a number of the tasks were not sound psychometrically. These suspect tasks showed little communality with tasks of their own type.

In addition to the substantial contribution to total variance of the general factor there was an easily identifiable academic achievement group factor and a Piagetian conservation factor. Neither described a very high proportion of the total variance, but both are so well defined that there is little doubt concerning their replicability. When one thinks in terms of the hierarchial model, most of the research involving Piagetian tasks is uninterpretable (i.e., one does not know whether a particular effect is related to the general factor or to a group Piagetian factor). This suggests the need for the use of multiple dependent variables in research concerned with cognitive development. From the present point of view also, relationships between independent variables and the general factor in Piagetian tasks would almost certainly be more important psychologically and socially than those with a group factor.

Other conclusions follow. The items in children's tests of intelligence can be used almost interchangeably with Piagetian tasks in describing cognitive development. Age scales would be especially useful for this purpose. One can also measure general intelligence by administering a series of Piagetian tasks almost interchangeably with any standard test of intelligence. Note that the latter are not completely interchangeable with each other because correlations corrected for attenuation are rarely unity. It also follows that a better measure of the general factor in cognitive abilities could be constructed using items from both approaches. A measure of the general factor should be as broad as its defining variables.

Social Selection and the General Factor. Quite a different aspect of the importance of the general factor in human abilities is furnished by the effects of social selection. There were many, many social forces that determined in 1960 whether a given child would be in one high school rather than in another. There were and are many demographic differences among the nation's high schools: rural–urban, sectional, socioeconomic, racial, public–private, and curriculum specialty, to name the obvious ones. We asked how these forces in toto affected the intercorrelations of the Project Talent cognitive tests. We added to the matrix selected demographic measures of the schools. We were able to obtain these intercorrelations for the means of 59 cognitive measures, one composite measure of the socioeconomic status (SES) of individual students, and 19 school demographic measures for more than 700 high schools from the Project Talent Data Bank. Data for 10th-grade students were requested to minimize the dropout problem and to avoid the junior-senior-high problem. (Humphreys, Parsons, & Park, 1979).

Our hypothesis was that social selection operated primarily on the general factor. Under these circumstances it would be difficult to define the traditional group factors. We were also interested in trying to determine whether the effect on the general factor would operate through primary selection on socioeconomic factors or whether selection was directly on the general factor. Support for the latter would require evidence that selection on socioeconomic factors was indirect.

The results are convincing. There is a large almost general factor on which tests that are known to be good measures of g have loadings from .9 to .95 for both boys and girls. For example, General Vocabulary and Reading Comprehension define the upper level. Three highly speeded clerical type tests, which in this research were scored by number right only, are the only ones that do not have appreciable loadings on this factor in either sex. Hunting and fishing information for the girls are also not loaded appreciably on this factor. The socioeconomic index for the students' families has a loading on this same factor in the seventies. The amount of selection on the SES index is about at the mean of the cognitive tests (i.e., selection on socioeconomic factors appears to be indirect). Of the school variables, rate of college going has the highest factor loading, but several school variables have almost zero loadings. The factor is not general in the factor analytic sense, but it can be identified with the general factor in intelligence.

Only one of the three small-group factors was identified with confidence and this one did not represent a so-called primary mental ability. Variables loading on this factor included, especially for boys, hunting, fishing, farming, and mechanical information, a shorter school year, small classes, and relatively few students in the school. A designation of rural high schools seems apt. A second group factor was defined by the three highly speeded tests. It is not certain what factors produce student selection in high schools on speed of performance unrelated to g. On the grounds that the very broad difference on cognitive tests between blacks and whites disappears when there is no correction for errors on tests of this type, a tentative identification of this factor with black schools was made. Identification of the third group factor was even more tenuous. Information about the Bible covaries with low teacher salaries and low student per capita expenditures. These may be private sectarian schools.

Another method of gauging the amount of social selection that determines school enrollment is to compare the standard deviations of schools with the standard deviations of individuals within the schools. The medians of these ratios for both boys and girls approaches .60 and is just under the ratio for the socioeconomic index. Because many of the Project Talent tests were of very modest reliability—tests had to be kept short because of restrictions on total testing time—the size of many of their variance ratios is substantially attenuated by errors of measurement. In contrast the socioeconomic index is undoubtedly highly reliable and had little attentuation of its variance ratio. We concluded that the amount of selection was large, that selection was on the general factor primarily, and that selection of the socioeconomic index was mediated by its correlation with the general factor. We had only speculation to offer, however, concerning the bases for general factor selection.

Possible Applications.   Use of the hierarchial model and intepretation of the broader factors that ensue is not restricted to cognitive tests. Whenever a psychologist is faced with the problem of multiple criterion measures, for example, it is appropriate to turn to the hierarchial model. If one obtains two or more supervisor ratings, two or more peer ratings, and administers multiple objective tests of proficiency on the job, a minimum of three first-order factors will be found. Furthermore, if the investigator has used varimax rotations, a conclusion that there are three "independent" dimensions in job proficiency is likely to follow. It should now be obvious that this is a naive conclusion.

The model also has applicability outside the cognitive and proficiency domains. The conflicting views concerning personality factors (Eysenck, 1960) are based on Eysenck's emphasis on broad factors and Cattell's emphasis on narrow factors. The two points of view come much closer together when Cattell's second-order factors are compared with Eysenck's first-order factors. Note that the use of the hierarchial model does not assume that a general factor will be found. It only allows one to be defined if supported by the data. When applied in the noncognitive domain, higher-order factoring may stop with two or more orthogonal factors in the highest order.

It should also be useful to view diverse measures of job satisfaction as constituting a possible hierarchy. As a general rule a factor analyst should always look for possible higher-order factors on the excellent grounds that higher-order factors are very likely to be the most important factors psychologically. It does not matter very much how many factors can be identified in the testing room that are based on the nuances of wording of test items unless it can be shown that measures of these narrow factors furnish differential information about behavior in the real world.

THE INTERPRETATION OF GENERAL INTELLIGENCE

Acceptance of a general factor in human abilities as a descriptive construct does not lead automatically to an interpretation of g along the lines of Charles Spearman, who discussed the construct in terms of "mental energy" (1914, 1927). Although most psychologists today would reject his terminology, many would still think of a factor, either general or group, as an entity, or as a unitary "thing" within the organism (Guilford, 1967). Factors at all levels and of all types are readily reified in this way. There is, however, a more acceptable alternative that can be traced most directly to Godfrey Thomson (1919). Others who have discussed factors in this more acceptable fashion are Edward Thorndike (1926), Robert Tryon (1935), and George Ferguson (1954).

The Nature of "g". Thomson discussed *g* in terms of multiple overlapping neural bonds. Thorndike brought in multiple stimulus–response bonds. Ferguson discussed group factors in terms of transfer of training resulting from environmental experiences. Their approach is closer to observables both anatomically and behaviorally than constructs that are discussed as entities.

I have translated the point of view of Thomson and the others in the following way. To the extent that there is a genetic contribution to individual differences in general intelligence, that contribution is polygenic. Environmental contributions are also multiple. To coin a term, we might call these contributions polyenvironmental. Similarly, the biological substrate for general intelligence is polyneural, and the behavioral observations that define the phenotypic construct are polybehavioral. Intelligence is the resultant of the processes of acquiring, storing in memory, retrieving, combining, comparing, and using in new contexts information and conceptual skills; it is an abstraction.

In order to sample these behaviors adequately, intelligence tests must be composed of a large number of items heterogeneous in content and having only moderate levels of interitem correlations. Imposing a criterion of high homogeneity impairs the construct validity of the intelligence test and converts it into a measure of a phenotypic trait subordinate in the ability hierarchy.

Heredity and Intelligence. Although it is theoretically possible to estimate the genotypic level of a person from a continuously distributed phenotypic trait such as general intelligence, a dependable estimate of the correlation between genotype and phenotype in a specified population is required. Present estimates for the general factor are not dependable, and I do not anticipate any change in this state of affairs in the foreseeable future. Accepting evolutionery continuity in animal behavior as well as in structure, I am 99% confident that the square of this correlation, the heritability coefficient, lies between .2 and .8. The pattern of family resemblance coefficients suggests, but does not demonstrate a value toward the high end of this range. Other data, or more precisely the lack of adequate data on the effects of prenatal, perinatal, and early postnatal environmental conditions, suggests the need for the wide range of possible values.

Interpretations of intelligence test scores that involve inferences concerning native ability compound that error, for error it is, by equating phenotypic level with genotypic level. Whatever the correlation may be, it is surely less than unity. If we knew the correlation, the estimation of genotype would be made by means of an ordinary regression equation in which standard scores with a mean of zero and SD of 1.0 would be the sensible choice for the genotypic scale. Estimation of genotypes would necessarily involve regression toward the population mean of zero from extreme phenotypes. This regression would be accentuated by the presence of measurement error in the phenotypic measure.

The problem of inferring genotype from phenotype is complicated further in children and adolescents in ways that make the equation of phenotypic score with native ability even more erroneous. It is probable that the phenotypic–genotypic correlation varies with chronological age, and it is quite certain that there are individual differences in the rate of development. Differences in rate, whether produced by genetic or environmental causes, result in a simplex matrix in intercorrelations of true scores on intelligence tests administered over successive occasions. (Humphreys, 1960.) Estimates of individual genotypes would be everchanging during development and would not become relatively stable until maturity.

Intelligence and Adaptability to One's Environment. Criticisms of the construct of general intelligence have been expressed in recent years along one or more of the following lines: the tests measure the content of middle-class white culture; adaptability to the environment is more important than measured intelligence and is highly relative from culture to culture; survival in the ghetto is a more important criterion of intelligence than inability to read and write.

There is a modest amount of validity in such statements. The construct of general intelligence is itself adaptable to cultures other than our own, but the measuring instruments must of necessity be geared to the culture. On the other hand, to accept some degree of cultural relativity does not and should not equate intelligence to adaptability to the environment. Survival in some cultures may be heavily dependent on size, strength, muscular coordination, and sensory acuity. For a given group also, whether a separate species, or merely an isolated subset of a particular species, fertility rate contributes heavily to group survival.

One can isolate a contribution of general intelligence to survival even though the cultural group has no books nor a number system. There were individual differences among the Polynesians who colonized the Pacific in their accuracy of navigation. Similarly there were individual differences among American Indians in hunting and warring skills that went beyond size, strength, coordination, and sensory acuity. Once books and numbers are introduced and evaluated highly by a society, those who would otherwise have been the most successful navigators or the most successful strategists in the hunt or in war become most successful in reading comprehension and in the manipulation of numbers and mathematical symbols. Our so-called middle-class intelligence tests reflect behavior this society considers important, but intelligence can be manifest in other behaviors. Survival in the ghetto does require intelligence, but it also requires size, strength, coordination, and sensory acuity. In the American culture, also, with the availability of public education, radio, TV, newspapers, and books the intelligence component of survival in the ghetto is tapped by scores on standard tests of intelligence. Individual differences within the black population as measured by present tests provide valid information about individuals even though there is no adequate explanation of the difference between the black and white means.

Fluid Ability and General Intelligence. This interpretation of general intelligence is very similar to Cattell's description of fluid ability. Cattell's measures of fluid ability, however, are not the only nor possibly even the best measures of general intelligence. Intelligence is too fluid to be tied to a particular subset of cognitive tests, and there is a fluid (general) component in the variance of the most crystallized information or achievement test.

ACKNOWLEDGMENTS

Much of the research reported here was supported by a grant from the National Institute of Mental Health, MH 23612-04, Studies of Intellectual Development and Organization. Thanks are also due to the Project Talent Data Bank of the American Institutes for Research, to the Educational Testing Service, and to Professor Beth Stephens for some of the data analyzed.

REFERENCES

Atkin, R., Bray, R., Davison, M., Herzberger, S., Humphreys, L. G., & Selzer, U. Ability factor differentiation, grades 5 through 11. *Applied Psychological* Measurement, 1977, *1*, 65-76. (a)

Atkin, R., Bray, R., Davison, M., Herzberger, S., Humphreys, L. G., & Selzer, U. Cross-lagged panel analysis of 16 cognitive measures. *Journal for Research in Child Development*, 1977, *48*, 944-952. (b)

Burt, C. *The factors of the mind: An introduction to factor analysis in psychology.* New York: MacMillan, 1941.

Cattell, R. B. *Abilities: Their structure, growth, and action.* Boston: Houghton Mifflin, 1971.

Eysenck, H. J. *The structure of human personality* (2nd ed.) London: Methuen, 1960.

Ferguson, G. A. On learning and human ability. *Canadian Journal of Psychology.* 1954. *8*, 95-112.

Flanagan, J. C., Davis, F. B., Dailey, J. T., Shayt, M. F., Orr, D. B., Goldberg, I., & Neyman, C. A. Jr. *The American high school student.* Project Talent Office, University of Pittsburgh, Pittsburgh, 1964.

Guilford, J. P. *The nature of human intelligence.* New York: McGraw-Hill, 1967.

Humphreys, L. G. Investigations of the simplex. *Psychometrika*, 1960, *25*, 313-323.

Humphreys, L. G. The organization of human abilities. *American Psychologist*, 1962, *17*, 475-483.

Humphreys, L. G., Ilgen, D., McGrath, D., & Montanelli, R. Capitalization on chance in rotation of factors. *Educational and Psychological Measurement*, 1969, *29*, 259-272.

Humphreys, L. G., & Montanelli, R. G. An investigation of the parallel analysis criterion for determining the number of common factors. *Multivariate Behavioral Research*, 1975, *10*, 193-206.

Humphreys, L. G., & Parsons, C. *Piagetian tasks measure intelligence and intelligence tests assess cognitive development. Intelligence*, 1979, *3*, 369-382.

Humphreys, L. G., Parsons, C., & Park, K. *Dimensions involved in differences among means of cognitive measures. Journal of Educational Measurement*, 1979, *16*, 63-76.

Humphreys, L. G., Tucker, L. R., & Dachler, P. Evaluating the importance of factors in any given order of factoring. *Multivariate Behavioral Research*, 1970, *5*, 209–215.

Jöreskog, K. G. A general method for analysis of covariance structures. *Biometrika*, 1970, *57*, 239–511.

Kaiser, H. F., & Dickman, K. W. Analytic determination of common factors. *American Psychologist*, 1959, *14*, 425. (Abstract)

Montanelli, R. G., & Humphreys, L. G. Latent roots of random data correlation matrices with squared multiple correlations on the diagonal: A Monte Carlo study. *Psychometrika*, 1976, *41*, 341–348.

Schmid, J., & Leiman, J. The development of hierarchial factor solutions. *Psychometrika*, 1957, *22*, 53–61.

Spearman, C. The theory of two factors. *Psychological Review*, 1914, *21*, 101–115.

Spearman, C. *The abilities of man*. New York: MacMillan, 1927.

Thomson, G. On the cause of hierarchial order among correlation coefficients, *Proceedings of the Royal Society, A*, 1919, *95*.

Thorndike, E. L. *The measurement of intelligence*. New York: Bureau of Publications, Teachers College, Columbia University, 1926.

Thurstone, L. L. *Primary mental abilities*. Chicago: University of Chicago Press, 1938. (Psychometric Monograph No. 1)

Tryon, R. C. A theory of psychological components—an alternative to "mathematical factors." *Psychological Review*, 1935, *42*, 425–454.

Tucker, L. R. Personal communication, 1978.

Tucker, L. R., Koopman, R. F., & Linn, R. L. Evaluation of factor analytic research procedures by means of simulated correlation matrices. *Psychometrika*, 1969, *34*, 421–459.

Vernon, P. E. *The structure of human abilities*. New York: Wiley, 1950.

Wechsler, D. Intelligence: Definition, theory, and the IQ. In R. Cancro (Ed.). Intelligence: *Genetic and environmental influences*. New York: Grune and Stratton, 1971.

12 Multivariate Diagnostic Information Processing by Computer

Benjamin Kleinmuntz
University of Illinois at Chicago

Don N. Kleinmuntz
Center for Decision Research University of Chicago

Introduction

A minor legend of the old country doctor was that he could diagnose a disease by smelling it when he was near one of his patients. Some lesser physicians were reputed to have diagnostic dogs as traveling companions, dogs that would bark a certain number of times when in the presence of various types of diseases. Such folklore was undoubtedly intended to account for the mysterious and sometimes miraculously intuitive powers of these specially trained healers. Present-day diagnosticians still earn formidable reputations for correctly diagnosing diseases when given only minimal pathognomonic cues. Unfortunately not much more is known today about clinical judgment than at the time of the old country doctor—sorry state of affairs indeed.

This chapter attempts to remedy this gap in knowledge by demonstrating that clinical judgment can be subjected to the rigors of scientific scrutiny. For purposes of the chapter, we assume that clinical judgment is a problem-solving enterprise that is amenable to computerized multivariate information-processing strategies not unlike those espoused by Newell and Simon (1972). But first, some preliminary remarks and definitions seem in order.

At the outset, it is important to emphasize that we consider clinical judgment a special instance of problem solving in which the diagnostician is confronted by an array of variables through which he sifts, rejecting some aspects of the available information and calling for more information to supplement existing data. The starting point of this problem solving is the information about the patient, which may be in the form of biographical data, symptoms, signs, laboratory test results, psychometric data, or other observable and elicited cues. The end result or the solution to this multivariate problem is a judgment about, or a classification of the patient into a diagnostic category. The fact that different clinical specialities deal with different symptoms, signs, and tests, and use different tools does not alter the fact that similar problem-solving behaviors may underlie them all. At the same time, it is recognized that the cognitive behaviors that intervene between beginning and end may be for each diagnostician a highly idiosyncratic process.

Second, it is important to emphasize that the question of how the clinician processes information is clearly within the domain of psychological studies that concern themselves with problem solving, judgment, and thinking. It is only recently that there has been a resurgence of concern within psychology with the central topic of thinking. Much of this renewed interest has been due to the appearance of the electronic digital computer and the emergence of the concept of a computer program. The significance of the computer for diagnostic decision making does not lie in its mechanical ability to process clinical data; it lies rather in the fact that this machine has forced clinicians to specify rigorously the processes that are involved in thinking. Instructions can then be given to the computer (i.e., programs can be written) that combine these processes in such a way that the machine executes each of the instructions in solving the most complicated multivariate problems. Obviously, if we can be precise enough about a process to describe it in terms that can be programmed for machine operations, then we know quite a bit about that process.

We shall now describe three seemingly disparate but related instances in which the computer was used for solving multivariate diagnostic problems. The first of these deals with personality test interpretation by computer. Clinical neurology diagnosis is the topic of the second computer use. And the third has no substantive subject matter or problems to solve other than those that we design for the computer. These studies are interrelated in that they use the computer as a noncomputational tool for processing multivariate information. It is noncomputational in the sense that the machine's main purpose is not to compute, but rather to follow and initiate actions (e.g., compare two symbols and branch left if equal, branch right if not) that are programmed for it. If the program is innovative the computer can show such intelligent behavior as playing chess and understanding natural language. Our interest, however, is in clinical information processing.

Personality Assessment as a Multivariate Problem

Some years ago, we chose to study the thinking of an experienced clinical psychologist interpreting the results of a personality test (Kleinmuntz, 1963a, 1963b). The test was the Minnesota Multiphasic Personality Inventory (MMPI), which is convenient for our purposes because it yields a multivariate, patterned profile. The MMPI was designed to classify most of the known diagnostic categories along about 13 dimensions or scales; a correct interpretation of the configuration of these scales is essential for arriving at a correct diagnosis. The task of test interpretation would be immeasurably simpler if the diagnosis depended merely on the elevation of a single scale; but this is not the case. Profile interpretation therefore can be a highly subjective business.

1. Thinking Aloud Protocol. We devised a scheme that enabled and even forced the test interpreter to "think aloud" and give us a running commentary of his or her thinking as he or she solved the MMPI profile problem. The Q-sort technique developed by William Stephenson at the University of Chicago (1953) lent itself well to the task we had in mind. Conventional use of Stephenson's method calls for the preparation of a set of phrases covering, for example, a set of descriptive personality traits. These phrases are then prepared on a deck of cards and the rater is instructed to sort the cards by placing a specified number of cards in each of several piles. The number of cards and the piles into which they are to be sorted vary from one study to the next, but an invariant of the method is that the cards must be placed along the continuum of a forced normal distribution. In our study, instead of using cards with printed phrases or statements, we used MMPI profiles as cards to be sorted. The experienced MMPI user was instructed to Q-sort the profiles of emotionally maladjusted students ($N = 45$) and adjusted college students ($N = 81$) along a 14-step continuum. He or she was told to place the two least maladjusted profiles on the farthest left-hand pile, and to place to the right of these three slightly less maladjusted profiles, and so forth until the two most adjusted profiles were placed on the farthest pile to the right.

While the test interpreter was placing the profiles in one pile or the other, he or she was encouraged to think aloud. In other words, the sorter was instructed to give reasons for placing particular profiles along the continuum of piles. It was imperative not to allow the sorter to make any decisions without giving a rationale. Typically, a statement would be made such as the following: "Now I'm going to divide these into two piles . . . on the left (least adjusted) I'm throwing MMPIs with at least four scales elevated above the score of 70" (Table 12.1). These "thinking aloud" sessions were tape-recorded, and the protocols of one expert (there were 10 experts in all) were studied intensively. The information obtained from this test interpreter after about 30 hours of Q-sorting was edited, compiled, flow-charted (Fig. 12.1) and then programmed into computer language so that an electronic digital computer could make decisions about profiles similar to those made by the Q-sorter. In other words, the computer was given the sorter's information and strategies for processing the information.

2. The Decision Rules. The success rate of the programmed decision rules were quite similar to that of the MMPI expert. They both had about an 80% hit rate in classifying correctly the profiles of persons who were maladjusted; and they had about a 70% hit rate in the correct classification of the adjusted persons.

TABLE 12.1
MMPI Decision Rules and Tape-Recorded Protocol

Rule	Protocol
1. If four or more clinical scales T-Score $\geq$ 70, call maladjusted.	1. Now I'm going to divide these into two piles. . . on the left (least adjusted) I'm throwing all Mults with at least four scales printed.
2. If scales Hs, D, Hy, Pd, Mf, Ps, Pt, Sc, and Si are $\leq$ 60 and if Ma $\leq$ 80 and Mt $\leq$ 10_R, then call adjusted.	2. I'll throw all Mults to the right (most adjusted) if there's no clinical scale above a T-score of 60. . . I'll let Ma go up as high as 80. . . maybe a raw score of 10 on Mt would be playing it safe. . . so I'm looking at three things now and sorting according to these conditions.
3. If the first two scales in the Hathaway code includes Pd, Pa, or Sc, and at least one of these is $\geq$ 70, then call maladjusted (if Mf is among the first two scales, then examine the first three scales in the Hathaway code).	3. If either Pd, Pa, or Sc is primed, I'm putting it on the left side (least adjusted). . . it would also be nice to have all of these scales slightly more elevated than the others.
4. If Pa or Sc $\geq$ 70 and Pa, Pt, or Sc $\geq$ Hs, D, or Hy, call maladjusted.	4. If the elevations are popsided to the right with the left side of the profile fairly low, I'm throwing the Mults to the left (least adjusted).
5. Call maladjusted if Pa $\geq$ 70 unless Mt $\leq$ $.6_R$ and K $\geq$ 65.	5. Here's a paranoid character. . . I wish his K score were not quite so high. . . and he could use more Mt . . . when that Mt score is less than 10, I figure something must be stabilizing him. . . I like an inverted V with F high on the validity scales.
6. If Mt $\leq$ 6, call adjusted.	6. Boy, I don't know that Mt is too low to call her maladjusted. . . I'll settle for calling them adjusted if Mt is at a raw score of 6 or lower.
7. Call maladjusted if $(Pa + Sc - 2\ Pt)$ $\geq$ 20 and Pa or Sc $\geq$ 65.	7. Here's a nice valley between scales 6 and 8 and both 6 and 8 are high . . . I'll call this one maladjusted.
8. If D or Pt are the primary elevations and Es $\geq$ 45_R, call adjusted.	8. These 27 profiles are giving me a pain. . . if 2 or 7 is too elevated like, say, higher than a T-score of 80 and if the Es scale is approaching a raw score of 50. . . I'll call it adjusted.

(*continued*)

TABLE 12.1—*Continued*

Rule	Protocol
9. If *Pd* 70 and (a) male: *Mt* 15$_R$ or (b) female: *Mt* 17$_R$, call maladjusted.	9. A primed *Pd* and an *Mt* raw score of 15 or more is going over to the left pile (least adjusted). . . I guess on a male profile an *Mt* of 15 or more will do. . . and an *Mt* of 17 or more on a female profile.
10. If *Mt* 23$_R$ and *Es* 45$_R$, call maladjusted.	10. With *Mt* high and *Es* low, I'll call maladjusted at this stage of the game.
11. If 5 or more clinical scales 65 and if either *Pa* or *Sc* 65, call maladjusted.	11. Everything's up on this girl's MM PI. . . . I'm especially bothered by the high *Pa*. . . here's a high *Sc*. . . everything else is up too. . . over to the left (least adjusted).
12. Call adjusted if at least 5 clinical scales are between 40 and 60 and *Es* 45$_R$.	12. Here are a couple of nice, normal-looking Mults. . . all scales hugging a *T*-score of 50, and *Es* is nice and high. . . over to the right (most adjusted).
13. Call maladjusted if the profile is male and *Mf* 70 and *Sc* *Pt* and *Sc* 60.	13. An elevated *Mf* is pretty common for boys around colleges, but when it's primed and when *Sc* is up and is higher than *Pt*, I.ll throw it to the left (least adjusted).
14. If *Si* 60 and *Pa* 60 or *Sc* 70, call maladjusted.	14. That's a fairly high *Si*. . . and *Pa* is up, I'll call it maladjusted. . . here's one with a high *Si* and *Sc* is also up, I'll call this maladjusted.
15. Call maladjusted if *Es* 35$_R$.	15. Here's a pretty good-looking MMPI, but that low *Es* makes me think something might be wrong . . . to the left (least adjusted).
16. Call adjusted if *Mt* 10$_R$.	16. These are all pretty bad-looking Mults. . . I'll call adjusted if the *Mt* is lower than 10.

The set of 16 MMPI decision rules and tape-recorded protocol are shown in Table 12.1. The flow chart for these rules appear in Fig. 12.1.

Perhaps the most important lesson learned from this project was that clinicians can be forced to explicate their problem-solving strategies. In fact, one test interpreter gave us sufficient information to enable us to program his decisions. However, it must be noted that although the programmed sequential decision rules were surprisingly similar to those of the MMPI expert, there were depar-

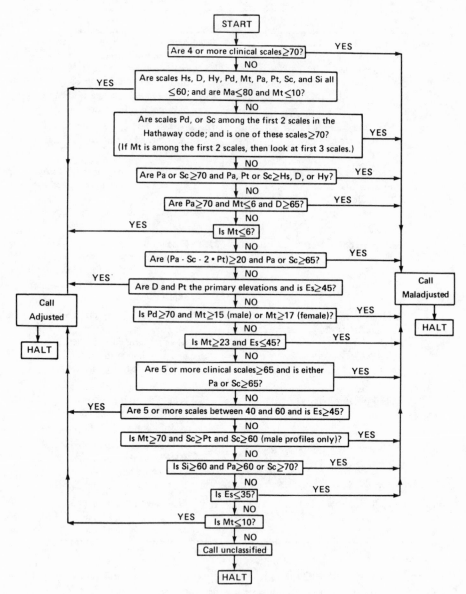

FIG. 12.1.   Flow chart of edited MMPI rules.

tures in the computer program from the expert's taped protocol. Interpretive rules of thumb and procedural tricks of the trade were borrowed from the expert and were used in the computer program only if they maximized the success rate of the MMPI decision rules. In other words, due to a focus at that time on the pragmatic problem of devising a set of "best" rules for performing the profile analytic job, we decided to depart from perfect simulation. Mathematicians call these shortcut solutions *heuristics*. An approach that would have aimed at reproducing the MMPI expert's every decision, down to its minutest detail, would have been a *simulation* of profile analytic decision making. Such an approach, although impractical from the point of view of yielding a set of workable interpretive rules, might have given us more insight into, and perhaps even the beginnings of, a theory of the pattern analytic behavior of the clinical decision maker. On the other hand, an approach that would have relied entirely on mathematical formulas is the *artificial intelligence* approach. It would yield very little information about the cognitive processes involved in profile interpretation, but might lead to quick and optimal solutions to MMPI interpretation.

Neurology Diagnosis as a Multivariate Problem

The next study had as its main objective the direct simulation of diagnostic judgment (Kleinmuntz, 1968, 1975). We chose to focus on the cognitive activities of clinical neurologists. This was not an arbitrary choice: The highly structured nature of the multivariate clinical data within that speciality, and the emphasis among neurologists on coming up with *the* correct diagnosis, made that area a tempting one for scientific study.

1. Twenty Questions. In order to force the neurologist to "think aloud" during diagnostic searching, a scheme had to be devised that was similar to the Q-sort procedure described earlier, and that would be more appropriate than the Q-sort for clinical neurology. For this purpose, we elected to use a variant of the childhood game of "Twenty Questions," a technique that lends itself to the systematic study of a number of decision-making variables. The game is played by having one player, called the experimenter, think of a disease while the other player, or subject, tries to diagnose the disease the experimenter has in mind. The experimenter can assume any of a number of roles. For example, the experimenter could pretend that he or she is a patient suffering with symptoms *a, b,* and *c;* or he or she could assume the role of the omniscient neurologist who is thinking of a cerebral disorder that is characterized by symptoms *a, b,* and *c.* The diagnostician's task in either case is to ask about the presence or absence of other symptoms, signs, or biographical data and to call for specific laboratory tests and inquire about their results. Again as in the case of the MMPI decision rule study, the subject's questions and the experimenter's answers were tape-recorded.

2. *Binary Trees.*   The end product of the diagnostic neurology game resembles a tree structure (Fig. 12.2). The way the game was described in the foregoing, we would obtain binary trees in which each point or node in the tree has exactly one connection to a point closer to the root of the tree. The starting point or the root of the tree is the subject's first question; all subsequent questions are the tests that are performed at the various nodes of the tree. Unless a node is an endpoint—that is, unless a diagnosis has been made on the basis of the questions asked (i.e., tests performed up to that point)—it is connected to two lower nodes, and through them to any number of still lower nodes. A test is associated with each nonterminal node, and, depending on the result of the test, a particular branch to a lower node is taken. A path is a collection of lines from the root of the tree to an endpoint or terminal node, and the path is the representation of the search strategy that the clinician used in arriving at the diagnostic solution.

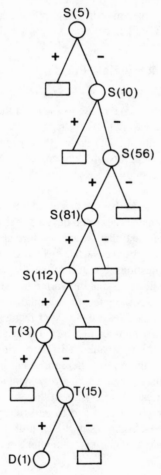

FIG. 12.2.   A binary tree structure for representing the search strategy of a diagnostician.

For illustrative purposes, consider the game represented in Fig. 12.2, in which the experimenter asserted that he has a disease in mind, let us call it $D(1)$, and the subject, inquiring about the presence or absence of a number of symptoms, asks whether a certain symptom is present in that disease. The subject's first question is whether $S(5)$ is present in the particular disease the experimenter has in mind. He or she receives a negative reply. Then the subject asks whether $S(10)$ is a symptom of the disease. Again he or she receives a negative reply. The next question, presumably based on information obtained from prior questions, concerns the presence of $S(56)$. An affirmative reply to that question leads to the question about the presence of $S(81)$ and $S(112)$. Confirmation of the presence of these symptoms then leads the subject to call for laboratory tests $T(3)$ and $T(15)$. The experimenter in our example replied that the results of the first test were negative, but that $T(15)$ yielded positive results. The subject then ventures a diagnosis, $D(1)$, which in our example happens to be a correct diagnosis, and the game is terminated. Because the game was tape-recorded, the tree structure is ready for computer programming.

From inspection of this tree we can readily see the number and types of questions that the subject had to ask to arrive at a diagnosis. In the game represented in Fig. 12.2, the binary tree that begins with the root $S(5)$ has exactly eight nodes, all except the last of which are test nodes. The path from $S(5)$ to $D(1)$ has seven branches, of which three are negative and all the rest are positive.

3. Variations on the Diagnostic Game.   The constraints of the game can be varied along several dimensions. For example, the amount of information that the experimenter gives the subject at the outset of the game, and the role that the experimenter assumes, affect the tree structure obtained from the subject. If the experimenter assumes the role of the inarticulate patient, he or she might start the game by stating that he or she hasn't been feeling well for the past 2 or 3 days. It is then the subject's (i.e., the diagnostician's) task to elicit as many symptoms and call for as many laboratory tests as seem to be essential for a diagnosis. On the other hand, the experimenter can play the role of the articulate patient and initiate the inquiry by stating that he or she has been having a low-grade fever for the past several days and has noticed an increased stiffening of the neck over that period of time. The more articulate patient, in addition to greater amounts of helpful information, may create noise in the diagnostician's system by offering surplus and sometimes misleading information. This method of controlling the kinds and amounts of information available to the diagnostician permits a systematic study of the effects of these variables on diagnostic accuracy.

4. Enter the Computer.   Now what does the computer have to do with all this? So far, not very much. Mainly the storage capacity of the machine has been used to accumulate our tree structure information. This information allows us a glimpse of the manner in which a clinician (or several different ones) utilizes cues and combines diagnostic information before arriving at a decision. The tree structure approach facilitates the testing of hypotheses about methods of combination, individual differences in judgment ability, effects of misleading cues on diagnosis, and many other variables yet to be specified. But for all of this, no computer was really necessary. We might very well have stored our information on a large revolving blackboard, or perhaps we could have left it on the magnetic tapes of our recording machine. Analyses of the tree structures would have been possible in those forms, but the computer is a more convenient storage bin because it allows us ready access to the information. More importantly, the rigors of computer programming forced us to devise a scheme that compelled the careful spelling-out of the thought processes under study.

The digital computer allows us a refinement in addition to those mentioned in the foregoing, and we must admit that this refinement was the really intriguing one that has helped to motivate the direction and the course of our work; it allows us to construct a model of the clinical decision maker that, if the model is a good one, functions in precisely the same manner as the human decision maker. Once we have a collection of one subject's tree structures, it should be possible to write programs that will enable the machine to utilize diagnostic search strategies in much the same manner as did the human decision maker. In principle, if we have a large enough collection of trees from one subject or from a group of diagnosticians, and if this collection includes most of what is kown about clinical neurology, then we can challenge the machine in the same way that patients challenge neurologists—i.e., by confronting them with a set of symptoms and complaints.

In fact, that is exactly what we did, in the sense that we collected the thinking-aloud information from one neurologist who diagnosed a large number of disorders. Figure 12.3 is a "tree of trees" that depicts the overall diagnostic strategies of that clinician. This summary tree, as it were, represents how one

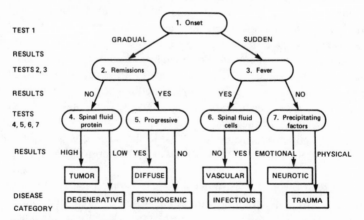

FIG. 12.3. A tree of trees based on the search strategy of a neurologist over many diagnostic games.

particular neurologist coped with the multivariate information of many disorders presented to her during many games of Twenty Questions. Thus, when presented with any set of symptoms and complaints, our neurologist typically began to solve the diagnostic problem by asking about whether the symptoms were of gradual or sudden onset. If the answer (e.g., results) was "gradual," she then pursued a specific line of inquiry (e.g., left branch) that ultimately led her to diseases that were either a tumor, degenerative, diffuse, or psychogenic. If the answer to the first question was "sudden," the possible diseases were of vascular, infectuous, neurotic, or traumatic origin. In any case, the important feature to note about such a tree of trees is that it is a model of one nuerologist's diagnostic strategies.

Hypothetical Diagnostic Problem Spaces

Having used real-world diagnostic problems such as the foregoing, we experienced a certain dissatisfaction with the contraints imposed by the particulars of the disciplines with which we dealt. What we seemed to lack was adequate control of the parameters of the problem space that contained the information to be diagnosed. Consequently, we decided to develop a completely hypothetical multivariate problem environment and, in turn, to design clinicians (e.g., strategies) for diagnosing these problems of our own creation. Such a hypothetical diagnostic system, we believe, also has the advantage over real environments in that it permits us to change the features of the problem spaces and to compare human versus mathematical solutions to the given problems.

Moreover, the complexity of real-world environments has resulted in research that focuses on selected manageable subtasks rather than on its full range of possibilities. Thus, our work with the MMPI, described above, was limited to that task and incorporated no data from other possible sources of psychodiagnostic information. Likewise in the neurology task we had to radically reduce the complexity of the neurologist's clinical speciality in order to gain some insight into the inferential processes operating in diagnostic decision making.

So that we can demonstrate the possibilities inherent in this approach, we will describe one hypothetical environment. Also, three possible decision strategies will be designed, and their performance compared.

We design our task by specifying the probabilistic relationships among all symptoms, diseases, and treatments. For each "case," the doctor is presented with a patient complaining of three symptoms. Each patient is suffering from a single disease, labelled Di. There are a limited number of possible diseases, denoted as $D1$, $D2$, $D3$, etc. Also, for the general population, there is a base-rate probability for each Di, called $P(Di)$. Each patient is represented as a vector of symptoms, each of which can be either present (positive) or absent (negative). Given the patient has Di, we denote the conditional probability of symptom j (Sj) being positive as $P(Sj+ \mid Di)$. The complementary probability of Sj being negative is $P(Sj- \mid Di) = 1 - P(Sj+ \mid Di)$. Also, assume that the likelihood of a patient's having any two symptoms is conditionally independent [i.e., $P(Sj+ \mid Di, Sk+) = P(Sj+ \mid Di)$, for all i, and $j \neq k$].

Next, the patient's condition is represented by a variable Ct, which changes over time (Ct denotes the condition in time period t). Ct is represented on a 0–100 scale, corresponding to "percentage of full health." In particular, as Ct increases, the patient is said to be healthier, whereas a value of Ct below zero indicates death. Clearly, the doctor's task is to prevent death, and improve the patient's condition as much as possible. Factors that influence the patient's health are: (1) the disease; (2) the effect of treatments given to the patient; and (3) the cost to the patient's health of diagnostic tests. These will be explained in turn.

The disease generally causes the patient to get progressively closer to death. This is represented by a linear trend, with random variation. Thus, each period, Ct is decremented by an amount $\delta + \epsilon$ where ϵ is a normally distributed error term, with zero mean. δ is a constant. Because of random variation, in any single period the patient may improve on his or her own. However, on average, his or her condition will deteriorate.

- The doctor has a number of treatments available and, in any one period, may select one treatment (Tk) to apply to the patient. The effectiveness is denoted by the random variables $\mu(k, i)$, with a normal distribution whose parameters depend on which Tk was selected, as well as which Di the patient has. The same treatment will have vastly different effect, depending on Di. Thus, a Tk may have either a positive or negative effect.

The patient's symptoms are initially unknown to the doctor. However, once each period, just before selecting a Tk, it is possible to test for the presence or absence of a single Sj. The tests provide reliable results (an assumption that can be relaxed), but also have a detrimental effect on the patient's health, called ϕ. As a simplification, the effect ϕ will be assumed uniform over all the possible tests and, also, ϕ will be relatively small. The doctor need not test for a symptom every period, but rather, only as necessary.

The sequence of events is as follows: The patient is presented to the doctor, with an unknown disease, complaining of three (positive) symptoms. In addition, the doctor is informed of the patient's initial condition, CO. Then, each time period t, the doctor may do two things. First, he may request a test for some symptom Sj. Because test reports are reliable, Sj will always be a symptom that has not previously been searched for. Once the test results are received (with no time lag), a treatment Tk is selected. The doctor then receives immediate feedback about the change in the patient's condition following treatment. However, no information is provided about the extent to which results are due to chance events versus treatment effects. This concludes period t. The doctor then starts period $t + 1$, requesting a test, and so on. Generally, the process continues until either: (1) the patient dies ($Ct \leq 0$); (2) the patient achieves perfect health ($Ct \geq 100$); or (3) some arbitrary stopping point is reached (in this case $t = 60$).

The next step is to develop decision strategies, and test their performance. Three such strategies will be described: (1) an expected utility maximizer, using Bayes theorem to update probabilities; (2) a strategy that uses heuristics to arrive at diagnoses, and then picks an acceptable treatment; and (3) a generate-and-test strategy, which picks treatments randomly, until an acceptable one is found.

1. Expected Utility-Bayesian Revision. This strategy assumes the doctor has a utility function over the patient's health: $U(Ct) = \exp(-cCt)$. This function denotes an aversion to taking risks, with this aversion increasing as the constant c does. We will assume a small amount of risk aversion, $c = .2$. Clearly, overly strong risk aversion is undesirable, as there is always a "safe" short-run action—complete inaction. In the long run, for this particular environment, inaction will hurt the patient. A second critical assumption for this strategy is that the doctor has complete knowledge of all the relevant task parameters (base rates, conditional probabilities, distributions of all random variables, etc.).

At each stage, the decision maker updates the posterior probabilities for each Di, using Bayes theorem. Starting with the base rates, the posterior probability in stage t becomes the prior for stage $t + 1$. These posteriors are used to take expectations across utilities of possible outcomes. Actions are chosen that maximize expected utility.

The procedure for making each decision follows the methods of statistical decision theory (Raiffa & Schlaifer, 1961). Generally the expected utility (EU) of a treatment in period t is:

$$EU(Tk = \Sigma \ Pt(Di) \int U[Ct \mid C(t - 1), i, k] f[Ct \mid C(t - 1), i, k] \ dCt \quad (1)$$

where $Ct = C(t - 1) - \delta + \epsilon - \phi + \mu(k, i)$, or $Ct = C(t - 1) - \delta + \epsilon + \mu(k, i)$ if no symptom is tested for, and $Pt(Di)$ is the most current posterior probability for Di. The distribution of Ct is normal with expectation $E(Ct \mid i, k) = C(t - 1) - \delta - \phi + E[\mu(k, i)]$, and variance $V(Ct \mid i, k) = V(\epsilon) + V[\mu(k, i)]$. Again, the constant ϕ is presently only if a decision is made to test for a symptom.

Given this distribution, and the exponential utility function it is possible to show (Keeney & Raiffa, 1976, pp. 200–202) that:

$$EU(Tk) = -\Sigma \ Pt(Di) \exp\{cE[Ct \mid i, k] + \tfrac{1}{2} c^2 V[Ct \mid i, k]\}. \quad (2)$$

We can then compute the expected utility of not searching for a symptom.

$$EU \ (\text{no test}) = \max EU(Tk), \quad (3)$$

because no new information would be revealed before the treatment selection. The EU of searching for Sj will be averaged over two allternatives corresponding to the test outcomes:

$$EU \ (\text{test for } Sj) = P(Sj +) \max\{EU[Tk]\} + P(Sj-) \max\{EU[Tk]\} \quad (4)$$

The quantity $EU[Tk]$ is calculated by equations 1 and 2, using different posterior probabilities. The two quantities $Pt(Di \mid Sj+)$ and $Pt(Di \mid Sj-)$ are the posterior probabilities that will result if either $Sj+$ or $Sj-$ is subsequently observed. The formula for the first quantity is:

$$Pt(Di \mid Sj+) = P(Sj+ \mid Di)Pt(Di)/\Sigma \ P(Sj+ \mid Dq)Pt(Dq). \tag{5}$$

The calculation for $Sj-$ is analogous. The quantities $P(Sj+)$ and $P(Sj-)$ are the likelihoods of observing those two results if the decision maker decides to test for Sj. The computation is:

$$P(Sj+) = \Sigma \ P(Sj+ \mid Dq)Pt(Dq), \tag{6}$$

and $P(Sj-) = 1 - P(Sj+)$. Finally, we want to maximize the expected utility of searching, given Equations 3 and 4:

$$EU \text{ [best test]} = \max \ [EU \ (\text{test for } Sj), \ (\text{no test})]. \tag{7}$$

Thus, the choice may be to test for some Sj, or not to test at all. Once the results are observed, the posterior can be updated: $Pt(Di) = Pt(Di \mid Sj+)$, or $Pt(Di \mid Sj-)$, or no update at all, as appropriate.

The next step is to pick a treatment Tk. Using the current $Pt(Di)$, and Equation 2, the best treatment is:

$$EU \text{ [best treatment]} = \max \ [EU(Tk)]. \tag{8}$$

This treatment is selected, and a result Ct observed. The final step to update the posteriors based on this observed result. The likelihood of the observed result, conditional on each disease [denoted $P(Ct \mid Di)$], is derived from the normal density function. The updated probabilities are:

$$Pt'(Di) = P(Ct \mid Di)Pt(Di)/\Sigma \ P(Ct \mid Dq)Pt(Dq). \tag{9}$$

$Pt'(Di)$ becomes the prior probability used in period $t + 1$.

This type of EU-Bayesian strategy optimizes only for the current time period. Because the actions taken in one period may change the situation to be faced later, the results may not be optimal over the entire time frame. An optimal strategy would have to look ahead to future time periods, possibly at a considerable computational cost.

2. *Heuristic Decision Strategy.*   If one considers the EU strategy developed in the foregoing, it becomes apparent that even then the computational demands are considerable. The heuristic decision strategy will proceed with more informal rules, requiring less complete computations for comparisons. This strategy indulges in a limited amount of search until it reaches a *satisfactory* rather than an optimal solution.

In particular, assume the decision maker has limited computational abilities, and limited knowledge about the task, assumptions that are probably valid for most human decision makers. The knowledge base consists of: $P(Sj+ \mid Di)$, a measure of the extent to which $Sj+$ is diagnostic of Di (measured on a 0-1 scale); $E[\mu(k, i)]$, the average effectiveness of Tk given Di; and $E[\mu(k, i)] - 2\sqrt{V[\mu(k, i)]}$, a measure of the "worst case" outcome of applying Tk to a patient with Di.

The general procedure is to develop a hypothesis about the patient's disease, Dh, and to try to confirm that hypothesis. The type of evidence that is most salient consists of symptoms that are strongly diagnostic if present, and are in fact present. Although the absence of undiagnostic symptoms might be equally strong support for Dh, it is assumed that only positive evidence is sought.

The criterion for picking a test is that, if positive, that symptom will provide reasonably strong confirmation of Dh. Thus, if $P(Sj+ \mid Dh)$ is above some level of aspiration, then that Sj will be tested. Furthermore, if the body of positive evidence is strong (as represented by the sum of the $P(Sj+ \mid Dh)$ for all symptoms observed present), no further testing is done.

If the resulting test for Sj is positive, this merely reinforces the current Dh. If the evidence is disconfirming $(Sj-)$, then a new hypothesis might be adopted. The Di with the largest sum of $P(Sj+ \mid Di)$, over observed symptoms, becomes the new Dh. Note that it is possible for the Dh to remain the same, if no better candidate exists.

Treatment selection is made randomly from treatments that meet the following criteria: (1) $E[\mu(k, h)]$, the expected effectiveness of Tk given Dh, exceeds a minimal level; (2) the "worse case" outcome of Tk, given Dh, exceeds a minimal level; and (3) previous applications of this treatment to this patient have not been negative. This last condition prevents the clinician from making the same mistakes over and over.

If the selected treatment works well according to prespecified criteria (e.g., has the patient improved, on average, using this treatment?), it is kept and applied in later periods. When the results for any treatment are observed to be unfavorable, then a new Tk is selected and, possibly, a new Dh formulated. The minimal levels of the treatment selection criteria are lowered as needed, so some treatment can always be found. The principal advantage to this strategy is that it uses simple rules to make its decision, and once a good treatment has been found, further decision-making activity is halted. Fig. 12.4 presents this strategy in a flow chart.

3. Generate-and-Test Treatment Strategy.   This strategy makes minimal demands on the decision maker. It requires negligible knowledge, and very little in the way of cognitive effort. A treatment is generated at random and is tested for favorable results. If the observed effectiveness of a treatment falls below a minimal level, a new treatment is selected. This continues, always keeping a treatment as long as it seems to be effective. The symptoms of the patient are ignored, no attempt is made to diagnose. This strategy is a very simple example

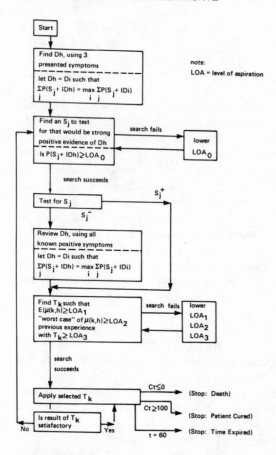

FIG. 12.4.   Heuristic decision strategy.

of trial and error learning, and again, looks for a satisfactory, rather than optimal solution. Fig. 12.5 flow-charts this strategy.

4. Simulation results.   Each of the three strategies was simulated for 100 cases. The diseases were observed in proportion to their base rates, and symptoms randomly assigned according to their likelihoods. The results are given in Table 12.2. The comparison point taken was $C60$, the condition after 60 periods. In cases where the patient died earlier, $C60$ was assumed to be zero. In cases where the patient was cured earlier, $C60$ was assumed to be 100. The results are also graphed in Fig. 12.6.

The major insight to be gained from this analysis is the apparent trade-off between effort and decision quality. The increasingly complex strategies also performed better. However, the huge increase in complexity for the *EU* strategy was offset with only a relatively small improvement in results. Conclusions are tentative, with only these three strategies, but these results suggest that there are diminishing returns to cognitive effort in the effort–error trade-off.

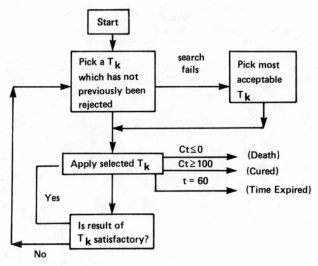

FIG. 12.5. Generate-and-test strategy.

TABLE 12.2
Summary of Simulation Results

Disease	Strategy:	Generate & Test	Heuristic	EU-Bayesian
D1	median	77.8	100	100
n = 35	mean	72.89	90.21	89.13
	s.d.	20.83	16.24	14.81
D2	median	41.7	24.7	57.2
n = 25	mean	43.41	30.90	57.20
	s.d.	42.10	22.92	17.34
D3	median	100	100	100
n = 20	mean	98.50	96.92	100
	s.d.	4.16	13.77	0
D4	median	100	100	100
n = 15	mean	95.86	100	100
	s.d.	16.03	0	0
D5	median	100	100	100
n = 5	mean	81.60	93.82	100
	s.d.	26.11	13.82	0
total	median	89.7	100	100
n = 100	mean	74.52	78.37	85.50
	s.d.	32.85	32.14	20.98

TABLE 12.3
Frequency Table of Simulation Results

Disease	Strategy	Cure 100+	80–100	60–80	40–60	20–40	0–20	Death 0–
				Results, by Category				
D1	G	6	7	12	6	4	9	0
n = 35	H	20	7	7	0	1	0	0
	B	18	9	6	2	0	0	0
D2	G	5	2	5	1	1	1	10
n = 25	H	0	0	3	8	6	3	5
	B	1	1	9	11	3	0	0
D3	G	16	4	0	0	0	0	0
n = 20	H	19	0	0	0	1	0	0
	B	20	0	0	0	0	0	0
D4	G	15	0	0	0	1	0	0
n = 15	H	15	0	0	0	0	0	0
	B	15	0	0	0	0	0	0
D5	G	3	0	1	1	0	0	0
n = 5	H	4	0	1	0	0	0	0
	B	5	0	0	0	0	0	0
Total	G	44	13	18	8	6	1	10
n = 100	H	58	7	11	8	8	3	5
	B	59	10	15	13	3	0	0

Note: G = generate and test strategy
H = heuristic strategy
B = Bayesian-EU strategy

Another important difference among the strategies is the amount of knowledge required about the task. The *EU*-Bayesian strategy seems most sensitive, because it utilizes a large amount of detailed information. This points out an important advantage of trial and error strategies. As the features of the task change, those strategies will be able to *adapt* to the new environment. Without a complete respecification of the task parameters, an *EU* strategy would be unable to perform well.

Care should be taken in interpreting any of these strategies as "best" or "optimal" in any sense. For instance, a whole class of potentially useful strategies has been overlooked. These are strategies that can learn from experience, not just within individual cases, but across cases as well. In examining the simulation results, it is apparent that treatment $T11$ was quite effective in treating both $D1$ and $D2$, the two most common diseases. A "smart" trial and error learner would notice that $T11$ turns out to be effective in a majority of cases and would *always* apply that treatment first. This is analogous to a doctor always treating an

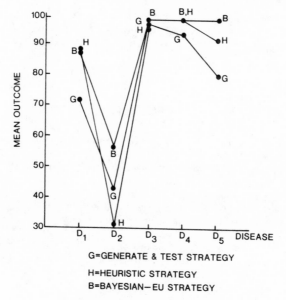

FIG. 12.6. Simulation results.

infection with a broad spectrum antibiotic and considering other treatments only if the patient does not respond to the drug. Other, more sophisticated learning strategies may be feasible also, and the effects of various feedback modes on learning should be instructive (for a more detailed discussion of the learning capabilities and more generally of hypothetical problem spaces, see Kleinmuntz & Kleinmuntz, 1981).

Summary and Conclusion

Clinicians in many areas of diagnostics are engaged in a form of problem solving in which the multivariate information is highly configural and complex. All too often their clinical decision making has an aura of the mysterious about it which removes it from scientific scrutiny.

We presented three examples of how clinical diagnosis can be reinstated into the scientific arena. The first example dealt with computer studies of a personality test interpreter's diagnostic decision about MMPI profiles. The second had as its subject a clinical neurologist whose multivariate diagnostic problem solving was tape-recorded and modeled on the computer. And the third example consisted of designing hypothetical problem environments that were solved by several diagnostic strategies.

The primary significance of these studies lies in their demonstration of how the computer can be used to study and to build models of diagnostic decision making. Secondarily, these studies can provide insights about the practical aspects of how best to arrive at accurate diagnosis. And finally, these studies can provide comparative data about how humans and machines perform in certain diagnostic problems.

REFERENCES

Feigenbaum, E. A. The simulation of verbal learning behavior. *Proceedings of the Western Joint Computer Conference*, 1961, 121–132.

Keeney, R. L., & Raiffa. H. *Decisions with multiple objectives: Preferences and value tradeoffs.* New York: Wiley, 1976.

Kleinmuntz, B. MMPI decision rules for the identification of college maladjustment: A digital computer approach. *Psychological Monographs*, 1963, No. 14. (a)

Kleinmuntz, B. Personality test interpretation by digital computer. *Science*, 1963, *139*, 416–418. (b)

Kleinmuntz, B. The processing of clinical information by man and machine. In Kleinmuntz, B. (Ed.), *Formal representation of human judgment.* New York: John Wiley & Sons, 1968.

Kleinmuntz, B. The computer as clinician. *American Psychologist*, 1975, *30*, 379–387.

Kleinmuntz, D. N., & Kleinmuntz, B. Decision strategies in simulated environments. *Behavior Science*, 1981, *26*, 294–305.

Newell, A., & Simon, H. A. *Problem solving*, Englewood Cliffs, N.J.: Prentice-Hall, 1972.

Raiffa, H., & Schlaifer, R. *Applied statistical decision theory.* Cambridge, Mass.: MIT Press, 1961.

Stephenson, W. *The study of behavior: Q-technique and its methodology.* Chicago: University of Chicago Press, 1953.

13

Process Models of Social Behavior

L. Rowell Huesmann
University of Illinois at Chicago Circle

Not surprisingly, most of the literature on multivariate methods in psychology concerns techniques for analyzing empirical data. Yet the simultaneous study of a large number of variables presents as many thorny problems for the theorist as for the empiricist. Theoretical models that could pass scrutiny when all but a few variables were ignored frequently fail in attempting to explain the interactions among a large set of variables. Too often the solution has been to present a set of simple models describing the observed relations between pairs of variables. Although such descriptive models are sometimes accepted as psychological theories, they usually provide little information about underlying psychological processes.

An alternative approach for the construction of formal models to explain multivariate data is "process modeling." This approach aims directly at the specification of psychological processes underlying the observed behavior. The presumption is that a formal model of subjects' information-processing behaviors allows the clearest understanding of the observed multivariate data. Furthermore, the specification of such a process model in an algorithmic form permits the validation of the model through computer simulation.

In cognitive psychology, process modeling has become perhaps the dominant mode of theorizing, but in social psychology its inroads have been small. The objective of this chapter is to illustrate the advantages of algorithmic process models in theorizing about multivariate data collected from experimental, quasi-experimental, and observational studies of social behavior.

The use of process models and simulation in psychology is now over 20 years old. Beginning with the classic models of problem solving developed by Newell, Shaw, and Simon (1958), the occurrence of process models in cognitive psychology expanded with models of various cognitive phenomena developed by their students and others (Feigenbaum & Feldman, 1963; Minsky, 1968) and reached fruition with the emergence of dominant theories of memory and problem solving stated as process models (Anderson, 1976; Newell & Simon, 1972). The use of process models in social psychology has not followed a parallel course. A number of early process models of social behavior were stimulated by the work of Simon and Newell (Gullahorn & Gullahorn, 1963; Loehlin, 1965), and Abelson's excellent 1968 paper on computer simulation (Abelson, 1968) in social psychology made the methodology widely known among social psychologists. However, process models, with a few exceptions, have not yet had a great impact on social or clinical psychology. Abelson's and Schank's models of belief systems (Abelson & Carroll, 1965; Abelson, 1973, 1975; Schank & Abelson, 1975), Huesmann and Levinger's models of dyadic social interaction (1976; Levinger & Huesmann, 1980), and Colby's (1964, 1973) models of paranoia are exceptions that have influenced the content areas studied. However, the impact of even these models has been limited, perhaps because such process models are still considered to be impractical "tricks" by many researchers in these areas. Nevertheless, process models may provide the best chance for progress in modeling multivariate social phenomena.

My aim in this chapter is to provide an introduction to the use of algorithmic processes to model multivariate social phenomena. After a discussion of the characteristics by which formal models can be evaluated, I compare algorithmic process models with the type of descriptive structural models most commonly seen in social psychology. This comparison is illustrated with an example of a model of causal attribution. Then the methodology of process modeling is elaborated and a second, more complex example of an algorithmic model is presented to introduce some common information-processing operations and to demonstrate the level of precision that actual simulations require.

EVALUATING MODELS

In evaluating the utility of a general class of models, one must consider a number of different factors. Although the validity of any specific model ultimately rests on how accurately it predicts observed data, what constitutes *meaningful* accuracy depends on other properties of the model. In particular, one must look at the falsifiability of the model. Falsifiability is a measure of the ease with which a model could be negated by empirical data. All other things being equal, a scientist should prefer the more easily falsifiable of two equally predictive models until it is, in fact, negated.

The preference for the more falsifiable theory is derived from the logic of the scientific method. If a theory T predicts an observed behavior B ($T \rightarrow B$), then the *nonoccurrence* of B implies that the theory T is *false* ($\bar{B} \rightarrow \bar{T}$); but the *occurrence* of the behavior B does not allow any definitive conclusion to be drawn about T according to the laws of logic. Hence, a theory can never be proven true; it can only be proven false. If one could also assume that $\overline{T} \rightarrow \overline{B}$, one could reach the definitive conclusion that T is true when B ocurs. However, the assumption $\overline{T} \rightarrow \overline{B}$ is equivalent to saying that no other theory except T predicts B, and such a premise is seldom warranted. How then does a theory gain support?

One common view is that the plausibility of a theory relative to other theories increases as a function of the number and rigor of the tests to which it is subjected without being falsified. A theory's increase in plausibility after passing a test depends on the probability that it could have failed. If the model is formulated in such a way that falsification is almost impossible, then passing another test does little to enhance its plausibility. Therefore, unfalsifiable models have little value. Unfortunately, these models persist because their low falsifiability is overshadowed by the number of tests they seemingly pass. Perhaps the best way to detect such models is by asking the author what evidence would be accepted as negating the model. If the author has difficulty conceiving of negative evidence, the model is not very falsifiable.

Components of Falsifiability

What contributes to a model's falsifiability? The most important factors are its precision and universality. Consider a theory frequently stated in the media, "All aspirin is alike." Let us compare it with the similar statement, "All pain reducers have the same ingredients." The second theory is the more precise and universal and, therefore, the more readily falsifiable. It is more precise because it replaces the word "alike" with "have the same ingredients," and it is more universal because it applies to "all pain reducers." On the other hand, the universality and precision of the first theory are so low that it is essentially unfalsifiable. Of course, falsifiability is not the only characteristic on which models should be evaluated. Two other frequently cited factors are simplicity and a priori plausibility. Other things being equal, the simpler model and the more plausible model on the basis of existing evidence is the preferred model. Although a priori plausibility is sometimes overlooked, a clear implication of Bayesian logic is that the greater a model's plausibility before it is tested, the greater its plausibility after it passes a test.

To formulate a precise, unambiguous model is not easy. Natural languages are designed to allow ambiguities. Not only are words such as attitude, reward, dissonance, and attribution ambiguous, but attempts to give them more precise definitions using natural language usually only replace one ambiguity with another. Thus, to say, as do Krech and Crutchfield (1948) that an attitude is: "an enduring organization of motivational, emotional, perceptual, and cognitive processes with respect to some aspect of the individual's world [p. 152]" introduces as many ambiguities as it resolves. In addition, there seems to be a reluctance to strive toward precision in theories precisely because precision enhances falsifiability. Sometimes a model that appears reasonably falsifiable is transformed into a less falsifiable model through revisions introduced to account for failed tests. For example, Seligman's (1975) learned helplessness model of depression originally hypothesized a direct connection between a perception of noncontingent reinforcement and depression. In order to explain contradictory data, however, a revision has been offered that requires certain attributions be made for the connection to form (Abramson, Seligman, & Teasdale, 1978). Although the revision accounts for the contradictory data, it accomplishes this by introducing attributions as a mediating construct. The result is that the theory's precision and falsifiability are reduced (Huesmann, 1978). Revisions of this type are not unusual in social psychology. When dealing with social science data, it is difficult to propose any precise model that is not contradicted by some data. By default, then, those models that seem to be the most predictive are often the least precise.

PROCESS AND DESCRIPTIVE MODELS

How can these deficiencies in social-psychological theorizing be remedied? The central thesis of the chapter is that social psychologists should turn more toward algorithmic process models to explain relations in multivariate data. There are two components to such a turn—a change from describing relations between variables to explaining relations by specifying processes, and a change from informal models in natural language to formal models in algorithmic languages. Both these changes lead to enhanced falsifiability for the models.[1]

Describing the processes underlying observed behaviors instead of simply describing relations between variables usually results in a greater universe of predictions. Predictions are deduced from the process specifications that might otherwise not be noted. At the same time, because processes are specified in an algorithmic language, there is little room for ambiguity. A command for a computer to perform a process cannot have multiple meanings. Furthermore, the model, when executed on a computer, generates observable data rather than simple summary statistics of relations between variables. As a result, an algorithmic process model of a psychological phenomenon must be at least as falsifiable as any equivalent formal descriptive model. For example, suppose M is a mathematical model expressing certain formal relationships between observable environmental variables and observable behaviors. Now generally there will be a number of process models: $P_1 \ldots P_m$ that would imply the mathematical model M. The theorist may or may not state a process model (usually one is

---

[1]The word algorithmic is used generically to denote a class of models. Any model formalized in an algorithmic language is included even if it is a heuristic model.

suggested but not formalized), but at least one undoubtedly exists as diagramed below:

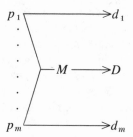

If the predicted relationships D do not occur, M is falsified, and all the process models $P_1 \ldots P_m$ are falsified. If the relationship D occurs, the plausibility of M increases and the plausibility of each of $P_1 \ldots P_m$ increases equally. But $P_1 \ldots P_m$ are not identical; they propose different processes. To the extent that these processes are reflected in observable data, these models make the additional predictions $d_1 \ldots d_m$, which, if unfulfilled, lead to falsification of the process models without falsification of M. Thus, each is more readily falsifiable than the mathematical model derived from it.

Granted that a process model is bound to be more precise and falsifiable than an equivalent formal descriptive model, one might argue that a process model nevertheless requires too large a sacrifice in simplicity. Furthermore, some argue that a computer program has so many free parameters that it is trivial to model any behavior. This argument overlooks two factors. First, a process model seldom has any completely free parameters. Each parameter is tied to a process and must be plausible for that process. One cannot, for example, plausibly propose a model with a memory capacity divergent from existing norms. In fact, because parameters are tied to processes, it is usually easier to judge the a priori plausibility of a process model than a descriptive model. Secondly, one should not confuse the complexity of the formal language used to express the model with the complexity of the model. In fact, objective attempts to measure simplicity (Gregg & Simon, 1967) have indicated that process models are not significantly more complex than descriptive models.

Process modeling requires one to specify psychological processes that cannot be directly observed. The detail needed to model social behavior at the lowest level of information processing would be enormous. But process models can be developed at varying levels of detail and may build on the process models developed for lower levels. A psychologist modeling dyadic interactions may desire to have the simulated subjects learn in a manner consistent with cognitive theory, but probably does not want or need to incorporate a process model of learning into the model of dyadic interaction. Therefore, a process model designed to explain one phenomenon may incorporate descriptive, nonprocess representations of lower-level phenomena. A good analogy can be drawn with a computer scientist who is attempting to explain the execution time of a program. The scientist would hardly begin by attempting to show the microelectronic operations required by each step in a flow chart. Rather, the flow chart would be modeled by a program, the program by its machine language equivalent, the machine language program by the microprocesser operations, the microprocesser operations by their electronic constituents, and so on. Such hierarchical decomposability, some have argued (Simon, 1969), is in fact most likely a necessary characteristic of any information-processing system. Without such decomposability, the development of a complex system would be too susceptible to destruction due to random interference.

In order to better explicate the argument for process models, let us examine in more detail one common class of *formal* descriptive models: structural models. The purpose is not to discourage the use of formal descriptive models, but rather to show the advantages that occur from the statement of a theory as an algorithmic process model either in isolation or in conjunction with a descriptive model.

Structural Models

Linear structural models are perhaps the most commonly occurring type of descriptive model in explaining multivariate relations. Such models represent relations between variables by sets of linear equalities. Each equality relates a criterion variable to a linear function of several predictor variables. Many widely used multivariate techniques are based on the assumption of such a model, (e.g., factor analysis, analysis of variance, and regression analysis). Nonlinearities and interactions can be introduced easily by adding nonlinear functions of the predictor variables into the structural equation. Still, the basic model is additive and descriptive. No assumptions need be made (though there frequently are) about the processes generating the relations, and if such assumptions are made, they are not necessarily reflected by the structural equation. Factor analytic studies of personality, cognitive skills, and social and abnormal behavior yield structural, not process, descriptions of multivariate data.

In the past decade, the term structural model has taken on a more specific connotation than the one implied in the foregoing, being used almost exclusively to refer to models implying a causal relation between variables (Bentler, 1980). This type of structural model was introduced to the social sciences primarily through the work of Wright (1934) and Simon (1953, 1954). Such models, most often called path models, attempt to represent the causal relations between variables with a set of linear equations. Clearly a path model is more process oriented than a simple structural model, but still far removed from a process model of the underlying psychological mechanisms.

To illustrate some of these differences, let us consider a simple structural model that represents one kind of causal relation between two variables x and y:

$$y_2 = b_{y_2 x_1} x_1 + b_{y_2 y_1} y_1 + e_{y_2};$$

$$x_2 = b_{x_2 x_1} x_1 + e_{x_2}.$$

The subscripts denote time; so the model specifies that y at time 2 is influenced by x at time 1 but that the converse is not true. In other words, x is a cause of y. For example, the model might represent the relation between height and weight in children. Weight (y_2) depends on earlier weight (y_1) and height (x_1), but height (x_2) depends only on earlier height (x_1). The other sources of variance in x_2 and y_2 are included in the error terms e_{x_2} and e_{y_2}. These error terms are assumed to be independently distributed about zero; so

$$E(e_{x_2}),\ E(e_{y_2}) = 0$$

$$\text{Cov } (e_{x_2},\ e_{y_2}),\ \text{Cov } (e_{x_2},\ x_1),\ \text{Cov } (e_{y_2},\ x_1),\ \text{Cov } (e_{y_2},\ y_1) = 0.$$

Although this model denotes a directed relation between variables, it does not specify a process. A considerable variety of observed data could be consistent with the model. In terms of manipulations of variables, the model indicates that on the average, a one-unit change in x_1 (height) will result in a $b_{y_2 x_1}$ unit change in y_2 (later weight) and a $b_{x_2 x_1}$ unit change in x_2 (later height),whereas a manipulation of y_1 (weight) should not affect x_2 (later height). Unfortunately, in the situations in which such structural models are applied, manipulation of variables is often not practical and testing of the model must be based on observational data. Two common methodologies for testing structural models of this simple type are path analysis and cross-lagged correlational analysis.

Path Analysis. With path analysis, one estimates the coefficients in the structural equations from the data. One can then reject or accept the model depending on how close the estimated coefficients are to the hypothesized coefficients. One may also compare competing path models (e.g., a y causes x model) to see which fits the data more accurately. In principle, path analyses can be applied to almost any structural model. In practice, however, several problems arise. First, the structural model is almost never specified a priori with specific coefficients. The more common approach is to estimate the path coefficients from the data and then to hypothesize *those* coefficients for the structural model. Most often, the only inference that is made is the rejection of the null hypothesis of a zero coefficient. The lack of an a priori specification of coefficients often reflects the lack of an underlying process model. This lack contributes to a second difficulty. A fundamental assumption of path analysis is that there are no exogenous variables correlated with both x and y. But when a structural model is considered in the abstract without reference to the underlying processes, such an assumption is difficult to support. Thirdly, any number of processes of quite different psychological import could imply the same structural model. Therefore, the goodness of fit of a structural model to data may be a weak test of the validity of an underlying process model.

Cross-lagged Correlations. Another common technique for testing simple causal structural models is cross-lagged correlation analysis. For the height and weight example, one would compare the correlation $r_{x_1y_2}$ with the correlation $r_{y_1x_2}$. If x (height) is a cause of y (weight), the argument goes, it should be true that $r_{x_1y_2} > ry_1x_2$. The validity of this argument, however, depends upon a number of assumptions about reliability, variances, and covariances which are seldom specified in the model or tested. By manipulating these parameters, it is possible to construct a model in which x causes y, but $rx_1y_2 < ry_1x_2$. For example, in the aforementioned model for the relation between height and weight, suppose

$$b_{y_2x_1} = .1 \qquad by_2y_1 = .9 \qquad b_{x_2x_1} = .9$$

$$\text{so } y_2 = .1x_1 + .9y_1 + e_{y_2}$$

$$x_2 = .9x_1 + e_{x_2},$$

then suppose

$$\sigma_{y_1}^2 = 1 \qquad \sigma_{x_1}^2 = 1 \qquad \sigma_{e_{y_2}}^2 = 1 \qquad \sigma_{e_{x_2}}^2 = .1.$$

These parameters denote a weak causal effect for x (height) on y (weight) ($b_{y_2x_1} = .1$). However, x_2 has much less error variance than y_2, and, therefore, x will be much more stable over time than y.

From this model we can derive equations for the two cross-lagged correlations, $r_{x_1y_2}$ and $r_{y_1x_2}$.

$$r_{x_1y_2} = \frac{\text{Cov}(x_1, y_2)}{\sigma_{x_1}\sigma_{y_2}}$$

$$= \frac{E\{X_1(by_2x_1X_1 + by_2y_1Y_1 + e_{y_2})\} - E\{x_1\}E\{b_{y_2x_1}x_1 + b_{y_2y_1}y_1 + e_{y_2}\}}{\sigma_{x_1}\sqrt{\text{Var}\{b_{y_2x_1}x_1 + b_{y_2y_1}y_1 + e_{y_2}\}}}.$$

Because the covariances of x_1 and y_1 with the error components are 0, we find

$$= \frac{b_{y_2x_1}(E\{x_1^2\} - E^2\{x_1\}) + b_{y_2y_1}(E\{x_1y_1\} - E\{x_1\}E\{y_1\}) + (E\{x_1e_{y_2}\} - E\{x_1\}E\{e_{y_2}\})}{\sigma_{x_1}\sqrt{b_{y_2x_1}^2\text{Var}\{x_1\} + b_{y_2y_1}^2\text{Var}\{y_1\} + \text{Var}\{e_{y_2}\} + 2b_{y_2x_1}b_{y_2y_1}\text{Cov}(x_1, y_1)}}$$

$$= \frac{b_{y_2x_1}\sigma_{x_1}^2 + b_{y_2y_1}\text{Cov}(x_1, y_1)}{\sigma_{x_1}\sqrt{b_{y_2x_1}^2\sigma_{x_1}^2 + b_{y_2y_1}^2\sigma_{y_1}^2 + \sigma_{e_{y_2}}^2 + 2b_{y_2x_1}b_{y_2y_1}\text{Cov}(x_1, y_1)}}$$

Substituting the parameter values, and using $\sigma_{x_1} = \sigma_{y_1} = 1$, we find

$$= \frac{.1 + .9r_{x_1y_1}}{\sqrt{.01 + .81 + 1 + 2(.1)(.9)(r_{x_1y_1})}} = \frac{.1 + .9r_{x_1y_1}}{\sqrt{1.82 + .18r_{x_1y_1}}}$$

Similarly,

$$r_{y_1 x_2} = \frac{\text{Cov}(y_1, x_2)}{\sigma_{y_1} \sigma_{x_2}}$$

$$= \frac{b_{x_1 x_2} \text{Cov}(x_1, y_1)}{\sigma_{y_1} \sqrt{b_{x_2 x_1}^2 \sigma_{x_1}^2 + \sigma_{ex_2}^2}}$$

$$= \frac{.9 r_{x_1 y_1}}{\sqrt{.81 + .1}} = \frac{.9 r_{x_1 y_1}}{\sqrt{.91}}$$

It follows from these two equations that whenever $r_{x_1 y_1} > .26$, then $r_{x_1 y_2} < r_{y_1 x_2}$ despite the fact that x_1 is a cause of y_2. In other words, the cross-lagged analysis yields exactly the wrong conclusion in this case. While this example is somewhat contrived, it is symptomatic of problems in cross-lagged analyses (Rogosa, 1980).

The difficulties inherent in the analysis techniques used with structural models (e.g., path analysis and cross-lagged analysis) stem in great part from the fact that the models describe relations between variables rather than processes and describe these relations imprecisely with parameters to be estimated. My thesis is not that these techniques should never be used. Rather it is that the value of structural models and their associated analysis techniques depends greatly on the precision with which an underlying process model is specified. The more completely a process model can be specified, the more exactly the parameters of the structural model can be hypothesized, and the more valuable will be path analysis or cross-lagged analysis in understanding the relations in multivariate data.

An Example of a Structural Model

To explicate this argument let me now take a real structural model and construct some corresponding process models. A good recent example of the use of structural modeling appears in Fiske, Kenny, and Taylors' (1981) study of stimulus saliency effects in attributions of causality. These authors were concerned with explaining why salient social stimuli have an impact on causal attributions that is disproportionate to their logical relevance. They proposed and tested empirically several possible structural models for explaining the phenomenon. Their most complex structural model is diagrammed in Fig. 13.1.

The paradigm to which the model applies is a two-actor conversation observed by the subjects. On the surface the model allows for three types of mediation between the subject's attention and attributions: behavior recall, visual recall, and verbal recall. From Fiske et al.'s discussion it is clear that considerable process-oriented theorizing is behind the model. However, the general theory as denoted by the path diagram is that attention affects attributions (as measured by the four manifest questions on the right of the figure) by enhancing recall of an

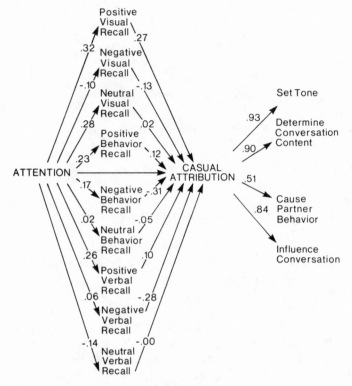

FIG. 13.1. The structural model proposed by Fiske, Kenny, and Taylor (1980) to explain effects in causal attributions about a conversation.

actor's behavior, an actor's utterances, or an actor's visual appearance, or directly in some other manner. No parameters are specified a priori for the model that has one latent variable (causal attribution), 13 measured variables, and one exogenous variable (attention).

In a series of clever experiments the authors manipulate which actor a subject faces (attention) and estimate the parameters of the structural model. The derived parameters (Fig. 13.1) suggest that attention exerts its influence on attributions by enhancing the recall of evidence the subject considers relevant to causality. Of course the parameters derived in such path analyses can only be viewed as suggestive until cross-validated. As with other least-squares techniques, colinearity among variables can make the estimates of the parameters unstable. Another problem is that some causal variables that might be correlated with variables in the model are not in the model themselves (e.g., an actor's physical attractiveness). Nevertheless, Fiske et al.'s (1981) conclusion that recall mediates the attention effect seems the most plausible.

However, the authors would like to extent their conclusions considerably beyond the simple causal relations suggested by the path diagram. Their descriptive structural model was based on a process model of social cognition, and they attempt to draw conclusions about this process model. Unfortunately, as is often the case with descriptive models, the underlying process model was not formalized in information-processing notation but only outlined in the text.

Fiske et al. assume that "salient stimuli attract attention [p. 1]." To surmount the circularity of this definition, they specify some characteristics that would make a stimulus more salient. They then propose several possible ways in which increased attention might affect attributions. First, they suggest that salient (verbal) information may be taken in selectively or recalled more easily or possibly both. But because previous attempts to interfere with the encoding or decoding stage apparently have not attenuated salience effects, Fiske et al. (1981) also offer the alternative that:

> The subject has been essentially deaf to the conversation, but is left with particularly vivid images of the salient person animatedly talking and gesturing. Accordingly, the subject rates that person as more influential, because images of that person come to mind more often or more easily, [p. 3].

Another possibility the authors propose is that people use only part of the evidence they recall in making attributions—namely, the "representative" evidence that fits the perceiver's preconceptions about who should be causal in the conversation (Tversky & Kahneman, 1980). In other words: ". . . salience effects are mediated only by that recall perceived as appropriate data, on the basis of each subject's prior causal schemas [p. 4]."

Although these theories underlying the structural model are couched in information-processing terms, they are not specified in any formal manner. As a result the structural model and these theories are subject to most of the criticisms of descriptive models reviewed in the first section of this chapter. The processes are summarized imprecisely and ambiguously. Exactly how are details of an actor's conversation encoded? Different encoding processes would yield different predictions about interference and recall. The authors say: "if a perceiver takes in a greater quantity of details about . . . the salient actor . . . , the person can access more instances of the salient actor causing the conversation [p. 2]." This need not be true, but depends on the encoding and recall processes. For the visual recall process, is the visual information stored separately for each actor or in one schema for the conversation? For the availability hypothesis, why should primacy make information more available than recency? If equal amounts of information are encoded about both actors, what process produces differential recall? Availability does not describe a process but an empirical fact. For the representative causal schema model, when does the causal schema exert its influence (at encoding, recall, or both) and how? The point is that formal specification of these process models could clarify these ambiguities and provide stronger predictions than the structural model does by itself. As it stands, there are a number of different process models, all of which are consistent with the structural model but imply quite different mediation effects.

Some Corresponding Process Models

Let us now formulate some of the process models that are consistent with Fiske et al.'s structural model. In particular, let us formally specify some algorithms for how a causal schema could influence attributions. The objective is to show how interrelations in multivariate data can be better understood when formal process models for the relations are specified.

Fiske et al. (1981) say: "Perceivers employ a priori theories about what constitutes appropriate evidence for causality; the evidence may not in fact be causally relevant, but if it fits with people's expectations, then they use it [p. 3]." But exactly how does this process work? Do subjects evaluate information as they observe it, encode it if it fits the causal schema, and discard it otherwise; or do they encode all information and evaluate it upon recall? Does increased attention raise the likelihood of encoding any information or only causally relevant information? What is the form of the causal schema? Is it a schema for conversations? There are too many alternatives for consideration in a methodological paper; so only a few illustrative process models will be described.

Encoding and Recall.   There are two different encoding and recall models we will consider. The simplest, shown in Table 13.1, assumes that subjects process the verbal, visual, and behavioral information in the sequence in which it

TABLE 13.1

An Algorithm for Encoding and Recalling a Conversation Without Reference to a Causal Schema for a Conversation

Encoding

E1:   Visual and verbal information enters short-term memory (STM) in observed temporal order. Least attended-to information is lost from STM.

E2:   Each piece of information in STM is rehearsed proportionately to the extent that attention is focused on it.

E3:   Each piece of information that is rehearsed for a sufficient period of time is encoded more permanently into a knowledge structure for the conversation that is kept in long-term memory (LTM).

E4:   Go to E1.

Recall

R1:   Access the entry node in LTM for the conversation's knowledge structure.

R2:   Search from the entry node for a behavior, utterance, or image (depending on the recall question). If one can be found that has not been previously recalled then call it node X and mark it "recalled"; otherwise stop the recall process.

R3:   Find the actor of X. If the recall question was asked about this actor, then output node X.

R4:   Search from node X for another behavior, utterance, or image. If one can be found that has not been previously recalled, then call it node X, mark it "recalled," and go to R3; otherwise go to R2.

TABLE 13.2

An Algorithm for Encoding and Recalling a Conversation with
Reference to a Causal Schema for Conversations

Encoding

E1: Retrieve a causal schema for conversations from long-term memory (LTM).
Let it be the CURRENT-SCHEMA.

E2: Visual and verbal information enters short-term memory (STM) in observed
temporal order. Least attended-to information is lost from STM.

E3: Each piece of information in STM is processed proportionately to the extent
that attention is focused on it.

E4: Can attended information be integrated into CURRENT-SCHEMA? If "yes"
then remove it from STM and store it in CURRENT-SCHEMA in LTM. Mark
it "episodic" information.

E5: Search memory for a causal schema that fits episodic information in CUR-
RENT-SCHEMA and STM more accurately than CURRENT-SCHEMA. If
none found, try to derive one. If none derived, go to E2.

E6: If a new schema is found, then integrate as much information as possible from
CURRENT-SCHEMA and STM into new schema. Let CURRENT-SCHEMA =
new schema and go to E2.

Recall

R1: Access the entry node in LTM for the conversation's causal schema.

R2: Search from the entry node for a behavior, utterance, or image (depending on
the recall question). If one can be found that has not been previously recalled
then call it node X and mark it "recalled"; otherwise stop the recall process.

R3: Find the actor of X. If the recall question was asked about this actor, then
output node X.

R4: Search from node X for another behavior, utterance, or image. If one can be
found that has not been previously recalled, then call it node X, mark it
"recalled," and go to R3; otherwise go to R2.

occurs and attempt to organize it into a coherent knowledge structure in long-
term memory. Attention influences rehearsal, which influences likelihood of
successful encoding into long-term memory. Recall of information from the
conversation would be accomplished by accessing the knowledge structure and
retrieving the most readily available information about the conversation sequence. One possible variation of this encoding and recall model would differ in
organizing information into two separate knowledge structures—one for each
actor. Such encoding would be more time-consuming but would permit more
rapid retrieval of information about an actor.

The second encoding and recall algorithm is shown in Table 13.2. Under this
model only information that fits the subject's causal schema for a conversation is
encoded, and therefore only that information could be recalled.

Attributions. Four algorithms are presented in Table 13.3 for how attributions might be made within these encoding and recall models. The first two
assume that attributions about causality are computed from recalled information

TABLE 13.3
Four Algorithms for Making Causal Attributions about an Actor's Role in a Conversation

Models for Causal Attributions Based on Recall (Known Questions)

Schema-Dependent

A1: Retrieve the causal schema for the conversation
A2: CAUSAL-CONTRIB(ACTOR$_i$) = 0
A3: Execute the RECALL algorithm for ACTOR$_i$
     For each node X that is recalled,
     do;
          If node X is relevant to the specific causal question ask, then
               If node X is consistent with the causal schema for the conversation, then
                    CAUSAL-CONTRIB(ACTOR$_i$) = CAUSAL-CONTRIB(ACTOR$_i$)
                                                + CAUSAL-WEIGHT (X, from schema).
     end;
A4: Make a causal attribution proportional to CAUSAL-CONTRIB(ACTOR$_i$).

Schema-Independent

A2: CAUSAL-CONTRIB(ACTOR$_i$) = 0
A3: Execute the RECALL algorithm for ACTOR$_i$
     For each node X that is recalled,
     do;
          If node X is relevant to the specific causal question ask, then
               CAUSAL-CONTRIB(ACTOR$_i$) = CAUSAL-CONTRIB(ACTOR$_i$) + 1.
A4: Make a causal attribution proportional to CAUSAL-CONTRIB (ACTOR$_i$).

Models for Causal Attributions, Made During Encoding (Unknown Questions)

Schema-Dependent

A1: Let CURRENT-SCHEMA be the current causal schema used by the encoding process, or for schema-independent encoding let it be one for conversations that has been retrieved from LTM.
A2: CAUSAL-CONTRIB (ACTOR$_i$) = 0
A3: For each behavior, utterance, or image (X) of ACTOR$_i$ doing something that is attended to by the subject, do;
          If X is consistent with the CURRENT-SCHEMA, then
               CAUSAL-CONTRIB (ACTOR$_i$) = CAUSAL-CONTRIB (ACTOR$_i$) +
                                            CAUSAL-WEIGHT (X, from CURRENT-SCHEMA).
     end;
A4: Store a causal attribution proportional to CAUSAL-CONTRIB (ACTOR$_i$) in LTM.

Schema-Independent

A2: CAUSAL-CONTRIB (ACTOR$_i$) = 0
A3: For each behavior, utterance, or image (X) of ACTOR$_i$ doing something that is attended to by the subject, do;
               CAUSAL-CONTRIB (ACTOR$_i$) = CAUSAL-CONTRIB (ACTOR$_i$) + 1.
     end;
A4: Store a causal attribution proportional to CAUSAL-CONTRIB (ACTOR$_i$) in LTM.

after the causal questions are asked. The second two assume that the attributions are made during encoding and are stored in memory for later retrieval. In each of these cases one algorithm (schema-dependent) causes the subject to reject any recalled or observed information that is not compatible with his/her current causal schema for the conversation and causes the subject to weigh each piece of compatible evidence according to the causal schema. The other algorithm (schema-independent) causes the subject to weigh equally every behavior, utterance, or image of an actor doing something as proof of their causal contribution to the conversation. Of course, there could be many variations of these attribution algorithms, but these are representative of the two extremes.

What are the predictions of these models? They are summarized in Table 13.4. All the models predict that attention affects encoding and hence recall. Attended-to information is more likely to be recalled, so all the models predict positive path coefficients from attention to the recall of utterances, behaviors, or images. Such coefficients were obtained for Actor A but not for Actor B. If we constrain ourselves to the universe of process models specified, the only reasonable conclusion is that the attention manipulation (having the subject face Actor B) did not work perhaps because other aspects of Actor A were more salient.

While both encoding algorithms predict that attention enhances recall, under schema-based encoding, the effect of attention on recall could be eliminated if the information were inconsistent with the causal schema. Inconsistent or irrelevant information would not be encoded under this model even if attended to. Because Fiske et al.'s data suggest that attention affects only the recall of causally relevant information, the appropriate algorithm for encoding would seem to be the schema-dependent model. Additional support for schema-based encoding derives from the fact that only weak primacy effects were found for recall. Under schema-independent encoding, normal primacy and recency effects would be expected, but under the schema-dependent model, sequential position of information in the conversation would be less important than its "representativeness" of causality.

Give that schema-based encoding seems to be used, the next question is whether attributions about causality are made during encoding and saved or are made when the causal questions are asked and are based on recall. It is clear from Fiske et al.'s data (Fig. 13.1) that recall of positive information is related to causal attributions. Furthermore, they find that the responses on the four causal questions cannot be fit very well with a single dimension of causality. Both these results point to attributions being based on recall after the causal questions are asked.

In summary, the process model utilizing schema-dependent encoding and attributions based on recall best fits the data. Stimulus saliency affects attributions because the subject is more likely to encode causally consistent stimuli to which attention is directed and is therefore more likely to recall them when asked to make an attribution. These conclusions do not contradict Fiske et al., but they

TABLE 13,4
Predictions of the Process Models for Causal Attributions

Schema-Independent Encoding
1. Attention increases the likelihood of encoding and hence recall of any kind of information.
2. Recall of information is unaffected by its causal relevance.

Attributions Made During Encoding
1. Attributions are not affected by recall
2. Attributions are very similar for all causal questions

　Schema-Independent Attributions
　1. Attributions are affected by all information to which attention is directed during encoding.

　Schema-Dependent Attributions
　1. Attributions are affected by all information consistent with the subject's causal schema for a conversation to which attention is directed during encoding.

Attributions Made During Recall
1. Attributions are affected by recall and hence by attention during encoding.
2. Attributions may be very different for different causal questions.

　Schema-Independent Attributions
　1. Attributions are affected by all recalled information.

　Schema-Dependent Attributions
　1. Attributions are affected only by recalled information that is consistent with the subject's causal schema for a conversation.

Schema-Dependent Encoding
1. Only information consistent with subject's causal schema for a conversation is encoded and hence can be recalled.
2. Attention increases the likelihood of encoding and hence recalling only causally consistent information.

Attributions Made During Encoding
1. Attributions are not affected by recall.
2. Attributions are very similar for all causal questions.
3. Attributions are affected by attended-to information consistent with the subject's *current* causal schema for a conversation.

Attributions Made During Recall
1. Attributions are affected by recalled information and hence by attention during encoding.
2. Attributions may be very different for different causal questions.
3. Attributions are affected only by recalled information that is consistent with the subject's *final* causal schema for the conversation.

---

are more precise. The process model is less ambiguous than the structural model, is consistent with existing models of cognitive processing, and provides additional predictions that could be tested with additional data. For example, the clustering of information recalled during the free-recall task should reflect the subjective organization of the encoded information (i.e., the causal schema).

Also, if the schema-dependent encoding model is correct, one should be able to manipulate whether or not a particular utterance from the conversation is recalled by inducing a comparable or incompatible causal schema with the beginning of the conversation. Similarly, interference with the encoding of *relevant causal* information would have to change the subject's attributions under this model.

The lesson of these examples should not be that structural modeling is to be avoided. Far from it. Rather it is that the greatest power can be obtained from the use of structural or other descriptive models (e.g., stochastic) if the underlying process models are formally specified as algorithms. The resulting theory will be more powerful and yield more predictions for empirical tests.

MECHANISMS OF PROCESS MODELING

Having seen how algorithmic specifications of psychological processes can aid in understanding the relations in multivariate data, let us examine in more detail the mechanisms of process modeling. The simple examples presented in the foregoing do not do justice to the complexities of process modeling. Each of the algorithms presented and the knowledge structures on which they operate would have to be described even more precisely before simulations could have been run. Yet the traditional summary statistics collected in empirical studies usually do not provide sufficient information for a theorist to decide what algorithm a subject is using. One of the advantages of a process model is that computer simulations of the model will generate actual behaviors, not just summary statistics. But, as a result, one needs to analyze actual behaviors, not simply summary statistics, in order to develop an algorithmic process model. One needs to gain insight into the processes subjects are using, processes that often are not directly observable. A technique that has become widely used to gather such data is called protocol analysis.

Protocol Analysis

Most generally protocol analysis can be viewed as the study of transcripts of subjects' concurrent verbalizations of their thinking. To obtain a protocol, one asks (and sometimes trains) a subject to "think aloud" while performing a task. It is important to distinguish a protocol obtained in this manner from a retrospective description. Retrospective descriptions may be easier to obtain, but certainly are less reliable.

Protocol analysis, like process modeling, has been used extensively within cognitive psychology, and a well-developed methodology has emerged (Newell & Simon, 1972). The objective of protocol analysis is to derive a process model of a subject's behavior at successively higher levels of abstraction. The analyst begins with a complete transcript of the subject's verbal and observed nonverbal behaviors during the task being studied. The analyst proceeds as a detective whose aim is to induce what processes the subject has used. The analyst may accept the subject's verbal statements about a process at face value or infer quite different processes, depending on all the available data. From this initial analysis, a "problem behavior graph" is constructed that represents each process the subject employed in an ordered graph. The graph is not a flow chart or model; it simply displays the trajectory of the processes the subject used. Behavior graphs can be constructed successively at finer and finer levels of process specification. There is nothing mysterious about the analysis technique. With a sufficiently well-defined task environment and information-processing system, the induction of a problem behavior graph can even be performed by a computer program (Waterman & Newell, 1971).

Given an initial behavior graph, the analyst may wish to aggregate or disaggregate processes to achieve finer or coarser levels of explanation. Either when gathering data for testing an existing model or when collecting data for constructing a model, the analyst will have an a priori conception of the subject's processes that will influence the level of aggregation chosen. The next step for the analyst is to construct an algorithmic model that would generate the behavior graph obtained. Actually, it is almost never the case that one could construct an algorithmic model that generates a behavior graph perfectly. The analyst may choose to disregard certain aspects of the graph that seem questionable and may choose a model that approximates the graphs of many subjects over a model that more precisely predicts one subject's graph. The essential methodology for measuring the goodness of fit of the resulting process model is to generate actual protocols and compare these with observed protocols.

Protocol analysis has not been applied widely in social psychology though verbal self-reports are frequently collected. Nisbett and Wilson (1977) have justifiably criticized many of these procedures, but unfortunately they fail to make the necessary distinctions between protocol analysis and other verbal reports. Furthermore, they neglect the large body of literature available in cognitive psychology on mental processes and process modeling. As a result, many readers may incorrectly conclude that process modeling and protocol analysis are inappropriate for social psychology. Smith and Miller (1978) and Ericsson and Simon (1978, 1980) have persuasively attacked these conclusions. For example, although Nisbett and Wilson (1977) do not discriminate different types of mental processes, recent cognitive theorists have distinguished certain automatic information processes that are relatively inaccessible to subjects' awareness from more controlled accessible processes (Schneider & Shiffrin, 1977; Shiffren & Schneider, 1977). In any case, because protocol analysis infers processes from verbalizations (as opposed to accepting verbalizations as processes), information about any type of process could be derived from protocols. Ericsson and Simon (1980) argue that, if certain precautions are taken, even retrospective verbalizations can be validly analyzed. The important constraint, they suggest, is that subjects not be required to recode or interpret the retrospective information. Recently, Taylor and Fiske (1980) have presented an analysis of the potential of protocol analysis for social psychology.

Information Structures and Operations

In order to develop almost any process model of behavior one must postulate at least the outline of the information-processing systems with which one is dealing. This fact inextricably links all process models of social behavior to cognitive psychology. It would seem foolish to postulate an information-processing system whose operation violates the known data on cognitive processing, but such foolishness is sometimes seen.

Among cognitive psychologists a consensus has emerged about the general outlines of the human information-processing system. One can best describe the general model of the system in the terminology of the computation sciences. The general model can be divided into two parts—the data structures postulated for the representation of information and the processes that are performed on these data structures. Let us now look at the major types of data structures assumed to be used and a few of the algorithms postulated for processing these data structures.

The representation system postulated most often is known as a *node-link* memory. Its central elements are *nodes* representing discrete entities (e.g., objects, events, actions, descriptions, or even processes). These nodes are connected into networks by *links* that represent named (e.g., superordinate, color, time) or unnamed associations between nodes. The "meaning" of a node is given by its network of links (associations). Some special types of networks are particularly important—ordered lists in which each node is associated with a "next" or "previous" node, trees in which a root node is linked to a number of nodes, which in turn are linked to a number of other nodes, and description lists in which attribute–value pairs are linked to a node being described. It is quite time-consuming to model a node-link memory with the data structures provided by simple algorithmic languages designed for numeric operations (e.g., FOR-TRAN); so special list or string-processing languages have been developed for representing such structures and carrying out symbol manipulation operations on them (e.g., LISP, SNOBOL).

The elementary information processes operate on these data structures directly. Among them are operations for creating and linking nodes, accessing nodes via links, comparing nodes, and assigning designating symbols to nodes. Although these elementary operations are the building blocks of all process models, most models of social behavior would begin with the assumption of more complex structures and processes.

Representations of Knowledge

When one attempts to specify the processes underlying an individual's social behavior, one must assume some representation for the individual's knowledge. Several similar representations for knowledge have been developed by information-processing theorists (Anderson, 1976). A complete exploration of them is beyond the scope of this chapter, but we can briefly consider an example whose central characteristics are typical of the class. The Norman and Rummelhart (1975) network model can serve this purpose. Knowledge is encoded as a set of interrelated propositions about the state of the world and procedures for accomplishing certain states. Winograd (1972) was perhaps the first to introduce this principle that much of our knowledge can best be represented as procedures. Within the information-processing system the propositions and procedures are represented by an active structural network. This node-link network is modified as new knowledge is encountered. Each link in the network is a specific type expressing a relation between nodes. As an example, Fig. 13.2 shows a part of the knowledge structure of Leon-Gabor, one of Rokeach's (1964) patients who believed himself to be Christ. This sample diagram is only suggestive of the

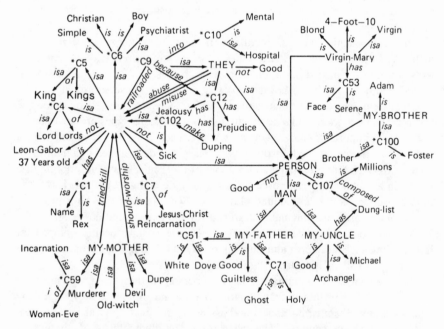

FIG. 13.2.   A representation of the knowledge structure of Leon-Gabor, one of Rokeach's Three Christs of Ypsilanti (1964). (From *Human Information Processing* by P. H. Lindsay & D. A. Norman, with permission of Academic Press. Copyright 1972).

complexities one encounters in applying such representations to modeling social behaviors. Inevitably, computer simulations are needed to handle the intricacies. But the intricacies of these and other schemes (Kintsch, 1974; Schank, 1975) only reflect the complexities that humans face in storing knowledge.

Heuristic Search

A central operation in process models of behavior is often a search through a knowledge structure. The knowledge structure might represent a subject's attitudes, a subject's causal schemata, a subject's perception of social relationships, a subject's perception of outcomes of social behaviors, or any other type of knowledge. Regardless of how the knowledge structure is represented, search processes become very tedious and time-consuming as the structures become even moderately large. As a result, information-processing psychologists have devoted a fair amount of thought to how knowledge structures are searched. The general theory that has evolved is that searches are conducted heuristically—that is, they are guided by "rules of thumb" that allow the searcher a reasonable chance of finding what is sought while examining only a small portion of the knowledge structure. Such searches appear in many process models.

AN EXAMPLE: A HEURISTIC SEARCH MODEL FOR SOCIAL DECISIONS

Having reviewed some fundamentals of constructing process models, let us now examine a model that is detailed enough to have been simulated—a model of how a person decides what to do or say when involved in a competitive social interaction. The model is worth studying for several reasons. Although our analysis of the causal attribution theories demonstrated the value of process models in explaining multivariate relations, that example did not show how information-processing constraints may force the direction that a process model takes. Yet frequently, as in the example that follows, the need for reasonably rapid processing leaves few alternatives for an algorithmic model. Second, this decision-making model incorporates many of the elementary information processes and knowledge structures commonly used in process models. Third, the core of the model is a heuristic search algorithm widely used in artificial intelligence research but seldomly used in modeling psychological processes. It is an algorithm whose variants could be utilized in any number of models of social–psychological processes. Finally, this model serves as a good example of how process modeling often clarifies one's thinking. The model is not easy to understand at first because of the wealth of detail necessary to specify unambiguously and precisely what seems at first to be a relatively simple process. But if one expends the effort required to understand it, one will probably understand the search problem that subjects face more deeply than before. In fact, to some people, the intensity of thinking that algorithmic models require is the best argument in their favor.

Consider the case of a person who is interacting socially with another person. How does he or she decide what to do or say next? How is information about what might happen organized? How does a person evaluate potential outcomes? A structural-modeling approach would entail outlining the potential relations between variables and behaviors relevant to these questions. However, the process-modeling approach requires the scientist to hypothesize answers to the foregoing questions in terms of information processes and organizations. One such model (Huesmann & Levinger, 1976) represents the person's knowledge about the interactions as an inverted tree. The branches descending from the root node represent the subject's possible behaviors, and the branches descending below those represent the coactor's possible responses. The resulting nodes symbolize the possible states of the relationship after one interaction. From each of these nodes, branches descend in the same manner, leading to the potential states of the relationship after two interactions. One level of a tree of this type is shown in Fig. 13.3. If there are m possible behaviors by each actor in each state, then, after d interactions, the tree will have m^{2d} tip nodes (final states). The model presumes there is a payoff for the actor associated with each outcome of an interaction, and the actor wishes to find the sequence of behaviors that will maximize his or her payoffs. For any realistic case this tree would become enormous if the subject tried to look very far into the future. For example, if there were only four different behaviors available to each person in each interaction, to

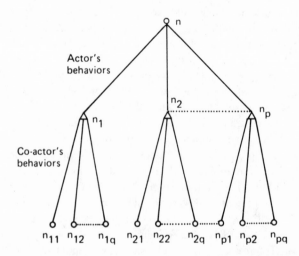

FIG. 13.3. Two levels of a tree representing a single interaction by two actors. Node n_{ij} is reached when the actor selects behavior i and the coactor behavior j. From each of these nodes branches would descend representing the next interaction.

look ahead five interactions would require searching a tree with $4^{2(5)} = 4^{10} =$ 1,048,576 tip nodes. How can a subject search through such a tree? The heuristic search model suggests that the actor limits the breadth and depth of search in the tree with rules that direct the search down the paths that seem likely to be the best ones (have the most payoffs). In this context a heuristic can be viewed as a function for evaluating the likelihood that a node is on the best path.

Let me describe the heuristic search model more formally for an actor in a competitive dyadic interaction. By competitive I mean that the sum of the actor's and coactor's payoffs is a constant for all outcomes. Therefore, what one actor gains, the other actor loses, though both actors may receive highly positive payoffs. Actors try to maximize their own sum of payoffs and assume that their coactors will try to do the same. Huesmann and Levinger (1976) have already presented a model for a noncompetitive interaction. The model for a competitive interaction is similar, but allows for a greater use of heuristics by the actors.

As shown in Fig. 13.3, a single interaction is represented by two levels of the tree—the first level representing the actor's behavior and the second representing the coactor's behavior, though in fact both behaviors may occur simulatneously. The heuristic search algorithm presented in Table 13.5 is called a dynamically ordered minimax search with alpha–beta cutoffs. It is widely used in models of competitive interactions, and variations are used in process models of other situations. The procedure is called a minimax process because it selects the behavior for the actor that will maximize his or her own sum of payoffs when the coactor is trying his best to minimize them. It is guaranteed to find the best behavior for the actor to choose under this assumption, and it uses a heuristic rule to alter dynamically the direction of the search to find the best behavior as quickly as possible. A variation using a ''satisficing'' heuristic would differ only in when search terminates.

Let h represent the actor's heuristic estimate of the value of a particular node. The algorithm directs the actor's search down the tree along the path with the greatest h-values. No part of the tree is even created until it is needed. At each new level where a new interaction occurs, the h-values are backed up, replacing the older (and probably less accurate) h-values higher up on the tree. If a different path has a higher value as a result of this computation, it is followed. When the search has progressed down some path to the maximum level to be searched (maxdepth), actual values (value) are computed and summed up the tree as far as the actor is certain of nodes' values. The search down the tree resumes from that point along the unsearched path with the best h-values. Eventually the actual values will be summed up all the way to the start of the tree, and the best path will be found. Then the actor chooses the immediate behavior on the best path. Of course, what appears to be the best path at one time may turn out to be not so good later.

This algorithm is detailed in Table 13.5, and an example of the application of this algorithm is shown in Fig. 13.4. To understand the algorithm one must

TABLE 13.5

The Heuristic Search Model for Decision Making during a
Competitive Social Interaction

Let *Pay (n)* be the payoff received by the actor at node n. Inasmuch as the interaction is competitive, the coactor's payoff can be represented as *Totalpay (n)* – *Pay (n)*.

Let *Sumpay (n)* be the sum of payoffs the actor receives down to and including the payoff at node n.

Let *Maxdepth* be the number of levels (interactions) down the tree that the actor searches.

Let *Value (n)* be the value of node n computed by backing up the sum of payoffs from *Maxdepth* using the minimax procedure. When *Value* is finally computed for the initial node, the procedure is finished.

Let *h (n)* be the heuristic estimate of *Value (n)* used to guide the search through the tree. For example, if one thought that the payoff from any single interaction were likely to be *Minpay*, one might use $h(n) = Sumpay(n) + Minpay \times (Maxdepth - Depth(n))$.

Let *Greatestvalue (n)* be an upper bound on *Value (n)*. It is determined for the actor's decision nodes from backed-up values using the minimax procedure, and it gradually decreases until it becomes *Value (n)*.

Let *Leastvalue (n)* be a lower bound on *Value (n)*. It is determined for the coactor's decision nodes from backed-up values using the minimax procedure, and it gradually increases until it becomes *Value (n)*.

1. Let $n \leftarrow$ initial node
   Currentdepth $\leftarrow 0$
   $h(n) \leftarrow$ Minpay $\times$ Maxdepth

2. Follow the apparent best path from n until a node is reached whose successors have not yet been generated. Use the following procedure:

   a. Let n be the current node.
   b. If n has no successors, go to *3* to generate successors.
   c. Name the immediate successors $n_1 \ldots n_p$.
   d. Move down from n to the n_i with the *largest $h(n_i)$*.
   e. Currentdepth $\leftarrow$ Currentdepth + 1.
   f. If n_i has no successors, go to *5* to generate successors.
   g. Name the immediate successors $n_{i1} \ldots n_{iq}$.
   h. Move down from n_i to the n_{ij} with the *smallest $h(n_{ij})$*.
   i. If Currentdepth = Maxdepth then Value $(n_{ij}) \leftarrow h(n_{ij})$. Go to *7* to back-up values.
   j. Go to *a*.

3. Generate the immediate successors of the current node n. Call them $n_1 - - - n_p$. Each corresponds to a different behavior for the actor. For each generated node n_i, let $h(n_i) \leftarrow h(n)$
   Greatestvalue $(n_i) \leftarrow + \infty$
   Currentdepth $\leftarrow$ Currentdepth + 1

4. Randomly select a node n_i (actor's behavior) for initial consideration

5. Generate the immediate successors of n_i. Call the $mn_{i1} \ldots n_{iq}$. Each corresponds to a different behavior by the coactor. For each generated node n_{ij}, let Sumpay(n_{ij}) $\leftarrow$ Sumpay(n_i) + Pay(n_{ij})
   $h(n_{ij}) \leftarrow$ Sumpay(n_{ij}) + Minpay $\times$ (Maxdepth - Currentdepth)
   Leastvalue $(n_{ij}) \leftarrow - \infty$

(continued)

TABLE 13.5—*Continued*

---

6. "Back up" *h*-values, according to minimax procedure, as far as possible up the tree. Use the following procedure:

   a. Currentdepth ← Currentdepth - 1
   b. If $h(n_i)$ = min $h(n_{ij})$ then go to *2e* and start back down the tree.
   c. $h(n_i)$ ← min $h(n_{ij})$
   d. If $h(n)$ = max $h(n_i)$ then go to *2a* and start back down the tree.
   e. $h(n)$ ← max $h(n_i)$
   f. If *n* = initial node then go to *2a* and start back down the tree.
   g. Relabel *n* as n_{ij}. Call its immediate ancestor n_i and its grandparent *n*. Go to *a* and back up higher in tree.

7. Maxdepth has been reached. "Back up" actual sum of payoff values as far as possible up the tree. Use alpha-beta procedure to close off dead branches. Set $h(n)$ so dead and already searched nodes will not be searched again. Use the following procedure:

   a. Currentdepth ← Currentdepth -1
   b. Greatestvalue(n_i) ← min Value(n_{ik}) over all successor nodes of n_i for which Value (n_{ik}) exists
   c. If Value(n_{ik}) exists for all successors of n_i or Greatestvalue(n_i) < Least-value (immediate ancestor(n_i))
      then
         Value(n_i) ← Greatestvalue(n_i)
         $h(n_i)$ ← $- \infty$ so this branch won't be searched again
      else
         go to *2e* to start back down tree.
   d. Leastvalue(n) ← Max Value(n_k) over all successor nodes of *n* for which Value(n_k) exists
   e. If Value(n_k) exists for all successors of *n* or Leastvalue(n) > Greatestvalue (immediate ancestor(n))
      then
         Value(n) ← Leastvalue(n)
         $h(n)$ ← $+ \infty$ so this branch won't be searched again
      else
         go to *2a* to start back down the tree.
   f. If *n* = initial node then go to *8* because we have found the best path.
   g. Relabel *n* as n_{ij}. Call its immediate ancestor n_i and its grandparent *n*. Go to *a* and back up higher in tree.

8. The best path has been found. The actor selects the immediate behavior with the greatest value Value(n_i).

---

follow it through such an example. The tree being searched is for two levels of an interaction. In the first level, each actor has three behavior options and in the second level, two. The payoffs are shown at the end of each branch. However, only the portion of the tree was diagrammed that was generated by the algorithm. The remainder of the tree, no matter what its payoffs, could not provide a better solution than the one outlined in dark on the figure. The final backed-up values

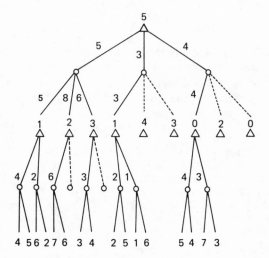

FIG. 13.4.   A portion of a tree representing a continuing dyadic interaction. The nodes drawn are those generated by the actor in looking ahead two interactions with a dynamically ordered heuristic search algorithm. The dashed branches lead to nodes generated but not evaluated. The optimal path solution for the actor is darkened.

are shown alongside the branches and the order in which the algorithm searched the tree is denoted by the left-to-right ordering. The dashed branches were generated but never searched. The complete tree has 66 nodes and the heuristic search algorithm processed only 32 of them in finding the optimal path. The optimal path is the left-most path which has a backed up value of 5.

This algorithmic model of a social decision illustrates several important points about the utility of algorithmic process models in explaining multivariate social data. First, if it is actually to be simulated, such a model must be extremely precise and detailed. To many psychologists, such precision is anathema— perhaps because so many unknowns must be guessed. Second, the requirement for precision often forces the theorist to hypothesize processes that seem implausible, but he or she cannot conceive of any other way to perform the task (e.g., the heuristic search). Although these are problems, one must remember that descriptive models simply beg these issues; they do not resolve them any more satisfactorily. Third, the decision model demonstrates some of the most common data structures and operations used in process models. Finally, and perhaps most importantly, the example should have given the reader an insight into how process modeling affects our thinking about multivariate relations. The constraints of precision and process specification force one to make explicit latent assumptions, however distasteful, and eliminate "fuzzy" thinking about the relations between variables. In such a way, a clearer understanding of multivariate data is obtained than with descriptive structural models.

SUMMARY

In this chapter I have argued that process models of behavior are needed in social psychology, where multivariate studies often lack an adequate theoretical orientation. Process models specified in the language of the information sciences are more precise, less ambiguous, and more readily falsifiable than most theories of social behavior stated in natural languages. Although structural models of behavior are useful descriptive devices, their utility as models can be greatly enhanced by the specification of an underlying process model. A common general representation of the human information-processing system has been developed by cognitive psychologists for process modeling and could be employed in process models of social behavior. Knowledge is represented by linked list structures in a node-link memory. Heuristic search in such a knowledge structure would form an important part of many process models of social behavior, and a common model for heuristic search was presented at the end of the chapter.

REFERENCES

Abelson, R. P. Simulation of social behavior. In G. Lindzey & E. Aronson (Eds.), *Handbook of Social Psychology* (Vol. 2). Reading, Mass.: Addison-Wesley, 1968.

Abelson, R. P. The structure of belief systems. In R. C. Schank & K. M. Colby (Eds.), *Computer models of thought and language*. San Francisco: Freeman, 1973.

Abelson, R. P. Concepts for representing mundane reality in plans. In D. G. Bobrow & A. M. Collins (Eds.), *Representation and understanding*. New York: Academic Press, 1975.

Abelson, R. P., & Carroll, J. D. Computer simulation of individual belief systems. *American Behavioral Scientist*, 1965, *8*, 24–30.

Abramson, L. Y., Seligman, M. E. P., & Teasdale, J. D. Learned helplessness in humans: Critique and reformulation. *Journal of Abnormal Psychology*, 1978, *87*, 49–74.

Anderson, J. *Language, memory and thought*. Hillsdale, N.J.: Lawrence Erlbaum Associates, 1976.

Bentler, P. Multivariate analysis with latent variables: Causal modeling. *Annual Review of Psychology*, 1980, *31*, 419–456.

Colby, K. M. Experimental treatment of neurotic computer programs. *Archives of General Psychiatry*, 1964, *10*, 220–227.

Colby, K. M. *Simulations of belief systems*. In R. C. Schank & K. M. Colby (Eds.), Computer models of thought and language. San Francisco: Freeman, 1973.

Ericsson, K. A., & Simon, H. A. *Retrospective verbal reports as data*. C. I. P. Working Paper No. 388, Department of Psychology, Carnegie-Mellon University, 1978.

Ericsson, K. A., & Simon, H. A. Verbal reports as data. *Psychological Review*, 1980, *87*(3), 215–251.

Feigenbaum, E. A., & Feldman, J. *Computers and thought*. New York: McGraw-Hill, 1963.

Fiske, S. T., Kenny, D., & Taylor, S. E. Structural models for the mediation of salience effects on attribution. *Journal of Experimental Social Psychology*, 1981.

Gregg, L. W., & Simon, H. A. Process models and stochastic theories of simple concept formation. *Journal of Mathematical Psychology*, 1967, *4*, 246–276.

Gullahorn, J. T., & Gullahorn, J. E. A computer model of elementary social behavior. *Behavior Science*, 1963, *8*, 354–362.

Huesmann, L. R. Cognitive processes and models of depression. *Journal of Abnormal Psychology*, 1978, *87*, 194–198.

Huesmann, L. R., & Levinger, G. Incremental exchange theory: A formal model for progression in dyadic social interaction. In L. Berkowitz & E. Walster (Eds.), *Advances in Experimental Social Psychology* (Vol. 9). New York: Academic Press, 1976.

Kintsch, W. *The representation of meaning in memory.* Hillsdale, N.J.: Lawrence Erlbaum Associates, 1974.

Krech, D., & Crutchfield, R. S. *Theory and problems in social psychology.* New York: McGraw-Hill, 1948.

Levinger, G., & Huesmann, L. R. An incremental exchange perspective on the pair relationship: Interpersonal reward and level of involvement. In K. J. Gergen, M. C. Greenberg, & R. H. Willis (Eds.), *Social exchange: Advances in theory and research.* New York: Plenum, 1980.

Lindsay, P. H., & Norman, D. A. *Human information processing.* New York: Academic Press, 1972.

Loehlen, J. C. Interpersonal experiments with a computer model of personality. *Journal of Personality and Social Psychology,* 1965, *2,* 580–584.

Minsky, M. *Semantic information processing.* Cambridge: MIT Press, 1968.

Newell, A., Shaw, J. C., & Simon, H. Elements of a theory of human problem solving. *Psychological Review,* 1958, *65,* 151–166.

Newell, A., & Simon, H. A. *Human problem solving.* Englewood Cliffs, N.J.: Prentice–Hall, 1972.

Nisbett, R. E., & Wilson, T. D. Telling more than we can know: Verbal report on mental processes. *Psychological Review,* 1977, *84,* 231–259.

Norman, D. A., Rumelhart, D. E., & the LNR Research Group. *Explorations in cognition.* San Francisco: Freeman, 1975.

Rogosa, D. A critique of cross-lagged correlation. *Psychological Bulletin,* 1980, *88,* 245–258.

Rokeach, M. *The Three Crists of Ypsilanti,* New York: Knopf, 1964.

Schank, R. C. *Conceptual information processing.* Amsterdam: North–Holland, 1975.

Schank, R. C., & Abelson, R. P. *Scripts, plans and knowledge.* Presented at 4th International Joint Conference on Artificial Intelligence, Tbilisi, USSR, 1975.

Schneider, W., & Shiffrin, R. M. Controlled and automatic human information processing: I. Detection search and attention. *Psychological Review,* 1977, *84,* 1–66.

Seligman, M. E. P. *Helplessness.* San Francisco: Freeman, 1975.

Shiffrin, R. M., & Schneider, W. Controlled and automatic human information processing: II. Perceptual learning, automatic attending and a general theory. *Psychological Review,* 1977, *84,* 127–189.

Simon, H. A. Causal ordering and identifiability. In W. C. Hood & T. C. Koopmans (Eds.), *Studies in econometric method.* New York: Wiley, 1953.

Simon, H. A. Spurious correlation: A causal interpretation. *Journal of the American Statistical Association,* 1954, *49,* 467–479.

Simon, H. A. *The sceinces of the artificial.* Cambridge: MIT Press, 1969.

Smith, E. R., & Miller, F. S. Limits on perception of cognitive processes: A reply to Nisbett and Wilson. *Psychological Review,* 1978, *85,* 355–362.

Tversky, A., & Kahneman, D. Causal schemata in judgments under uncertainty. In M. Fishbein (Ed.), *Progress in Social Psychology,* Hillsdale, N.J.: Lawrence Erlbaum Associates, 1980.

Waterman, D., & Newell, A. Protocol analysis at a task for artificial intelligence. *Artificial Intelligence,* 1971, *2,* 285–318.

Winograd, T. Understanding natural language. *Cognitive Psychology,* 1972, *3,* 1–191.

Wright, S. The method of path coefficients. *Annals of Mathematical Statistics,* 1934, September, 161–215.

Author Index

Subject Index